'Van Gogh's letters ... are one of the [...]
literature, not only for the inherent beauty of the prose and the
sharpness of the observations but also for their portrait of the
artist as a man wholly and selflessly devoted to the work he had
to set himself to' – *Washington Post*

'Fascinating ... letter after letter sizzles with colorful, exacting
descriptions ... This absorbing collection elaborates yet another
side of this beuiling and brilliant artist'
– *The New York Times Book Review*

'Ronald de Leeuw's magnificent achievement here is to make
the letters accessible in English to general readers rather than
art historians, in a new translation so excellent I found myself
reading even the well-known letters as if for the first time ...
It will be surprising if a more impressive volume of letters
appears this year' – *Observer*

'Any selection of Van Gogh's letters is bound to be full of
marvellous things, and this is no exception' – *Sunday Telegraph*

'With this new translation of Van Gogh's letters, his literary
brilliance and his statement of what amounts to prophetic art
theories will remain as a force in literary and art history'
– *Philadelphia Inquirer*

'De Leeuw's collection is likely to remain the definitive volume
for many years, both for the excellent selection and for the
accurate translation' – *The Times Literary Supplement*

'Vincent's letters are a journal, a meditative autobiography ...
You are able to take in Vincent's extraordinary literary qualities
... Unputdownable' – *Daily Telegraph*

VINCENT WILLEM VAN GOGH was born in Holland in 1853. He became an assistant with an international firm of art-dealers and in 1881 he went to Brussels to study art. After an unsuccessful love affair with his cousin he returned to Holland and in 1885 he painted his first masterpiece, *The Potato Eaters*, a haunting scene of domestic poverty. A year later his brother Theo, an art dealer, enabled him to study in Paris, where he met Gauguin, Toulouse-Lautrec and Seurat, who became very important influences on his work. In 1888 he left Paris for the Provençal landscape at Arles, the subject of many of his best works, including *Sunflowers* and *The Chair and the Pipe*. It was here Van Gogh cut off his ear, in remorse for threatening Gauguin with a razor during a quarrel, and he was placed in an asylum for a year. On 27 July 1890 Van Gogh shot himself at the scene of his last painting, the foreboding *Cornfields with Flight of Birds*, and he died two days later.

RONALD DE LEEUW has been the director of the Van Gogh Museum in Amsterdam since 1986. He trained as an art historian at the universities of Los Angeles, California, and of Leiden, The Netherlands. As a specialist in nineteenth-century painting, he has been responsible for numerous exhibitions in The Netherlands and abroad, including the 1990 Vincent Van Gogh Centennial retrospective in Amsterdam. Since 1990 Ronald de Leeuw has also directed the Museum Mesdag in The Hague, known for its fine Barbizon and Hague School holdings. In 1994 he was appointed professor extraordinary in the history of collecting at the Free University of Amsterdam.

ARNOLD POMERANS was born in 1920 and was educated in South Africa. He emigrated to England in 1948, and from 1948 to 1955 taught physics in London. In 1955 he became a full-time translator and has had just under two hundred major works issued by leading British and US publishers. Among the authors translated by him are Louis de Broglie, Anne Frank, Sigmund Freud, George Grosz, Jan Huizinga, Jean Piaget and Jules Romain.

THE LETTERS OF
VINCENT VAN GOGH

Selected and Edited by Ronald de Leeuw

Translated by Arnold Pomerans

PENGUIN BOOKS

Published by the Penguin Group
Penguin Books Ltd, 80 Strand, London WC2R 0RL, England
Penguin Putnam Inc., 375 Hudson Street, New York, New York 10014, USA
Penguin Books Australia Ltd, 250 Camberwell Road, Camberwell, Victoria 3124, Australia
Penguin Books Canada Ltd, 10 Alcorn Avenue, Toronto, Ontario, Canada M4V 3B2
Penguin Books India (P) Ltd, 11 Community Centre, Panchsheel Park, New Delhi – 110 017, India
Penguin Books (NZ) Ltd, Cnr Rosedale and Airborne Roads, Albany, Auckland, New Zealand
Penguin Books (South Africa) (Pty) Ltd, 24 Sturdee Avenue, Rosebank 2196, South Africa

Penguin Books Ltd, Registered Offices: 80 Strand, London WC2R 0RL, England

www.penguin.com

First published by Allen Lane The Penguin Press 1996
Published in Penguin Books 1997

049

This collection copyright © Ronald de Leeuw, 1996
This translation copyright © Sdu Publishers, 1996
All rights reserved

The moral right of the author and translator has been asserted

Printed and bound in Great Britain by Clays Ltd, Elcograf S.p.A.

Except in the United States of America, this book is sold subject
to the condition that it shall not, by way of trade or otherwise, be lent,
re-sold, hired out, or otherwise circulated without the publisher's
prior consent in any form of binding or cover other than that in
which it is published and without a similar condition including this
condition being imposed on the subsequent purchaser

ISBN-13: 978-0-140-44674-6

www.greenpenguin.co.uk

Penguin Books is committed to a sustainable
future for our business, our readers and our planet.
This book is made from Forest Stewardship
Council™ certified paper.

Contents

For Gerlof

About This Edition

The text of this selection of letters is based on *De Brieven van Vincent van Gogh* (*The Letters of Vincent van Gogh*), edited by Han van Crimpen and Monique Berends-Albert and published in 1990 by the Van Gogh Museum in collaboration with Sdu (the Netherlands state publishing house). The translation of letters originally written in French is based on a new transcription specially prepared for this edition. The letters D, F and E in square brackets indicate whether a particular letter was originally written in Dutch, French or English.

Van Gogh's letters have come down to us largely undated. In most cases, however, the correct sequence and date have been determined satisfactorily, though some problems with dates remain, especially in letters from the Arles period. In all these cases the dates given in the Sdu edition have been provisionally retained.

Drawings have been included only when the letters selected here were illustrated by the artist himself.

The greatly improved and enlarged 1990 edition of the *Letters* is still obtainable only in Dutch, so the numbering of the letters used here is based on the 1914/1953/1973 edition, which has been the basis of all translations to date. As a result, this book can be used in conjunction with the existing Van Gogh literature, in which that numbering is commonly found.

The letters to Van Rappard bear an R-number, those to Émile Bernard a B-number and those to his sister Wil a W-number. The recently discovered letter from Wil van Gogh to her girlfriend Line Kruysse, which is quoted here at some length, was first published in the *Bulletin van het Van Gogh Museum* (1992/3, Vol. 7).

This edition is not primarily intended for readers well versed in art history, so no attempt has been made to relate the pictures mentioned in the text to the oeuvre catalogues of Baart de la Faille and Jan Hulsker. Dates of birth and death of the dramatis personae are given in the Index.

Translator's Note

Quotations from letters Van Gogh wrote in French that appear in the linking text and in the Introduction have been translated from the Dutch, unless the letters in question are included in this book. Quotations from Johanna van Gogh-Bonger appear in her English. Translations of French words or phrases used by Van Gogh in his Dutch letters have been provided in notes, except where they are already familiar in English.

Introduction

Nothing annoyed Van Gogh more than 'acting as a pedestal for something you do not know'; being misused for an end he himself did not pursue. Although the circumstances of his life often gave him good cause, he stated emphatically that '... on no account would I choose the life of a martyr. For I have always striven for something other than heroism, which I do not have in me ...'

The story of any artist's rise to fame makes fascinating reading and none is more fascinating than Van Gogh's. His contemporaries' alleged failure to appreciate his talent, the claim that he sold only a single painting in his lifetime and his death under intriguing and not yet fully explained circumstances have all fired the imagination.

In 1913, when Johanna van Gogh-Bonger, the widow of Van Gogh's brother Theo, put the finishing touches to the first complete edition of Vincent van Gogh's letters to her husband, she did so with some trepidation. In her Introduction she expressed the wish that the letters should be read 'with consideration'; at the same time she hoped that his dramatic life would not obscure the perception of his oeuvre. For the serious reader and the art historian, the publication of these letters added a fresh dimension to the understanding of Van Gogh's artistic achievement, an understanding granted us by virtually no other painter.

Van Gogh himself was an avid reader of artists' biographies, devouring whatever he could find on the lives of painters he admired – Delacroix, Corot, Millet and Monticelli – and he expected conduct from artists in keeping with the character of their art. At the beginning of his own artistic career, he treated Alfred Sensier's biography of Millet, *La vie et l'œuvre de J.-F. Millet*, published in 1881, almost as if it were Thomas à Kempis's *Imitation of Christ*. He could hardly have imagined that his own letters to Theo would in their turn fulfil a similar role for a host of readers, and countless artists in particular.

The century that has passed since Van Gogh's suicide in July 1890 in the village of Auvers-sur-Oise in northern France has brought, in addition to posthumous acclaim, a distortion of many of the ideas and values Van Gogh upheld as an artist. A Van Gogh mythology – and Johanna van Gogh feared just that – has become an impediment to direct access to Van Gogh's creative work. Irving Stone's book *Lust for Life*, followed later by the film version and the world-wide dissemination of Van Gogh reproductions, has in one respect fulfilled his ambition to be a people's artist, albeit in an ironical sense. However, it has also served to isolate him once more from other artists by placing him in a special position.

One year before his death Van Gogh himself discerned in the – positive – critiques of Albert Aurier and J. J. Isaäcson the first symptoms of a misrepresentation of his work. The emphasis his early critics placed on his obsession, if not his madness, eclipsed the message he himself wanted to convey. His ambition to become known as a painter of peasant life and as 'the painter of modern portraits' is at odds with the prevailing image of a madman who died a martyr to art. That a painting such as *The Bedroom*, intended as a welcome to Gauguin and a homage to Seurat, in which he strove to convey an image of *rest* and *simplicity*, should nowadays be considered a model of colour enhancement and distorted perspective is something that would have astonished him. His paintings have an expressive force that not even the most confident disclaimers in his own letters can fully gainsay. For the serious reader, Van Gogh's correspondence nevertheless provides appropriate material for refuting most, if not all, of the myths surrounding his work. As against the cliché of Van Gogh the impulsive and frenetic painter who plants his easel in the Provençal landscape and flings his impressions on to canvas while battling against the mistral, the letters reveal a more complex and captivating personality. Familiarity with the Vincent of the letters, moreover, leads irrevocably to sympathy for, if not identification with, this struggling seeker after God, for this toiling artist who set himself such high ethical standards.

Rarely are readers welcomed as wholeheartedly and intimately into the process of creation of truly great art as they are through Van Gogh's letters. It is thanks to their accessibility that Van Gogh, among all the fathers of modern art – Cézanne, Gauguin, Seurat – has become the most universally loved. His letters are also virtually the only ones of their kind with sufficient intrinsic appeal to be read outside the professional circles of art historians.

That Van Gogh's range of ideas is not seen as dated, as the musings of an historical figure, a hundred years after his death is in part due to the fact that he made no concession to the anecdotal or modish, to the temporal nature of things. Although he frequented metropolitan centres such as Paris and London, and associated with the great artists of his day, he never became a chronicler of outward appearances like the de Goncourt brothers. Whether his particular concern was religious or artistic, he invariably cultivated his inner universe and confidently sought the eternal in the temporal. In his art no less than in his letters he aimed at the greatest possible authenticity of form, because '[when] the object represented is, as far as style is concerned, in harmony with and at one with the manner of representation, isn't it just that which gives a work of art its quality?'

As a result of his hunger for friendship and contact with fellow artists, Van Gogh came to know many of them in the course of his life. Small wonder, then, that so many memories of Van Gogh were recorded after his death. Whatever the value of these often conflicting character sketches, they are a warning against accepting the artist's own view of himself as the last word. Even so, the world knows Van Gogh's outward appearance mainly from his self-portraits, and his personality from the image that emerges from his correspondence. Although Van Gogh himself realized that 'it is difficult to know oneself – but it isn't easy to paint oneself either', the picture that emerges from his letters has proved infinitely more subtle and hence more powerful than those his contemporaries have left us. It must, however, be borne in mind that Van Gogh's version, too, cannot be considered a complete and true reflection of his life. Moreover, if we had more of his letters to such fellow artists as Bernard and Gauguin, then we might well have discovered other facets of his personality. What he wanted to share with Theo, or intended for Theo in particular, was bound to be subject to certain constraints. It is as well to remember that the letters to his brother were not so much written as an autobiographical record as for a very specific purpose – namely to maintain good relations with one who supported him financially all his life. The phrases at the beginning of so many letters, acknowledging receipt of his brother's last remittance and thanking him for it, have the sound of an incantation. Beyond that, Van Gogh himself knew perfectly well that one and the same individual can provide material for the most divergent portraits, and in his relations with Theo he stressed the artistic aspect.

Only through Theo could he hope to convince the world of his merit. Far from being objective, the letters thus constitute an eloquent apologia in which Van Gogh pleads his own cause. The critical reader will now and then discover contradictions in his argument, but like every good writer Van Gogh ultimately forces us to accept the world on his own terms and succeeds in persuading quite a few to share his ideals.

Publication history

'When as Theo's young wife I entered in April, 1889, our flat in the Cité Pigalle in Paris, I found in the bottom of a small desk a drawer full of letters from Vincent, and week after week I saw the soon familiar yellow envelopes with the characteristic hand-writing increase in number' (from the Preface, written by Johanna van Gogh-Bonger, to the first edition of *The Complete Letters of Vincent van Gogh*, in the English version published by Thames & Hudson in London in 1958, Vol. 1, p. xiii). The publication of these letters became Johanna van Gogh-Bonger's life's work. After Vincent's death, Theo himself had cherished the notion of publishing a selection of the letters and asked the critic Albert Aurier to write a book about Vincent based on them. Theo's own death, on 25 January 1891, followed by that of Aurier in 1892, thwarted these plans, and it was not until January 1914 that the letters were published almost in full – thanks to the efforts of Theo's widow. In the intervening years it was largely through the translation and publication of extracts by such artists as Émile Bernard and Henry van de Velde that the existence of the letters became more widely known. From an early stage, critics in France, the Netherlands and Belgium used quotations from the letters to throw light on various paintings. In 1893, Van Gogh's colleague and friend Émile Bernard was the first to publish a selection of letters addressed to himself, in the journal *Mercure de France*. In 1905 the Dutch critic Albert Plasschaert published sixteen letters to

Van Gogh's colleague Van Rappard. Not long after the artist's death, therefore, the letters began to be instrumental in shaping Van Gogh's reputation.

The 1914 edition, published partly in Dutch and partly in French – that is to say, in the languages in which the letters had been written – was quickly followed by a German edition, and somewhat later by editions in English and other languages. Over the years, moreover, other groups of letters addressed to his fellow artists and friends Émile Bernard and Anthon van Rappard and to his sister Wil were added to the *Verzamelde Brieven* (Collected Letters). Dr Vincent Willem van Gogh (1890–1978), Johanna and Theo's son, played an important part in encouraging the publication of later editions, not least in an editorial capacity.

In 1973 the opening of the Rijksmuseum Vincent van Gogh in Amsterdam was the occasion for a reissue of the *Verzamelde Brieven*. For it was here that Dr Vincent Willem van Gogh's former collection – and thus the great majority of the originals of Vincent's letters to Theo and Wil – found their final destination, as the property of the Vincent van Gogh Foundation, established in 1960. On the basis of this material, Douglas Cooper, in collaboration with the Van Gogh Museum and the Vincent van Gogh Foundation, went on to publish forty-five letters by Gauguin to Vincent, to Theo and to Johanna van Gogh in 1983.

A fully revised Dutch edition was prepared in 1990, under the auspices of the Rijksmuseum Vincent van Gogh, by Han van Crimpen and Monique Berends-Albert, and published on the centenary of Vincent van Gogh's death. It comprises a greatly revised, more comprehensive and newly transcribed edition in four volumes. Recently discovered letters have been added, and numerous passages, left out of the first edition for reasons of discretion, have been restored. In her 1914 edition Johanna van Gogh had, for obvious reasons, omitted references to such incidents as Pastor Van Gogh's threats to have his son locked up in a mental asylum. Similarly she carried out some thorough pruning of the numerous passages, especially in the early letters, filled with religious outpourings, possibly fearing that their long-windedness might deter early readers from persevering with the letters. The countless poems Van Gogh copied out for Theo and various friends, which were also omitted from, or severely cut in, the early editions, were included in full in the 1990 edition.

Innumerable selections of letters have preceded the present one. The most important published recently was that compiled by Jan Hulsker, who aimed to provide a nearly complete picture of the main events in Van Gogh's life through letters and extracts from letters. Although the selection offered here is scarcely less extensive, its purpose is entirely different. The present book is an attempt to present complete letters whenever possible, the better to convey a full picture of their tone and structure. The desire to follow Van Gogh's train of thought has informed this attempt, rather than the wish to present all the relevant details. The selection is spread as evenly as possible over the various periods of his life. His great humanitarian, religious and artistic passions, whether they revolved around God, love or the painter's Muse, have taken precedence over the chronicling of facts. Thus several letters bearing witness to Van Gogh's desperate courtship of his cousin Kee Vos are included virtually uncut, not to present the sequence of events as such, but to show how an ill-fated obsession was exorcized.

In the passages linking successive groups of letters I have tried to keep the reader informed of what was preoccupying Vincent during the intervening periods, not least by quoting from the correspondence. Only when these quotations contain too much miscellaneous material concerning irrelevant subjects have small cuts, indicated by [. . .], been made.

One problem for readers of a selection of letters such as this is that it fails to depict the author's paramount concern – the paintings. In this respect the early letters, which demand less familiarity with the pictures, are somewhat easier to follow than the later ones. However, readers can take comfort from the fact that even Theo had yet to see the paintings and drawings mentioned in the letters and had to make do with pen-and-ink sketches of them. All such sketches incorporated in the relevant letters and all drawings enclosed in them are, wherever possible, reproduced in full in this selection.

The letters as Vincent's and Theo's joint work of art

To the art historian Van Gogh's letters naturally constitute a vital source for identifying and dating the majority of the paintings, and also give insights into their genesis and background. Thus the letters make it clear that Van Gogh's later paintings must be placed against the background of a broader conception of his oeuvre as a coherent whole. What is striking is the continuity of ideas, the consistency with which Van Gogh, on the various halts in his pilgrimage – for those are the terms in which he viewed his life from the 1870s onwards – faced up to the world and to art. If ever a painter knew where he was going and how to present his progress, that painter was Vincent van Gogh.

From our point of view Theo was, of course, an ideal correspondent. Thanks to his position in Goupil & Cie, a firm of leading international art dealers, he was extremely well informed about what was happening in the contemporary art world. Vincent, with his own experiences in the picture trade, used the same frame of reference, so that the brothers needed no more than a hint to be able to communicate with each other, the geographic distance between them proving no obstacle. Theo, in turn, was receptive enough to Vincent's ideas to make his brother's contacts among the younger Parisian avant-garde his own – after some initial differences of opinion. Although in social respects the brothers' lives drew increasingly apart, the artistic bond between them remained close.

Theo van Gogh was the kind of man who saved even the smallest scrap of paper, and it is to this trait that we owe the almost complete series of more than 600 letters from Vincent. We remain relatively uninformed about the Parisian period alone, for at that time the brothers were sharing an apartment and had no need to correspond. There are other gaps in the correspondence as well, but these pale into insignificance when compared to the almost total absence of letters from Theo. Only about forty or so of these, written after October 1888, have come down to us. In Vincent's letters we now possess a mere echo of Theo's, and 'What Theo really thought about Vincent', as an article by Jan Hulsker puts it, is something we can at best only vaguely surmise.

We know that Vincent thought highly of Theo's observations and that he now and then lauded the merits of his brother's letters. It has been suggested that in their correspondence Vincent and Theo modelled themselves on the de Goncourt brothers. As Vincent often took the lives of other artists as his model, it would not be surprising to find that as a letter-writer also he should have wanted to follow an illustrious example. The notion is an appealing one since it reflects Vincent's cherished dream to be joined with his brother in a 'work of art'. Towards the end of December 1885, Vincent referred to 'what the de Goncourts went through – and of how, at the end of their lives, they were pessimistic, yes – but also sure of themselves, knowing that they had done something, that their work would last. What fellows they were! If only we got on together better than we do now, if only we too could be in complete accord – we could be the same, couldn't we?'

When Vincent tried during his Drenthe period to persuade Theo to turn his back on the art trade and to opt for the artist's life, he used these French naturalist writers as an example, and, referring to what he had read about their diary (then not published), he wrote, '... I wish that we too might walk together somewhere at the end of our lives and, looking back, say, "Et d'un" [firstly] we have done this, "et de deux" [and secondly] that, "et de trois" [and thirdly]...' The acquisition of their joint collection of Japanese prints, too, may well have been partly inspired by the 'maison d'artiste' set up by the de Goncourts, whose love of Japanese art was proverbial.

Nevertheless, Vincent seemingly failed to keep Theo's letters. This suggests that much as Theo played a part in the creation of the drawings and paintings through his role as art dealer, so he participated in the creation of the letters by being their principal and ideal recipient. However, it would no doubt have given the brothers great satisfaction to discover that their correspondence, besides being an autobiographical document, now also serves as an exemplary source for anyone seeking to reach to the very heart of late nineteenth-century artistic life, thus playing much the same role in art as the diaries of the de Goncourts play in literature.

Literary features

Among the literary qualities that have earned Van Gogh's letters their place in world literature, power of expression and integrity take pride of place. The letters convince because they are fashioned by inner compulsion and broach subjects of existential concern to the artist. From the outset the letters strike an authentic note. When he addresses his brother or colleagues, for whom a hint was enough in matters of art,

Van Gogh's tone is naturally different from the one he adopts to address his parents or Wil. The companionable and humorous sides of his personality come out most strongly in his letters to such fellow artists as Bernard and Van Rappard. The tone is further influenced by his passions of the moment. During the periods of his involvement with Kee Vos and Sien Hoornik he is sometimes wound up to fever pitch. At his moments of religious fanaticism a pedagogic and sermonizing tone alternates with the intense passions of the zealot. During his later years in France his language grows appreciably less exalted. The descriptions of landscapes, for instance, are less elaborate and have less of a literary veneer than those from his English and Borinage periods. It would seem that the shorthand of Impressionism also rendered his prose more concise.

Although the letters are full of shrewd observations and crisply formulated images, Van Gogh was no coiner of the aperçu. The expressive force of his prose lies more in the accumulation of arguments by which he attempts to ward off the threats of this world than in short, brilliant sayings. Much as he never considered a quick sketch in oils as an end in itself but aimed at a fully rounded picture, so he never considered a subject closed in his letters until it had been lit up from all sides. Not infrequently he returns to the same subject in various passages of one and the same letter, or develops the thoughts that preoccupy him over a series of letters. This can sometimes make for long-windedness, but at inspired moments the result reads like a beguiling 'variation on a theme'.

Long before Van Gogh aspired to a career as an artist, his letters contained passages of great intrinsic beauty. Although it is well known that his father was no inspired preacher, the word of the Bible must have formed Vincent's first literary training. His letters from the late 1870s – that is, from his intensely religious period – seem at times like so many exercises in the writing of sermons. They are riddled with the biblical texts Vincent had made his own, and with passages from religious tracts which he applied to the most diverse situations. He had a good memory and often quoted long passages by heart, as well as many poems.

Van Gogh's landscape descriptions during his English period (1873–6) betray an eye already schooled in the art trade. While he developed as an artist, he also learned to express his ideas more succinctly and pithily in his letters, with the same telling effect we find in his sketches and rough drawings. His descriptions of landscapes, people or situations fascinate by their colourfully drawn comparisons, as when he portrays the Zouave as 'a young man with a small face, a bull neck, the eyes of a tiger', or when he writes of the *Night Café*: 'I have tried to depict man's terrible passions with red and green. The room is blood red and dull yellow, a green billiard table in the middle and four lemon-yellow lamps radiating orange and green. There is a clash and a contrast throughout, between the most diverse reds and greens, in the figures of the little sleeping tramps, in the bleak empty room, in purple and blue.'

Van Gogh's special talent lay in his creative imagination, his powers of association being the most essential component of his literary repertoire. Even at times of crisis in his relations with Theo he prefers to resort to metaphor. Thus he compares their conflicting views to the actions of soldiers firing at one another from behind barricades, because they, too, belonged to distinct camps – artists and art dealers. Because of their private frame of reference, a simple allusion to a novel both brothers had read sufficed. Thus when Vincent informed Theo of the attempted suicide of Margot Begemann in Nuenen, he compared her to 'the first Madame Bovary'.

The Bible, history and literature yielded a host of such references, but the true heroes and martyrs of their mythology were painters, living or dead. Van Gogh's idols were Millet and Delacroix, and – in later letters – Monticelli and Puvis de Chavannes.

That the act of reading itself was turned into a metaphor in some of Van Gogh's paintings can be seen from the frequency with which books appear in his work, from the *Still Life with Bible*, in which Zola's *La Joie de vivre* forms an ironic commentary on the open Bible representing the world of his father, and from his homage in the *Romans parisiens* to the naturalists, to his never-realized dream of painting the display window of a bookshop as the main motif of a triptych.

The illness

Against all expectations, the symptoms of Van Gogh's mental illness are conspicuous by their almost complete absence from his letters. Much as he chose not to paint before he had fully recovered from one of his attacks, so he refrained from writing at times of crisis. Throughout his life, admittedly, his letters bear witness to a man possessed, frequently agitated, enraged, dejected, obsessed, but never deranged, or emotionally or intellectually unstable. We learn about his crises after the event – through the analyses he himself was wont to give of them. Whether describing his stay in the hospital in The Hague, where he was being treated for a venereal disease, or in the hospital in Arles, or in the institution in Saint-Rémy, he writes clearly, rationally and with a marked lack of sentimentality about his illness. And though he is familiar with the prevailing views on the supposed borderland between genius and madness and sometimes flirts with them, he studiously refuses to grant mental illness any positive influence on artistic creation. When, after an attack, he feels that he is not yet well enough to live a normal life, he keeps his letters short and tries to come to terms with the condition that was to remain his mortal foe. Whenever there is mention of madness in artists – a subject on which he is remarkably well informed – Van Gogh contends that the main cause lies in society's rejection of painters, which forces them into isolation and treats them 'as madmen, and because of this treatment [they] actually [go] insane, at least as far as their social life is concerned'.

Literature as inspiration

Frequent reference has been made to the dominant role of literary inspiration in the genesis of Van Gogh's paintings. Apart from providing a key to the meaning he attached to the subjects he depicted, an analysis of his reading also explains much of his writing style.

Whether and to what extent the writers with whose work Van Gogh was familiar helped form that style has been, incidentally, the subject of very few studies. But even without thorough analysis it seems likely that his long familiarity with literature – in his parental home and later in Amsterdam and again as an apprentice preacher, associating with clergymen – had a profound influence on his outlook. His letters from the time clearly reflect the influence of religious texts and his attendance at several sermons every Sunday. The influence of Dutch literature, by contrast, seems relatively slight, not least because Van Gogh had learned

French, German and English at high school (the Hogere Burgerschool) in Tilburg and because all his friends and acquaintances read a great deal of foreign literature. His move to the London branch of Goupil in 1873 increased his familiarity with English writers. In George Eliot and Dickens he discovered 'plastic' qualities 'just as powerful as, for instance, a drawing by Herkomer, or Fildes or Israëls'.

He was at first drawn particularly to Balzac and the historian Michelet among the French writers, until he discovered the French naturalists, especially Zola and the de Goncourts, in the 1880s. What humour he missed in these 'bitter' naturalists, he made up for with the more congenial Daudet, Voltaire (whose Pangloss in *Candide* was one of his favourite characters) and Flaubert's *Bouvard et Pécuchet*. How sensitive he was to linguistic nuances, even in foreign languages, may be seen from his praise of the style of Ernest Renan, a writer of 'a French that nobody else speaks. A French in which one hears, <u>in the sound of the words</u>, the blue sky, the soft rustling of the olive trees . . .'

Van Gogh's frequent comparison of people to animals has been linked to Zola's similarly inventive imagery. Thus Zola's *Germinal* may well have inspired Van Gogh's description of a woman mine worker as having the 'expression of a lowing cow'. He compared himself to a 'tired coach horse', or, laden with painting gear, to a 'porcupine'. His metaphors became grimmer during his stay at the Saint-Rémy institution, when he likened the 'continuous horrible screaming and screeching' of the inmates to that 'of animals in a zoo'.

Characteristic of his way of thinking, writing and painting is the habit of generalizing highly personal experiences and turning the specific into the typical, sometimes with philosophical overtones. Under his pen and brush Madame Ginoux becomes *the* Arlésienne, his friend Boch *the* poet and the soldier Milliet *the* lover. Van Gogh discovered the same approach in Victor Hugo's *Les Misérables*. In common with many 'realists' of his generation, he went to extraordinary lengths to depict the bare facts of everyday life, without gloss. Beyond that, he felt that his subjects, humble and commonplace though they might be, must carry a symbolic charge, often underlined with a literary reference. In this way he managed to effect a reconciliation or, as he put it under the influence of Puvis de Chavannes's picture *Inter Artes et Naturam*, to arrange 'a strange and happy meeting of far distant antiquities and crude modernity'. For the most part this layer of meaning cannot be gleaned from the pictures alone but must be reconstructed with the help of the letters.

The unknown Van Gogh

Anyone familiar with the drawings and paintings Van Gogh produced during his short, intense life will discover that the letters highlight many facets of his personality that are suggested by his work as a visual artist. From the Antwerp period onwards, the letters reflect his love of Japanese art, a love borne out by the use of colour, the composition and the stylized presentation found in many of his paintings. His enthusiasm for English literature and woodcuts is reflected in his drawings and paintings, from the peasant heads produced at Nuenen and inspired by the 'Heads of the People' in English magazines to the painting entitled, in English, *At Eternity's Gate*. Now and then, however, the letters afford us glimpses of an 'unknown Van Gogh', whose interests cannot be directly linked to particular paintings and drawings, or to particular literary creations.

That Van Gogh idolized such popular contemporary artists as Scheffer, Decamps and Delaroche in his youth need not surprise us, nor the fact that they eventually made way for new heroes. What is remarkable, however, is the loyalty he continued to feel for his old idols. No matter how radically his tastes changed, he remained constant to artists once admitted to his heart. A relative unknown such as the Anglo-American historical and genre painter George Henry Boughton, first extolled in letters in the 1870s for the noble sentiment of his art, is still being mentioned with much appreciation during the Nuenen period – albeit for technical reasons. Conversely, Van Gogh's later allegiance to the Impressionists did not blind him to their shortcomings, and he never considered their discoveries concerning the laws of colour the only way forward. Though he counted himself one of their number – it was not until much later that his art came to be labelled 'Post-Impressionist' – he found them wanting in the long run. The letters show how he fell back on his earliest loves time and again. These included not only such widely admired masters as Millet and Delacroix, but also Meissonier, a painter of fine historical detail whom his avant-garde colleagues despised, and the fashionable Tissot.

Theo realized early in 1888 that Vincent did not embrace the new and the modish alone, recognizing that he saw as his special mission the upholding of the achievements of an earlier generation of artists – 'the regeneration of the old ideas that have been corrupted and diminished by wear and tear'.

In the past, ignorance of this conservative side of his nature has often given rise to a false interpretation of the work Van Gogh did after he left Arles. Because of their loss of colour, the pictures he made in Saint-Rémy and Auvers-sur-Oise have been considered an artistic relapse largely associated with his mental illness. That, following his 'dark' Brabant period, Van Gogh should have discovered the vivid, richly contrasting colours of France – 'the high yellow note' – matched the prevailing view of the evolution of art in the late nineteenth century. In contrast to the oversimplified picture of an artist who abandoned the earth-bound art of the Barbizon and Hague Schools under the impact of Impressionism and the scorching southern sun and who, following mental decline at the end of his life, was unable to maintain the 'high yellow note', the letters convey a far more consistent story. They show us how Van Gogh, after the liberation of colour in his Arles period, finally tried once more to channel his art along the lines of his original ideal, still his aim, of becoming a northern painter of peasant life. It is increasingly being appreciated that the paintings he did during the last year of his life demonstrated much breaking of new ground.

We see a similar development in his literary taste. In notes and letters, the young, 'unknown' Van Gogh reveals his delight in the fairy-tales of Hans Christian Andersen and copies out whole pages of poems by Jan van Beers, Joseph Autran, Pierre Jean de Béranger, François Coppée, Rückert, Uhland, Heine and Goethe. And just as his taste in painting evolves from Scheffer and Delaroche to the Impressionists and Seurat, so the above-named romantic poets are ousted from their places of honour by Balzac, Flaubert, Zola and the de Goncourt brothers. But even here Van Gogh remains loyal to a number of youthful passions, rereading Dickens and Harriet Beecher Stowe. Now and then the memory of a favourite poem loved in his youth seems to find an echo in one of his later paintings. Thus the lyrical references in the early letters to Dickens's descriptions of ivy receive belated homage in the splendid series of 'sousbois' (undergrowth) painted in Paris and Saint-Rémy.

Some of his favourite books are incorporated into his paintings with their titles clearly displayed, as, for instance, *Uncle Tom's Cabin* in the portrait of Madame Ginoux and the de Goncourts' *Manette Salomon* in the portrait of Dr Gachet. Other literary preferences go without mention in his work. Thus his paintings do not testify to his interest in the French Revolution or in Tolstoy's revolutionary ideas, evinced in the letters and reflected in the cuttings he collected from illustrated magazines. The letters do record how engrossed he was in Victor Hugo's *Les Misérables* and *Quatre Vingt Treize*, as well as in what Michelet, Dickens and Carlyle had to say about the French Revolution. Van Gogh saw his own period, too, as an age on the brink of major upheavals, and this was something upon which he frequently ruminated. We can picture him in heated discussions on the subject in Parisian artists' cafés or with his friend Roulin in Arles.

A life in letters

Van Gogh's 'life in letters' satisfies a number of literary criteria which render its reading particularly gratifying. Oscar Wilde remarked that life imitates art far more than art imitates life, but in Van Gogh's case all the ingredients of life seem to have gone into literary expression. The very fact that he himself used the lives of artists as a model for his own is significant. The linear development of his own life story through the halts. if not the stations of the cross, on his pilgrimage – Brabant, London, Paris, London, The Hague, Drenthe, Nuenen, Antwerp, Paris, Arles, Saint-Rémy, Auvers – seems made for literature. The dramatic dénouement in Arles and the associated mental crisis, so close on the heels of the peak of his artistic achievement, are as potent in their impact as the last act of a tragedy by Shakespeare (whose historical plays Van Gogh read in Saint-Rémy). Even the reason for his return to the north, and with it the closing of a geographical circle at the end of his life, could not be improved upon by a writer of fiction.

That Van Gogh's life did not simply and relentlessly speed towards madness and the abyss but that, precisely towards the end of his life, the circle closed with his wish to return to the great loves of his youth, to Millet and Delacroix, and that even in Saint-Rémy he still tried to produce a new version of his first masterpiece, *The Potato Eaters*, all ensured that his life had an 'artistically' perfect rounding off.

The handling of the recurring motifs in his life – for instance, the succession of unhappy love affairs, the role of his various friendships with fellow artists (and also their development), the transformation of his love of God, through his humanitarian phase in the Borinage, into his love of art – as well as the many emotional crises, which, with hindsight, the reader is bound to consider as portents of the ultimate tragedy, Van Gogh would have been unable to improve upon as a writer. The letters are full of such leitmotivs. In his Brabant period, Van Gogh himself compared his paintings to the weaving of cloth. The number of recurring themes and the striking consistency of his range of ideas as reflected in the letters find their artistic counterpart in his striving after coherent decorations for the Yellow House and – in a broader sense – the construction of his 'oeuvre'. In that respect he proved to be, and much more so than he realized, a true contemporary of Richard Wagner, whose attempt to produce a *Gesamtkunstwerk* – a synthesis of all the arts – he so admired. Thus, referring to Wagner, he exclaimed, 'How we need the same thing in painting!'

The discovery of these repeated leitmotivs in his letters lends an extra dimension to the interpretation of comparable situations during various periods of his life. A case in point was his attitude to friendship. From Harry Gladwell, the young man with whom he would read the Bible in the evening after work during his first stay in Paris, to his fellow artists Van Rappard, Bernard and Gauguin, and the postman Roulin, Van Gogh cultivated intense friendships. They give the lie to the oversimplified view that he was an antisocial human being. True, at times his behaviour disturbed nearly everyone who came into contact with him, and differences in artistic opinion could at times lead to bitter disputes with other painters, but Dr Mendes da Costa, his Latin teacher in Amsterdam, later charitably described Van Gogh's 'inappropriate behaviour' as 'charming oddity'.

The ambivalent attitude to sexuality that prevailed in the nineteenth century is clearly reflected in Van Gogh's frustrated love life. Nearly all his amorous overtures were spurned, and even when he believed that he might lay claim to a very modest portion of happiness, as with Sien Hoornik or Margot Begemann, the social gulf between them seemed so great that the relationships were doomed to failure. Brothels and the use of tobacco and alcohol, dubbed 'anti-aphrodisiacs' by Van Gogh, remained his only stimulants, sublimation by art his only solace.

Although the letters merely skim the surface of this subject, they can nevertheless prove most revealing. Vincent's delight when Theo makes him privy to the perils of his own love life is a poignant sign of the brothers' great intimacy, and it was with bitter resignation that Vincent renounced his right to earthly love in some of his later letters.

Much as Van Gogh's mature art was dominated by a radical use of complementary colours, so many of the recurring themes in the letters constitute a system of strict polarities. In his relationship with his brother there was the continual tension between artist and art dealer. In his dealings with his father he contrasted the hypocritical practices of the cloth with the true humanity he saw embodied in Christ. Van Gogh's sense of isolation found its counterpart in his dream of establishing a painters' fraternity based on what he thought was the Japanese model. In the visual arts themselves he saw a constant conflict between drawing and painting, between his talent for making quick sketches and his ideal of the finished tableau, between the pull of the landscape and that of the figure. His great aim of becoming a painter of peasant life was regularly at odds with his penchant for city life, and Van Gogh the realist was forever struggling with the temptations of symbolism, 'style' and abstraction.

After a youth full of false starts and disappointments, his decision to become an artist was unconditional. He accepted the social implications even when madness was the price that had to be paid. He preferred to go hungry in The Hague to producing 'saleable watercolours' before he was ready to do so. In Arles, he fell briefly under the spell of Gauguin's tempting abstractions, but abruptly forswore them because they offended his deepest convictions as a realist. Although he was prepared to try everything honestly, his inability to compromise invariably triumphed in the end. This inflexibility alienated him from his fellow men. His letters to Isaäcson and Aurier prove that – following in Millet's footsteps – he did not even like to be praised when he felt unworthy or when such praise mistook the essence of his work.

Shortly after Vincent's departure for Arles, Theo wrote to their sister, Wil, that their brother's art was far from self-centred: 'Through him I came into contact with many painters who held him in high regard [...]. Moreover, his heart is so big that he is constantly trying to do things for others. Tant pis for all those who cannot or will not understand him.' It was Vincent's hope, in a Utopian brotherhood of artists, to purge hostile society – and the practices of the art trade! – of every vestige of improbity.

Without wishing to detract in any way from the tragic isolation in which Van Gogh's self-taught skill matured and briefly came to rich fruition, it is not going too far to claim that his letters bear at least equal witness to his affinity with the world he had created around him. For every belief he lost, for every clash with society, he found his own compensation. While his visits to museums were necessarily few and far between, he created his own Louvre on his walls with photographs, woodcuts and Japanese prints. When the people of Nuenen refused to pose for him, he discovered the beauty of birds' nests. When canvas and paint ran out in Arles he used his reed pen to effect a revolution in Western draughtsmanship. Van Gogh may rarely have sold a picture, but all the greater was the number of friends who valued his work and exchanged canvases with him. At the moment of his greatest existential anguish, Delacroix and Millet watched over him, and Theo was almost constantly there. The times when he was racked with doubt about Theo's solidarity were probably the most tragic of his intense life.

Ronald de Leeuw
Amsterdam

Biographical Outline

1853   Vincent Willem van Gogh born at Groot-Zundert on 30 March, the eldest son of the Reverend Theodorus van Gogh and Anna Cornelia Carbentus (1819–1907)

1857   Birth of his favourite brother, Theodorus (Theo), on 1 May

1861–8   Sketchy school education: one year at Zundert village school (1861); two years at boarding school in Zevenbergen (1864–6), and one and a half years at Rijks Hogere Burgerschool Willem II in Tilburg (September 1866–March 1868)

1869   On 30 July, he joins the international art dealers, Goupil & Cie, in The Hague as their youngest employee, under H. G. Tersteeg

1872   In August, he starts regular correspondence from The Hague with his brother Theo, who is four years his junior

1873   Theo joins the Brussels branch of Goupil & Cie on 1 January; Vincent is transferred to Goupil's London branch in June; Theo starts to work for Goupil in The Hague in November

1874   From October to December, Vincent is temporarily transferred to Goupil's main branch in Paris, then returns to London

1875   Second transfer to Goupil's main branch in Paris on 15 May

1876   Dismissed from Goupil & Cie at the end of March; he becomes a teacher in Ramsgate on 16 April and an assistant preacher in Isleworth in the middle of July

1877   From January to late April he works for Blussé & Van Braam, a bookshop in Dordrecht, then moves to Amsterdam in May to prepare for the entrance examination to the theological faculty

1878   In July he formally abandons his studies in Theology and, after a short training period in Laeken near Brussels during the autumn, moves to the Borinage in December to work as an evangelist among the miners

1879   In July Van Gogh decides to become an artist

1880   Moves to Brussels, where he meets the painter Anthon van Rappard through Theo, who has meanwhile been transferred to Goupil's main branch in Paris

1881   Moves into his parents' house in April and practises drawing from live models; in August, he falls violently in love with his cousin Kee Vos-Stricker but is rejected; at the end of November, he starts several weeks' work in The Hague with Anton Mauve, his cousin by marriage and a member of the Hague School; after a violent quarrel with his parents at Christmas time, he moves to The Hague

1882   In January he rents a studio in the Schenkweg, The Hague; initially both Tersteeg – his former branch manager at Goupil's – and Mauve prove very helpful, Mauve even giving him drawing lessons, but both men turn against him when he takes his model, Sien Hoornik, a pregnant, unmarried mother, and her small daughter into his house and even considers marrying her (Theo, however, continues to give him financial support); in March, he receives his first commission, for twelve views of The Hague, from his uncle Cornelis ('C. M.'); following a stay in the City Hospital in June, he produces his first watercolours in July and his first painted studies in August; studies lithography in November, in the hope of finding work as an illustrator

1883   Living with Sien Hoornik becomes increasingly difficult and when it also dawns on him that city life is beyond his financial means, he breaks with her; on 11 September he leaves for Drenthe, where he takes lodgings successively in Hoogeveen and Nieuw Amsterdam; although the Drenthe landscape proves a revelation to him, his working conditions are miserable: the weather is bad, he has no studio, and there is a shortage of painting and drawing materials; moreover, Theo's money is late reaching him and he is troubled by loneliness; after three months, he decides to go to his parents in Nuenen and arrives there on 5 December

1884   At first his relationship with his parents is tense, but matters improve when he takes care of his sick mother in January; he decides to become a painter of peasant life and produces numerous painted and colour-washed studies of weavers in January-February; in May, he rents a study from Schafrat, the verger of the Catholic church; in the summer, Margot Begemann forms an attachment with him, but marriage is not forthcoming; in the autumn, he teaches still-life painting to several amateurs and works in the genre himself

1885   In the winter, he starts painting a series of fifty peasants' heads and develops his conception for *The Potato Eaters*; his father dies suddenly on 26 March; he completes the definitive version of *The Potato Eaters* at the end of April and moves into his studio in May; in the summer he draws peasants working on the land; in September the Catholic priest instructs his parishioners not to pose for Vincent any longer; he moves to Antwerp on 24 November and hopes to earn a living there with townscapes and portraits; the busy seaport makes an overwhelming impression on him, especially the art galleries, where Rubens's use of colour and brush technique have a particular attraction for him

1886   He enrols in the Antwerp Academy on 18 January and attends lessons in figure painting and in drawing from plaster casts; he meets the English painter Horace Mann Livens; he leaves for Paris on about 1 March and moves in with Theo; he works in Fernand Cormon's studio, where he makes friends with Henri de Toulouse-Lautrec, Émile Bernard, John Peter Russell and Archibald Standish Hartrick; he discovers the true meaning of Impressionism; in the summer, he paints a series of still lifes with flowers as colour studies; he meets Louis Anquetin and Charles Angrand; he becomes an admirer of the work of Adolphe Monticelli

1887   In March–April he organizes an exhibition of Japanese prints in the Café Le Tambourin; in April–May he paints many pictures along the Seine at Asnières, accompanied by Paul Signac; in November he organizes an exhibition of the 'impressionistes [*sic*] du Petit Boulevard' in the Restaurant du Chalet, where his own work appears side by side with that of An-quetin, Bernard, Arnold Koning and Toulouse-Lautrec; he meets Gauguin, Guillaumin, Pissarro and Seurat during the exhibition; he exhibits a painting in the Théâtre Libre d'Antoine (December 1887–January 1888)

1888   On 19 February, exhausted by the pressures of life in Paris and driven by a great longing for rest and a warm climate, he leaves for Arles in the south of France and takes a room at the Restaurant Carrel; in April he paints orchards in bloom; on 1 May he rents four rooms in the Yellow House but does not have enough money to make them habitable; he leaves the Restaurant Carrel for a room in the Café de la Gare; at the beginning of June, he briefly visits Les-Saintes-Maries-de-la-Mer on the Mediterranean coast; he paints harvest scenes and portraits during the summer; he plans to turn the Yellow House into a studio of the south, and invites Gauguin to live and work in it; in expectation of Gauguin's arrival he moves into the Yellow House on 16 September; Gauguin finally arrives in Arles on 23 October; in the middle of November he turns down an invitation to exhibit in the offices of the *Revue Indépendante*; in late November and early December he paints the portraits of the entire family of Joseph Roulin, the post-man; during December, conflicting views on art make working with Gauguin increasingly difficult; following a violent argu-ment with Gauguin, he cuts off part of his ear on 23 December and Gauguin leaves precipitately for Paris; he is admitted to the hospital in Arles and treated by Dr Félix Rey

1889   Contrary to all expectations, he recovers quickly and returns to the Yellow House on 7 January; following a petition by his neighbours, he is readmitted to hospital in February; on 23 March he is visited by Paul Signac, to whom he shows his work at his studio; on 17 April Theo marries Johanna Gesina Bonger in Amsterdam; at the end of April Vincent decides to become a voluntary patient at Saint-Paul-de-Mausole, a psychiatric institution in nearby Saint-Rémy-de-Provence, where he arrives on 8 May; he has a sudden attack in mid-July while out painting in the fields and is unable to return to work until early September; in September two of his paintings are shown at the fifth exhibition of the Société des Artistes Indépendants in Paris; in the autumn, he 'translates' work by Millet, Delacroix and Rembrandt into colour, including Millet's *Les travaux des champs*; at the end of December he has another attack, lasting one week

1890   On 18 January the seventh annual exhibition of the Vingtistes in Brussels, which includes six of his paintings, opens; at the end of January he has another attack lasting a week; on 25 January he receives Albert Aurier's laudatory article entitled 'Les Isolés: Vincent van Gogh'; Theo's son, named Vincent Willem after him, is born on 31 January; he visits Arles on 22 February and has another attack, which lasts until the end of April; having been declared fit to do so, he leaves for Auvers-sur-Oise on 16 May; while passing through Paris, he visits Theo and meets Theo's wife, Johanna; he arrives in Auvers on 20 May and is placed in the care of Dr Paul Gachet, a physician and amateur artist; he rents a room in Ravoux's inn and starts painting prolifically; on 8 June Theo, Johanna and their child visit Auvers; he travels to Paris for the last time on 6 July in order to discuss Theo's problems at Boussod & Valadon; he shoots himself in the chest on 27 July and dies of his wounds on 29 July in Theo's presence; his funeral in Auvers on 30 July is attended by many friends

1891   On 25 January Theo dies at the age of thirty-three

Early Letters

Vincent Willem van Gogh was born on 30 March 1853 in Groot-Zundert, a village in Brabant on the Belgian border, the oldest son of Theodorus van Gogh and his amiable wife, Anna Cornelia Carbentus (their first child, also named Vincent, had been stillborn exactly one year earlier). He was named Vincent Willem after his two grandfathers. A daughter, Anna, followed in 1855, and in 1857 a second son, Theo, with reddish hair and blue eyes just like Vincent, but of slighter build. The family was further enlarged by two daughters, Lies and Willemien, and a late arrival, a son called Cor.

Vincent's father was a Protestant clergyman in the predominantly Catholic southern Netherlands. Little is known of the young Vincent other than that he was a rather trying, sometimes troublesome boy – probably because his mother tended to spoil her children – and that he loved animals and flowers. Vincent and Theo kept each other company a good deal and their childhood against the background of 'the wheat fields, the heath and the pine forests, in that peculiarly intense atmosphere of a village parsonage' was later described by Johanna van Gogh-Bonger as a poetic age, a Brabant idyll. Association with the somewhat unruly peasant lads of the neighbourhood did little to detract from this. For a short time Vincent attended the village school in Zundert, but when he was eleven he was sent to a boarding school in Zevenbergen for two years, followed by a year and a half at the Hogere Burgerschool in Tilburg. In late July 1869, he became the youngest employee of the Hague branch of Goupil & Cie, a well-known firm of art dealers, also established in London, Paris, New York and Brussels. In addition to paintings and drawings, the firm specialized in the sale of reproductions. That the son of a Brabant clergyman should have chosen a career in the international art trade is not as strange as it might at first seem; no fewer than three of his father's brothers – 'C. M.', Cent and Hein – held prominent positions in that field. It seems the recommendation of his Uncle Vincent, his father's favourite brother, who lived in nearby Prinsenhage, was decisive in Vincent's choice of profession.

In The Hague, Vincent took lodgings with the Roos family on the Beestenmarkt and paid regular visits to various Hague relatives and friends of his mother. Regards from these families – the Haanebeeks, the Van Stockums and the Carbentuses (Aunt Fie) – can be found conscientiously included at the end of his letters.

The earliest of Van Gogh's letters to have come down to us is dated August 1872, three years after he joined Goupil, and is addressed to his brother Theo, then at school in Oisterwijk, a small town in Brabant. Theo had paid a short visit to him in The Hague, and Vincent recalls the walks they took together. Diffident though this first letter may be, in a sense it foreshadows their later relationship, in which such walks were above all the occasion for confidential talks at critical periods.

I [D]

[18] August 72

[My dear] Theo,

Many thanks for your letter, I was glad you arrived back safely. I missed you the first few days & it felt strange not to find you there when I came home in the afternoons.

We have had some enjoyable days together, and managed to take a few walks & see one or two sights between the spots of rain.

What terrible weather. You must have <u>sweltered</u> on your walks to Oisterwijk. There was harness racing yesterday for the exhibition, but the illuminations & the fireworks were put off because of the bad weather, so it's just as well you didn't stay on to see them. Regards from the Haanebeek & Roos families.

Always your loving
<u>Vincent</u>

The second letter from Van Gogh to have survived is dated 13 December of the same year. He congratulates Theo on the fact that he too will be working in the art trade as from January 1873, at the Brussels branch of Goupil & Cie. The idea that they would both then be 'in the same profession' lent a fresh dimension to their relationship and led Vincent to open his regular correspondence with his younger brother: 'We must be sure to write to each other often.'

2 [D]

The Hague, 13 December 1872

Dear Theo,

What good news I've just read in Father's letter. I wish you luck with all my heart. I'm sure you will like it there, it's such a fine firm. It will be quite a change for you.

I am so glad that both of us are now to be in the same profession & in the same firm. We must be sure to write to each other often.

I hope I'll see you before you leave, we still have a lot to talk about. I believe Brussels is a very pleasant city, but it's bound to feel strange at first. Write to me soon in any case. Well, goodbye for now, this is just a brief note dashed off in haste, but I had to tell you how delighted I am at the news. Best wishes, & believe me, always,

Your loving brother
<u>Vincent</u>

I don't envy your having to go to Oisterwijk every day in this awful weather. Regards from the Roos family.

Van Gogh was very happy to be working in the Hague branch of Goupil & Cie under H. G. Tersteeg. 'My new year has begun well,' he wrote at the beginning of January 1873. He had just had a rise in salary and this gave him reason to hope that he would be able to stand on his own feet from then on. The brothers wrote to each other at length about art, expressing their admiration for the old Dutch masters, as well as for Corot and such fashionable contemporary artists as Alfred Stevens, Rotta and Cluysenaer. They also exchanged information about reproductions, and while Vincent gave reports of his visits to Amsterdam museums and galleries, he pressed Theo continually for news of exhibitions in Brussels. Meanwhile, he advised his younger brother to smoke a pipe if he felt downcast, an idea he had taken from Dickens, who recommended tobacco as a remedy for suicide.

In March he informed Theo that he was about to be promoted and transferred from The Hague to London. He journeyed by way of Paris and made use of the opportunity to visit the main museums and galleries. Proudly he reported how distinguished Goupil's Paris offices were, 'splendid and much bigger than I had imagined, especially [the one in] the Place de l'Opéra'.

Vincent arrived in London on 13 June 1873, and remained there for just under two years, until 15 May 1875. Goupil's premises were at 17 Southampton Street, just off Covent Garden. Their main trade was in reproductions, for which there was a keen demand. His new manager was Charles Obach.

At his first London address, which is not known to us but which was, he wrote, in a 'quiet, pleasant and airy' neighbourhood, there were also three German boarders 'who are very fond of music & play the piano & sing, which makes the evenings very enjoyable'. On his salary of £90 a year, however, he had to be careful, and this made it difficult for him to go out and about with them.

In August 1873 Vincent moved and took lodgings with the Loyer family in Hackford Road in Brixton, south London. A sketch of the houses in this street, the setting for the first of a whole series of disappointments in love, is the earliest English drawing of Van Gogh's to come down to us.

For the time being, it seemed, London continued to please him. Vincent made excursions with his German friends, went rowing on the Thames and discovered the joys of gardening. He urged Theo to read the *Gazette des Beaux-Arts* and William Bürger's book on French and Dutch museums and galleries. He himself visited gallery after gallery in London, from the Royal Academy to the Dulwich Picture Gallery. He discovered that some of the French painters he admired, including James Tissot, Otto Weber and Ferdinand Heilbuth, lived in London, but English painting itself did not appeal to him at first – he deemed the work 'with few exceptions very nasty, poor stuff'. Those exceptions were the Victorian masters John Everett Millais and George Henry Boughton, and 'among the older painters' Turner, Crome and Constable. Again, at the beginning of 1874, when Vincent compiled a list of all the artists he especially liked, there were few English names on it. Instead, the list included several artists who were to play a dominant role in his later letters, chief amongst them the painters of peasant life Jean-François Millet and Jules Breton, and the landscape painters of the Barbizon School and their Dutch counterparts in the Hague School. During this London period, he did not scorn the work of such popular Salon painters as Meissonier or such sentimentalists as Ary Scheffer and Albert Anker. He even praised the voluptuous pieces of Adolphe Bouguereau. It was certainly no accident that his taste was not at odds with that of the Goupil 'stable'.

At this time he was reading, amongst other things, the poems of Jan van Beers, which reminded him of Brabant, as well as savouring the works of Keats – 'the favourite of the painters here & so I found the time to read him' – whose 'The Eve of Saint Mark' he copied out in one of his letters. His favourite author was Jules Michelet, whose *L'Amour* – and in particular the chapter called '*Les aspirations de l'automne*' – he frequently quoted and called 'both a revelation and a gospel'.

In November 1873 Theo was transferred to Goupil in The Hague, and in March 1874 Vincent heard the 'wonderful' news that his young sister, Anna, would be coming to London to find a job.

13 [D]

London, January 1874

My dear Theo,

Many thanks for your letter. My warm good wishes for a very happy New Year. I know you are doing well in the firm, because Mr Tersteeg told me so. I can see from your letter that you are taking a keen interest in art, & that's a good thing, old fellow.

I'm glad you like Millet, Jacque, Schreyer, Lambinet, Frans Hals, &c., because, as Mauve says, 'That's it.' That painting by Millet, L'angélus du soir, 'that's it', indeed – that's magnificent, that's poetry. How I wish I could have another talk with you about art, but we'll just have to keep writing to each other about it. <u>Admire</u> as much as you can, most people <u>don't admire enough</u>.

Here are the names of a few painters I particularly like. Scheffer, Delaroche, Hébert, Hamon, Leys, Tissot, Lagye, Boughton, Millais, Thys Maris, De Groux, De Braekeleer Jr, Millet, Jules Breton, Feyen-Perrin, Eugène Feyen, Brion, Jundt, George Saal, Israëls, Anker, Knaus, Vautier, Jourdan, Jalabert, Antigna, Compte-Calix, Rochussen, Meissonier, Zamacois, Madrazo, Ziem, Boudin, Gérôme, Fromentin, de Tournemine, Pasini, Decamps, Bonington, Diaz, Th. Rousseau, Troyon, Dupré, Paul Huet, Corot, Schreyer, Jacque, Otto Weber, Daubigny, Wahlberg, Bernier, Émile Breton, Chenu, Cézar de Cocq, Mlle Collart, Bodmer, Koekkoek, Schelfhout, Weissenbruch, & last [but] not least Maris & Mauve.[1]

But I could carry on like that for I don't know how long, & then there are still all the old ones & I am sure I have overlooked some of the best of the modern.

Do go on doing a lot of walking & keep up your love of nature, for that is the right way to understand art better & better. Painters understand nature & love her & <u>teach us to see</u>.

And then there are painters who never do anything that is no good, who cannot do anything bad, just as there are ordinary people who can do nothing but good.

I'm getting on well here, I've got a lovely home & I'm finding it very pleasurable taking a look at London & the English way of life & the English people themselves, & then I've got nature & art & poetry, & if that isn't enough, what is? But I haven't forgotten Holland & especially not The Hague & Brabant.

We are busy at work doing the stocktaking, but it will all be over in 5 days, we got off more lightly than you did in The Hague.

1 'last ... least': in English.

I hope that, like me, you had a happy Christmas.

And so, my boy, best wishes & write soon, I've put down whatever came into my head in this letter. I hope you'll be able to make some sense out of it.

Goodbye, regards to everybody at work & to anyone else who asks after me, especially everybody at Aunt Fie's & at the Haanebeeks'.

Vincent

I am enclosing a few lines for Mr Roos.

20 [D]

London, 31 July 1874

My dear Theo,

I'm glad you've been reading Michelet & that you understand him so well. If that kind of book teaches us anything it is that there is much more to love than people generally suppose. To me, this book has been both a revelation and a gospel.

'Il n'y a pas de vieille femme!'[1] (That does not mean there are no old women, only that a woman does not grow old as long as she loves & is loved.) And then a chapter like Les aspirations de l'automne, how rich that is ... That a woman is a 'quite different being' from a man, & a being we do not yet know, or at best only superficially, as you put it, yes, that I am sure of. And that a woman & a man can become one, that is, one whole & not two halves, I believe that too.

Anna is bearing up well, we go on marvellous walks together. It is so beautiful here, if one just has a good & single eye without too many beams in it. And if one does have that eye, then it is beautiful everywhere.

Father is far from well, although he & Mother say that he's better. Yesterday we received a letter with all sorts of plans

---

1 There are no old women!

(wouldn't we just try this & that) which will prove to be unworkable & certainly useless & at the end Father said once again that he leaves it all to us, &c., &c. Rather petty and disagreeable, Theo, & it reminded me so much of Grandfather's letters, but qu'y faire.[2] Our beloved Aunts are staying there now & are no doubt doing much good! Things are as they are & what can a person do about it, as Jong Jochem said.

Anna & I look at the newspaper faithfully every day & reply to whatever advertisements there are. On top of that we have already registered with a Governess agency.[3] So we are doing what we can. More haste less speed.

I'm glad that you go round to the Haanebeeks so often, give them all my kindest regards & tell them some of my news.

The painting by Thys Maris that Mr Tersteeg has bought must be beautiful. I had already heard about it & have myself bought & sold one in the same genre.

My interest in drawing has died down here in England, but maybe I'll be in the mood again some day. Right now I am doing a great deal of reading.

On 1st January 1875 we shall probably be moving to another, larger shop. Mr Obach is in Paris at the moment deciding whether or not we should take that other firm over. Don't mention it to anybody for the time being.

Best wishes & write to us again soon. Anna is learning to appreciate paintings & has quite a good eye, admiring Boughton, Maris & Jacquet already, for instance, so that is a good start. Between you and me, I think we are going to have a difficult time finding something for her, they say everywhere that she is too young, & they require German, too, but be that as it may, she certainly has a better chance here than in Holland. Goodbye,

Vincent

You can imagine how delighted I am to be here together with

2 What can one do?
3 'Governess agency': in English.

Anna. Tell H. T.[4] that the pictures have duly arrived & that I shall be writing to him soon.

After a year in England, Van Gogh returned to the Netherlands to spend two weeks with his parents, who had meanwhile moved to Helvoirt, still in Brabant. Here he devoted part of his time to landscape sketches and to filling a little sketchbook for Betsy Tersteeg, the small daughter of his Hague employer. This sketchbook is now in the Van Gogh Museum. On 15 July he returned to London with Anna, who also moved in with the Loyers.

Michelet's dictum in *'Les aspirations de l'automne'*, as quoted by Van Gogh, that 'a woman is a "quite different being" from a man, & a being we do not yet know' became harsh reality for Van Gogh during this period, when he expressed his feelings for Eugenie Loyer, the nineteen-year-old daughter of his landlady, by proposing to her. There are no letters extant in which Van Gogh refers to being in love, but the situation may be inferred from the family correspondence. We have only one letter from Vincent himself mentioning Eugenie. In it he describes her as 'a girl with whom I have agreed that we should be as brother and sister to each other'. When Van Gogh asked for her hand, it transpired that Eugenie was secretly engaged to someone else and that there could be no question of a serious relationship between them. When he nevertheless continued to press Eugenie to call off her engagement, the situation became intolerable and Vincent and his sister were obliged to move out.

Following a very enthusiastic and harmonious start to his stay in London, at most marked by a little homesickness, Van Gogh's unrequited love for Eugenie cast a shadow over the second half of his London period. Vincent and Anna moved to lodgings at Ivy Cottage, 395 Kennington Road, but very soon afterwards Anna found a post as a lady's companion, whereupon she moved again, this time to Welwyn, then a village some twenty-five miles north of London. Her new home, too, happened to be called Ivy Cottage. Left behind alone in London, Vincent sent his parents gloomy letters. His father judged it high time to

4 Herman Tersteeg.

take a hand and once again consulted his brother. 'Uncle Cent' arranged a posting for his nephew to Paris, for which Vincent departed very reluctantly in the middle of November. Though put out at his parents' interference, he went home to Helvoirt for Christmas and had an emotional reunion there with Theo, which strengthened their bond even further. Then he returned with Anna to London.

In the middle of May 1875, Van Gogh was again transferred to Goupil in Paris, this time ostensibly for one or two months. However, it was eventually decided to keep him on longer and in the end he remained until March of the following year. At first this was very much against his will, and his parents received grumpy and somewhat confused letters, which worried them. He seemed to be overworked. However, these problems proved to be short-lived and it was not long before he clearly began to enjoy Paris. He lived in Montmartre, then still a semi-rural part of the capital, in a small room not far from Goupil's establishment in the rue Chaptal. He went to the annual exhibition at the Salon, and visited the Louvre and the museum of modern art in the Palais du Luxembourg. At a Corot exhibition he was greatly impressed by a painting whose subject matter was to preoccupy him later – *Le jardin des oliviers*. A high point of his stay in Paris was a visit to the sale of Millet drawings at the auctioneering firm Drouot. In the presence of these masterpieces he felt as awed as Moses had before the burning bush: 'When I stepped into the hall of the Drouot salerooms, I felt like telling myself, take off your shoes, for the place where you are standing is holy ground.'

His preferences can, as ever, be gathered from the prints and photographs of paintings he stuck to the walls of his small room. The work of artists from The Hague and Barbizon Schools rubbed shoulders with that of Ruysdael and with Rembrandt's *Lecture de la Bible*.

30 [D]

[letterhead] Goupil & Cie, Paris
Paris, 6 July 1875

My dear Theo,

Many thanks for your letter. Yes, my boy, I thought as much. You must let me know how your English is getting on. Have you done anything about it? If not, it's not the end of the world.

I'm renting a little room in Montmartre I'm sure you'd like. It's small, but it looks out over a little garden full of ivy & Virginia creeper. I'll tell you what prints I have on the wall:

Ruysdael, Le buisson
d° Blanchisseries
Rembrandt, Lecture de la bible (a large Old-Dutch room, evening, a candle on the table. A young mother sits reading the Bible beside her baby's cradle. An old woman is listening. It reminds one of, 'Verily I say unto you, where 2 or 3 are gathered together in my name, there am I in the midst of them'. It's an old copper engraving as big as Le buisson, superb).
Ph. de Champaigne, Portrait d'une dame
Corot, Soir
d°   d°
Bodmer, Fontainebleau
Bonington, Une Route
Troyon, Le Matin
Jules Dupré, Le Soir (la halte)
Maris, Blanchisseuse
d° Un baptême
Millet, (woodcuts, 4 proofs) Les heures de la journée
v. d. Maaten, Enterrement dans les blés
Daubigny, L'aurore (coq chantant)
Charlet, L'hospitalité, Ferme entourée de sapins, l'hiver dans la nuit, Un paysan & un soldat devant la porte
Ed. Frère, Couturières
d° Un tonnelier

Anyway, my boy, look after yourself, you know how, be as meek & mild as you can. Let us always remain good friends. Goodbye,

Vincent

Theo sent him a poem by Rückert, but Vincent was beginning to show a preference for devotional texts. The tone of the letters from Paris began to change. Passages with a religious slant appeared more and more often alongside innumerable accounts of his favourite paintings and reproductions. Museum and church visits went hand in hand, and in the letters art and religion were increasingly bracketed together. 'When I have the opportunity,' he wrote to Theo, 'I shall send you a French Bible & [Thomas à Kempis's] l'Imitation de Jésus Christ, which was probably the favourite book of that lady painted by Ph. de Champaigne. There is a portrait of her daughter, a nun, in the Louvre, also by Ph. de Ch. She has l'Imitation on the chair beside her.' The letters to Theo began to sound appreciably more austere and didactic, and he now expressly advised his brother not to read Michelet, an author he himself had so warmly commended. A note of religious fanaticism was gaining the upper hand in his correspondence.

38 [D]

Paris, 17 Sept. 1875

My dear Theo,

A feeling, even a fine feeling, for the beauties of nature is not the same as a religious feeling, though I believe these two are connected.*

* The same is true of the feeling for art. Do not succumb too much to that either. Above all, save some love for the business & for your work, & respect for Mr Tersteeg. One day you will appreciate, better than now, how much he deserves that. No need to overdo it, though.

Nearly everyone has a feeling for nature, some more, some less, but there are some who feel: God is a Spirit, and they that worship Him must worship Him in spirit and in truth. Father is one of those few, Mother too, and Uncle Vt[1] as well, I think.

You know that it is written, 'The world passeth away, and the lust thereof', and that on the other hand we are also told about 'that good part which shall not be taken away', and about 'a well of water springing up into everlasting life'. Let us also pray that we may grow rich in God. Still, do not dwell too deeply on these matters – in the fullness of time they will become clearer to you of their own accord – and just take the advice I have given you.

Let us ask that it may fall to us to become the poor in the Kingdom of God, God's servants. We are still a long way from that, however, since there are often beams in our eye that we know not of. Let us therefore ask that our eye may become single, for then we ourselves shall become wholly single.

Regards to Roos & to anyone who may ask after me, and believe me, always,

Your loving brother
<u>Vincent</u>

You are eating properly, aren't you? In particular eat as much bread as you can. Sleep well, I must go and polish my boots for tomorrow.

43 [D]

[letterhead] Goupil & Cie, Paris
Paris, 14 October 1875

My dear Theo,

Just another few words to cheer myself up as well as you. I advised you to dispose of your books, and advise it still. Be sure

1 Vincent.

to do it, it will give you peace of mind. But at the same time be careful not to become narrow-minded, or afraid of reading what is well written, quite the contrary, such writings are a source of comfort in life.

'Que toutes les choses qui sont véritables, toutes les choses qui sont honnêtes, toutes les choses qui sont justes, toutes les choses qui sont pures, toutes les choses qui sont aimables, toutes les choses qui sont de bonne réputation, et où il y a quelque vertu, et qui sont dignes de louange; que toutes ces choses occupent vos pensées.'[1]

Seek only light and freedom and do not immerse yourself too deeply in the worldly mire.

How I should like to have you here, to show you the Luxembourg and the Louvre, &c., but I have the feeling that you, too, will be coming here one day.

I have had quite a good letter from Anna, I am sending it on to you, but please let me have it back when you have read it.

Father once wrote to me, 'Do not forget the story of Icarus, who wanted to fly to the sun, and having reached a certain height lost his wings & fell into the sea.' You may often feel that neither Anna nor I are what we hope to become and that we still lag a long way behind Father and other people, that we lack soundness and simplicity and sincerity. One does not become simple and true overnight. But let us persevere, and above all have patience. He who believes, does not hasten. Still, there is a difference between our desire to become Christians and that of Icarus to fly to the sun.

To my mind, there is nothing wrong with having a reasonably strong body, so make sure you feed yourself properly, and if you feel very hungry sometimes, or rather, have a good appetite, then eat well. I assure you that that is what I do myself often enough, and above all used to do. Especially bread, in my opinion, my boy, and don't be too shy about it. 'Bread is the staff

1 Whatsoever things are true, whatsoever things are honest, whatsoever things are just, whatsoever things are pure, whatsoever things are lovely, whatsoever things are of good report; if there be any virtue, and if there be any praise, think on these things (Epistle to the Philippians 4:8).

of life',[2] the English say (although they like meat as well, on the whole far too much).

And now, write again soon and about everyday matters, too, for a change. Take care of yourself and give my regards to anyone who asks after me. Let us hope we see each other in a month or two. I shake you warmly by the hand in my thoughts, and am always,

Your loving brother
Vincent

Theo was to receive a whole series of such edifying epistles and notes, all seemingly written with the intention of bolstering his faith.

In 1875 Van Gogh again spent Christmas with his family in Brabant. However, when he returned to Paris in January he was summoned by his employer, given a serious talking to and dismissed as from 1 April. The official explanation was his absence during the busy Christmas season, but that was plainly not the whole story. Van Gogh's increasing religiosity had gone hand in hand with a growing aversion to the art trade, nor had he become more adroit in his dealings with clients. He apparently took his dismissal as inevitable, for his report of the matter to Theo is fairly laconic. 'When the apple is ripe, a soft breeze will make it fall from the tree, and such was the case here. I have probably done things that in a certain sense have been very wrong, so I cannot complain [...]. Well, my boy, I am not at all clear what I should do next, but we shall try to maintain hope and courage.' Only later, during his Drenthe period, would he look back on this episode with some bitterness. If only they had given him a little more guidance, if only they had given him another chance, then everything might have turned out better.

Reading seemed to be the best remedy for this setback. The writers to engage his attention during these last months in Paris included Heine, Uhland, Erckmann-Chatrian, Jules Breton (a writer as well as a painter), Hans Christian Andersen, Longfellow and George Eliot. The last-named's *Scenes of Clerical Life* appealed to him particularly because the book told 'the story of a clergyman who lived chiefly amongst the inhabitants of the back streets of a town'. Literature helped his search for the paths that were open to him in real life. Knowing that his days with Goupil were now numbered, he immersed himself in Bulwer-Lytton's *Kenhelm Chillingly*, which seemed to parallel his own situation: it told of the 'adventures of a rich Englishman's son who could find no rest or peace in his own social circles and sought it among other walks of life. He ended up returning to his own class, but did not regret what he'd done.' This strong identification with literary characters is a recurrent feature of Van Gogh's letters. The Bible, however, prevailed over all other writings. Although his future course was not yet clear to him, Van Gogh came gradually to look on life as a pilgrimage and upon the Lord as his shepherd.

He read the Bible at night, after work, with his English friend Harry Gladwell. The way in which he describes this friend in a letter to Theo has all the plasticity of the portraits he was to paint later: '... a young <u>Englishman</u>, Harry Gladwell, an employee in the business, 18 years old, the son of a London art dealer, who will probably join his father's business later. He had never been away from home before and was fearfully uncouth, especially during his first weeks here, for instance eating 4 to 6 sous' worth of bread morning, noon and night [...] and filling up with pounds of apples & pears, &c. For all that as thin as a rake, with two strong rows of teeth, big red lips, sparkling eyes, a pair of large, usually red, protruding ears, a close-cropped head (black hair), &c., &c. A quite different being from the Lady by Philippe de Champaigne, I can assure you.'

Having at the very last moment bought a few etchings after Millet in Paris, Van Gogh returned to Brabant when his job with Goupil ended and lived for a short time with his parents, who had moved to Etten the previous October. For the first time we read that he had already started to toy with the idea of becoming an artist. However, even before his departure from Paris, he had received a letter from one William Stokes, a schoolmaster in the small English town of Ramsgate, offering him the post of assistant at his boarding school. On 4 April 1876 Van Gogh wrote to Theo from their parents' home: 'As you know, Ramsgate is a seaside resort. I saw in a book that there are 12,000 inhabitants, but I know no more about it.' A fortnight later he enthusiastically sent his brother a small piece of seaweed from there. A letter to Theo at the end of May betrayed the painter's eye with a beautiful description of a storm off the Kent coast.

Ramsgate and Isleworth

67 [D]

Ramsgate, 31 May 1876

My dear Theo,

Bravo on going to Etten on 21 May, so that happily 4 of the 6 were at home. Father wrote to me at length how everything went on the day. Thanks also for your last letter.

Did I write to you about the storm I watched not long ago? The sea was yellowish, especially close to the shore. On the horizon a streak of light and above it immensely large dark grey clouds, from which one could see the rain coming down in slanting streaks. The wind blew the dust from the little white path among the rocks into the sea and shook the hawthorn bushes in bloom and the wallflowers that grow on the rocks. To the right, fields of young green corn, and in the distance the town, which, with its towers, mills, slate roofs, Gothic-style houses and the harbour below, between 2 jetties sticking out into the sea, looked like the towns Albert Dürer used to etch.

I watched the sea last Sunday night as well. Everything was dark grey, but on the horizon the day was beginning to break. It was still very early and yet a skylark was already singing. And the nightingales in the gardens by the sea. In the distance, the light of the lighthouse, the guard-ship, &c.

That same night I looked out of the window of my room at the roofs of the houses you can see from there, and at the tops of the elms, dark against the night sky. Above the roofs, a single star, but a beautiful, big, friendly one. And I thought of us all and I thought of my own years gone by and of our home, and these words and this sentiment sprang to my mind, 'Keep me from being a son who brings shame, give me Thy blessing, not because I deserve it but for my Mother's sake. Thou art Love, cover all things. Without Thy constant blessing we shall succeed in nothing.'

Enclosed is a little drawing of the view from the school window through which the boys follow their parents with their eyes as they go back to the station after a visit. Many a one will never forget the view from that window.

You really ought to have seen it this week, when we had rainy days, especially at dusk when the lamps are lit and their light is reflected in the wet streets. On such days Mr Stokes can sometimes be in a bad temper, and if the boys make more of a noise than he likes they occasionally have to go without their bread and tea in the evening. You ought to see them looking out of the window then, there is something so melancholy about it. They have so little apart from their meals to look forward to and to see them through from one day to the next.

I wish you could also see them going down the dark stairs and through the narrow passage to where they have their dinner. The sun does shine pleasantly in there. Another peculiar place is a room with a rotten floor where there are 6 basins in which they wash, and a dim light is all that reaches the washstand through the broken panes of the window. That is certainly quite a melancholy sight. I should like to spend, or to have spent, a winter with them, just to see what it is like.

The youngsters have made an oil stain on your little drawing, please forgive them.

Enclosed, a few lines for Uncle Jan. And now, good night. Should anyone ask after me, my greetings to them. Do you still visit Borchers from time to time? If you see him, remember me to him as well as to Willem Valkis and everybody at the Rooses'. A handshake in my thoughts from

Your loving
Vincent

[67]: enclosed sketch.

Van Gogh was a formidable walker. At the end of March he had written to Theo from Paris about the pleasure with which he thought back on his walking-tour to Brighton during an earlier stay in England. This time he went on a few brisk walks from Ramsgate to London. He saw life in the metropolis largely from the point of view of his religious faith, informing Theo that there was a great 'longing for religion among the people in the large cities. Many a worker in a factory or shop has had a strange, beautiful and pious youth. But city life sometimes removes "the early dew of morning". Even so, the longing for "the old, old story" remains. What is at the bottom of the heart stays at the bottom of the heart. In one of her books, [George] Eliot describes the life of factory workers, &c., who have formed a small community and hold religious services in a chapel in "Lantern Yard", and she says of it, "It is the Kingdom of God on earth, no more and no less."'

After his trial month with Mr Stokes, Van Gogh had to make up his mind whether or not he would stay on. Mr Stokes had plans for moving his school to Isleworth, near London, and had asked Vincent to go along, too, but could not promise him any pay beyond his board and lodging. Once again Van Gogh began looking for another post and – perhaps mindful of Eliot's *Scenes of Clerical Life* – he wrote to Theo that it was likely to be 'a job between clergyman and missionary among working people in the suburbs of London'. In a note to a prospective employer he gave a fair résumé of his position at the time.

[D] [enclosed with letter 69]

[17 June 1876]

Dear Sir,

A clergyman's son who, because he has to work for his living, has neither the money nor the time to keep up studies at King's College, and is in any case already a few years older than is usual for those who go there and has not yet even started the preliminary studies in Latin and Greek, would, all this notwithstanding, be very glad to find a position connected with the church, albeit the position of a university-educated clergyman is beyond his reach.

My father is a clergyman in a village in Holland. I went to school when I was 11, staying on until I was 16. I then had to choose a profession and did not know which to choose. Through the kind offices of one of my uncles, a partner in the firm of Goupil & Cie, art dealers and publishers of engravings, I obtained a position in his business in The Hague. I was employed in this business for 3 years. From there I went to London to learn English and, after 2 years, moved on to Paris. Various circumstances have, however, compelled me to leave Messrs G. & Cie, and for the past 2 months I have been teaching at Mr Stokes's school in Ramsgate. But since my aim is a position in connection with the church, I must look elsewhere.

Although I have not been trained for the church, perhaps my past experience of travels, of living in different countries, of association with various people, poor and rich, religious and irreligious, of work of various kinds, days of manual labour followed by days of office work, &c., perhaps also my ability to speak various languages, may in part make up for my not having been to a university.

But the reason I would much sooner give for commending myself to you is my innate love of the church and everything to do with the church, which may lie dormant from time to time but always reawakens; and, if I may say so, although with a sense of great inadequacy and imperfection: the Love of God and of man.

And also, when I think of my past life and of my father's house in the village in Holland, the sense of: 'Father, I have sinned against heaven, and before thee, and am no more worthy to be called thy Son: make me as one of thy hired servants. Be merciful to me a sinner.'

When I lived in London I often attended your church and have not forgotten you. Now I would ask for your recommendation as I look for a position, and also that you keep your fatherly eye on me should I find such a position. I have been left a good deal to myself, and I believe your fatherly eye will do me good, now that:

> The early dew of morning
> has passed away at noon.[1]

Thanking you in anticipation for what you may feel able to do for me –

In July 1876 Van Gogh, who had meanwhile turned twenty-three, was finally offered a post as an assistant preacher by the Reverend Thomas Slade-Jones, a Methodist minister in Isleworth. Vincent lived with his employer and his wife, Annie, in their house, Holme Court. Between giving lessons to his pupils, he wrote long letters to his brother full of atmospheric descriptions of the local landscape. He relished English poetry and hymns, copying them out at length in letters and poetry albums for family and friends.

He enjoyed the city, 'especially the streets in the evening when it is more or less foggy and the lamps are lit', or when the sun went down in a park 'behind the elm trees, whose leaves are now coloured bronze. Over the grass lay that mist Anna wrote about, and a stream runs through the park in which you can see swans swimming. The acacia trees in the playground have already lost many of their leaves; they can be seen through the window in front of my desk – sometimes they stand

1 'The early . . . noon': in English.

out dark against the sky, sometimes the sun can be seen rising red in the mist behind them.'

Van Gogh's favourite reading at this period was John Bunyan's *The Pilgrim's Progress*. He associated it with a painting by the Victorian artist George Henry Boughton, which reminded him of a walk he made to Canterbury in June. The pilgrim in the painting seemed evocative of his own path through life and inspired his first sermon, which he gave at the end of October.

74 [D] [part]

Isleworth, 26 Aug. 1876

My dear Theo,

[. . .] It is towards evening. A sandy path leads over the hills to a mountain on which one can see the Holy City, lit by the sun setting red behind the grey evening clouds. On the path, a pilgrim on his way to the city. He is already tired and asks a woman in black, who is standing on the path and whose name is 'Sorrowful yet alway rejoicing':

> Does the road go uphill then all the way?
> 'Yes to the very end.'
> And will the journey take all day long?
> 'From morn till night my friend.'[1]

The landscape through which the path runs is very beautiful, brown heathland with birches and pine trees here and there and patches of yellow sand, and in the distance the mountains against the sun. Truly, it is not a picture but an inspiration.

I am writing to you between lessons. Today I took a few moments off to go for a walk between the hedgerows with 'John and Theogenes' to study it. How I wish you could just see the playground and the garden beyond, now, in the twilight. The gas

---

1 Slight misquotation (in English) from Christina Rossetti's 'Up-Hill'. Van Gogh had already quoted this poem earlier, in a letter to Theo from Paris on 6 October 1875.

is flickering in the school and one can hear the companionable sound of the boys at their lessons. Now and then one of them starts to hum a snatch of some hymn or other, and then there is something of the 'old faith' in me. I am still far from being what I want to be, but with God's help I shall succeed. I want – to be bound to Christ with unbreakable bonds and to feel these bonds. To be sorrowful yet alway rejoicing. To live in and for Christ, to be one of the poor in His kingdom, steeped in the leaven, filled with His spirit, impelled by His Love, reposing in the Father with the repose of which I wrote to you in my last letter. To become one who finds repose in Him alone, who desires nothing but Him on earth, and who abides in the Love of God and Christ, in whom we are fervently bound to one another. [...]

79 [D]

Isleworth [31 October 1876]

Dear Theo,

It is high time you heard from me again. Thank God the recovery is continuing. I am longing so much for Christmas – it will probably be upon us before we know it, though it still seems so far away.

Theo, last Sunday your brother preached for the first time in God's house, in the place of which it is written: 'In this place will I give peace'. Enclosed is a copy of what I said – may it be the first of many.

It was a bright autumn day and a beautiful walk from here to Richmond along the Thames, in which were mirrored the tall chestnut trees with their burden of yellow leaves and the bright blue sky, and through the tops of those trees the part of Richmond that lies on the hill, the houses with their red roofs and uncurtained windows and green gardens and the grey spire above them, and below, the great grey bridge, with the tall poplars on either side, over which the people could be seen going by as small black figures.

When I stood in the pulpit I felt like someone emerging from a dark vault underground into the friendly light of day, and it is a wonderful thought that wherever I shall go from this day forward I shall be preaching the Gospel. To do that <u>well</u>, one must have the Gospel in one's heart; may He grant that. God says, Let there be light! And there is light. He speaks and it is there. He commands and there it stands and stands firm. He, who calls us, is faithful, and shall accomplish it.

You know enough of the world, Theo, to realize that a poor preacher is quite alone as far as the world is concerned – but He can increasingly arouse in us awareness and belief. 'And yet I am not alone because the Father is with me.'

> I know in whom to place my trust
> Though day and night may come and go.
> I know the rock on which I build:
> He never fails who saves me yet.
> And come the evening of my life,
> Worn out with care and strife I will,
> For each day granted me on earth,
> The air with praises to Thee fill.
> (Evangelical Hymns 280: 5).

> Glory, Christians by your left
> and by your right side God abides!
> Where helplessly I lose my way
> Or suffer sorely, God is there!
> Where dear friends' hands in vain reach out
> to help me, God is there!
> In death and in death's thrall,
> Yes, God is everywhere.
> (Evangelical Hymns 143: 3).

But my boy, how I long for Christmas and for all of you. Once again I feel as if I have grown years older in these few months.

> The panting hart who slipped the chase,
> Craves no more fiercely for the joys
> of the refreshing water brooks,

Than doth my soul now long for God.
Aye, my soul is athirst for God:
Dear God of life, oh when, oh when
Shall I Thy countenance approach
And magnify Thy name with praise?

Oh, my soul why art cast down,
and so disquieted withal?
Trust thou in God as didst of yore,
Seek in His praises all thy joy,
How oft hath not in days gone by
He changed thy fortune for the best.
Hope thou in God, lift up your eyes,
For yet I shall his praises sing.
(After Psalm 42: 1 and 5).

Whenever we meet disappointment and sickness and trouble, my boy, let us thank Him for having brought us this hour, and let us not forget meekness, for it is written: 'On this man will I look, even on him who is poor and sorrowful and who trembleth at My word.'[1] I was in Richmond again yesterday evening and walked across a large grassy field there surrounded by trees and houses, with the spire rising high above them. The dew lay on the grass and it was growing dusk. On one side the sky was still aglow from the setting sun, on the other side the moon was rising. An old lady (dressed in black) with beautiful grey hair was walking under the trees. In the middle of the field boys had lit a big bonfire which one could see flickering in the distance. I thought of the lines 'And come the evening of my life, Worn out with care and strife I will, For each day granted me on earth, The air with praises to Thee fill'. Goodbye, a handshake in my thoughts,

Your very loving brother
Vincent

I hope to preach on John and Theogenes in Mr Jones's church a

1 Quotation in English. Based on Isaiah 66:2.

week this Thursday: 'And the Lord added daily to the church such as should be saved.'[2]

Your brother was very deeply moved when he stood at the foot of the pulpit and bowed his head and prayed, 'Abba, Father, in Thy name be our beginning.'

Regards to Mr and Mrs Tersteeg, Haanebeek, Van Stockum and all at the Rooses' and Van Iterson[3] and anyone else you may see whom I know.

[E] [enclosed with letter 79: sermon given by Van Gogh in English, on 29 October 1876, and written down for Theo[4]]

[31 October 1876]

Psalm 119: 19: 'I am a stranger in the earth, hide not Thy commandments from me.'

It is an old faith and it is a good faith that our life is a pilgrims progress – that we are strangers in the earth, but that though this be so, yet we are not alone for our Father is with us. We are pilgrims, our life is a long walk or journey from earth to heaven.

The beginning of this life is this. There is one who remembereth no more Her sorrow and Her anguish for joy that a man is born into the world. She is our Mother. The end of our pilgrimage is the entering in Our Father's house, where are many mansions, where He has gone before us to prepare a place for us. The end of this life is what we call death, it is an hour in which words are spoken, things are seen and felt that are kept in the secret chambers of the hearts of those who stand by, – it is so that all of us have such things in our hearts or forebodings of such things.

There is sorrow in the hour when a man is born into the

2 Quotation in English. Based on Acts 2:47.
3 Teunis van Iterson, Tersteeg's assistant at Goupil's in The Hague.
4 Reproduced here as Vincent wrote it.

world, but also joy – deep and unspeakable – thankfulness so great that it reacheth the highest Heavens. Yes the Angels of God they smile they hope and they rejoice when a man is born in the world. There is sorrow in the hour of death – but there too joy unspeakable when it is the hour of death of one who has fought a good fight. There is One who has said, I am the resurrection and the life, if any man believe in Me, though he were dead yet shall he live. There was an Apostle who heard a voice from heaven saying: Blessed are they that die in the Lord, for they rest from their labour and their works follow them.

There is joy when a man is born in the world, but there is greater joy when a Spirit has passed through great tribulation, when an Angel is born in Heaven.

Sorrow is better than joy – and even in mirth the heart is sad – and it is better to go to the house of mourning than to the house of feasts, for by the sadness of the countenance the heart is made better. Our nature is sorrowfull but for those who have learnt and are learning to look at Jesus Christ, there is always reason to rejoice.

It is a good word that of St. Paul's: As being sorrowful yet always rejoicing. For those who believe in Jesus Christ, there is no death and no sorrow that is not mixed with hope – no dispair – there is only a constantly being born again, a constantly going from darkness into light. They do not mourn as those who have no hope – Christian Faith makes life to evergreen life.

We are pilgrims in the earth and strangers – we come from afar and we are going far. The journey of our life goes from the loving breast of our Mother on earth to the arms of our Father in heaven. Everything on earth changes – we have no abiding city here – it is the experience of everybody: That it is God's will that we should part with what we dearest have on earth – we ourselves we change in many respects, we are not what we once were, we shall not remain what we are now. From infancy we grow up to boys and girls – young men and young women – and if God spares us and helps us, to husbands and wives, Fathers and Mothers in our turn, and then, slowly but surely the face that once had the early dew of morning, gets its wrinkles, the eyes that once beamed with youth and gladness speak of a sincere deep and earnest sadness – though they may keep the fire of Faith, Hope and Charity – though they may beam with God's spirit. The hair turns grey or we loose it – ah – indeed we only pass through the earth, we only pass through life – we are strangers and pilgrims in the earth. The world passes and all its glory. Let our later days be nearer to Thee and therefore better than these.

Yet we may not live on just anyhow – no, we have a strife to strive and a fight to fight. What is it we must do? We must love God with all our strength, with all our might, with all our heart, with all our soul, we must love our neighbour as ourselves. These two commandments we must keep and if we follow after these, if we are devoted to this, we are not alone, for our Father in Heaven is with us, helps us and guides us, gives us strength day by day, hour by hour, and so we can do all things through Christ who gives us might.

We are strangers in the earth, hide not Thy commandments from us. Open Thou our eyes that we may behold wondrous things out of Thy law. Teach us to do Thy will and influence our hearts that the love of Christ may constrain us and that we may be brought to do what we must do to be saved.

> On the road from earth to Heaven
> Do Thou guide us with Thine eye
> We are weak but Thou art mighty
> Hold us with Thy powerful hand.

Our life we might compare it to a journey, we go from the place where we were born to a far off haven. Our earlier life might be compared to sailing on a river, but very soon the waves become higher, the wind more violent, we are at sea almost before we are aware of it – and the prayer from the heart ariseth to God: Protect me o God, for my bark is so small and Thy sea is so great. The heart of man is very much like the sea, it has its storms, it has its tides and in its depths it has its pearls too. The heart that seeks for God and for a Godly life has more storms than any other. Let us see how the Psalmist describes a storm at sea. He must have felt the storm in his heart to describe it so. We read in the 107th Psalm: They that go down to the sea in ships that do business in great waters, these see the works of the Lord and His wonders in the deep. For He commandeth and raiseth up a stormy wind which lifteth up the waves thereof. They mount up to Heaven they go down again to the depth, their soul melteth in them because of their trouble. Then they cry unto the Lord in their trouble and He bringeth them out of their distress. He bringeth them unto their desired haven.

Do we not feel this sometimes on the sea of our lives? Does not everyone of you feel with me the storms of life or their forebodings or their recollections?

And now let us read a description of another storm at sea in the New Testament, as we find it in the VIth Chapter of the Gospel according to St. John in the 17th to the 21th verse. And the disciples entered into a ship and went over the sea towards Capernaum. And the sea arose by reason of a great wind that blew. So when they had rowed about five and twenty or thirty furlongs, they see Jesus walking on the sea and drawing nigh unto the ship and they were afraid. Then they willingly received Him into the ship and immediately the ship was at the land whither they went. You who have experienced the great storms of life, you over whom all the waves and all the billows of the Lord have gone – have you not heard when your heart failed for fear the beloved well-known voice – with something in its tone that reminded you of the voices that charmed your childhood – the voice of Him whose name is Saviour and Prince of peace, saying as it were to you personally – mind to you personally: 'It is I, be not afraid.' Fear not. Let not your heart be troubled.

And we whose lives have been calm up to now, calm in comparison of what others have felt – let us not fear the storms of life, amidst the high waves of the sea and under the grey clouds of the sky we shall see Him approaching for Whom, we have so often longed and watched. Him we need so – and we shall hear His voice: 'It is I, be not afraid.'

And if after an hour or season of anguish or distress or great difficulty or pain or sorrow we hear Him ask us: 'Dost Thou love me?' then let us say: Lord, Thou knowest all things, Thou knowest that I love Thee. And let us keep that heart full of the love of Christ and may from thence issue a life which the love of Christ constraineth. Lord Thou knowest all things, Thou knowest that I love Thee. When we look back on our past, we feel sometimes as if we did love Thee, for whatsoever we have loved, we loved in Thy name.

Have we not often felt as a widow and an orphan – in joy and prosperity as well and more even than under grief, because the thought of Thee. Truly our soul waiteth for Thee more than they that watch for the morning – our eyes are up unto Thee, o Thou who dwellest in Heavens. In our days too there can be such a thing as seeking the Lord.

What is it we ask of God – is it a great thing? Yes it is a great thing: peace for the ground of our heart, rest for our soul – give us that one thing and then we want not much more, then we can do without many things, then can we suffer great things for Thy name's sake. We want to know that we are Thine and that Thou art ours, we want to be thine – to be Christians. We want a Father, a Father's love and a Father's approval. May the experience of life make our eye single and fix it on Thee. May we grow better as we go on in life.

We have spoken of the storms on the journey of life, but now let us speak of the calms and joys of Christian life. And yet, my dear friends, let us rather cling to the seasons of difficulty and work and sorrow even for the calms are treacherous often. The heart has its storms, has its seasons of drooping, but also its calms and even its times of exaltation. There is a time of sighing and of praying, but there is also a time of answer to prayer. Weeping may endure for a night, but joy cometh in the morning.

> The heart that is fainting
> May grow full to o'erflowing

And they that behold it
Shall wonder and know not
That God at its fountains
Far off has been raining

My peace I leave with you – we saw how there is peace even in the storm. Thanks be to God who has given us to be born and to live in a Christian country. Has any of us forgotten the golden hours of our early days at home, and since we left that home – for many of us have had to leave that home and to earn their living and to make their way in the world? Has He not brought us thus far? Have we lacked anything? We believe, Lord, help Thou our unbelief. I still feel the rapture, the thrill of joy I felt when for the first time I cast a deep look in the lives of my Parents, when I felt by instinct how much they were Christians. And I still feel that feeling of eternal youth and enthusiasm wherewith I went to God saying: 'I will be a Christian too.'

Are we what we dreamt we should be? No – but still – the sorrows of life, the multitude of things of daily life and of daily duties so much more numerous than we expected – the tossing to and fro in the world, they have covered it over – but it is not dead, it sleepeth. The old eternal faith and love of Christ it may sleep in us but it is not dead and God can revive it in us. But though to be born again to eternal life, to the life of Faith, Hope and Charity – and to an evergreen life – to the life of a Christian and of a Christian workman, be a gift of God, a work of God – and of God alone, yet let us put the hand to the plough on the field of our heart, let us cast out our net once more – let us try once more – God knows the intention of the spirit. God knows us better than we know ourselves, for He made us and not we ourselves. He knows of what things we have need. He knows what is good for us. May He give His blessing in the seed of His word that has been sown in our hearts.

God helping us, we shall get through life – with every temptation. He will give a way to escape.

Father we pray Thee not that Thou shouldest take us out of the world, but we pray Thee to keep us from evil. Give us neither poverty nor riches, feed us with bread convenient for us. And let Thy songs be our delight in the houses of our pilgrimage, God of our Fathers, be our God: may their people be our people, their Faith our faith. We are strangers in the earth, hide not Thy commandments from us, but may the love of Christ constrain us. Entreat us not to leave Thee or to refrain from following after Thee. Thy people shall be our people. Thou shalt be our God.

Our life is a pilgrim's progress. <u>I once saw a very beautiful picture</u>, it was a landscape at evening. In the distance on the right hand side a row of hills appearing blue in the evening mist. Above those hills the splendour of the sunset, the grey clouds with their linings of silver and gold and purple. The landscape is a plain or heath covered with grass and heather, here and there the white stem of a birch tree and its yellow leaves, for it was in Autumn. Through the landscape a road leads to a high mountain, far, far away. On the top of that mountain a city whereon the setting sun casts a glory. On the road walks a pilgrim, staff in hand. He has been walking for a good long while already and he is very tired. And now he meets a woman, a figure in black that makes one think of St. Paul's word: 'As being sorrowful yet always rejoicing.' That Angel of God has been placed there to encourage the pilgrims and to answer their questions.

And the pilgrim asks her: 'Does the road go up hill then all the way?' And the answer is: 'Yes to the very end.' And he asks again: 'And will the journey take all day long?' And the answer is: 'From morn till night my friend.'

And the pilgrim goes on sorrowful yet always rejoicing, sorrowful because it is so far off and the road so long. Hopeful as he looks up to the eternal city far away, resplendent in the evening glow and he thinks of two old sayings, he has heard long ago, the one is:

> There must much strife be striven
> There must much suffering be suffered
> There must much prayer be prayed
> And then the end will be peace.

and the other:

> The water comes up to the lips
> But higher comes it not.

And he says, I shall be more and more tired, but also nearer and nearer to Thee. Has not man a strife on earth? But there is a consolation from God in this life, an angel of God comforting men, that is the Angel of Charity. Let us not forget Her. And when everyone of us goes back to daily things and daily duties, let us not forget that – that things are not what they seem, that God by the things of daily life teacheth us higher things, that our life is a pilgrim's progress and that we are strangers in the earth, but that we have a God and Father who preserveth strangers, and that we are all bretheren. Amen.

And now the grace of our Lord Jesus Christ, and the love of God our Father, and the fellowship of the Holy Ghost, be with us for evermore. Amen.

(Reading: Psalm 91)

> Tossed with rough winds and faint with fear
> Above the tempest soft and clear
> What still small accents greet mine ear
> 't Is I, be not afraid!
>
> 't Is I, who washed thy spirit white;
> 't Is I, who gave thy blind eyes sight,
> 't Is I, thy Lord, thy life, thy light,
> 't Is I, be not afraid.
>
> These raging winds, this surging sea
> Have spent their deadly force on me
> They bear no breath of wrath to Thee
> 't Is I, be not afraid.
>
> This bitter cup I drank it first
> To Thee it is no draught accurst
> The hand that gives it thee is pierced
> 't Is I, be not afraid.

When on the otherside thy feet
Shall rest, mid thousand welcomes sweet;
One wellknown voice thy heart shall greet -
't Is I, be not afraid.

Mine eyes are watching by thy bed
Mine arms are underneath, thy head
My blessing is around Thee shed
't Is I, be not afraid.

Once more, a handshake in my thoughts. Yesterday evening I went to Turnham Common to take the service for Mr Jones, who was not well. I walked there with the oldest of the boys, he is 17 but as tall as I am and has a beard. He is due to go into business later, his father has a large factory. He has an honest, good, sensitive heart and a great need of religion. His hope and desire are to do good among the working people when he is older. I recommended Eliot's Felix Holt to him.

It was beautiful in the park with the old elm trees in the moonlight and the dew on the grass. It felt so good speaking in the little church – it is a wooden church.

Bye, Theo, bye, my boy, I hope I have written this so you are able to read it. Keep your spirits up and get better soon.

Dordrecht

Van Gogh's stay in England ended as abruptly as it had begun. By Christmas 1876 he was back in Holland, where family discussions culminated in the decision that he must give up his English post because it held too few long-term prospects. His mother seemed to understand him when she sighed, 'I wish that he could work with nature or art,' but his own solution, again after mediation by his Uncle Vincent, was to take a job as a bookseller. In January 1877 Van Gogh was to be found in Dordrecht, the town where his beloved Ary Scheffer was born. There he started work in Blussé & Van Braam's bookshop. One of the first places in the Netherlands to embrace the reformed religion, Dordrecht was fertile soil for his fanatical faith and he never missed a service, of whatever denomination. Beyond that, he delighted in the 'golden glow' of the town, birthplace of Aelbert Cuyp, whose paintings captured the special quality of the light there. Writing from memory, he gave astonishingly vivid descriptions of a painting by Daubigny and of London in the rain.

In a letter dated 22 March 1877, written soon after a brief meeting with Theo in Amsterdam, Van Gogh explained that his religious vocation was a hereditary trait. 'In our family, which is a Christian family in the full sense of the term, there has always been, as far as one can tell, someone from generation to generation who was a preacher of the Gospel.'

85 [D] [part]

[7/8 February 1877]

My dear Theo,

[...] Last Sunday I was in the French church here, which is very solemn and dignified and has something most attractive about it. The text was: 'Hold that fast which thou hast, that no man take thy crown.' The sermon closed with: 'If I forget thee, O Jerusalem, let my right hand forget her cunning.' After church I went for a lovely walk along a dyke past the mills; the glittering sky over the meadows was reflected in the ditches.

There are some special things in other countries, for instance the French coast I saw near Dieppe: the falaises[1] topped with green grass, the sea and the sky, the harbour with the old boats as if painted by Daubigny, with brown nets and sails, the small houses, among them a few restaurants, with little white curtains and green pine branches in the windows, the carts with white horses harnessed in large blue halters and red tassels, the drivers with their blue smocks, the fishermen with their beards and oilskins and the French women with pale faces, dark, often rather deep-set eyes, black dresses and white caps. And, for instance, the streets of London in the rain with the lamps, and a night spent there on the steps of a little old grey church, as happened to me this summer after that trip from Ramsgate.

There are indeed some special things in other countries, but last Sunday, when I walked on that dyke, I thought how good it felt to be on Dutch soil, and I felt something like, 'Now it is in mine heart to make a covenant with the Lord God!' For the memory of old times came back to me, among other things how we used to walk with Father to Rijsbergen, etc., during the last days of February and heard the lark above the black fields with the young green corn, beheld the sparkling blue sky with the white clouds above, and then the paved road with the beech trees.

1 Chalk cliffs.

Oh, Jerusalem, Jerusalem! Or rather, oh, Zundert, oh, Zundert! Who knows if we might not walk together beside the sea this summer! We must stay good friends, anyway, Theo, and just believe in God and trust with an abiding trust in Him who presides over prayer and over thought – who can tell to what heights grace can rise?

Warmest congratulations on today – it is already half past one and so it is already 8 February. May God spare us our father for a long time yet and may 'He bind us closely to one another, and may our love for Him strengthen our bonds ever more'.

Father wrote he had already seen starlings. Do you still remember how they used to perch on the church in Zundert? So far I have not noticed any here, but I did see a great many crows on the Great Church in the morning. Now it will soon be spring again and the larks, too, will be returning. 'He reneweth the face of the earth,' and it is written: 'Behold, I make all things new,' and much as He renews the face of the earth, so He can also renew and strengthen man's soul and heart and mind. The nature of every true son does indeed bear some resemblance to that of the son who was dead and came back to life.

Let us not forget the text 'sorrowful yet alway rejoicing', 'unknown and yet well known', and write the word weemoed[2] as two words, wee[3] and moed[4] and faith in God, who in His time can cause the loneliness which we sometimes feel even in the midst of a crowd, to fall from us. He, of whom Joseph said, 'He hath made me forget all my toil, and all my father's house.' And yet Joseph had not forgotten his father, as well you know, but you also know what he meant by his words.

Take care of yourself, give my regards to all at the Rooses' and above all to Mr and Mrs Tersteeg, and accept a handshake in my thoughts and believe me,

Your very loving brother
Vincent

2 Melancholy.
3 Woe.
4 Courage.

Tell Mr Tersteeg not to take it amiss that the drawing samples have been kept for so long. They are for the H. B. school,[5] and there are 30 already there. But they also want to choose some for the evening classes and so they need to keep them for about a week longer. You will have them back as soon as possible.

Send me that page from Michelet again, my boy. The one you sent me before is in the box in my desk and I need it. Write again soon.

89 [D]

Dordrecht, 22 March 1877

My dear Theo,

I want to make sure you have a letter to take on your journey. What a good day we spent together in Amsterdam. I stayed and watched your train until it was out of sight. We are such old friends already – how often haven't we walked the black fields with the young green corn together at Zundert, where at this time of year we would hear the lark with Father.

This morning I went to Uncle Stricker's with Uncle Cor and had a long talk there on you know what subject. In the evening at half past six Uncle Cor took me to the station. It was a beautiful evening and everything seemed so full of expression, it was still and the streets were a little foggy, as they so often are in London. Uncle had had toothache in the morning, but luckily it didn't last. We passed the flower market on the way. How right it is to love flowers and the greenery of pines and ivy and hawthorn hedges; they have been with us from the very beginning.

Have written home to tell them what we did in Amsterdam and what we talked about. On arrival here I found a letter from home at the Rijkens'. Father was unable to preach last Sunday

5 Hogere Burgerschool (high school).

and the Rev. Mr Kam stood in for him. I know that his heart burns for something to happen that will allow me to follow in his footsteps, not just some of the way, but all the way. Father has always expected it of me, oh, may it come about and blessings be upon it.

The print you gave me, 'Heaven and earth shall pass away, but my words shall not pass away', and the portrait of the Rev. Mr Heldring are already up in my little room, oh, how glad I am to have them, they fill me with hope.

Writing to you about my plans helps me to clarify and settle my thoughts. To begin with, I think of the text, 'It is my portion to keep Thy word'. I have such a craving to make the treasure of the Bible's word my own, to become thoroughly and lovingly familiar with all those old stories, and above all with everything we know about Christ.

In our family, which is a Christian family in the full sense of the term, there has always been, as far as one can tell, someone from generation to generation who was a preacher of the Gospel. Why should there not be a member of our family even now who feels called to that ministry, and who has some reason to suppose that he may, and must, declare himself and look for means of attaining that end? It is my prayer and fervent desire that the spirit of my Father and Grandfather may rest upon me, and that it may be granted me to become a Christian and a Christian labourer, that my life may come to resemble, the more the better, those of the people I have mentioned above – for behold, the old wine is good and I do not desire new. Let their God be my God and their people my people; let it be my lot to come to know Christ in His full worth and to be impelled by His charity.

It is so beautifully put in the text, 'As sorrowful, yet alway rejoicing', what that charity is, and in 1 Cor. 13 she 'beareth all things, believeth all things, hopeth all things, endureth all things. Charity never faileth.'

My heart is filled today with the text about those on the way to Emmaus, when it was toward evening and the sun was going down: 'But they constrained him, saying, Abide with us.'

It is dear to you, too, that 'sorrowful, yet alway rejoicing', keep it in mind, for it is a good text and a good cloak to wear in the storm of life, keep it in mind at this time now that you have been going through so much. And be careful, for though what you have been through is no small thing, yet as far as I can see there is something still greater ahead, and you too will be put in mind of the Lord's word: I have loved you with an everlasting Love, as one whom his mother comforteth, so will I comfort you. I shall comfort you as one who comforteth his Mother. I shall give you another Comforter, even the Spirit of truth. I will make a new covenant with you. Depart, touch no unclean thing, and I will take you to me for a people, and I will be to you a God. And I will be a Father unto you, and ye shall be my sons and daughters. <u>Hate</u> the evil and the places where it is rife, it draws you with its false splendour and will tempt you as the devil tried to tempt Christ by showing Him 'all the kingdoms of the world, and the glory of them'; and saying, 'All these things will I give thee, if thou wilt fall down and worship me.' There is something better than the glory of the things of this world, namely the feeling when our heart burns within us upon hearing His word, faith in God, love of Christ, belief in immortality, in the life hereafter.

Hold on to what you have, Theo, my boy, brother whom I love, I long so fervently for the goal you know of, but how can I attain it? If only everything were already behind me, as it is behind Father, but it takes so much hard work to become a Christian labourer and a preacher of the Gospel and a sower of the Word. You see, Father can count his religious services and Bible readings and visits to the sick and the poor and his written sermons by the thousand, and yet he does not look back, but carries on doing good.

Cast your eye up on high and ask that it be granted to me, as I ask it for you. May He grant your heart's desire, He who knows us better than we know ourselves, and is above prayer and above thought, since His ways are higher than our ways and His thoughts higher than our thoughts, as high as Heaven is above earth. And may the thought of Christ as a Comforter and of God as a lofty dwelling be with you.

Best wishes on your journey, write soon and accept a handshake in my thoughts. Goodbye, and believe me, always,

Your loving brother
<u>Vincent</u>

I hope Father will soon be better. Try to be in Etten for Easter, it will be so good to be together again.

It may be said of many things in the past, and also of what you have been through: 'Thou shalt find it after many days.'

A week earlier he had written, 'I hope and believe that my life will be changed and that my longing for Him will be satisfied.' His family was far from happy – one of his sisters said he was 'groggy with piety'.

Amsterdam

Van Gogh's desire to become a clergyman finally persuaded him to move to Amsterdam in May and there, under the vigilant eye of his uncle, the Reverend J. P. Stricker, to prepare for the state examination he had to pass before he could study theology. He tackled Latin and Greek with gusto under the guidance of Dr M. B. Mendes da Costa and again attended as many sermons as he could from dawn to dusk every Sunday.

Amsterdam, with its picturesque harbours and canals, reminded him both of Ramsgate and of Rembrandt's etchings. The reproductions on the walls of his room showed that his love of God was matched by his love of art.

95 [D]

Amsterdam, 19 May 1877

My dear Theo,

What a fine day we spent together, one we shall not easily forget. I want to make sure you find a letter on your return from Etten. You no doubt had a good time at home too, so write soon and tell me how you spent the day.

I am enclosing something for your portfolio, viz. a lithograph after J. Maris, which might well be called <u>A Poor Man in the Kingdom of God</u>, and a lith. after Mollinger – have you ever seen it before? I have not. At a Jewish bookseller's, where I buy all the Latin and Greek books I need, I had the chance of picking prints cheaply from a large batch, 13 pictures for 70 cents. I thought I would take a few for my little room, to give it some atmosphere, which is needed if I am to get new ideas and freshen my mind.

I will tell you what they are, so that you can have some idea of what it all looks like now and what I have hanging up. 1 after Jamin (which is also hanging in your room), one after M. Maris: that little boy going to school. 5 pictures after Bosboom. Van der Maaten, Funeral Procession in the Cornfields. Israëls, a poor man on a snowy winter road, and Ostade, Studio. Then Allebé as well, a little old woman on a winter morning fetching hot water and coals with the snow lying on the streets – I sent that one to Cor for his birthday. The Jewish bookseller still had a great many more excellent ones, but I cannot afford any more, and though I do hang up one or two things I am not, after all, making a collection.

Yesterday Uncle Cor sent me a batch of old paper, like the sheet I'm using to write to you, won't it be wonderful for working on? There's a lot of work to do already and it isn't easy, but with steadfastness one should get used to it. I hope to keep in mind the ivy 'which stealeth on though he wears no wings'[1]; as the ivy climbs along the walls, so must the pen along the paper.

Every day I do some walking. Recently I went through a very pleasant district – when I walked down the Buitenkant to the Dutch railway station one could see men working there & alongside the IJ[2] with sand carts – and went along all sorts of little narrow streets with gardens full of ivy. It had a feel of Ramsgate about it. At the station I turned left, where most of the windmills are, on to a road along a canal with elm trees. Everything there reminds one of Rembrandt's etchings.

One of these days I shall make a start with Streckfuss's Algemene Geschiedenis,[3] or rather I have started it already. It isn't easy, but I certainly hope that taking it one step at a time and doing the best one can will pay off. But it will take time –

1 '"which ... wings"': in English.
2 IJ: lake near Amsterdam.
3 General History.

many testify to that, and not just Corot alone: 'Il n'a fallu pour cela que quarante ans de travail, de pensée et d'attention.'⁴ The work of men such as Father, the Rev. Mr Keller van Hoorn, Uncle Stricker and so many others requires a great deal of study, and the same is true of painting. And a man may well ask himself: how shall I ever manage that?

For one's own work, thoughts and observation are not enough, we need the comfort and blessing and guidance of a higher power, and that is something anyone who is at all serious and who longs to lift up his soul to the light is sure to recognize and experience. Pining for God works like leaven on dough. May it also prove to be true in the story of both our lives.

Let us just believe in God and, clinging to that belief, confide in Him:

> God said: Set there on rock and mountain,
> this in eternal writ,
> Let all who there behold it
> Read what it was He said:
> One day hard rock will crumble
> The greatest mount cave in,
> Yet My covenant with you
> In truth it wavers not.
> (Evangelical Hymns 188: 1–2)

> > Who but the good Lord leaves to care
> > And trusts in Him in direst need,
> > Is safe and shelterèd in Him,
> > Is godly, marvellously spared,
> > Who but in God on high does trust,
> > Cannot have built on sand.
> > (Evangelical Hymns 194: 1)

Doing what needs to be done, and, if we are thrust in the right direction and, as it were, a door is opened for us, proceeding in that direction, we may acquire something of the old faith which

4 It took only forty years' work, thought and attention.

God pours into many a heart, into that of the simple no less than into that of the great, into that of Aertsen no less than into that of Father or Uncle Jan or Uncle Cor – the same also happened to Rembrandt, Millet, Bosboom and who knows how many others, indeed, we can discover it in greater or lesser measure in almost everyone, or at least traces of it. He is not far from any of us.

Is Mrs Tersteeg still keeping well and have you been round to see Mauve yet? Keep your spirits up, as you are no doubt doing, good times may be in store for us, if God spares us and bestows His blessing on what we do.

Will you ever be joining me in some little church or other? God grant that you may, and I believe that He will grant it. Meanwhile, let us be grateful for our ordinary lives – if nothing out of the ordinary ever happens to us, and the only thing we know is a good prayer, let us then pray it, as Father once prayed on a New Year's Eve, when it was bitterly cold and the winter not easy for anybody, our own family included. That prayer came from the depths of his heart: 'Bind us, o Lord, closely to one another and let our Love for Thee strengthen these bonds ever more, preserve us from all evil, above all from the evil of sin. Father, we do not pray Thee to deliver us from the world, but to preserve us from evil. Preserve us from too much self-reproach. Grant us favour in the eyes of those to whom we are most closely bound and in the eyes of those who shall come after us.'

When I see a painting by Ruysdael, Van Goyen, Bosboom, or so many others, I am reminded again and again of the words, 'As sorrowful, yet alway rejoicing' – of wee-moed.[5]

Will you come to my little study again some Sunday and shall we go together to the little church in Scheveningen again? I hope so.

Regards to everyone at your place and accept a handshake in my thoughts from

Your very loving brother
Vincent

5 Melancholy.

Yesterday I saw a portrait of Michelet, looked at it carefully and thought of 'sa vie d'encre et de papier'.[6] I am tired at night and find it difficult to get up as early as I would like, but that will pass and I trust I shall be able to force myself to do it.

I hope to be at Uncle Stricker's on Whit Monday afternoon and evening.

120 [D]

Amsterdam, 3 March 1878

My dear Theo,

It is time to write to you again. How I should have liked to be with you today. It is such lovely weather here and one has the feeling that spring is on its way. The lark can probably already be heard in the country, but that's unlikely to happen in the city, unless one can detect its call in the voice of some old clergyman, whose words come from a heart that's in tune with the lark's.

Heard the Rev. Mr Laurillard preaching this morning in the Oudezijde Chapel. Uncle Stricker was at church as well and I had coffee with him. Uncle Jan had gone to the Nieuwe Diep this morning, but is back again now. Then to a Sunday School in the Barndesteeg and then walked around the outer embankments and, in passing, called in on three Roman Catholic churches.

Went round to see Vos last night, who is none too well. It was such a sad sight to find him sitting there moodily in front of the window, hollow-eyed and with his feet on a stove – he is afflicted with cold feet. Kee too is so pale and looks so tired. Went on from them to Uncle Cor's. He has had the salon repapered and a new grey carpet laid on the floor. Now those beautiful bookcases with the complete Gazette des Beaux Arts, etc., in their red bindings, stand out better than before. Uncle

6 His life of ink and paper.

told me that Daubigny had died. I freely confess that I was downcast when I heard the news, just as I was when I heard that Brion had died (his Bénédicité hangs in my room), because the work of such men, if it is understood, touches us more deeply than one realizes. It must be good to die in the knowledge that one has done some truthful work and to know that, as a result, one will live on in the memory of at least a few and leave a good example for those who come after. A work that is good may not last for ever, but the thought expressed by it will, and the work itself will surely survive for a very long time, and those who come later can do no better than follow in the footsteps of such predecessors and copy their example.

Speaking of good works, would you like to have a Flemish Imitation of Christ? I hope to send it to you shortly, in a small book which, if need be, can easily be slipped into the pocket.

When Uncle told me about Daubigny, I thought of his etchings after Ruysdael (Le buisson and Le coup de soleil), and Uncle has promised to get hold of them, as he did not know them at all.

Was at the Rev. Mr Gagnebin's last Monday night and met his wife and daughter as well and also went to his study, where we talked until about 11 o'clock. He told me, amongst other things, 'Qu'à certains temps de sa vie il s'était bien trouvé en s'oubliant entièrement et en se jetant dans le travail sans arrière pensée, qu'alors il avait fait beaucoup et s'était retrouvé plus tard fortifié et avancé dans ce qu'il s'était proposé et éclairé dans l'esprit. Que cependant, même maintenant, personne n'en savait rien combien ses sermons lui coûtaient de peine.'[1]

Have worked my way through the history of the Netherlands and have done an abstract of 30 closely written pages. (I was pleased to come across the battle of Waterloo and the 10-day campaign in it once again.) Do you know that Rochussen once

---

1 That at certain times in his life it did him good to forget himself completely and to throw himself into his work without reservation, that he then achieved a great deal and later felt strengthened and further along the road on which he had set out, and enlightened in spirit. For all that, no one knows even now how much effort his sermons cost him.

painted the siege of Leyden? I mean the picture owned by Mr De Vos. Am now also working on general hist.

I am looking forward more than a little to your coming here again. Do try your best to stay as long as possible. And if you can, write again soon, for you know how much pleasure your letters always give me.

Have you read anything good lately? Be sure to get hold of the works of George Eliot somehow, you won't be sorry if you do, <u>Adam Bede</u>, <u>Silas Marner</u>, Felix Holt, Romola (the life of Savonarola), <u>Scenes from Clerical Life</u>. You will remember that we gave the 3 underlined to Father for his birthday last year. When I have time for reading again, I shall reread them once more. Both the Rev. Mr McFarlane and Adler spoke to me about them, that is, they advised me to read them.

Wrote to Harry Gladwell this week, as he had not replied to my last letter and I so wanted to know what he was doing and what he was planning to do. I am still hoping he will become a clergyman, and if he does he will do a good job, of that I am certain. But it won't be an easy thing for him to achieve.

Did you ever see an original etching by Millet of a man wheeling a barrow of manure into a garden on a day like today, in early spring? And remember as well that he made an etching, 'Les becheurs'. If you ever do come across it you are unlikely to forget it in a hurry. I was thinking of the first this morning when Uncle Stricker was looking for texts in which the word manure, or dung, appears, e.g., 'Let it alone this year also, till I shall dig about it, and dung it'. Made a list recently of all the pictures by Brion I could remember. When you come here, you must tell me whether I have forgotten many of them. Lord, keep my memory green![2] That is something one should say over and over again.

Last Sunday went to see Cousin Vrijdag at the timber yards. There are still 7 children at home, a pleasant little bunch, most of them very young. Could you perhaps give me notice somewhat in advance of your arrival? Then I can do some of my work

2 'Lord ... green!': in English.

beforehand so that we'll have more time to spend together. Goodbye, a handshake in my thoughts, and believe me,

Your loving brother
Vincent

Uncle Jan sends you his regards.
Remember me to everyone at your house.

121 [D]

Amsterdam, 3 April 1878

I have been thinking about what we were discussing, and the saying sprang to mind: 'Nous sommes aujourd'hui ce que nous étions hier.'[1] That does not mean that one must stand still and may not try to improve oneself; on the contrary, it is a compelling reason for doing so and for being glad to do so. But to be true to the saying, one must not backslide, and once one has started to look at things freely and openly one must not face about or stray.

Those who said 'nous sommes aujourd'hui ce que nous étions hier' were honnêtes hommes,[2] as is apparent from the constitution they drew up, which will remain for all time and of which it has been well said that it was written 'avec le rayon d'en haut et d'un doigt de feu'.[3]

It is a good thing to be an 'honnête homme' and to try increasingly to be one, partly and wholly, and one does well to understand that this entails being an 'homme intérieur et spirituel'.[4]

He who is firmly convinced he is one of their band will always go about his business quietly and calmly, never doubting that all must end well. There once was a man who went to

1 We are today what we were yesterday.
2 Gentlemen.
3 With a ray of light from on high and a fiery finger.
4 Inward and spiritual man.

church and asked, 'Can it be that my ardour has deceived me, that I have taken a wrong turning and managed things badly? Oh, if only I could be rid of this doubt and know for certain I shall come out victorious and succeed in the end.' And then a voice answered him, 'And if you were certain, what would you do then? Act now as if you were certain and you will not be disappointed.' Then the man went on his way, not unbelieving but believing, and returned to his work no longer doubting or wavering.

As for being an 'homme intérieur et spirituel' might one not be able to develop into one through knowledge of history in general and of certain individuals from all ages in particular, from the history of the Bible to that of the Revolution and from the Odyssey to the books of Dickens and Michelet? And could we not learn something from the work of such men as Rembrandt or from Breton's Mauvaises herbes or Millet's Les heures de la journée, Le bénédicité by de Groux or Brion or Le conscrit by de Groux (or else by Conscience) or his Apothécaire or Les grands chênes by Dupré, or even from Michel's mills and sandy plains?

It is by continually holding fast to these thoughts and deeds that we are filled with a good leaven at the last, that of being sorrowful yet alway rejoicing, which will become apparent when our lives have come to fruition, bearing the fruits of good works.

Le rayon d'en haut does not always shine upon us and may well be hidden behind clouds, but without that light a man cannot live and is worth nothing and can do no good, and those who claim that man can live without faith in that higher light and need not trouble to acquire it, are sure to have their hopes dashed.

We have talked a good deal about our duty and how we may attain the right goal, and we have properly concluded that our first objective must be to find a specific position and a profession to which we can wholly devote ourselves. And I believe that we also agreed on this point, viz. that one must pay particular attention to the end, and that a victory gained after a whole life of work and effort is better than one gained with greater dispatch.

Anyone who leads an upright life and experiences real difficulty and disappointment and yet is not crushed by them is worth more than one for whom everything has always been plain sailing and who has known nothing but relative prosperity. For who are the most obviously superior of us? Those who merit the words, 'Laboureurs, votre vie est triste, laboureurs, vous souffrez dans la vie, laboureurs, vous êtes bienheureux'.[5] It is they who bear the marks of 'toute une vie de lutte et de travail soutenu sans flêchir jamais'.[6] It is right to try to become like that. So we go on our way 'undefessi favente Deo'.[7]

As for me, I must become a good preacher, who has something to say that is right and is of use to the world, and perhaps it is as well that I should spend a relatively long time on preparation and be securely confirmed in an unwavering faith before I am called to speak to others about it. (It is fitting that before one embarks upon that work, a treasure should be gathered up that others can enjoy.) Let us but go forth quietly, testing everything and holding fast to what is good, and trying all the time to learn more of what is useful and adds to our experience. Weemoed[8] may be a good experience, provided we write it as two words: wee,[9] which is in every man, each of us having reason enough, but it must be allied to moed,[10] and the more the better, for it is good to be someone who never despairs.

If only we try to live righteously, we shall fare well, even though we are bound to encounter genuine sadness and real disappointments and shall probably commit real mistakes and do things that are wrong, but it is certainly better to be ardent in spirit, even though one makes more mistakes, than narrow-minded and over-cautious.

It is good to love as many things as one can, for therein lies

---

5 Labourers, your life is bleak, labourers, your life is full of suffering, labourers, you are blessed.
6 A whole life of struggle and labour borne unflinchingly.
7 Should be *indefessi favente Deo* (by the grace of God unwearied).
8 Melancholy.
9 Woe.
10 Courage.

true strength, and those who love much, do much and accomplish much, and whatever is done with love is done well. If one is affected by some book or other, let us say by Michelet's 'L'hirondelle, L'alouette, Le rossignol, Les aspirations de l'automne, Je vois d'ici une dame, J'aimais cette petite ville singulière' – to mention just a few, then it is because that book was written from the heart in simplicity and meekness of spirit. Better to say but a few words, but filled with meaning, than to speak many that are but idle sounds and as easy to utter as they are useless.

Love is the best and the noblest thing in the human heart, especially when it is tested by life as gold is tested by fire. Happy is he who has loved much, and is sure of himself, and although he may have wavered and doubted, he has kept that divine spark alive and returned to what was in the beginning and ever shall be. If only one keeps loving faithfully what is truly worth loving and does not squander one's love on trivial and insignificant and meaningless things then one will gradually obtain more light and grow stronger.

The sooner one tries to become accomplished in a certain position in life and a certain field and adopts a relatively independent way of thinking and acting, and the more one keeps to set rules, the stronger in character one will grow, and that does not mean becoming narrow-minded. It is a wise thing to do this, because life is short and time passes quickly. If one is accomplished in one single thing, understanding one single thing well, then one has insight into and knowledge of many other things into the bargain.

It's as well to go out into the world from time to time and mix with other people (and sometimes one feels, in fact, obliged and called upon to do so) – or it may simply be one way 'de se jeter dans le travail sans arrière pensée et de toutes ses forces'[11] – but one who prefers to be quietly alone with his work and seems to need very few friends will go safest in the world and among people. One should never feel secure just because one has no difficulties or cares or handicaps, and one should never be too

11 Of throwing oneself into work unreservedly and with all one's strength.

easy-going. Even in the politest circles and the best surroundings and circumstances one should retain something of the original character of a Robinson Crusoe or of primitive man, for otherwise one cannot be rooted in oneself, and one must never let the fire in one's soul die, for the time will inevitably come when it will be needed. And he who chooses poverty for himself and loves it possesses a great treasure and will hear the voice of his conscience address him ever more clearly. He who hears that voice, which is God's greatest gift, in his innermost being and follows it, finds in it a friend at last, and he is never alone!

Happy is he who has faith in God, for he will in the end be tided over all life's difficulties, albeit not without trouble and sorrow. One cannot do better than hold on to the thought of God come what may, in all circumstances, in every place and at all times, and try to get to know Him better. One can learn this from the Bible as well as from all other things. It is good to go on believing that everything is more miraculous than one can ever begin to understand, for that is the truth; it is good to remain sensitive and humble and tender-hearted even though one may have to hide one's feelings, as is often necessary. It is good to be well versed in the things that are hidden from the wise and the learned of this world, but that are revealed as if by nature to the poor and the simple, to women and little children. For what can one learn which is better than that which God has given by nature to every human soul and which goes on living and loving, hoping and believing, in the depth of every soul, unless we wantonly destroy it.

The need is for nothing less than the infinite and the miraculous, and a man does well to be satisfied with nothing less, and not to feel easy until he has gained it.

That is what all great men have acknowledged in their works, all those who have thought a little more deeply and searched and worked and loved a little more than the rest, who have plumbed the depths of the sea of life. Plumb the depths, that is what we too must do if we want to make a catch, and if we sometimes have to work the whole night through without catching anything, then we do well not to give up and to cast the net once more at dawn.

So let us go forward quietly, each on his own path, forever making for the light, 'sursum corda',[12] and in the knowledge that we are as others are and that others are as we are and that it is right to love one another in the best possible way, believing all things, hoping for all things and enduring all things, and never failing. And not being too troubled by our weaknesses, for even he who has none, has one weakness, namely that he has none, and anyone who believes himself to be consummately wise would do well to be foolish all over again.

'Nous sommes aujourd'hui ce que nous étions hier', that is, 'honnêtes hommes', yet men who must be tested in the fire of life to become fortified inwardly are confirmed in what, by the grace of God, they are by nature.

So may it be with us, my boy, and may you fare well along your path and may God be with you in all things and help you to succeed, which, with a warm handshake on your departure, is the wish of

Your very loving brother

Vincent

It is only a very small light, the one in the little Sunday-school room in Barndesteeg, but let me keep it burning. Even if I should not, however, I do not think that Adler is the man to let it go out.

12 Lift up your hearts.

The Borinage

Much as Van Gogh, during his career in the art trade, came increasingly to consider the gulf between the practices of that trade and his own love of art as unbridgeable, so in his study of theology he was more and more torn between book learning (he had seven years of study ahead of him) and a yearning to spread the Gospel. In the end, following a year of extreme austerity and self-chastisement, he turned his back on formal theological studies in July 1878. Once again he was having to face a fresh start in a relatively short time. Later he would insist that the stumbling block had not been Latin, for he had proved time and again that he had a strong bent for languages. In August 1879 he was to call the Amsterdam episode 'the worst time of my life'.

To his father, Vincent's decision was a bitter blow. He acted as Vincent's go-between for new jobs, but came up against what he felt was his son's lack of ambition, for all Vincent now wanted was to resume the missionary work he had started in England. To that end, he enrolled in a Flemish school for prospective evangelists in Laeken near Brussels, but this attempt, too, came to nothing in the end: he was judged not to have the necessary qualifications for a missionary. Nevertheless, he found work almost immediately as a lay preacher in the village of Wasmes, among the coal miners of the Belgian Borinage. Van Gogh threw himself heart and soul into his new mission. Eloquently, he described the mine workers' hard existence and the sufferings of man and beast, while at the same time keeping an eye on what the surroundings offered in terms of the picturesque. At Christmas 1878, shortly after a visit from Theo, he sent his brother a description of the Borinage that sounds like an account of a scene in a painting by Pieter Brueghel.

127[D]

Petites Wasmes, 26 Dec. 1878
Borinage Hainaut

My dear Theo,

It is time I wrote to you again, to wish you, firstly, all the best at the start of a New Year. May many good things be your lot and may God's blessing rest on your work in the year on which we are now embarking.

I very much long for a letter from you, to hear how things are going and how you are, and also if you have <u>seen anything beautiful and remarkable of late</u>. As far as I am concerned, you'll be aware that there are no paintings here in the Borinage, that by and large they do not even know what a painting is, so obviously I have not seen anything in the way of art since my departure from Brussels. But that does not alter the fact that the country here is very special and very picturesque, everything speaks, as it were, and is full of character. Lately, during the dark days before Christmas, snow was lying on the ground. <u>Everything reminded one then of the medieval paintings by, say, Peasant Brueghel, and by so many others</u> who have known how to depict the singular effect of red & green, black & white so strikingly. And often the sights here have made me think of the work of, for example, <u>Thys Maris or Albrecht Dürer</u>. There are sunken roads here, overgrown with thornbushes and gnarled old trees with their freakish roots, which resemble perfectly that road on Dürer's etching, Le chevalier et la mort.

Thus, a few days ago, the miners returning home in the evening towards dusk in the white snow were a singular sight. These people are quite black when they emerge into the daylight from the dark mines, looking just like chimney sweeps. Their dwellings are usually small and should really be called huts; they lie scattered along the sunken roads, in the woods and on the slopes of the hills. Here and there one can still see moss-covered roofs, and in the evening a friendly light shines through the small-paned windows.

Much as we have coppices & shrubby oaks in Brabant and pollard willows in Holland, so one sees blackthorn hedges around the gardens, fields and meadows here. Lately, with the snow, the effect is that of black lettering on white paper, like pages of the Gospel.

I have already spoken several times here, both in a fairly large room especially designed for religious meetings and also at the meetings they usually hold in the evenings in the workmen's cottages, and which may best be called Bible classes. Among other things, I have spoken on the parable of the mustard seed, the barren fig tree and the man born blind. At Christmas, of course, on the stable in Bethlehem and Peace on earth. If, with God's blessing, I were to get a permanent position here, I should welcome that with all my heart.

Everywhere round here one sees the large chimneys & the tremendous mountains of coal at the entrance to the mines, the so-called charbonnages. You know that large drawing by Bosboom, Chaudfontaine – it gives a good impression of the countryside in these parts, except that here everything is coal while to the north of Hainaut there are stone quarries and in Chaudfontaine they have iron.

I still keep thinking of the day you came to Brussels and of our visit to the Museum. And I often wish you were a bit nearer and that we could be together more often. Do reply soon, I keep looking at that etching of Un jeune citoyen, over and over again.

The miners' talk is not very easy to make out, but they understand ordinary French well, provided it is spoken quickly and fluently enough, for then it automatically sounds like their patois, which comes out with amazing speed. At a meeting this week, my text was Acts 16: 9: 'Et Paul eut de nuit une vision d'un homme macédonien qui se présenta devant lui et la pria disant: "Passe en Macédonie et nous aide".'[1] And they listened

---

1 And a vision appeared to Paul in the night; There stood a man of Macedonia, and prayed him, saying Come over into Macedonia, and help us.

attentively when I tried to describe what that Macedonian was like who needed and longed for the comfort of the Gospel and for knowledge of the Only True God. That <u>we should think of him as a workman, with lines of sorrow and suffering and fatigue on his countenance, without pomp or glory</u> but with an immortal soul and needing the food that does not perish, namely God's word, because man liveth not by bread alone, but by all the words that flow from God's mouth. How Jesus X[2] is the Master who can strengthen and comfort and enlighten one like the Macedonian, a workman and labourer whose life is hard. Because He Himself is the great Man of Sorrows who knows our ills, Who was called the son of a carpenter, though He was the Son of God and the great Healer of sick souls. Who laboured for 30 years in a humble carpenter's shop to fulfil God's will. And God wills that in imitation of X, man should live and walk humbly on earth, not reaching for the sky, but bowing to humble things, learning from the Gospel to be meek & humble of heart.

I have already had occasion to visit some of the sick, since there are so many of them here. Wrote today to the President of the Committee of Evangelization asking him if my case could be dealt with at the next meeting of the committee.

It is thawing tonight. I can't tell you how picturesque the hilly country looks in the thaw, with the snow melting and now that the black fields with the green of the winter wheat can be seen again.

For a stranger, the villages here are real rabbit warrens with the countless narrow streets and alleyways of small workers' houses, at the foot of the hills as well as on the slopes and the tops. The nearest comparison is a village like Scheveningen, especially the back streets, or villages in Brittany as we know them from pictures. But you have travelled through these parts by train on your way to Paris and may have fleeting memories of them. The Protestant churches are small, like the one at De Hoeve though a little larger, but the place where I spoke was just a large bare room which could hold 100 people at most. I

2 Christ.

also attended a religious service in a stable or shed, so everything is simple and original enough.

Write soon if you can find the time, and know that you are again and again, indeed constantly, in my thoughts. Wishing once more that God's blessing be yours in the New Year, and shaking your hand in my thoughts, believe me, always,

Your very loving brother
Vincent

My regards to everyone at the Rooses' and wish them all the very best for the New Year, as well as anyone who may ask after me.

When you write, please address your letter care of M. van der Haegen, Colporteur, à Pâturages près de Mons (Borinage Hainaut).

I have just visited a little old woman in a charcoal-burner's home. She is terribly ill but full of faith and patience. I read a chapter with her and prayed with them all. The people here have something unique and attractive about them thanks to their simplicity and good nature, not unlike the Brabant people in Zundert & Etten.

In the middle of July 1879 Van Gogh was told that his appointment in Wasmes could not be extended and so he moved to the nearby village of Cuesmes. He read a great deal of Dickens (*Hard Times!*), though drawing had meanwhile become his main interest. He asked Theo for books on the basic principles of draughtsmanship and he was sent a box of paints by Mr Tersteeg, his former employer at Goupil's. One sketchbook after another was filled. In the middle of August Theo paid him a visit and, as after all such meetings between the brothers, Vincent wrote a revealing letter soon afterwards. Its principal themes were gratitude for the visit and uncertainty about the permanence of the close relationship he now enjoyed with his brother, his 'compagnon de voyage', travelling companion.

132 [D] [part]

[c. 15 August 1879]

My dear Theo,

I am writing to you expressly to tell you how grateful I am for your visit. It had been quite a long time since we had seen each other or had written as we used to do. Still, it is better to be close than dead to each other, the more so as, until one is truly entitled to be called dead by virtue of one's legal demise, it smacks of hypocrisy or at least childishness to carry on as if one were. Childish in the manner of a young man of 14 who believes that his dignity and rank in society oblige him to wear a top hat.

The hours we spent together have at least assured us that we are both still in the land of the living. When I saw you again and walked with you, I had a feeling I used to have more often than I do now, namely that life is something good and precious which one should value, and I felt more cheerful and alive than I have been feeling for a long time, because in spite of myself my life has gradually become much less precious, much less important and more a matter of indifference to me, or so it has seemed.

When one lives with others and is bound by feelings of affection, then one realizes that one has a reason for living, that one may not be utterly worthless and expendable, but is perhaps good for something, since we need one another and are journeying together as compagnons de voyage. But our proper sense of self-esteem is also highly dependent upon our relationship with others.

A prisoner who is condemned to solitude, who is prevented from working, &c., will in the long run, especially if the run is too long, suffer from the effects as surely as one who has gone hungry for too long. Like everyone else, I need friendly or affectionate relationships or intimate companionship, and am not made of stone or iron like a pump or a lamppost, and like any man of culture or decency I cannot do without these things and not feel a void, a lack of something – and I tell you all this to let you know how much good your visit has done me.

And just as I would not want us to become estranged, so I would want to keep in with all at home. For the moment, however, I am not very keen on going back there and would much rather stay on here. Yet it may well all have been my own fault and you could be right about my not seeing things straight. And so, despite my great reluctance and though it is a hard course for me to take, I may yet go to Etten, at least for a few days.

As I think back with gratitude to your visit, my thoughts return to our discussions as well, of course. I have had similar ones before, even a good many and often. Plans for improvement and change and generating energy – and yet, do not be offended, I am a little frightened by them, not least because I have sometimes acted upon them only to have my hopes dashed.

[...]

A change for the better in my life, shouldn't I long for that, or are there times when one has no need for betterment? I hope I do become much improved. But precisely because that is what I long for, I am afraid of remèdes pires que le mal.[1] Can you blame a patient for standing up to his doctor and preferring not to be given the wrong treatment or quack remedies?

Is it wrong for someone suffering from consumption or typhus to insist that a more potent remedy than barley water might be indicated, might indeed be essential, or, while finding nothing wrong with barley water as such, to question its effectiveness and potency in his particular case? The doctor who prescribed the barley water would be wrong to say: this patient is an obstinate mule who is courting his own destruction because he refuses to take his medicine – no, it is not that the man is unwilling, but that the so-called remedy is worthless, because though it might well be good for something, it does not fit the case.

Can you blame a person for remaining indifferent to a painting listed in the catalogue as a Memling, but having nothing more in

1 Cures worse than the disease.

common with a Memling than that it has a similar subject from the Gothic period, but without artistic merit?

And if you should conclude from these remarks that I meant to suggest your advice was worthy of a quack, then you have completely misunderstood me, as I have no such thoughts or opinions about you. If, on the other hand, you believe that I would do well to follow your advice literally to become an engraver of invoice headings & visiting cards or a bookkeeper or a factotum – or the advice of my very dear sister Anna to devote myself to the baker's trade or many other suchlike things, curiously at odds and hardly compatible – you would be making another mistake.

[...]

And now, all joking aside, it is my honest opinion that it would be better if the relationship between us were to become closer on both sides. If ever I came to believe seriously that I was being a nuisance or a burden to you or to those at home, of no use to anyone, and were obliged to look upon myself as an intruder or to feel superfluous so far as you are concerned, so that it would be better if I were not there at all, and if I should have to try all the time to keep out of other people's way – were I really to think that, then I should be overwhelmed by a feeling of sadness and should have to wrestle with despair.

I find it hard to bear this thought and even harder to bear the thought that so much dissension, misery and sorrow between us, and in our home, may have been caused by me. Should that indeed be the case, then I might wish it were granted me not to have much longer to live.

Yet when this thought sometimes depresses me beyond measure, far too deeply, then after a long time another occurs too: 'Perhaps it is only an awful, frightening dream and later we may learn to see and understand it more clearly.' Or is it real, and will it ever get better rather than worse? Many people would undoubtedly consider it foolish and superstitious to go on believing in a change for the better.

It is sometimes so bitterly cold in the winter that one says, 'The cold is too awful for me to care whether summer is coming or not; the harm outdoes the good.' But with or without our approval, the severe weather does come to an end eventually and one fine morning the wind changes and there is a thaw. When I compare the state of the weather to our state of mind and our circumstances, subject to change and fluctuation like the weather, then I still have some hope that things may get better.

If you wete to write again soon, you would make me very happy. Should you do so, please address your letter care of J. B. Denis, Rue du Petit Wasmes à Wasmes (Hainaut).

Walked to Wasmes the evening after you left. Have drawn yet another portrait since. Goodbye, accept a handshake in my thoughts and believe me,

Yours truly,[2]
<u>Vincent</u>

Shortly after writing this letter, Van Gogh visited his parents in Etten, despite the reluctance he had confessed to Theo. For a whole year his correspondence with Theo then came to an end, and other family letters, too, are almost entirely lacking. This void seems to have been connected with the bad feeling between father and son during this period, the Reverend Theodorus van Gogh even threatening to have his son locked up in a mental institution in Gheel. All references to this painful incident were later cut from the letters by Johanna van Gogh-Bonger. Only recently have these passages been restored, though letters written in this period from 1879 to 1880 seem to have been irretrievably lost.

After a further stay with his parents in the spring of 1880, Van Gogh returned to the Borinage in the summer to become a full-time artist. It was not until July 1880, however, that he wrote to Theo again. Though he did so 'rather reluctantly' and considering Theo 'a stranger', his highly individual letter nevertheless ends with the grudging confession: 'and know that it will do me good to hear from you.'

2 'Yours truly': in English.

133 [F]

[July 1880]

My dear Theo,

I am writing to you rather reluctantly because, for a good many reasons, I have kept silent for such a long time. To some extent you have become a stranger to me, and I to you perhaps more than you think. It is probably better for us not to go on like that. It is probable that I would not have written to you even now, were it not that I feel obliged, compelled, to do so – because, be it noted, you yourself have compelled me to.

I heard in Etten that you had sent fifty francs for me. Well, I have accepted them. With reluctance, of course, with a feeling of some despondency, of course, but I have reached a sort of impasse, am in trouble, what else can I do? And so I am writing to thank you.

As you may know, I am back in the Borinage. Father said he would prefer me to stay somewhere near Etten, but I refused and I believe I was right to do so. To the family, I have, willy-nilly, become a more or less objectionable and shady sort of character, at any rate a bad lot. How could I then be of any use to anyone? And so I am inclined to think the best and most sensible solution all round would be for me to go away and to keep my distance, to cease to be, as it were. What the moulting season is for birds – the time when they lose their feathers – setbacks, misfortune and hard times are for us human beings. You can cling on to the moulting season, you can also emerge from it reborn, but it must not be done in public. The thing is far from amusing, not very exhilarating, and so one should take care to keep out of the way. Well, so be it.

Now, although it is a fairly hopeless task to regain the trust of an entire family, one which has perhaps never been wholly weaned from prejudice and other equally honourable and respectable qualities, I am not entirely without hope that, bit by bit, slowly but surely, the good relationship between one and all may be restored. In the first place I should be glad to see this good relationship – to put it no more strongly than that – restored at least between Father and me, and further, I set great store by seeing it restored between the two of us. A good relationship is infinitely preferable to a misunderstanding.

Now I must trouble you with certain abstract matters, hoping that you will listen to them patiently. I am a man of passions, capable of and given to doing more or less outrageous things for which I sometimes feel a little sorry. Every so often I say or do something too hastily, when it would have been better to have shown a little more patience. Other people also act rashly at times, I think.

This being the case, what can be done about it? Should I consider myself a dangerous person, unfit for anything? I think not. Rather, every means should be tried to put these very passions to good effect.

To mention just one by way of an example, I have a more or less irresistible passion for books and the constant need to improve my mind, to study if you like, just as I have a need to eat bread. You will understand that. When I lived in other surroundings, surroundings full of pictures and works of art, I conceived a violent, almost fanatical passion for those surroundings, as you know. And I do not regret that, and even now, <u>far from home, I often feel homesick for the land of pictures</u>.

You may remember that I knew very well (and it may be that I know it still) what Rembrandt was or what Millet was or Jules Dupré or Delacroix or Millais or Matthijs Maris.

Well, today I am no longer in those surroundings, yet they say that what is known as the soul never dies but lives on for ever, continuing to seek for ever and again.

So instead of succumbing to my homesickness I told myself: your land, your fatherland, is all around. So instead of giving in to despair I chose active melancholy, in so far as I was capable of activity, in other words I chose the kind of melancholy that hopes, that strives and that seeks, in preference to the melancholy that despairs numbly and in distress. I accordingly made a more or less serious study of the books within my reach, such as the

Bible and Michelet's La révolution française, and then last winter Shakespeare and a little Victor Hugo and Dickens and Beecher Stowe and recently Aeschylus and then various less classical writers, a few great minor masters. You know, don't you, that Fabritius and Bida are counted among the minor masters?

Now anyone who becomes absorbed in all this is sometimes considered outrageous, 'shocking',[1] sinning more or less unwittingly against certain forms and customs and proprieties. It is a pity that people take that amiss.

You know, for example, that I have often neglected my appearance. I admit it, and I also admit that it is 'shocking'. But look here, lack of money and poverty have something to do with it too, as well as a profound disillusionment, and besides, it is sometimes a good way of ensuring the solitude you need, of concentrating more or less on whatever study you are immersed in. One essential study is that of medicine. There is scarcely anybody who does not try to acquire some knowledge of it, who does not at least try to grasp what it is about (and you see, I still know absolutely nothing about it). And all these things absorb you, preoccupy you, set you dreaming, musing and thinking.

Now for the past 5 years or so, I don't know how long exactly, I have been more or less without permanent employment, wandering from pillar to post. You will say, ever since such and such a time you have been going downhill, you have been feeble, you have done nothing. Is that entirely true?

What is true is that I have at times earned my own crust, and at other times a friend has given it to me out of the goodness of his heart. I have lived whatever way I could, for better or for worse, taking things just as they came. It is true that I have forfeited the trust of various people, it is true that my financial affairs are in a sorry state, it is true that my future looks rather bleak, it is true that I might have done better, it is true that I have wasted time when it comes to earning a living, it is true that my studies are in a fairly lamentable and appalling state,

1 '"shocking"': in English.

and that my needs are greater, infinitely greater than my resources. But does that mean going downhill and doing nothing?

You might say, but why didn't you go through with university, continue as they wanted you to? To that I can only reply that it was too expensive, and besides, the future then looked no better than it does now, along the path I am now taking.

And I must continue to follow the path I take now. If I do nothing, if I study nothing, if I cease searching, then, woe is me, I am lost. That is how I look at it – keep going, keep going come what may.

But what is your final goal, you may ask. That goal will become clearer, will emerge slowly but surely, much as the draft turns into the sketch and the sketch into the painting through the serious work done on it, through the elaboration of the original vague idea and through the consolidation of the first fleeting and passing thought.

You should know that it is the same with evangelists as it is with artists. There is an old academic school, often odious and tyrannical, the 'abomination of desolation', in short, men who dress, as it were, in a suit of steel armour, a cuirass, of prejudice and convention. Where they are in charge, it is they who hand out the jobs and try, with much red tape, to keep them for their protégés and to exclude the man with an open mind.

Their God is like the God of Shakespeare's drunken Falstaff, 'the inside of a church'.[2] Indeed, by a strange coincidence, some evangelical (???) gentlemen have the same view of matters spiritual as that drunkard (which might surprise them somewhat were they capable of human emotion). But there is little fear that their blindness will ever turn to insight.

This is a bad state of affairs for anyone who differs from them and protests with heart and soul and all the indignation he can muster. For my part, I hold those academicians who are not like these academicians in high esteem, but the decent ones are thinner on the ground than you might think.

Now, one of the reasons why I have no regular job, and why I

2 '"the inside of a church"': in English.

have not had a regular job for years, is quite simply that my ideas differ from those of the gentlemen who hand out the jobs to individuals who think as they do. It is not just a question of my appearance, which is what they have sanctimoniously reproached me with. It goes deeper, I do assure you.

I am telling you all this not to complain, not to make excuses for matters in which I may perhaps have been somewhat at fault, but very simply to tell you the following: during your final visit last summer when we were walking together near that abandoned mineshaft which they call La Sorcière, you reminded me of another walk we once took at another time near the old canal and the mill at Rijswijk, and, you said, we used to agree about many things, but, you added, 'You have changed since then, you are no longer the same.' Well, that is not entirely true. What has changed is that my life then was less difficult and my future seemingly less gloomy, but as far as my inner self, my way of looking at things and of thinking is concerned, that has not changed. But if there has indeed been a change, then it is that I think, believe and love more seriously now what I thought, believed and loved even then.

So you would be mistaken should you continue to think that I have become less keen on, say, Rembrandt, Millet or Delacroix or whoever or whatever, for the reverse is the case, but there are many different things worth believing and loving, you see – there is something of Rembrandt in Shakespeare, something of Correggio in Michelet and something of Delacroix in V. Hugo, and there is also something of Rembrandt in the Gospel or, if you prefer, something of the Gospel in Rembrandt, it comes to much the same thing, provided you understand it properly, do not try to distort it and bear in mind that the elements of the comparisons are not intended to detract in any way from the merits of the original individuals.

And there is something of M. Maris or of Millet in Bunyan, a reality that, in a manner of speaking, is more real than reality itself, something hitherto unknown that, if only you can read it, will tell you untold things. And in Beecher Stowe there is something of Ary Scheffer or of Sarto.

Now, if you can forgive someone for immersing himself in pictures, perhaps you will also grant that the love of books is as sacred as that of Rembrandt, indeed, I believe that the two complement each other.

I very much admire the portrait of a man by Fabritius that we stood looking at for a long time in the gallery in Haarlem one day when we took another walk together. Admittedly, I am as fond of Dickens's 'Richard Cartone' in his Paris & Londres in 1793,[3] and I could point to other particularly gripping characters in other books with a more or less striking resemblance. And I think that Kent, a character in Shakespeare's King Lear, is as noble and distinguished a man as that figure by Th. de Keyser, though Kent and King Lear are reputed to have lived much earlier.

Let me stop there, but my God, how beautiful Shakespeare is, who else is as mysterious as he is; his language and method are like a brush trembling with excitement and ecstasy. But one must learn to read, just as one must learn to see and learn to live.

So please don't think that I am renouncing anything, I am reasonably faithful in my unfaithfulness and although I have changed, I am still the same, and what preys on my mind is simply this one question: what am I good for, could I not be of service or use in some way, how can I become more knowledge-able and study some subject or other in depth? That is what keeps preying on my mind, you see, and then one feels impris-oned by poverty, barred from taking part in this or that project and all sorts of necessities are out of one's reach. As a result one cannot rid oneself of melancholy, one feels emptiness where there might have been friendship and sublime and genuine affection, and one feels dreadful disappointment gnawing at one's spiritual energy, fate seems to stand in the way of affection or one feels a wave of disgust welling up inside. And then one says, 'How long, my God!'

Well, that's how it is, can you tell what goes on within by looking at what happens without? There may be a great fire in

3 Sydney Carton in *A Tale of Two Cities*.

your soul, but no one ever comes to warm himself by it, all that passers-by can see is a little smoke coming out of the chimney and they walk on.

All right, then, what is to be done, should one tend that inner fire, turn to oneself for strength, wait patiently – yet with how much impatience! – wait, I say, for the moment when someone who wants to comes and sits down beside one's fire and perhaps stays on? Let him who believes in God await the moment that will sooner or later arrive.

Well, right now it seems that things are going badly for me, have been doing so for some considerable time, and may continue to do so well into the future. But it is possible that everything will get better after it has all seemed to go wrong. I am not counting on it, it may never happen, but if there should be a change for the better I should regard that as a gain, I should rejoice, I should say, at last! So there was something after all!

But, you will say, what a dreadful person you are, with your impossible religious notions and idiotic scruples. If my ideas are impossible or idiotic then I would like nothing better than to be rid of them. But this is roughly the way I actually see things. In Le philosophe sous les toits by Souvestre you can read what a man of the people, a simple craftsman, pitiful if you will, thinks of his country: 'Tu n'as peut-être jamais pensé à ce que c'est la patrie, reprit-il, en me posant une main sur l'épaule; c'est tout ce qui t'entoure, tout ce qui t'a élevé et nourri, tout ce que tu as aimé. Cette campagne que tu vois, ces maisons, ces arbres, ces jeunes filles qui passent là en riant, c'est la patrie! Les lois qui te protègent, le pain qui paye ton travail, les paroles que tu échanges, la joie et la tristesse qui te viennent des hommes et des choses parmi lesquels tu vis, c'est la patrie! La petite chambre où tu as autrefois vu ta mère, les souvenirs qu'elle t'a laissés, la terre où elle repose, c'est la patrie! Tu la vois, tu la respires partout! Figure toi, tes droits et tes devoirs, tes affections et tes besoins, tes souvenirs et ta reconnaissance, réunis tout ça sous un seul nom et ce nom sera la patrie.'4

4 You may never have thought what your country really is, he continued, placing his

In the same way I think that everything that is really good and beautiful, the inner, moral, spiritual and sublime beauty in men and their works, comes from God, and everything that is bad and evil in the works of men and in men is not from God, and God does not approve of it.

But I cannot help thinking that the best way of knowing God is to love many things. Love this friend, this person, this thing, whatever you like, and you will be on the right road to understanding Him better, that is what I keep telling myself. But you must love with a sublime, genuine, profound sympathy, with devotion, with intelligence, and you must try all the time to understand Him more, better and yet more. That will lead to God, that will lead to an unshakeable faith.

To take an example, one man will love Rembrandt, genuinely, and that man will surely know there is a God, he will really believe it. Another will make a thorough study of the French Revolution – he will not be an unbeliever, he will see that there is a supreme authority that manifests itself in great affairs. Yet another has recently attended a free course of lectures at the great university of sorrow and has heeded the things he saw with his eyes and heard with his ears, and has reflected upon them. He too will come to believe in the end and will perhaps have learned more than he can tell.

Try to grasp the essence of what the great artists, the serious masters, say in their masterpieces, and you will again find God in them. One man has written or said it in a book, another in a painting. Just read the Bible and the Gospel, that will start you thinking, thinking about many things, thinking about everything,

---

hand on my shoulder; it is everything around you, everything that has raised and nourished you, everything that you have loved. This countryside that you see, these houses, these trees, these young girls laughing as they pass, that is your country! The laws that protect you, the bread that rewards your labour, the words you speak, the joy and sorrow that come from the people and things in whose midst you live, that is your country! The little room where you used in days gone by to see your mother, the memories she left you, the earth in which she rests, that is your country! You see it, you breathe it, everywhere! Imagine your rights and your duties, your affections and your needs, your memories and your gratitude, gather all that together under a single name and that name will be your country.

well then, think about many things, think about everything, that will lift your thoughts above the humdrum despite yourself. We know how to read, so let us read!

Now then, you may well have bouts of being a little absent-minded, a little dreamy, indeed there are some who become a little too absent-minded, a little too dreamy. That may indeed have happened with me, but all in all that is my own fault, maybe there was a reason for it, perhaps I was lost in thought for one reason or another, anxious, worried, but one gets over that in the end. The dreamer sometimes falls into the doldrums, but is said to emerge from them again. And the absent-minded person also makes up for it with bouts of perspicacity. Sometimes he is a person whose right to exist has a justification that is not always immediately obvious to you, or more usually, you may absent-mindedly allow it to slip from your mind. Someone who has been wandering about for a long time, tossed to and fro on a stormy sea, will in the end reach his destination. Someone who has seemed to be good for nothing, unable to fill any job, any appointment, will find one in the end and, energetic and capable, will prove himself quite different from what he seemed at first.

I am writing somewhat at random, writing whatever flows from my pen. I should be very happy if you could see in me something more than a kind of ne'er-do-well. For there is a great difference between one ne'er-do-well and another ne'er-do-well. There is someone who is a ne'er-do-well out of laziness and lack of character, owing to the baseness of his nature. If you like, you may take me for one of those. Then there is the other kind of ne'er-do-well, the ne'er-do-well despite himself, who is inwardly consumed by a great longing for action, who does nothing because his hands are tied, because he is, so to speak, imprisoned somewhere, because he lacks what he needs to be productive, because disastrous circumstances have brought him forcibly to this end. Such a one does not always know what he can do, but he nevertheless instinctively feels, I am good for something! My existence is not without reason! I know that I could be a quite different person! How can I be of use, how can I be of service? There is something inside me, but what can it be? He is quite another ne'er-do-well. If you like you may take me for one of those.

A caged bird in spring knows perfectly well that there is some way in which he should be able to serve. He is well aware that there is something to be done, but he is unable to do it. What is it? He cannot quite remember, but then he gets a vague inkling and he says to himself, 'The others are building their nests and hatching their young and bringing them up,' and then he bangs his head against the bars of the cage. But the cage does not give way and the bird is maddened by pain. 'What a ne'er-do-well,' says another bird passing by – what an idler. Yet the prisoner lives and does not die. There are no outward signs of what is going on inside him, he is doing well, he is quite cheerful in the sunshine.

But then the season of the great migration arrives: an attack of melancholy. He has everything he needs, say the children who tend him in his cage – but he looks out, at the heavy thundery sky, and in his heart of hearts he rebels against his fate. I am caged, I am caged and you say I need nothing, you idiots! I have everything I need, indeed! Oh, please give me the freedom to be a bird like other birds.

That kind of ne'er-do-well of a person resembles that kind of ne'er-do-well of a bird. And people are often unable to do anything, imprisoned as they are in I don't know what kind of terrible, terrible, oh, such terrible cage.

I do know that there is a release, the belated release. A justly or unjustly ruined reputation, poverty, disastrous circumstances, misfortune, they all turn you into a prisoner. You cannot always tell what keeps you confined, what immures you, what seems to bury you, and yet you can feel those elusive bars, railings, walls. Is all this illusion, imagination? I don't think so. And then one asks: my God, will it be for long, will it be for ever, will it be for eternity?

Do you know what makes the prison disappear? Every deep, genuine affection. Being friends, being brothers, loving, that is what opens the prison, with supreme power, by some magic force. Without these one stays dead. But wherever affection is revived, there life revives. Moreover, the prison is sometimes called prejudice, misunderstanding, fatal ignorance of one thing or another, suspicion, false modesty.

But to change the subject – if I have come down in the world, you have in a different way come up in it. And if I have forfeited sympathy, you have gained it. I am glad of that, I say that in all sincerity, and it will always give me pleasure. If you lacked seriousness or consideration, I would be fearful that it might not last, but since I think that you are very serious and very considerate, I tend to believe it will!

But if you could see me as something other than a ne'er-do-well of the bad sort, I should be very happy.

For the rest, if I can ever do anything for you, be of some use to you, know that I am at your disposal. Now that I have accepted what you have given me, you are, should I be able to render you some service, in a position to ask me. It would make me happy and I should take it as a sign of trust. We have moved rather far apart and may in certain respects have different views, but some time, some day, one of us may be of service to the other.

For now I shake your hand, thanking you once again for having been so good to me. If, one of these days, you feel like writing, my address is, chez Ch. Decrucq, Rue du Pavillon 8, Cuesmes, near Mons, and know that it will do me good to hear from you.

Yours,
Vincent.

Van Gogh must have taken the decision to turn his back on preaching and to make his living as an artist as early as 1879. Theo promised him financial support. Having made up his mind to become an artist, his next step was to obtain the necessary professional training. Although Van Gogh did a lot of copying from anatomy and perspective textbooks and from Bargue's *Cours de dessin*, he felt a strong need for personal tuition. To that end he first consulted the Dutch landscape painter,

Willem Roelofs, who was working in Brussels, and then, on Theo's advice, he called on the young Dutch artist Anthon van Rappard, a contact that was later to develop into a close friendship. As far as his artistic training was concerned, however, Vincent remained in essence an autodidact.

He found the Borinage no less picturesque than Venice or Arabia, but now looked upon the miners, to whom he had previously wanted to bring the Gospel, more as 'types' than as his flock. Painting having ousted religion as his vocation, he made a pilgrimage on foot to the village of Courrières, the home of the painter Jules Breton, whom he revered. Though he lacked the means to stay in the art centres, Paris or Barbizon, he was determined to cling to his muse, and this decision is reflected memorably in his letter of 24 September 1880, which reads like a credo.

136 [F]

Cuesmes, 24 Sept. 1880

Dear Theo,

Your letter has done me good and I thank you for having written to me in the way you have.

The roll with a new selection of etchings & various prints has just arrived. First and foremost the masterly etching, Le buisson, by Daubigny/Ruysdael. Well! I propose to make two drawings, in sepia or something else, one after that etching, the other after Le four dans les Landes by Th. Rousseau. Indeed, I have already done a sepia of the latter, but if you compare it with Daubigny's etching you will see that it contrasts feebly, although considered on its own the sepia may betray some tone & sentiment. I shall have to return to it & tackle it again.

I am still working on Bargue's Cours de dessin & intend to finish it before I go on to anything else, for both my hand and my mind are growing daily more supple & strong as a result, & I cannot thank Mr Tersteeg enough for having been so kind as to lend it to me. The models are outstanding. Meanwhile I am reading one book on anatomy & another on perspective, which Mr Tersteeg also sent me. These studies are demanding & sometimes the books are extremely tedious, but I think all the same that it's doing me good to study them.

So you see that I am working away hard, though for the moment it is not yielding particularly gratifying results. But I have every hope that these thorns will bear white blooms in due course & that these apparently fruitless struggles are nothing but labour pains. First the pain, then the joy.

You mention Lessore. I think I remember some very elegant watercolour landscapes by him in a blond tone, worked with an apparent ease & a light touch, yet with accuracy & distinction, & a somewhat decorative effect (that is not meant badly, but on the contrary, in a favourable sense). So I know a little about his work & you mention someone not entirely unknown to me.

I admire the portrait of Victor Hugo. It is done very conscientiously with the evident intention of portraying the truth without straining after effect. That is precisely what makes it so effective.

Last winter I pored over some of Hugo's works, Le dernier jour d'un condamné & an excellent book on Shakespeare. I first started studying this writer long ago. He is just as splendid as Rembrandt. Shakespeare is to Charles Dickens or V. Hugo what Ruysdael is to Daubigny, & Rembrandt to Millet.

What you say in your letter about Barbizon is perfectly true & I can tell you one or two things that will make it clear how much I share your view. I haven't been to Barbizon, but though I haven't been there, I did to go Courrières last winter. I went on a walking tour in the Pas-de-Calais, not the English Channel but the department, or province. I had gone on this trip in the hope of perhaps finding some sort of work there, if possible – I would have accepted anything – but in fact I set out a bit reluctantly, though I can't say exactly why. But I had told myself, you must see Courrières. I had just 10 francs in my pocket and because I had started out by taking the train, that was soon gone, & as I was on the road for a week, it was a rather gruelling trip.

Anyway, I saw Courrières & the outside of M. Jules Breton's studio. The outside of the studio was a bit of a disappointment, seeing that it is a brand-new studio, recently built of brick, of a Methodist regularity, with an inhospitable, stone-cold & forbidding aspect, just like C. M.'s Jovinda, which, between ourselves, I am none too keen on either, for the same reason. If I could have seen the inside, I am quite certain that I should have given no further thought to the outside, but there you are, I could not see the inside because I dared not introduce myself and go in. Elsewhere in Courrières I looked for traces of Jules Breton or any other artist. All I was able to find was a portrait of him at a photographer's & a copy of Titian's Entombment in a corner of the old church which looked very beautiful to me in the darkness & masterly in tone. Was it by him? I don't know because I was unable to make out any signature.

But of any living artist, no trace, just a café called the Café des Beaux Arts, also of new, inhospitable, stone-cold, repulsive brick – the café was decorated with a kind of fresco or mural depicting episodes from the life of that illustrious knight, Don Quixote.

To tell the truth, the frescos seemed to me rather poor consolation and fairly mediocre at the time. I don't know who did them.

But anyway I did see the country around Courrières then, the haystacks, the brown farmland or the marled earth, almost coffee-coloured (with whitish spots where the marl shows through), which seems somewhat unusual to people like us who are used to a blackish soil. And the French sky looked to me much finer & brighter than the smoky & foggy sky of the Borinage. What's more, there were farms & barns that, God be praised, still retained their mossy thatched roofs. I also saw the flocks of crows made famous by the pictures of Daubigny & Millet. Not to mention, as I ought to have done in the first place, the characteristic & picturesque figures of all manner of workmen, diggers, woodcutters, a farmhand driving his wagon & a silhouette of a woman with a white cap. Even in Courrières there was still a coal mine or pit, I saw the day shift come up at nightfall, but there were no women workers in men's clothes as in the Borinage, just the miners looking tired & careworn, black with coal dust, dressed in ragged miners' clothes, one of them in an old army cape.

Although this trip nearly killed me & though I came back spent with fatigue, with crippled feet & in a more or less depressed state of mind, I do not regret it, because I saw some interesting things and the terrible ordeals of suffering are what teach you to look at things through different eyes.

I earned a few crusts here and there en route in exchange for a picture or a drawing or two I had in my bag. But when my ten francs ran out I tried to bivouac in the open the last 3 nights, once in an abandoned carriage which was completely white with hoarfrost the next morning, not the best accommodation, once in a pile of faggots, and once, & that was a slight improvement, in a haystack that had been opened up, where I succeeded in making myself a slightly more comfortable little hideaway, though the drizzle did not exactly add to my enjoyment.

Well, even in these depths of misery I felt my energy revive & said to myself, I shall get over it somehow, I shall set to work again with my pencil, which I had cast aside in my deep dejection, & I shall draw again, & ever since I have had the feeling that everything has changed for me, & now I am in my stride & my pencil has become slightly more willing & seems to be getting more so by the day. My over-long & over-intense misery had discouraged me so much that I was unable to do anything.

I saw something else during the trip – the weavers' villages.

The miners & the weavers still form a race somehow apart from other workers & artisans and I have much fellow-feeling for them & should consider myself fortunate if I could draw them one day, for then these as yet unknown, or virtually unknown, types would be brought out into the light of day.

The man from the depths, from the abyss, 'de profundis', that is the miner. The other with the faraway look, almost daydreaming, almost a sleepwalker, that is the weaver. I have been living among them now for nearly 2 years & have learned a little of their special character, in particular that of the miners. And increasingly I find something touching & even pathetic in these poor, humble workers, the lowest of the low in a manner of speaking, and the most despised, who, owing to a possibly widely held but quite baseless and inaccurate presumption, are usually considered a race of knaves & scoundrels. Knaves, drunkards & scoundrels may be found here, of course, just as elsewhere, but the real type is nothing at all like that.

You refer vaguely in your letter to my coming sooner or later to Paris or its environs, if it were possible & if I wanted to. It is of course my eager & fervent wish to go either to Paris or to Barbizon, or somewhere else, but how can I, when I do not earn a cent and when, though I work hard, it will still be some time before I reach the point at which I can give any thought to something like going to Paris. For honestly, to be able to work properly I need at least a hundred francs a month. You can certainly live on less, but then you really are hard up, much too hard up in fact!

Poverty stops the best minds in their tracks, the old Palizzi saying goes, which has some truth in it & is entirely true if you understand its real meaning and import. For the moment I do not see how it could be feasible, and the best thing is for me to stay here & work as hard as I can, & after all, it is cheaper to live here.

At the same time I must tell you that I cannot remain very much longer in the little room where I live now. It is very small indeed, and then there are the two beds as well, the children's & my own. And now that I am working on Bargue's fairly large sheets I cannot tell you how difficult it is. I don't want to upset these people's domestic arrangements. They have already told me that I couldn't have the other room in the house under any circumstances, not even if I paid more, for the woman needs it for her washing, which in a miner's house has to be done almost every day. In short, I should like to rent a small workman's cottage. It costs about 9 francs a month.

I cannot tell you (though fresh problems arise & will continue to arise every day), I cannot tell you how happy I am that I have taken up drawing again. I had been thinking about it for a long time, but always considered it impossible & beyond my abilities. But now, though I continue to be conscious of my failings & of my depressing dependence on a great many things, now I have recovered my peace of mind & my energy increases by the day.

As far as coming to Paris is concerned, it would be of particular advantage to me if we could manage to establish contact with some good & able artist, but to be quite blunt about it, it might only be a repetition on a large scale of my trip to Courrières, where I hoped to come across a living example of the species Artist and found none. For me the object is to learn to draw well, to gain control of my pencil, my charcoal or my brush. Once I have achieved that I shall be able to do good work almost anywhere and the Borinage is as picturesque as old Venice, as Arabia, as Brittany, Normandy, Picardy or Brie.

Should my work be no good, it will be my own fault. But in Barbizon, you most certainly have a better chance than elsewhere of meeting a good artist who would be as an angel sent by God, should such a happy meeting take place. I say this in all seriousness and without exaggeration. So if, sometime or other, you should see the means & the opportunity, please think of me. Meanwhile I'll stay here quietly in some small workman's cottage and work as hard as I can.

You mentioned Meryon again. What you say about him is quite true. I know his etchings slightly. If you want to see something curious, then place one of his meticulous & powerful sketches next to a print by Viollet-le-Duc or anyone else engaged in architecture. If you do, then you will see Meryon in his true light, thanks to the other etching which will serve, whether you like it or not, as a foil or contrast. Right, so what do you see? This. Even when he draws bricks, granite, iron bars or the railing of a bridge, Meryon puts into his etchings something of the human soul, moved by I know not what inner sorrow. I have seen V. Hugo's drawings of Gothic buildings. Well, though they lacked Meryon's powerful and masterly technique, they had something of the same sentiment. What sort of sentiment is that? It is akin to what Albrecht Dürer expressed in his Melancholia, and James Tissot and M. Maris (different though these two may be) in our own day. A discerning critic once rightly said of James Tissot, 'He is a troubled soul.' However this may be, there is something of the human soul in his work and that is why he is great, immense, infinite. But place Viollet-le-Duc alongside and he is stone, while the other, that is, Meryon, is Spirit.

Meryon is said to have had so much love that, just like Dickens's Sydney Carton, he loved even the stones of certain places. But in Millet, in Jules Breton, in Jozef Israëls, the precious pearl, the human soul, is even more in evidence and better expressed, in a noble, worthier, & if you will allow me, more evangelical tone.

But to return to Meryon, in my view he also has a distant kinship with Jongkind & perhaps with Seymour Haden, since at times these two artists have been extremely good.

Just wait, and perhaps you'll see that I too am a workman. Though I cannot predict what I shall be able to do, I hope to make a few sketches with perhaps something human in them, but first I must do the Bargue drawings and other more or less difficult things. Narrow is the way & strait the gate & there are only a few who find it.

Thanking you for your kindness, especially for Le buisson, I shake your hand,

Vincent.

I have now taken your whole collection, but you will get it back later and in addition I've got some very fine things for your collection of wood engravings, which I hope you will continue, in the 2 volumes of the Musée Universal which I am keeping for you.

Etten

In April 1881 Van Gogh returned to the Netherlands and moved in with his parents in Etten at the start of a lengthy stay. Theo supplied him with paper, and Vincent spent most of his time making figure studies, until new clashes with his father – Vincent refused to join the family at church for Christmas – led to his being shown the door.

Van Gogh had an enduring need to enlist the support of other artists, of the older generation no less than of his own. He attached great importance to the opinion of Anton Mauve, both a leading figure in the Hague School and, by virtue of his marriage to Jet Carbentus, a relative. He also had regular contacts with Théophile de Bock, a contemporary and a great admirer of Corot.

150 [D]

[c. September 1881]

My dear Theo,

Though it is only a short time since I wrote to you, I have something more to tell you now.

For there has been a change in my drawings, both in the way I set about them and in the result.

Also, as a consequence of some of the things Mauve told me, I have started to work with live models again. Luckily I have been able to get several people to sit here for me, including Piet Kaufman, the labourer.

Careful study and the constant & repeated copying of Bargue's Exercices au fusain have given me a better insight into figure-drawing. I have learned to measure and to see and to look for the broad outlines, so that, thank God, what seemed utterly impossible to me before is gradually becoming possible now. I have drawn a man with a spade, that is 'un bêcheur',[1] 5 times over in a variety of poses, a sower twice, and a girl with a broom twice. Then a woman in a white cap peeling potatoes & a shepherd leaning on his crook and finally an old, sick peasant sitting on a chair by the hearth with his head in his hands and his elbows on his knees.

And it won't be left at that, of course. Once a few sheep have crossed the bridge, the whole flock follows.

Now I must draw diggers, sowers, men & women at the plough, without cease. Scrutinize & draw everything that is part of country life. Just as many others have done & are doing. I no longer stand as helpless before nature as I used to do.

I brought along some conté-crayon in wood (just like pencils) from The Hague and I work with them a great deal now.

I have also started to introduce the brush and the stump. With a little sepia or India ink, and now and then with a little colour.

What is quite certain is that the drawings I have been doing lately bear little resemblance to anything I have done before.

The size of the figures is about the same as that of an Exercice au fusain.

As for landscape, I don't see why it need suffer in any way as a result. On the contrary, it will gain. Enclosed are a few small sketches to give you an idea.

Of course I have to pay the people who pose. Not much, but because it happens every day it is one expense more until I manage to sell some drawings.

But since a figure is hardly ever a complete failure, I am sure that the outlay on the model will be recovered in full relatively soon.

For nowadays anyone who has learned to tackle a figure and hang on to it until it is safely down on paper, can earn quite a bit. I need hardly tell you that I am merely sending you these sketches to give you some idea of the pose. I dashed them off

1 A digger.

Waarde Theo,

Hoewel ik pas kort geleden U heb geschreven zoo heb ik
ditmaal U nog iets meer te zeggen.
Namelyk dat er eene verandering in myn teekenen is
gekomen zoowel in myn manier van doen als in het
resultaat daarvan.
Ook naar aanleiding van een ander dat Mauve my
zeide ben ik op nieuw begonnen te werken naar
levend model. Ik heb er onderscheiden personen hier
toe kunnen krygen gelukkig o.a. Piet Kaufman den
arbeider.
Het zorgvuldig bestudeeren het aanhoudend & herhaaldelyk
teekenen van de Exercices au fusain van Bargue
heeft my beter inzigt gegeven in het figuurteekenen.
Ik heb leeren meten en zien en groote lynen zoeken.
Zoodat 't geen my vroeger wanhopig onmogelyk
scheen my langzamerhand mogelyk gaat worden god dank.
Tot 5 maal toe heb ik een boer met een schop anders
un "bêcheur" geteekend en allerlei standen, twee
maal een zaaier; tweemaal een meisje met
een bezem. verder een vrouw met witte muts
die aardappelen schilt & een herder op zyn stok geleund
en eindelyk een ... boer op een stoel
by den haard gezeten met het hoofd in de handen en
de ellebogen op de knieën. —
En daar zal het natuurlyk niet by blyven.
als er eens een paar schapen over de brug zyn
volgt de heele kudde.
Spitters zaaiers ploegers mannen & vrouwen
moet ik nu onophoudelyk teekenen. Al wat tot het
boerenleven behoort onderzoeken & teekenen. Even als
veel anderen dat deden & doen. Ik sta nu niet meer
zoo magteloos voor de natuur als vroeger.

Uit den Haag bragt ik Conté in hout (even als potlood)
mede en daar werk ik nu veel mede
Ook begin ik met het penseel en den dweglauw er
in te werken. Met wat sepia of O. I. inkt en nu en
dan eens met wat klein.
Zeer zeker is het dat de teekeningen die ik dezen
laatsten tijd gemaakt heb weinig lijken op wat
anders wat ik tot nu toe maakte.
De grootte van de figuren is zoo ongeveer die
van een Exercices au fusain.
Wat betreft landschap. ik houd het er voor dat dat er
in geenen deele bij hoeft te lijden. integendeel het
zal er bij winnen. Hierbij een paar kleine schetsjes
om U een gedacht er van te geven.
Natuurlijk moet ik de menschen die poseeren betalen.
wel niet veel maar omdat het dagelijksch terug
komt is dit eene uitgave meer tot zoolang ik
er niet in slaag teekeningen te verkoopen.
Maar daar slechts zelden een figuur mij totaal
mislukt. zoo zullen de kosten van model er
naar 't mij voor komt reeds betrekkelijk spoedig
gansch en al kunnen uitgehaald worden.
Want voor iemand die een figuur heeft leeren
aanklampen en vasthouden tot 't op zijn pooten op
't papier staat is in den tegenwoordigen tijd nog wat te
verdienen ook. Ik hoef u wel niet te zeggen dat ik u deze
schetsjes alleen zend om U een gedacht te geven van de pose
ik heb ze vandaag gekrabbeld in korten tijd en merk dat er
heel wat op de proportie aan te merken valt zeker meer dan
op de eigenlijke teekeningen althans. Ik heb een goeden
brief van Rappard die druk aan 't werk schijnt te zijn
hij stuurde mij zeer aardige opstellen van een Rappard
Ik zou wel willen dat hij nog eens voor eenige
dagen naar hier kwam.

Dit is een akker of aardappelveld waar men aan 't ploegen
& zaaien is heb daarvan een vrij groote schets
met opkomend onweer

De twee andere schetsjes zijn poses van spitters.
Ik hoop er daarvan nog verscheiden te maken.

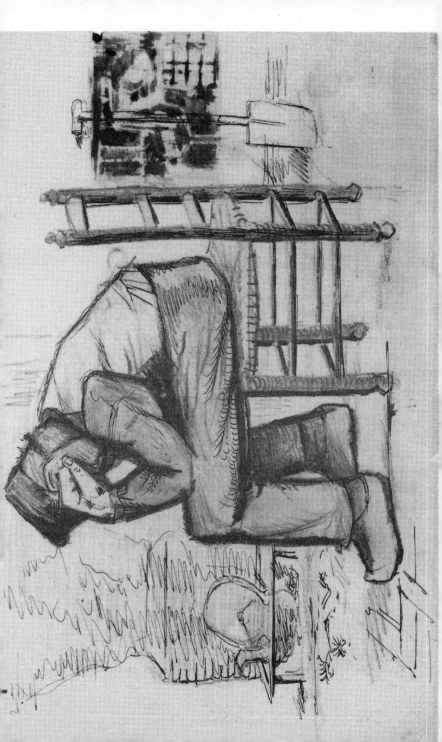

De andere zaaier heeft een korf.

Enorm graag zou ik eens een vrouw laten poseeren
met een zaaikorf om dat figuurtje te vinden dat ik
in 't voorjaar U heb laten zien en dat ge op den
voorgrond van 't eerste schetsje ziet

Enfin zooals Mauve zegt „de fabriek is in
volle werking".

Als ge wilt en kunt denk dan om het papier Ingres
van de kleur van ongebleekt linnen zoo mogelijk
het sterkere soort. Schrijf my eens spoedig als ge kunt
in elk geval, en ontvang een handdruk in gedachten.

t. à t.
Vincent

today in no time at all and can see that there is a lot wrong with the proportions, more so anyway than in the actual drawings. I've had a nice letter from Rappard, who seems to be hard at work. He sent me some very good landscape sketches. I wish he would come back here again for a few days.

This is a field or rather a stubble, where they are ploughing & sowing. Have made a fairly large sketch of it with a gathering thunderstorm.

The other two sketches are poses of diggers. I hope to do several more of them.

The other sower has a basket. I am tremendously anxious to get a woman to pose with a seed basket, so as to find a little figure like the one I showed you in the spring and which you can see in the foreground of the first little sketch.

Well, as Mauve says, the works are in full swing.

If you like and are able to, please remember the Ingres paper, the colour of unbleached linen, the stronger kind if possible. In any case, write as soon as you can, and accept a handshake in my thoughts,

Ever yours,
<u>Vincent</u>

152 [D]

[12–15 October 1881]

My dear Theo,

I was very pleased to get your letter just now, and as I intended to write to you anyhow in the next day or so, I am replying right away.

I'm so glad you've sent the Ingres paper. I've still got some left, but not the right colour.

I was happy to hear what Mr Tersteeg said to you about my drawings, and certainly no less glad that you saw progress yourself in the sketches I sent you. If that is indeed so, I mean to work to such effect that neither you nor Mr T. will have any reason to take back your more favourable opinions. I shall do my very best not to let you down.

The artist always comes up against resistance from nature in the beginning, but if he really takes her seriously he will not be put off by that opposition, on the contrary, it is all the more incentive to win her over – at heart, nature and the honest draughtsman are as one. (Nature is most certainly 'intangible',[1] yet one must come to grips with her and do so with a firm hand.) And having wrestled and struggled with nature for some time now, I find her more yielding and submissive, not that I have got there yet, no one is further from thinking that than I am, but things are beginning to come more easily.

The struggle with nature is sometimes a bit like what Shakespeare calls 'taming the shrew'[2] (which means wearing down the opposition, bon gré et mal gré[3]). In many fields, but especially in drawing, I think that 'serrer de près vaut mieux que lâcher'.[4]

I have come to feel more and more that figure drawing is an especially good thing to do, and that indirectly it also has a good

1 '"intangible"': in English.
2 '"taming ... shrew"': in English.
3 Willy-nilly.
4 Persistence is better than surrender.

effect on landscape drawing. If one draws a pollard willow as if it were a living being, which after all is what it is, then the surroundings follow almost by themselves, provided only that one has focused all one's attention on that particular tree and not rested until there was some life in it.

Enclosed are a few small sketches. I'm doing quite a bit of work on the Leurs road these days. Working with watercolour & sepia now and then too, but that isn't coming off too well yet.

Mauve has gone to Drenthe. We've agreed that I'll go and see him there as soon as he writes, but perhaps he'll come and spend a day at Prinsenhage first.

I went to see the Fabritius in Rotterdam on my last trip, and I'm glad you had a chance to see that Mesdag draw. among other things. If the drawing by Mrs Mesdag you mention is of yellow roses on a mossy ground, then I saw it at the exhibition and it is indeed very beautiful and artistic.

What you say about De Bock is, I think, true in every respect. I take the same view of him, but could not have put it as well as you did in your letter. If he could and wanted to concentrate, he would certainly be a better artist than he is. I told him straight out, 'De Bock, if you and I were to apply ourselves to figure drawing for a year, then we would both end up quite different from what we are now, but if we do not apply ourselves and simply carry on without learning anything new, then we won't even stay as we are but will lose ground. If we don't draw figures, or trees as if they were figures, then we have no backbone, or rather one that's too weak. Could Millet & Corot, of whom we both think so much, draw figures, or couldn't they? I think those Masters tackled just about anything.' And he agreed with me about this, in part at least.

In fact, I think he's been working very hard on the Panorama, and even though he refuses to admit it, that too will have a generally favourable effect on him.

He told me a very funny thing about the Panorama, which made me feel very warmly towards him. You know the painter Destrée. He went up to De Bock with a very superior air, and said to him, with great disdain, of course, yet in an unctuous and insufferably patronizing way, 'De Bock, they asked me to paint that Panorama, too, but seeing it was lacking in any artistic worth I felt I simply had to refuse.'

To which De Bock retorted, 'Mr Destrée, which is easier, painting a panorama or refusing to paint one? Which is more artistic, doing it or not doing it?' I'm not sure if those were his precise words, but that was certainly the gist of it, and I thought it straight to the point.

And I respect it as much as I respect your way of dealing with the older and wiser members of your society, whom you have left to their own old age and wisdom while you yourself have got on with things in your younger and more energetic way. That is true philosophy and makes us act as De Bock & you do when the need arises; it can be said of such philosophy that it is practical as well, in the same way as Mauve says, 'Painting is drawing as well.'

I've filled up my paper, so I shall end and go out for a walk. My warmest thanks for all your efforts on my behalf, a handshake in my thoughts, and believe me,

Ever yours,
<u>Vincent</u>

There followed a fascinating episode: Vincent's unrequited love for his cousin Kee Vos. These tender feelings had first appeared when Kee and her small child stayed with his parents in Etten in the summer of 1881. While studying theology in Amsterdam, Vincent had already given a warm account of the atmosphere in the home she had shared with her husband, writing in his letter to Theo dated 18 September 1877, 'I spent Monday evening with Vos and Kee, they are devoted to each other and one can readily see that where Love dwells the Lord commands His blessing. [...] When one sees them sitting together in the evening in the friendly light of the lamp in their small sitting room and close by the bedroom of their boy, who wakes up every so often to ask his mother for this or that, it is an idyll, though they have also known grim days and sleepless nights and fear and worry.'

Vincent was longing for just such sheltered family life and now projected that longing on to Kee Vos, who had meanwhile been widowed. She failed to notice Vincent's feelings for her until he made them unmistakably clear. Brusquely – at least in Vincent's eyes – she turned him down. Her rejection of him in three short, stinging words, 'Never, no, never', aggrieved and hurt him deeply. Though she left no room for doubt that it was pointless to entertain any hopes, Vincent did not give up. Moreover, his repeated attempts to contact her and his obstinate refusal to accept the obvious gave him a bad name among his relatives. But Van Gogh could not help himself. He opened his heart to Theo: 'If I did not give vent to my feelings every so often, then, I think, the boiler would burst.'

153 [D]

Etten, 3/9 1881[1]

My dear Theo,

There is something on my mind that I want to tell you about. You may perhaps know something of it already & it will not be news to you. I wanted to let you know that I fell so much in love with Kee Vos this summer that I can find no other words for it than, 'It is just as if Kee Vos were the closest person to me and I the closest person to Kee Vos,' and – those were the words I spoke to her. But when I told her this, she replied that her past and her future remained as one to her so that she could never return my feelings.

Then I was in a tremendous dilemma about what to do. Should I resign myself to that 'never, no, never', or consider the matter not yet settled & done with, keep in good heart and not give up.

I chose the latter. And to this day I do not regret this approach, although I am still up against that 'never, no, never'. Since then, of course, I have had to put up with quite a few

1 A mistake for 3/11 1881 (3 November 1881).

'petites misères de la vie humaine',[2] which, had they been written about in a book, might well have served to amuse some people, but which if one experiences them oneself must be deemed anything but pleasant.

However, to this day I am glad that I left the resignation – or the 'how <u>not</u> to do it'[3] method – to those who have a mind for it & for myself kept in good heart. You will understand that in a case like this it is surprisingly difficult to tell what one can, may & must do. Yet 'we pick up the scent as we wander about, not as we sit idly by'.

One of the reasons why I have not written to you before about all this is that my position was so uncertain & unsettled that I was unable to explain it to you. Now, however, we have reached the point where I have spoken about it, not only to her but to Father and Mother, to Uncle & Aunt Stricker & to our Uncle & Aunt at Prinsenhage.

The only one to say to me, and that very informally and privately, that there really might be a chance for me if I worked hard & made progress, was someone from whom I least expected it: Uncle Cent. He was pleased with the way in which I reacted to Kee's never, no, never, that is not making heavy weather of it but taking it in quite good humour, and said for instance, 'Don't give grist to the never, no, never mills which Kee has set up, I wish her all the best, but I rather hope those mills will go bankrupt.'

Similarly, I didn't take it amiss when Uncle Stricker said that there was the danger that I 'might be severing friendly relationships and old ties'. Whereupon I said that in my view the real issue, far from severing old ties, was to see if the old ties could not be renewed where they were in need of repair.

Anyway, that is what I hope to go on doing, to cast out despondency & gloom, meanwhile working hard – and ever since I met her, I have been getting on much better with my work.

2 Minor irritations of human life.
3 '"how . . . it"': in English.

I told you that the position has now become a bit more clear-cut. 1st – Kee says never, no, never, and then – I have the feeling that I'm going to have an immense amount of difficulty with the older people, who consider the matter settled & done with now and will try to force me to drop it.

For the time being, however, I think they'll go about it very gently, keeping me dangling and fobbing me off with fair words until Uncle & Aunt Stricker's big celebration (in December) is over. For they are anxious to avoid a scandal. After that, though, I fear they will be taking measures to get rid of me.

Forgive me for expressing myself somewhat harshly in order to make the position clear to you. I admit that the colours are somewhat glaring & the lines somewhat starkly drawn, but that will give you a clearer insight into the affair than if I were to beat about the bush. So do not suspect me of lacking in respect for the older people.

However, I do believe that they are positively <u>against</u> it & I wanted to make that clear to you. They will try to make sure that Kee & I can neither see nor speak nor write to each other, because they know very well that if we saw, spoke or wrote to each other, there would be a chance of Kee changing her mind. Kee herself thinks she will never change her mind, the older people are trying to convince me that she cannot change it, and yet they fear such a change.

The older people will change their minds about this affair, not when Kee changes her attitude but when I have become somebody who earns at least 1000 guilders a year. Once again, forgive the hard contours with which I am outlining matters. If I receive little sympathy from the older ones, I believe that some of the younger ones will be able to understand my position.

You may, Theo – you may hear it said of me that I want to force things, and expressions like that. Yet everyone knows how senseless force is in love! No, nothing is further from my thoughts.

But it is neither unfair nor unreasonable to wish that Kee and I, instead of not being allowed any contact with each other, might see, speak or write to each other so that we could come to know each other better, and <u>even</u> be able to tell whether or not we are suited to each other. A year of keeping in touch with each other would be salutary for her & for me, and yet the older people have really dug in their heels on this point. Were I rich, they would soon change their tune.

By now you will realize that I hope to leave no stone unturned that might bring me closer to her, and that it is my intention:

> To go on loving her
> Until in the end she loves me too.
> Plus elle disparait plus elle apparait.[4]

Theo, are you by any chance in love as well? I hope you are, for believe me, even its 'petites misères' have their value. One is sometimes in despair, there are moments when one is in hell, so to speak, yet there is also something different & better about it.

There are 3 stages –
1. Not loving & not being loved.
2. Loving & not being loved (the present case).
3. Loving & being loved.

Now, I tell you that the second stage is better than the first, but the third! That's <u>it</u>!

Well, old boy,[5] go and fall in love yourself and tell me about it some time. Keep your own counsel in the present case and have some sympathy for me. Of course I would much rather have had a yea and amen, but I am almost pleased with my 'never, no, never'. (I take it for <u>something</u>, though older & wiser heads say it is <u>nothing</u>.)

Rappard has been here, and brought some watercolours that are coming on well. Mauve will be calling soon, I hope, otherwise I shall go to him. I am doing a good deal of drawing and have the feeling it is improving. I am working much more with the brush than before. It is so cold now that I do almost nothing but

4 The more she disappears the more she appears.
5 'old boy': in English.

indoor figure-drawing, a seamstress, a basket-weaver, &c. A handshake in my thoughts & write soon and believe me,

Ever yours,
Vincent

If you ever do fall in love and get a never, no, never, don't resign yourself to it whatever you do! But you are such a lucky dog that nothing like that will ever happen to you, I hope.

They tried to make me promise that I would speak or write absolutely nothing more about this business, but I refused to promise that. In my opinion no one in the world should in fairness demand such a thing of me (or of anyone else in the same position). All I did do was to give Uncle Cent the assurance that for the time being I would cease writing to Uncle Stricker unless unforeseen circumstances should necessitate it. A lark cannot help singing in the spring.

156 [D]

[10 or 11 November 1881]

Dear brother,

I have received your letter, but think it is only an answer to my No. 1.

In No. 2 and No. 3 you will have found a 'talking-to' as my thanks for your advice, 'Take care not to build too many castles in the air before you are sure the work is not in vain.'

And since you have had that talking-to already, I shall not repeat it. Bien te fasse, old boy![1]

It's lucky at any rate that you haven't been guilty of 'in the meantime' thinking, isn't that so?

No, neither you nor I are guilty of that sort of thinking. To

---

1 Much good it may do you; 'old boy': in English.

the best of our belief, yours and mine, someone who lacks courage, or uses a won't-commit-myself approach, or doesn't dare stake his life with a smile, would be better off not even trying to win a real woman's heart. From the very beginning of this love I have felt that unless I threw myself into it sans arrière pensée,[2] committing myself totally and with all my heart, utterly and for ever, I had absolutely no chance, and that even if I do throw myself into it in this way the chance is very slight. But what do I care if my chance is great or small?

I mean, should I, can I, take that into account when I am in love? No, no reckoning up, one loves because one loves.

Being in love – quelle chose![3]

Imagine what a real woman would think if she found that someone was courting her with reservations; wouldn't she say something worse to him than 'never, no, never!'? Oh, Theo, don't let's talk about it, if you and I are in love then we are in love, voilà tout.[4] And we keep a clear head and do not becloud our mind, nor curb our feelings, nor douse the fire and the light, but simply say, 'Thank God, I am in love.'

Again, imagine what a real woman would think of a lover who came to her confident of success. I wouldn't give tuppence for his chances with someone like Kee Vos, and not for a hundred thousand guilders would I swap his chances for that 'no, never, ever'.

I sent you a few drawings because I thought you might find something of the look of Heike[5] about them. Now tell me, please, why don't they sell and how can I make them saleable? For I should like to earn some money now and then for the fare to go and look into that 'never, no, never'.

But be sure not to mention this plan of mine to the Most Rev. and Very Learned Mr J. P. S.![6] For when I do arrive entirely

2 Unreservedly.
3 What a business!
4 That's all there is to it.
5 A town near Etten in Noord-Brabant, also called St Willebrord.
6 Johannus Paulus Stricker, Uncle Stricker, the father of Kee.

unannounced, he might perhaps have no alternative but to turn a blind eye for the sake of peace.

Someone like the Most Rev. and Most Learned Mr J. P. S. becomes quite a different person from what he was before once one falls in love with his daughter, at least as far as the one involved in 'the present case' is concerned. He becomes quite gigantic and assumes unheard of proportions! But that does not alter the fact that, as one who loves his daughter, one is more afraid of <u>not going to him</u> than of <u>going to him</u>, even though one knows that he is capable of doing terrible things in the circumstances.

Anyway, right now I can't help feeling 'I have a draughtsman's fist', and I am very glad that I have such an implement, even though it is still unwieldy. The Ingres paper is really excellent.

And so you are popularly known as a lucky dog. For all the petites misères de la vie humaine.[7]

And you are not sure whether you really are one or not? But why should you doubt it?

Now look, what I should like to know is this: what sort of petites misères do you have? I know some of them in part or in full, others I don't.

Do you also have petites misères to do with a lady from time to time? Of course you do, but I should like to hear what they are! Surely none of the never, no, never sort? Or perhaps, on the contrary, too many heavy-handed yeas and amens?

Well, your petites misères with the ladies interest me exceedingly. Especially because I think of your petites misères what I think of my own, namely, that in many cases we do not quite know how to take them, when, in fact, they contain hidden treasure provided we know how to find and take possession of it. The petites or grandes misères are riddles. Finding the solution is well worth the trouble.

A lucky dog who complains – without reason! And they call me 'the melancholy one', and I ask you to congratulate me on my 'never, no, never'! And I get very cross when people tell me

7 Minor irritations of human life.

that it is dangerous to put out to sea, observing that one might drown in it. I don't get cross because I think they are wrong to say that, but because they seem to forget 'that there is safety in the very heart of danger'.[8]

So, you lucky dog: what is wrong with your luck? You were able to tell me with much piquancy what falling in love is like by your comparison with a strawberry. It was nicely put indeed, but to be in love in the teeth of a triple 'no never ever' as well as of a Most Rev. and Very Learned Mr J. P. S. who makes inquiries about the means of existence in the 'present case', as His Reverence calls it, or rather, does not even make inquiries about them because he (being into the bargain a Philistine when it comes to art) thinks that they are nonexistent – to be in love like that, I say, is not quite like picking strawberries in the spring.

And that 'never, no, never' is not balmy as spring air but bitter, bitter, bitter as the biting frost of winter. 'This is no flattery,'[9] Shakespeare would say. However Samson said something else: 'Out of the strong came forth sweetness.' And the question is very much whether Samson was not much wiser than I am. Proudly he seized hold of a lion and overpowered him, but could we do the same? 'You <u>must</u> be able to,' Samson would have said, and rightly so.

Enough, the strawberry season has not yet arrived, I can indeed see strawberry plants but they are frozen. Will spring arrive and thaw them out, and will they come into bloom, and then – then – who will pick them?

Still, that 'never, no, never' has taught me things I did not know: 1. It has brought home to me the enormity of my ignorance, and 2. women have a world of their own, and much more. Also that there are such things as means of existence.

I should think it more considerate of people if they said (as the Constitution says: 'Tout homme est considéré innocent jusqu'à sa culpabilité soit prouvée'[10]) that it should be assumed

8 '"that . . . danger"': in English.
9 '"This . . . flattery"': in English (from *As You Like It*).
10 Every man is considered innocent until proved guilty.

that others have the means of existence until the contrary is proved. It could be said: this man exists – I see him, he speaks to me, a proof of his actual existence is even that he is not uninvolved in a certain case, e.g. 'the present case'. His existence being clear and obvious to me (since I am aware that the person in question is not a mere ghost, but is made of real live flesh and bones) I shall take it as axiomatic thát he owes that existence to means he obtains in some way or other and for which he works. So I shall not suspect him of existing without any means of existence. However that is not the way people reason, least of all a certain person in question in Amsterdam. They have to see the means in order to believe in the existence of the person in question, but the existence of the person in question does not prove to them that he has means. Well, this being so, we are obliged to hold up a draughtsman's fist, though not to attack or even to threaten them with it. Then we must use that draughts-man's fist as best we can.

But the 'no never ever' riddle is still by no means solved in this way. Trying the direct opposite of certain pieces of advice can often prove practical and do one good. That is why it is in many cases so useful to ask for advice. But some pieces of advice can be used in their natural state and do not need to be turned inside-out or upside-down. This latter kind is very rare and desirable, however, for it still has some special characteristics. The former kind thrives everywhere in profusion. The latter sort is expensive. The former costs nothing and is sometimes delivered unsolicited to one's home by the sackful. 'In the meantime!!!'

Yours truly,[11]
<u>Vincent</u>

I close this letter with some advice of my own.

If ever you fall in love, do so without reservation, or rather, if you should fall in love simply give no thought to any reservation.

11 'Yours truly': in English.

Moreover, when you do fall in love, you will not 'feel certain' of success beforehand. You will be 'une âme en peine'[12] and yet you will smile.

Whoever feels so 'sure of his ground' that he rashly imagines 'she is mine', even before he has waged the soul's battle of love, even before, I say, he has become suspended between life and death on the high seas, in the midst of storm and tempest – there is one who knows little of what a real woman's heart is, and that will be brought home to him by a real woman in a very special way. When I was younger, one half of me once fancied that I was in love, and with the other half I really was. The result was many years of humiliation. Let me not have been humiliated in vain.

I speak as one '<u>Who has been down</u>',[13] from bitter experience, from learning the hard way.

Lucky dog! What's the matter? What aileth thee?[14] Perhaps, after all, you have not been such a lucky dog so far, but I think you are well on the way to becoming one. That much I gather from the tone of your letters.

It is just as if there is a small lump in your throat, in your voice. What kind of small lump is it? Could you not tell me for once, now that I have told you so much?

Theo, every girl's father has something called the key to the front door. A very terrible weapon, which can open and shut the aforesaid front door as Peter and Paul open and close the gates of heaven. Well, does that implement also fit the heart of the respective daughters in question? Can that be opened or shut with the key to the front door? I think not, God and love alone can open or close a woman's heart. Will hers open? Brother, will she ever let me in? Dieu le sait.[15] I cannot tell such things in advance.

---

12 A lost soul.
13 'I speak ... <u>down</u>'': in English.
14 'What's ... thee?': in English.
15 God knows.

158 [D]

Friday 18/9 – 1881[1]

Dear brother,

If I did not give vent to my feelings every so often, then, I think, the boiler would burst.

I must tell you something that, were I to keep it bottled up inside me, might distress me, but which, if I just come straight out with it, may turn out to be not too bad.

As you know, Father and Mother on the one hand and I on the other do not see eye to eye about what should or should not be done with regard to a certain 'no, never, ever'.

Well, after I'd been listening to the fairly strong expressions 'indelicate and inopportune' for some considerable time (just imagine that you were in love and they called your love 'indelicate', wouldn't you, with a certain amount of pride, take exception and say, 'Enough!'), at my urgent request that these expressions be no longer used, they stopped, but only to come up with a new order of the day. Now they say that 'I would be severing family ties'.

Well, I have told them over and over again, seriously, patiently and with feeling, that that is not the case at all. This helped for a time and then it started all over again. Now the complaint was that I kept 'writing letters'.

And when – rashly and wantonly in my view – they kept using that wretched expression 'severing ties', I did the following. For a few days I said not a word and took no notice at all of Father and Mother. A contrecoeur,[2] but I wanted them to see what it would be like if ties really had been severed.

Of course they were amazed at my behaviour, and when they said so, I replied, 'You see, <u>that's what it would be like</u> if there were no tie of affection between us, but luckily there is one and

1 A mistake for 18/11 (18 November 1881).
2 Reluctantly.

it will not be broken so easily, but I beg you to appreciate how dreadful that phrase "severing ties" really is, and not to use it any longer.' The result was, however, that Father grew very angry, ordered me out of the room, and, and cursed me, or at least that is exactly what it sounded like!

Now while I am very distressed and sorry about it all, I simply cannot agree that a father who curses his son and (remember last year) proposes to send him to a lunatic asylum (which naturally I resisted with all my might) and who calls his son's love 'inopportune and indelicate' (!!!), is in the right.

Whenever Father loses his temper he is used to having everyone, myself included, give in to him. However, I had made up my mind in God's name to let this fit of temper rage on for once.

In anger Father also said something about my having to move away somewhere else, but because it was said in anger I do not attach much importance to it. I have my models and my studio here, elsewhere life would be more expensive, working more difficult and the models dearer. But if Father and Mother were coolly and calmly to tell me, 'Go,' of course I would go.

There are things a man simply cannot let pass. If one hears people saying 'you are mad' or 'you are someone who severs family ties' or 'you are indelicate', then anyone with a heart in his body will protest with all his might. To be sure, I have told Father and Mother a thing or two as well, namely that they were quite wrong about this love of mine, that they had hardened their hearts, and seemed absolutely incapable of a gentler and more humane way of thinking. In a word, that to me their way of thinking seemed narrow-minded, neither full nor generous enough, and also that to me 'God' would ring nothing but hollow if one had to hide one's love and were not allowed to follow the dictates of one's heart.

Now I am quite ready to believe that there have been times when I have been unable to suppress my outrage upon hearing 'indelicate' or 'severing ties', but who would keep calm when that sort of thing never stops?

Quoi qu'il en soit.[3] In his anger, Father muttered nothing more nor less than a curse. But then, I had already heard something of the sort last year, and thank God, far from being properly damned, felt new life and new energy springing up within me. And I firmly believe that it will be the same this time, only more so, and more forcefully than last year.

Theo, I love her, her and no other, her for ever. And, and, and, Theo, although the 'no, never, ever' still 'seems' to be in full sway, there is a feeling of something like redemption within me, and it is as if she and I had stopped being two and were united for all eternity.

<u>Have my drawings arrived?</u> I made another yesterday, a peasant boy in the morning lighting the fire in the hearth with a kettle hanging over it, and another, an old man laying dry twigs on the hearth. I am sorry to say there is still something harsh and severe in my drawings, and I think that she, that is, her influence, is needed to soften that.

Well, my dear fellow, it seems to me there is no reason to take 'the curse' so terribly hard. Perhaps I used too harsh a method to make Father and Mother feel something they did not want to hear, yet is not 'a father's curse' a great deal stronger and harsher, going indeed a little too far? Enfin, je te serre la main, et crois-moi,[4]

Ever yours,
Vincent

Because of the estrangement from his parents through the Kee Vos affair, Vincent decided not to return to Etten for the time being. He reported instead to his cousin Anton Mauve for painting lessons in The Hague.

Unable for a moment to forget his feelings for Kee Vos and loving her still 'for a thousand reasons', Van Gogh forced his way unannounced

3 Be that as it may.
4 Well, I shake your hand, and believe me.

into her father's house in Amsterdam, where she was living at the time. His embarrassing account of that vain attempt to win Kee over makes it clear how overwrought he had meanwhile become. The affair also spelled the end of his religious faith. The clerical world, personified both by his own father and by Kee's father, the Reverend Mr Stricker, came in for some scathing remarks in his letters.

164 [D]

[*c.* 21 December 1881]

Sometimes, I'm afraid, you cast a book aside because it is too realistic. Have pity on, and patience with, this letter, and in any case read it through, even though you may think it a bit much.

My dear Theo,

As I wrote to you from The Hague, I still have one or two things to discuss with you now that I am back here again. It is not without emotion that I think back on my short trip to The Hague. When I arrived at M[auve]'s, my heart was beating quite hard, because I was thinking to myself, is he going to try to fob me off with fair words too or am I going to find something different here?

And well, what I found was that in all sorts of practical and friendly ways he helped and encouraged me. Mind you, not by approving of what I did or said all the time, on the contrary. But if he says to me, 'This or that is no good,' he immediately adds, 'but just try it this way or that,' which is a different matter altogether from criticizing for the sake of criticizing. If somebody says, 'You have this or that illness,' that's not a great deal of help, but if he says, 'Do this or that and you will get better,' and his advice is reliable, then you see, he has told you the truth, and, and, it's a help as well.

Anyway, I came away from him with some painted studies and a few watercolours. They are not masterpieces, of course, yet I really believe that there is some soundness and truth in them, more at any rate than what I've done up to now. And so I reckon that I am now at the beginning of the beginning of doing something serious. And because I can now call on a couple of technical resources, that is to say, paint and brush, everything seems fresh again, as it were.

But – now we have to put it all into practice. And so the first thing I must do is find a room large enough for me to keep at a proper distance.

As soon as he saw my studies Mauve told me, 'You are sitting too close to your model.' In many cases that means it's virtually impossible to achieve the proper proportions, and so that is definitely one of the first things I must attend to. I simply must find a large place to rent somewhere, be it a room or a shed. And it won't be all that terribly expensive. It costs 30 guilders a year to rent a workman's cottage in these parts, so I reckon that a room twice as large as one in a workman's cottage would come to, say, 60 guilders. And that is feasible.

I have already seen a shed, but it may have too many drawbacks, especially in wintertime. But I could work there, at least when the weather is a bit milder. And then there are models to be found here in Brabant, I think, and not just in Etten but in other villages too, should objections be raised here.

However, though I am very fond of Brabant I still have a feeling for figures other than the Brabant peasant type. Thus I still think Scheveningen is beautiful beyond words. But I happen to be here, and most probably it works out more cheaply here. In any case, I have promised M. to do my best to find a good studio, and besides, I must start using better paint and better paper now.

For studies and sketches, though, the Ingres paper is excellent. And it works out much cheaper to make my own sketchbooks in various sizes from that than to buy the sketchbooks ready-made.

I still have a small supply of Ingres paper, but if you could include some more of the same kind when you send those studies back to me, I should be greatly obliged to you. Not snow-white, but rather the colour of unbleached linen, no cold tones.

Theo, what a great thing tone & colour are. And those who fail to learn to have feelings for them will remain far removed from real life. M. has taught me to see so many things that I used not to see and one day I shall try to tell you what he has told me, as there may well be one or two things you do not see properly either. Anyway, I hope we'll have a good discussion about artistic matters some day.

And you cannot imagine the feeling of liberation I am beginning to have when I remember the things M. has told me about earning money. Just think of how I have been muddling along for years, always in a kind of fausse position.[1] And now there is a glimmering of real light.

I wish you could see the two watercolours I have brought back with me, for you would realize that they are watercolours just like any other watercolours. They may still be full of imperfections, que soit,[2] I am the first to say that I am still very dissatisfied with them, and yet they are quite different from what I have done before and look fresher and brighter. That doesn't alter the fact, however, that they must get fresher and brighter still, but one can't do everything one wants just like that. It will come little by little.

However, I need those two drawings I did, for I must be able to compare them with the ones I am going to do here, in order to keep the standard at least up to what I did at M.'s. Now although M. tells me that if I muddle along here for another few months and then go back to him, say in March, I shall be producing saleable drawings on a regular basis, I am still passing through a fairly difficult period right now. The cost of model, studio, drawing & painting materials keeps going up and I'm not earning any money yet.

To be sure, Father has said that I needn't worry about any unavoidable expenses, and he is pleased with what M. himself has told him and also with the studies and drawings I brought back. But I still think it is quite dreadful that Father should be

1 False position.
2 So be it.

out of pocket as a result. Of course, we hope it will turn out all right later on, but still, it is a load on my mind. For since I have been here Father has made really nothing at all out of me, and more than once, for instance, he has bought me a coat or a pair of trousers that I would really rather not have had, although I needed them, but Father should not have to be out of pocket because of that. The more so as the coat or trousers in question don't fit and are of little or no use. Well, here is yet another petite misère de la vie humaine.[3]

Besides, as I told you earlier, I loathe not being completely independent. For though Father doesn't expect me to account literally for every cent, he always knows exactly how much I spend and on what. And though as far as I am concerned I have no secrets, I still don't like showing my hand to people. As far as I am concerned even my secrets are not secrets to those with whom I am in sympathy. But Father is not someone for whom I can feel what I feel for, say, you or Mauve. I really do love Father and Mother, but it is quite a different feeling from the one I have for you or M. Father can't feel for or sympathize with me, and I can't settle into Father and Mother's system, it is too stifling and would suffocate me.

Whenever I tell Father anything, it goes in one ear and out of the other, and that certainly applies no less to Mother, and similarly I find Father and Mother's sermons and ideas about God, people, morality and virtue a lot of stuff and nonsense. I too read the Bible occasionally, just as I sometimes read Michelet or Balzac or Eliot, but I see quite different things in the Bible from what Father does, and what Father in his little academic way gleans from it I cannot find in it at all.

Now that the Rev. Mr ten Kate has translated Goethe's Faust, Father and Mother have read it, for since a clergyman has translated it, it cannot be all that immoral (???qu'est ce que ça?[4]). But they see it as no more than the disastrous consequence of an indelicate love.

3 Minor irritation of human life (see Letter 153).
4 What's that?

And they certainly understand the Bible no better. Take Mauve, for example. When he reads something profound, he doesn't immediately come out with: that man means this or that. For poetry is so deep and intangible[5] that one cannot define it systematically. But Mauve has a keen sensibility and, you see, I find that sensibility worth a great deal more than definitions and criticisms. And when I read, and actually I don't read all that much and then only a few writers, men whom I have discovered by accident, then I do so because they look at things more broadly and generously and with more love than I do and are acquainted better with reality, and because I can learn from them. But I really don't much care for all that twaddle about good and evil, morality and immorality. For to be sure, I find it impossible always to tell what is good and what is bad, what is moral and what is immoral.

Morality or immorality brings me back willy-nilly to K. V. Ah! I wrote to you at the time that it was beginning to seem less and less like eating strawberries in the spring. Well, that is indeed the case.

Forgive me if I repeat myself, but I don't know if I've already written to you exactly what happened to me in Amsterdam. I went there thinking, perhaps the no, never, ever will thaw, the weather is so mild.

And so one fine evening I trudged along the Keizersgracht looking for the house, and indeed I found it. And naturally I rang the doorbell and was told that the family were still at dinner. But then I was told to come in all the same. And all of them were there, including Jan and that very learned professor – except for Kee. And there was a plate in front of each person, but no extra plate. This small detail struck me. They had wanted to make me think that Kee wasn't there and had taken away her plate, but I knew that she was there, and I thought it all a bit of a farce or charade.

After a while I asked (after the usual small talk and greetings), 'But where is Kee?'

---

5 'intangible': in either French or English.

Then J. P. S. repeated my question to his wife, 'Mother, where is Kee?'

And Mother, the wife, said, 'Kee is out.'

So for the moment I inquired no further, but chatted with the professor about the exhibition at Arti which he had just seen. Well, then the professor disappeared and little Jan disappeared and J. P. S. and his spouse and yours truly remained alone and squared up to each other.

J. P. S. took the floor, as clergyman and father, and said that he had been on the point of sending yours truly a letter and that he would read that letter out.

First, however, interrupting the Rev. or Very Rev. gentleman, I asked again, 'Where is Kee?' (For I knew she was in town.)

Then J. P. S. said, 'Kee left the house the moment she heard you were here.' Now I know a few things about her and I must make clear to you that I did not know then nor do I know now with any certainty whether her coldness and rudeness are a good or a bad sign. This much I do know, that I have never seen her so apparently or actually cold and stern and rude to anyone else but me. So, staying perfectly calm, I did not say much.

'Let me hear the letter then,' I said, 'or not, I don't much care either way.'

Then came the epistle. The document was Very Reverend and Most Learned and so did not really amount to anything, but it did seem to say that I was requested to cease my correspondence and advised to make energetic efforts to put the matter out of my mind. Finally the reading came to an end. I felt just as if I had been listening to the clergyman, after his voice had been doing a sing-song, saying amen in church. It left me as cold as any ordinary sermon.

And then I began and said as calmly and civilly as I could, well, yes, I had heard this kind of argument very often before, but what now? – et après ça?[6] J. P. S. looked up then ... indeed, he seemed faintly alarmed that I was not completely convinced that the utmost limit of the human capacity to think and feel had

6 And after that?

been reached. According to him, no 'et après ça' was possible any longer.

And so we continued, and every so often Aunt M. would add a peculiarly Jesuitical word, and I got a bit steamed up and for once I did not pull my punches. And J. P. S. did not pull his punches either, going as far as a clergyman could. And although he did not exactly say 'God damn you', anyone other than a clergyman in J. P. S.'s mood would have expressed himself thus.

But you know that I love both Father and J. P. S. in my way, despite really detesting their system, and I shifted my ground a bit, and gave and took a little, so that at the end of the evening they told me I could stay for the night if I wished.

Then I said, 'Thank you very much, but if Kee walks out of the house as soon as I come calling, I don't think this is the right moment to spend the night here. I'll go to my lodgings.'

And then they asked, 'Where are you staying?'

I said, 'I don't know yet,' and then Uncle & Aunt insisted on taking me themselves to a good cheap hotel.

And my goodness, those two old people went with me through the cold, foggy, muddy streets and they did indeed show me a very good and very cheap hotel. I absolutely insisted on their not coming and they absolutely insisted on showing me. And, you see, I found something very human in that and it calmed me down a bit.

I stayed in Amsterdam another two days and had another talk with J. P. S., but I didn't see Kee, who spirited herself away every time. And I said that they ought to know that though they wanted me to consider the matter over and done with, I for my part was unable to do so. And to that they continually and steadily replied that I would learn to understand things better in time.

I saw the professor, too, again a few times, and I have to say he improves upon acquaintance, but, but, but, what else can I say about the gentleman? I told him I wished he might fall in love one day. There you are. Can professors fall in love? Do clergymen know what love is?

I read Michelet's La femme, la religion et le prêtre the other day.[7] Books like that are filled with reality, but what is more real than reality itself and where is there more life than in life itself? And we who are doing our best to live, if only we lived a great deal more!

Time hung heavily on my hands those three days in Amsterdam. I felt thoroughly miserable and found all that grudging kindness of Uncle's and Aunt's and all those discussions very hard to take. Until in the end I began to find myself hard to take as well and said to myself, 'You don't want to get melancholy again, do you?' And then I said to myself, 'Don't let yourself be browbeaten.'

And so it was that on a Sunday morning I went to see J. P. S. for the last time, and said, 'Look here, dear Uncle, if Kee V. were an angel, then she would be too exalted for me and I don't think I could stay in love with an angel. If she were a devil, I shouldn't want to have anything to do with her. In the present case I see in her a real woman, with feminine passions and whims and I love her very much indeed and that is a fact and I'm glad of it. As long as she doesn't become an angel or a devil, then the present case is not over.'

And J. P. S. couldn't add much to that and even said something about feminine passions, I don't quite know what he said, and then J. P. S. went off to church. No wonder one grows hardened there and turns to stone, as I know from my own experience.

And so, as far as the person in question, your brother, is concerned, he refused to allow himself to be browbeaten. But that didn't alter the fact that he had a browbeaten feeling, as if he had been standing too long against a cold, hard, whitewashed church wall.

And yes, if I may say so, my dear fellow, it is a little risky to remain a realist, but Theo, Theo, you are a realist yourself after all, well, please put up with my realism! I told you that as far as I am concerned even my secrets are no secrets, well, I am not taking that back, think of me what you will, and whether or not you approve of what I did does not really affect the issue.

---

7 The correct title is *Du prêtre, de la femme, de la famille.*

I continue – from Amsterdam I went to Haarlem and spent a very enjoyable time with our dear little sister Willemien and went for a walk with her and in the evening I left for The Hague and ended up at M.'s at about seven o'clock.

And I said, 'Look here, M., you were supposed to come to Etten to try to initiate me, more or less, into the mysteries of the palette. But it occurred to me that that would take more than just a few days, so I have come to you, and if you agree I shall stay here for about four to six weeks, or for as long or as short a time as you like, and then we shall see what is to be done. It's a bit impertinent of me to ask so much of you, but, well, j'ai l'épée dans les reins.'[8]

Anyway, then M. said, 'Have you brought anything with you?'

'Certainly, here are a few studies,' and then he said many, far too many, kind things about them, but he also made a few, far too few, criticisms. Well, the next day we set up a still life and he started by saying, 'This is how you must hold your palette.' And since then I have done a few painted studies and then later two watercolours.

So that is the summary of the work, but working with one's hands and head is not the whole of life.

I still felt chilled to the marrow, that is, to the marrow of my soul, by the above-mentioned imaginary or non-imaginary church wall. And I said to myself, you don't want to let that fatal feeling browbeat you. Then I thought to myself, I should like to be with a woman for a change, I cannot live without love, without a woman. I wouldn't give two cents for life if there were not something infinite, something deep, something real.

But, said I to myself then, you said 'she and no other' and now you want to go to another woman? But that's unreasonable, isn't it, that's illogical, isn't it?

And my answer to that was: who is the master, logic or I, does logic exist for me or do I exist for logic, and is there no reason or sense in my unreasonableness or my lack of sense? And whether I do right or wrong, I have no choice, that damned wall is too

8 I am under great pressure.

cold for me, I need a woman, I cannot, will not, may not, live without love. I am only a man and a man with passions, I must have a woman, otherwise I shall freeze or turn to stone or, in short, I shall have let things browbeat me.

I had in the circumstances, however, fought a great battle with myself and in that battle some of the things I believe concerning one's constitution and hygiene, that I have come to know more or less through bitter experience, gained the upper hand. One cannot forgo a woman for too long with impunity. And I do not believe that what some call God and others the supreme being and others nature, is unreasonable and pitiless, in short I came to the conclusion: I want to see whether I can find a woman.

And, my goodness, I didn't have to look all that far. I found a woman, by no means young, by no means beautiful, nothing special if you like. But perhaps you are a little curious. She was fairly tall, and strongly built, she didn't have the hands of a lady, like K. V., but the hands of a woman who does a great deal of work. But she was not coarse or common and had something very feminine about her. She reminded me of some quaint figure by Chardin or Frère or perhaps Jan Steen. Anyway, what the French call 'une ouvrière'.[9] She had had many cares, you could see, and life had been hard for her. Oh, nothing refined, nothing out of the ordinary, nothing unusual.

Toute femme à tout âge, si elle aime et si elle est bonne, peut donner à l'homme non l'infini du moment, mais le moment de l'infini.[10]

Theo, for me that faded je ne sais quoi,[11] that something over which life has passed, has infinite charm. Ah! for me she did have charm, something of Feyen-Perrin, of Perugino. See here, I am not quite as innocent as a 'bec blanc',[12] much less a baby in a cradle.

It was not the first time that I was unable to resist that feeling

9 A woman worker.
10 Any woman, at any age, if she loves and is a good woman, can give a man not the infinity of a moment, but a moment of infinity.
11 I don't know what.
12 Greenhorn.

of affection, that special affection and love for those women who are so damned and condemned and despised by clergymen from the lofty heights of their pulpits. I do not damn them, I do not condemn them, I do not despise them.

See here, I am nearly thirty and do you really think that [I] have never felt the need for love? K. V. is even older than I am, she has also known love in the past, but she is all the dearer to me for it. She is not inexperienced, but neither am I. If she wants to hold on to an old love and have nothing to do with a new, that is her affair, but if she insists on doing that and cold-shoulders me, I shan't stifle my energy and my mental powers on her account. No, I refuse to do that, I love her but I will not allow myself to become frozen and my mind crippled because of her. And the spur, the spark we need, is love, and not mystical love either.

That woman has not cheated me – oh, he who takes all such women for cheats is so wrong and has so little understanding. That woman was good to me, very good, very dear, very kind, in a way I shall not even tell my brother Theo, because I strongly suspect that my brother Theo has had a similar experience. Tant mieux pour lui.[13]

Did we spend much money? No, because I didn't have much, and I said to her, 'Look here, you and I don't have to make ourselves drunk to feel something for each other, you had best put what I can spare in your pocket.' And I wish I could have spared more, for she was worth it. And we talked about every-thing, about her life, about her worries, about her misery, about her health, and I had a more exhilarating conversation with her than, for instance, with my learned, professorial cousin Jan.

Now I am telling you these things not least because I hope you will realize that though I do have some sentiment, I don't want to be sentimental in a silly way. That I want quand bien même[14] to keep some warmth and vitality and my mind clear and my constitution sound in order to be able to work. And that

13 So much the better for him.
14 All the same.

I conceive my love for K. V. in this light, that for her sake I don't want to get down to work feeling melancholy and will not allow myself to be thrown off course.

That is something you will understand, you who have written something on the question of hygiene in your letter. You mentioned the fact that you haven't been enjoying good health lately – make every effort you can to get better again.

The clergymen call us sinners, conceived and born in sin. Bah! What confounded nonsense that is. Is it a sin to love, to feel the need for love, not to be able to live without love? I consider a life without love a sinful and immoral state.

If there is anything I regret then it is that period when I allowed mystical and theological profundities to mislead me into withdrawing too much into myself. I have gradually come to change my mind. When you wake up in the morning and find you are not alone but can see a fellow creature there in the half-light, it makes the world look so much more welcoming. Much more welcoming than the devotional journals and whitewashed church walls beloved of clergymen. She lived in a modest, simple little room lent a quiet grey tone by the plain wallpaper, yet warm like a picture by Chardin, a wooden floor with a mat and a piece of old dark-red carpet, an ordinary kitchen stove, a chest of drawers, a large, perfectly simple bed, in short, a real ouvrière's home. The next day she had to work at the washtub. Fair enough, I should have found her no more charming in a purple camisole jacket and a black skirt than I did now in a dress of brown or reddish-grey. And she was no longer young, perhaps the same age as K. V., and she had a child, yes, life had left its mark and her youth was gone. Gone? – il n'y a point de vieille femme.[15] Ah, and she was strong and healthy – and yet not coarse, not common.

Are those who set such great store by distinction always able to spot the distinguished? Good heavens, people search high and low for what is right under their noses, and I do too, now and then.

---

15 There are no old women.

I am glad I did as I did because I can think of no earthly reason that would keep me from my work or cause me to lose my good humour. When I think of K. V., then yes, I still say, 'she and no other', then I still think as I did in the summer about 'looking for another girl in the meanwhile'. But it isn't since yesterday that I have been taking a warm interest in those women whom the clergy condemn, despise and damn, indeed my love for them is rather older than that for Kee Vos. Many times when I walked the streets all alone with time hanging heavily on my hands, half sick and down in the dumps, with no money in my pocket, I would look at them and envy the people who could go with one, and I felt that those poor girls were my sisters in respect of circumstance and experience of life. And, you see, that is an old feeling of mine, and goes deep. Even as a boy I would often look up with infinite sympathy, indeed with respect, at a woman's face past its prime, inscribed as it were with the words: here life and reality have left their mark.

But my feeling for K. V. is quite new and something quite different. Sans le savoir,[16] she is in a kind of prison, she too is poor and cannot do as she pleases, she feels a kind of resignation, and it is my belief that the Jesuitisms of clergymen and devout ladies often make a greater impression on her than on me, Jesuitisms which, precisely because I have acquired some dessous de cartes,[17] no longer have any hold on me now. But she is devoted to them and would be unable to bear it if the system of resignation and sin and God and I know not what else, proved to be vain.

And I don't think it ever occurs to her that God may only appear once we say the words, those words with which Multatuli ends his prayer of an unbeliever: 'Oh God, there is no God.' You see, for me that God of the clergy is as dead as a doornail. But does that make me an atheist? Clergymen consider me one – que soit – but you see, I love, and how could I feel love if I were not alive myself or if others were not alive, and if we are alive there

16 Without realizing it.
17 Inside information.

is something wondrous about it. Now call that God or human nature or whatever you like, but there is a certain something I cannot define systematically, although it is very much alive and real, and you see, for me that something is God or as good as God. You see, when in due course my time comes, one way or other, to die, well, what will keep me going even then? Won't it be the thought of love (moral or immoral love, what do I know about it)?

And good heavens, I love Kee Vos for a thousand reasons, but precisely because I believe in life and in something real I am no longer as given to abstractions as before, when I had more or less the same ideas about God and religion as Kee Vos seems to have now. I am not giving her up, but that spiritual crisis with which she is perhaps struggling must be given time, and I am prepared to be patient about it and nothing she says or does now makes me angry. But while she cherishes and clings to the old, I must work and keep my mind clear for painting and drawing and for business. So I did what I did from a need for affection and for reasons of mental hygiene.

I am telling you all this so that you won't again think that I am in a melancholy or abstracted, brooding mood. On the contrary, most of the time I am fiddling around with and thinking about paints, making watercolours, looking for a studio, &c., &c. Old fellow, if only I could find a suitable studio!

Well, my letter has become rather long, but there you are. Sometimes I wish that the three months before I can go back to M. were already over, but as it is they may do me some good. But do write to me now and then. Is there any chance of your coming here this winter?

And believe me, I shan't rent a studio, &c., without first finding out what Mauve thinks. I shall send him the floor plan, as agreed, and he may come and have a look at it himself if need be. But Father must stay out of it. Father is not the man to get mixed up in artistic matters. And the less I am involved in dealings with Father, the better I get on with him. I must be free and independent in very many respects, that goes without saying.

I sometimes shudder when I think of K. V. and of her burying herself in her past and clinging to old and dead ideas. There is something fatal about it and, oh, it would not diminish her if she were to change her views. I think it quite possible that there will be some reaction, there is so much that is healthy and spirited in her.

And so in March I shall go back to The Hague and, and, to Amsterdam as well. But when I left Amsterdam that time, I told myself: under no circumstances will you become melancholy or allow things to get you down, letting your work suffer just when you have started to make some headway. Eating strawberries in the spring is indeed part of life, but it is only one short moment in the year and right now it is still a long way off.

And so you envy me for some reason or other? Oh, my dear fellow, no need for that, since what I seek can be found by everyone, perhaps even sooner by you than by me. And oh, I am so backward and narrow-minded in many things, if only I knew exactly where the trouble lay and how to go about putting it right. But alas, we often do not see the beams in our own eye.

Write to me soon and try to separate the wheat from the chaff in my letters. If there is some good in them, some truth, tant mieux,[18] but there is, of course, much in them that is more or less wrong, or exaggerated perhaps, without my always being aware of it. I am anything but a man of learning, and I am so amazingly ignorant, oh, just like so many others and even more so than others, but I am unable to judge that myself and can judge others even less than myself, and am often mistaken. But we pick up the scent as we wander about and il y a du bon en tout mouvement[19] (I chanced to hear Jules Breton say that, by the way, and remembered the remark).

Incidentally, have you ever heard Mauve preach? I've heard him mimicking several clergymen – once he preached about Peter's boat. The sermon was divided into 3 parts: 1st, was he given the boat or did he inherit it? 2nd, did he purchase it in

18 So much the better.
19 There is some good in every movement.

instalments or by taking out shares? 3rd, had he (dreadful thought) stolen it? Then he went on to preach about 'the Lord's good intentions' and about 'the Tigris and the Euphrates' and finally he mimicked J. P. S. marrying A.[20] and Lecomte.

But when I told him that I had once said during a discussion with Father that I believed that even in church, even in the pulpit, one could say something edifying, M. agreed. And then he mimicked Father Bernhard: 'God – God – is almighty – He has made the sea, He has made the earth and the sky and the stars and the sun and the moon, He can do everything – everything – everything – but – no, He is not almighty, there is one thing that He cannot do. What is that thing that God Almighty cannot do? God Almighty cannot cast out a sinner.'

Well, goodbye, Theo, write soon, a handshake in my thoughts, and believe me,

Ever yours,
<u>Vincent</u>

20 Anna Carbentus, Vincent's cousin.

The Hague

With money borrowed from Mauve, Van Gogh set up a studio at 138 Schenkweg, The Hague, not far from Rijnspoor railway station. This was the first of a long series of plainly furnished rooms which would form the background to his work and of which his *Bedroom in Arles* would later become a world-famous symbol: 'A room & alcove, the light is bright enough as the window is large, twice as large as an ordinary window.' The furniture was simple, with 'proper kitchen chairs and a really sturdy kitchen table'.

Theo supported Vincent's plan to stay in The Hague but remonstrated with him about the way he had treated his parents, 'people who have lived in the country all their lives & who have had no chance of participating in modern life'. Vincent, for his part, preferred to keep his contacts with his parents to a minimum: 'When I think of Etten it gives me the shudders, just as if I were in church.' He defended himself vigorously against Theo's claim that he had embittered his parents' life and rendered it 'almost impossible'. Numbering Theo's reproaches he vehemently refuted them one by one.

169 [D]

[7 or 8 January 1882]

Please don't think I'm sending your letter back to offend you, I simply believe this is the quickest way of answering it clearly. And if you didn't have your own letter to hand, you might not be able to understand quite so well what my answer refers to. Now the numbers will guide you. I'm short of time, I'm still expecting a model today.

Paris, 5 Jan. 1882

My dear Vincent,

I have received your two letters & thank you for keeping me in the picture. I think it is a very good thing that you have settled permanently in The Hague & hope to do as much as I can to help you out until you can start earning your own money. But what I do not approve of is the way in which you contrived to leave Father & Mother.[1]

That you could not bear it there is possible & that you should differ in your views from people who have lived in the country all their lives & who have had no chance of participating in modern life, is only too natural, but what the devil made you so childish & so shameless as to embitter Father & Father's life & render it almost impossible by setting about things in the way you did?[2] It isn't hard to fight with someone who is already weary.[3]

When Father wrote to me about it, I thought it must be a

misunderstanding, but you yourself say in your letter, 'As far as the relationship between Father & me is concerned, it will not be remedied in a hurry.'[4] Don't you know him then, & don't you realize that Father cannot live while there is all this bickering between the two of you?[5] Coûte que coûte,[1] you <u>are in duty bound</u> to ensure that matters are put right & I guarantee that one day you will be extremely sorry for having been so callous in this matter.[6]

It is Mauve who attracts you at the moment, &, carried away as usual, you find anyone who is not like him objectionable, because you look for the same qualities in everybody.[7] Is it not a bitter pill for Father to swallow to see himself belittled by someone who claims to be more of a freethinker,[8] and whom, au fond,[2] he possibly envies from time to time for his clearer insights?[9] Does his life count for nothing then?[10] I don't understand you.[11] Write to me again when you can[12] & give my regards to Mauve & Jet.

Ever yours,
<u>Theo</u>

[7 or 8 January 1882]

Because I have only a little time to spare, I can think of no better means of replying to your letter than by doing it in this way, answering your points one by one in orderly sequence.

(1) I did not 'contrive' anything, on the contrary, when Father was here, Mauve, Father & I talked about my renting a studio in Etten – spending the winter there – and returning to The Hague in the spring. Because of the models and because I had settled down to my work in Etten & had begun to make headway.

That does not alter the fact that I should have liked to prolong my stay in The Hague a bit more, seeing that I was here already, but it was nevertheless my definite intention to continue my studies of the Brabant peasant types. And when my plans

1 At all costs.
2 Deep down.

were thwarted, after they had been discussed with M. & I had already entered into correspondence with him about the studio in question (a shed in need of some repair), I could no longer contain my anger.

Do you recall a letter I wrote to you in which I expanded at some length on my plan to continue those studies? I mean the letter in which I asked you to impress upon Father & Mother once more in plain terms that working in Etten was of the greatest importance to me, &c. I remember the way I put it: it would be too bad if, because of a whim of Father's, I had to abandon work that had begun to make headway and on which I had been engaged for months. Give it some thought yourself – despite Mauve's help I am in much more of a fix here than at home, and I'll be blowed if I know how I am going to get through it.

(2) The reproach <u>that I set about embittering Father's & Mother's life</u> is not really your own. I know it, and of old, as one of Father's Jesuitisms and have told Father, & Mother too, that I considered it to be a Jesuitism and that I didn't take the slightest notice of it.

Whenever one says something to Father to which he has no reply, he comes out with a reproach of that sort and says, for example, 'You will be the death of me,' while he sits there perfectly calmly reading his newspaper and smoking his pipe. So I take such reproaches for what they are.

Or else Father flies into an enormous rage, is used to people being frightened by it and is astonished when somebody does not give way before his anger.

Father is extremely touchy and irritable and obstinate in domestic affairs and is used to having his way. And the heading 'the rules and regulations of this house', with which I am obliged to comply, includes literally anything that comes into Father's head.

(3) It's easy enough to fight with an old man, &c. Because Father is an old man, I have spared his feelings a hundred times & tolerated things that are little short of intolerable. Anyway, there wasn't any fighting this time either, but just an 'enough!',

and because he wouldn't listen to reason & common sense, I spoke straight out & it can only be to the good that for once Father should have heard a few home truths expressed that others too think now and then.

(4) That it will not be remedied in a hurry. For the sake of appearances I have put matters straight by writing to Father again and telling him that I have rented a studio, that I wished him a happy New Year, and that I hoped we would have no more quarrels of this or any other kind in that New Year. I shall do no more about it, nor do I need to.

If this last row had been an isolated case then it would be a different matter, but it was preceded by other rows, yet whenever I told Father a few things in a calmer though still resolute way, His Hon. would fling it all systematically to the winds. So as far as the things I have said in anger are concerned, I think the same even in a calmer mood, though for diplomatic reasons I have usually kept quiet about them or put them differently. But this time I lost my temper, my diplomacy went by the board, and well, for once I had my say. I offer no apology for that and while Father & Mother continue in this mood I shall take nothing back. Should they later behave in a more humane, more sensitive and more sincere way, then I shall be happy to take everything back. But I doubt if that will happen.

(5) That Father & Mother cannot live while there is all this bickering going on, &c., that's true, in so far as they are creating a desert around themselves and are earning themselves an unhappy old age when they could have a happy and contented one. But as to such expressions as 'I cannot bear it', 'it's killing me', 'my life is being embittered', I no longer attach any importance to them, for that's only their little way. And if they do not change, then, as I have already said, I'm afraid they are storing up many bad and lonely days for themselves.

(6) That I shall be sorry, &c. Before things came to their present pass, I used to have many regrets and be very sad and reproach myself because things between Father and Mother and me were going so badly. But now that matters have gone this far, well, so be it, and to tell you the truth, I have no regrets any

more, cannot help feeling a sense of deliverance. If I should later come to see that I did wrong, well, then I shall of course be sorry, but as it is I have been unable to see how else I could possibly have acted. When somebody tells me decisively, 'Get out of my house, the sooner the better, in half an hour rather than an hour,' well then, my dear fellow, it doesn't take a quarter of an hour for me to leave, never to return either. That was going too far, and you surely understand that, if only to spare you and others further financial trouble, I should not lightly have left of my own accord, but once that 'Get out' has been said, by them and not by me, well then, my course is clear enough.

(7) As for Mauve – yes indeed, I am very fond of M. and am in sympathy with him. I love his work – and I count myself fortunate to be learning from him, but I can no more withdraw into some system or school than Mauve can himself, and apart from Mauve and Mauve's work, I also love others who are quite different and work quite differently. And as for myself and my own work, perhaps there is a similarity between us at times, but there is certainly a difference as well. If I love someone or something, then I do so in earnest and sometimes with real passion and fire, but that doesn't make me think as a matter of course that only a few people are perfect and all the others worthless – far from it.

(8) Freethinker, that is really a word I detest, although I have to use it occasionally faute de mieux.[3] The fact is that I do my best to think things through and try in my actions to take account of reason and common sense. And trying to belittle someone would be quite contrary to that. So it is perfectly true that on occasion I have said to Father, 'Do try to think this or that through,' or, 'To my mind, this or that does not stand up,' but that is not trying to belittle someone. I am not Father's enemy if I tell him the truth for a change, not even that time I lost my temper and did so in salty language. Only it did no good, and Father took it amiss.

3 For want of anything better.

In case Father refers to my saying that, ever since I have acquired so much dessous les cartes,[4] I haven't given two pins for the morality and the religious system of the clergy and their academic ideas, then I absolutely refuse to take that back, for I truly mean it. It is just that when I am in a calm mood, I don't talk about it, although it is a different matter when they try to force me to go to church, for instance, or to attach importance to doing so, for then I naturally tell them that it is completely out of the question.

(10) Does Father's life count for nothing? I have already said that when I hear someone say, 'You will be the death of me,' while in the meantime that man is reading his paper and half a minute later is talking about goodness knows what advertisement or other, I consider that phrase fairly irrelevant and superfluous & take no notice of it. As soon as that kind of phrase is repeated to others, who are then going to consider me more or less a murderer or even a parricide, I say, these slanders are nothing more nor less than Jesuitisms. There you are. Anyway, the murderer has left the house now, and so, in short, I take not the slightest notice of any of it and even consider it ridiculous.

(11) You say, 'I don't understand you.' Well, I readily believe that, for writing is really a wretched way of explaining things to each other. And it takes up a great deal of time and you and I have a great deal to do as it is. But we must have a little patience with each other until we can see, and speak to each other.

(12) Write to me again. Yes, of course, but first we must agree how. Would you like me to write in a kind of businesslike style, dry and formal, weighing my words carefully and actually saying nothing at all? Or would you like me to continue to write as I have done recently, telling you all the thoughts that come into my head, without being afraid of rambling on now and then, without censoring my thoughts or holding them back? That's what I would prefer – that is, being free to write or say exactly what I mean.

So much for my direct answer to your letter, but I still have

4 Inside information.

some things to say to you about drawing, &c., &c., and I would sooner talk about that. Consider it a point in my favour that for the time being I am behaving as if Father and Mother did not exist. It would have been much better if I had spent this winter in Etten, and things would have been much easier for me, too, especially for financial reasons – if I were to start thinking & fretting about that again, it would make me melancholy, so that's over and done with, once and for all. I am here now and I must try to muddle through. If I wrote to Father about it again, it would be adding fuel to the fire, I don't ever want to get angry again and am throwing myself with might and main into life and affairs here, and, what can I do, Etten is lost and so is Heike, but I shall try to obtain something else in their stead.

———

Let me now thank you warmly for what you sent me. I don't need to add that I am still extremely anxious in spite of it. Of course my expenses are greater than in Etten and I cannot get down to work half as energetically as I should like and should be able to if I had greater resources.

But my studio is turning out well. I wish you could see it sometime. I have hung up all my studies and you must send me back those you still have because they could still be useful to me. They may not be saleable and I readily acknowledge all their faults, but there is something of nature in them because they were done with some passion.

And you know, I am toiling away at watercolours right now and when I have got my hand in, they will be saleable. But Theo, believe me, when I went to Mauve for the first time with my pen drawings and M. said, 'Now try it with charcoal & crayon & brush & stump,' I had the devil of a job working with that new material. I was patient, but that didn't seem to help, then I grew so impatient at times that I would stamp on my charcoal and become utterly dejected. And yet, a little while later, I sent you drawings done with chalk & charcoal & the brush, and I went back to Mauve with a whole lot of similar ones, in which, naturally, he found something to criticize, and with reason, and you did as well, but still, it was a step forward.

Now I am once again passing through a similar period of struggle and dejection, of patience and impatience, of hope and despair. But I have to struggle on and, well, in good time I shall understand watercolours better. If it were easy, there would be no pleasure in it. And ditto, ditto with painting.

Added to this, the weather is inclement so that I have yet to go out just for the fun of it this winter. Still, I am enjoying life, and in particular having a studio of my own is too glorious for words. When are you coming to have some tea or coffee with me? Soon, I hope. You can spend the night too, if necessary – how very nice and how enjoyable. And I even have some flowers too, a few small bowls of bulbs.

And what's more, I have obtained yet another ornament for my studio. I got an amazing bargain of splendid woodcuts from the Graphic, in part printed, not from the clichés, but from the blocks themselves. Just what I've been looking for for years. Drawings by Herkomer, Frank Holl, Walker and others. I bought them from Blok the Jewish bookseller, and for five guilders picked the best from an enormous pile of Graphics & London News. They include some superb things, for instance, the Houseless and homeless[5] by Fildes (poor people waiting outside a night shelter) and two large Herkomers and many small ones, and the Irish emigrants[6] by Frank Holl and the 'Old gate'[7] by Walker, and above all a girls' school by Frank Holl, and then another large Herkomer, The Invalids.

Anyway, it's just the stuff I need.

And I keep such beautiful things at home with some contentment because, my dear fellow, although I am still a long way from doing anything as beautiful myself, I have nevertheless hung a few of my studies of old peasants, etc., on the wall, which

5 Title in English.
6 Title in English.
7 Title in English.

proves that my enthusiasm for those artists is not mere vanity, but that I struggle and strive to make something myself that is realistic and yet done with feeling.

I've got about 12 figures of diggers and people working in the potato field, and I wonder if I couldn't do something with them. You still have a few of them, for instance a man putting potatoes into a sack. Well, I'm not sure when, but sooner or later I must get down to that, because last summer I made some careful observations, and here in the dunes I should be able to do a good study of the earth and the sky and then put in the figures boldly. Still, I'm not setting too much store by these studies, and hope, of course, to do something quite different and better, but the Brabant types are characteristic and who knows whether they can't still be used to good account. If there are any you would like to keep, feel at liberty to do so, but I should be very glad to have back those in which you are not interested. By studying new models I will automatically discover the mistakes in proportion I made in last summer's studies, and so they may yet prove useful to me.

When your letter took so long to come (since it went to Mauve first, I received it even later) I had to go to Mr Tersteeg, and he gave me 25 guilders until I received your letter. It might be a good idea if I, with your knowledge, or you, with my knowledge, made some sort of an arrangement with Mr T. For you realize, Theo, I must know with as much certainty as possible what to expect, and I must be able to calculate and be able to tell in advance whether I can do this or that or must give it up. So you will do me a great favour by agreeing with me to a definite arrangement, and I hope you will write to me about it soon.

Mauve has promised me to put my name forward immediately as an associate member of Pulchri,[8] because I shall then be able to draw from the model there 2 evenings a week and shall have more contact with artists. Then as soon as possible after that I

8 The artists' society and headquarters of the Hague School.

shall become a full member. Well, my dear fellow, thanks for what you sent, and believe me, with a handshake,

Ever yours,
Vincent

From Mauve, Vincent learned the principles of painting in watercolours and in oil. Mauve was one of the leading members of the Hague School, a movement predominant in the Dutch art world at the time. Its painters excelled in atmospheric landscapes of the Dutch polders and the everyday lives of peasants and fishermen. Mauve specialized in the painting of cattle and, with Weissenbruch, he was the most brilliant watercolourist of the Hague School.

Van Gogh benefited considerably from his lessons, but contact with the melancholy Mauve was not without its problems – the two artists sometimes got on each other's nerves. 'It isn't always very easy for me to get on with Mauve, any more than the other way around, because I believe both of us are of an equally nervous disposition.' Meanwhile, financial worries continued to plague Van Gogh. Sometimes he was 'feverish with nervous exhaustion' and did not know how he would get through the week. Luckily he was able to take advantage of the facilities of Pulchri Studio to do drawings from life. 'Drawing is becoming more and more a passion with me, a passion just like that of the sailor for the sea.' In addition, he found his models among the 'orphan' men and women, inhabitants of the Diaconessenhuis (a church-run almshouse and hospital), in the soup kitchens of The Hague, and – like Daumier before him – in third-class waiting rooms.

He did not lack support from colleagues during this early Hague period. In George Hendrik Breitner, who was to become the leader of the so-called Amsterdam Impressionists a few years later, he met a colleague at the beginning of his career who, like himself, was interested in the portrayal of simple working types. Van Gogh had hopes that drawings of this kind might sell as designs for magazine illustrations. He also benefited from the advice of the landscape painter Jan Hendrik Weissenbruch, one of the most congenial members of the Hague School, and drew confidence from the latter's appreciation of his pen drawings.

Théophile de Bock lent him a book that made a great impression on him, namely Alfred Sensier's biography of Jean-François Millet. Van Gogh saw his own path as a painter of peasants sketched out in this biography, much as, a few years earlier, he had seen his preacher's career mapped out in Bunyan's *Pilgrim's Progress*: 'It interests me so much that I am woken by it at night, light the lamp and carry on reading.' Sensier's biography of Millet was to remain Van Gogh's manual of true art until the day he died, and strengthened him in his resolve to become a painter of peasant life.

Vincent's relationship with Herman Tersteeg, who ran the Hague branch of Goupil & Cie, remained difficult and equivocal. The importance he attached to Tersteeg's opinion and sympathy is understandable, because Tersteeg wielded great influence in the art circles of his day. Vincent believed firmly that acceptance by him was the key to his breakthrough as an artist. It is true he made increasingly critical and indignant comments on Tersteeg's character, but at the same time he continued to vie for his favours and to bear his opinions in mind, even when they ran counter to his own deepest convictions. Years later, writing from Arles, Van Gogh was still trying to convince this pope of the arts in The Hague of his qualities as an artist.

Although Tersteeg bought one of his drawings, Van Gogh was deeply offended by such comments as, 'It's time you started to think about making a living.' Van Gogh refused to act on the suggestion that he should paint easily saleable watercolours – he was not yet ready to do this and preferred Mauve's advice to continue with his figure studies. He despised easy success: 'Surely, the true path is to delve deep into nature.'

Vincent refused to yield an inch when it came to matters of principle, even to his uncle, the art dealer Cornelis Marinus van Gogh, who called on him and gave him a commission to draw twelve views of The Hague. Thus when his uncle criticized the Belgian artist De Groux's way of life in his presence, Van Gogh felt almost personally attacked: 'It has always struck me that when an artist shows his work in public, he has the right to keep the inner conflicts of his private life (which is directly and fatally bound up with the peculiar difficulties involved in producing a work of art) to himself [. . .].'

The following letter conveys a good idea of the problems that exercised Van Gogh during his first period in The Hague. In it we also find mention for the first time of Clasina (Sien) Hoornik and her family, whom Vincent had taken on as models and who seemed at that time still 'splendidly willing'.

178 [D]

Friday 3 March [1882]

My dear Theo,

Since I received your letter & the money, I have had a model every day and am up to my ears in work.

I've a new model now, though I had done a hasty drawing of her once before. Or rather, there is more than one model, for I have already had 3 individuals from the same family, a woman of about 45 who is just like a figure by Ed. Frère, and her daughter, about 30, and a younger child of 10 or 12. They are poor people and, I must say, splendidly willing. I only managed to get them to agree to pose with some difficulty and on condition that I promise them regular work. Well, that was exactly what I wanted so badly myself, so I consider the deal a good one.

The younger woman's face isn't beautiful, because she has had smallpox, but the figure is very graceful and I find it rather charming. They have the right clothes, too, black merino and a nice style in bonnets and a beautiful shawl, &c.

You needn't worry too much about the money because I reached an agreement with them at the beginning. I promised that I would give them a guilder a day as soon as I sold something. And that I shall make up then for paying too little now.

But I simply must sell something. If I could afford to, I would keep everything that I am doing now for myself, since if I could just keep it for a year, I feel sure I would get more for it.

But anyway, in the circumstances I should find it very gratifying if Mr Tersteeg did take something now and then, if necessary on condition that it will be exchanged if it isn't sold. Mr

Tersteeg has promised to come round to see me as soon as he can find the time.

The reason I should like to keep them is simply this. When I draw individual figures, it is always with a view to a composition with more figures, for instance a 3rd-class waiting room, or a pawnshop, or an interior. But the larger compositions must mature gradually, and for a drawing with, let's say, 3 seamstresses, one might have to draw 90 seamstresses. Voilà l'affaire.[1]

I have had a kind note from C. M. with a promise that he will be coming to The Hague soon and visit me then. Well, it's just another promise, but perhaps something will come of it. We'll see.

For the rest I'm going to run after people less and less, dealers or painters, it doesn't matter who they are. The only people I shall run after will be models, since I'm sure that working without a model is quite wrong, at least for me.

It's gratifying, isn't it, Theo, when there's a little bit of light at the end of the tunnel, and I'm seeing a little bit of light now. It's gratifying to draw a human being, something alive – it may be damned difficult, but it's wonderful anyway.

Tomorrow I shall be giving a children's party, two children whom I have to entertain and draw at the same time. I want there to be some life in my studio and already have all sorts of acquaintances in the neighbourhood. On Sunday I am having a boy from the orphanage, a real type, but unfortunately I can only get him for a short time.

It may be true that I don't have the knack of getting on with people who are sticklers for etiquette, but on the other hand perhaps I get on better with poor or common folk, and what I lose on the one hand I gain on the other. Sometimes I just leave it at that and think: after all,[2] it's right and proper that I should live like an artist in the surroundings I'm sensitive to and am trying to express. Honni soit qui mal y pense.[3]

---

1 There you have it.
2 'after all': in English.
3 Shame to him who thinks ill of it; usually rendered 'evil be to him who evil thinks'.

Here we are at the beginning of another month, and although it's not yet a month since you sent me something, I would ask you to be kind enough to send me some more soon, if you can. It doesn't have to be 100 frs. all at once, but just a little to be going on with between now and when you can send the rest. I mention this because you said in a previous letter that you wouldn't be able to raise any money until after the stocktaking.

It grieves me sometimes when I realize I'm going to have to keep a model waiting, because they need it so badly. So far I have been paying them, but next week I shan't be able to. But I'll be able to get a model anyway, either the old woman or the younger one or the child.

Incidentally, Breitner mentioned you to me the other day, saying there was something he was very sorry for and which he thought you might still be cross about. Apparently, he still has a drawing that belongs to you, but I didn't understand exactly what it was all about. He is at work on a large affair, a market that will be full of figures. Last night I went out with him to look for different types of figures on the street so as to do a study of them later with a model in the studio. I've drawn an old woman in this way whom I saw on the Geest, where the madhouse is.

Well, bonsoir, I hope to hear from you soon,

Ever yours,
<u>Vincent</u>

I had to pay the rent too this week. Good-night, it's two o'clock already and I haven't finished yet.

Theo advised Vincent to keep on good terms with Tersteeg, because he was 'almost like an older brother to us'. Vincent, however, continued to be incensed at Tersteeg's condescending attitude to his work: 'For years now he has considered me a kind of duffer & dreamer. He still does, and even says of my drawing that "it's like a kind of opium you take so you won't feel the pain at not being able to do any more watercolours". Now then, that may be fine talk, but it is thoughtless, superficial and unfounded (the main reason for my not being able to do watercolours at this moment being that I must settle down even more seriously to my drawing and pay greater heed to proportion & perspective).' His own growing aversion to the practices of the art trade set Vincent thinking that Theo, too, would do better to retire from it and become a painter. The independence of an artist was greater than that of the art dealer. As an artist, Theo would experience a second flush of youth. 'Oh, Theo, why don't you throw everything overboard and become a painter, old fellow – you can if you want to. I sometimes suspect you of keeping a famous paysagiste [landscape painter] hidden inside you [. . .]. The two of us must become painters.'

   In countless letters to come Van Gogh continued to elaborate on his idea that Theo, too, would be well-advised to opt for life as an artist, an idea he was never to give up.

182 [D]

[*c.* 14–18 March 1882]

My dear Theo,

On second thoughts, it occurred to me that you must have found it odd to see a reference in my last letter to something I have never mentioned before, & a reference made, moreover, in a rather peremptory tone, something like: Theo, throw the whole lot overboard and become a painter, there is a famous paysagiste[1] inside you.

These words might well have escaped me at a moment when my passions were aroused. But that doesn't alter the fact that it happens like that with other things that I allow to slip out in spite of myself sometimes, once I've got in a passion or have been aroused in some way or other. In other words, what I say at such times is what I've been bottling up for a long time and then blurt out, sometimes quite bluntly. But although in a calmer mood I would put it better, or keep it to myself, the fact is that, especially in a calm mood, I am most decidedly of that particular opinion.

Now it is out, and out it must stay, I have said it at last in spite of myself – inadvertently – in short, bluntly – but now you know my innermost thoughts. And when I wrote, 'remain something better than H. G. T.', and when I intimated that I do not hold art dealers in general in high esteem – it's true, I could well have kept these things to myself, but now that my silence is broken and I have spoken – well then, that is how I will speak.

As to H. G. T., I knew His Hon. during a curious period of his life, when he had just 'worked his way up' as they say, and, moreover, was newly married. At the time he made a strong impression on me – he was a practical man, tremendously able and good-humoured, energetic in small & large things, in addition he radiated poetry, so to speak, but poetry of the genuine, unsentimental sort. I felt so much respect for him at the time that I always kept my distance & looked upon him as a being of a higher order.

Since – since – since then – I have come – more & more – to have my doubts – but I lacked the courage to take up an analytical scalpel to dissect him more closely. Now, however, having reached a point at which I must be very much on the qui vive and not allow my career to be ruined for no matter whom, the above-mentioned scalpel has not spared him. And all the time I sat in his small office or talked to him in the gallery with

1 Landscape painter.

a perfectly natural expression on my face and asked him some very ordinary questions, I was taking his measure as cold-bloodedly as I knew how.

I used to think he was the sort of person who put on the air of a man of means, of an homme du monde,[2] I don't know how to put it in one word, I'm sure you'll take my meaning, and who hid a great deal of feeling and a warm heart behind that iron mask. But I found his armour enormously thick, so thick that I cannot make up my mind for sure whether the man is made of solid metal, be it steel or silver, or whether deep, deep down inside the iron there is one small corner in which a human heart still beats. If there is no heart in him, then my affection for him has truly run its course, making way for a 'Qu'est ce que tu me fais – toi? Tu m'agaces'.[3] So that in six months or a year he will either leave me utterly cold, or, or I will perhaps have found a way of getting on better with His Hon. Meanwhile – he is still His Hon. to me. Those are not the terms in which one thinks of somebody for whom one feels warm sympathy. 'His Hon.' expresses something trite. Enough, suffit.[4]

Theo, I am definitely not a landscape painter, when I do landscapes <u>there will always be something of the figure in them</u>. However, it seems to me a very good thing that there are also people who are essentially 'paysagistes'. And – the thought that you might be just such a person – sans le savoir[5] – greatly preoccupies me. I am just as preoccupied with the antithesis, namely whether you, Theo, are really cut out to be a dealer.

If I had to prove the thesis, I might perhaps try to do so by indirect reduction. Quoi qu'il en soit,[6] do think it over. I don't need to tell you to consider carefully before you begin to paint, but perhaps you won't take it amiss if I add: Theo, until now you were free to do as you please but should you ever come to an arrangement with Messrs G. & Cie and promise to stay on in

2 Man of the world.
3 What are you doing to me? You are getting on my nerves.
4 That will do.
5 Without knowing it.
6 However that may be.

their business for the rest of your life, then you would be a free man no longer. And – it seems quite possible to me that there may come a moment in life when one regrets having committed oneself in that way.

You will no doubt tell me, the moment may well arrive when one regrets having become a painter. And what could I then reply on my own behalf? They who have such regrets are those who neglect solid study in the beginning and who race hurry-scurry to be top of the heap. Well, the men of the day are men of just one day, but whoever has enough faith and love to take pleasure in precisely what others find dull, namely the study of anatomy, perspective & proportion, will stay the course and mature slowly but surely.

When, pressed for money, I forgot myself for a moment and thought, I'll try to produce something with a particular appeal, the result was dreadful, I couldn't do it. And Mauve rightly became angry with me and said, that's not how to do it, tear that stuff up. At first I found that too hard to do, but later I did cut them up. Then when I began to draw more seriously, Tersteeg took exception and became angry – and overlooked the good things in my drawings and asked straight out for ones that were 'saleable'.

Well, you can see immediately from this that there is a difference between Mauve & Tersteeg. Mauve appears more and more serious the more one thinks about him, but is Tersteeg going to be able to pass this test? I hope so, but doubt if he will stand up to it as well as M. And how about those who are serious at heart, although they often have something disagreeable about them? One gets to like them and to feel at home with them – one quickly gets bored with those who are not serious enough.

You mustn't imagine that I have overlooked the change in your financial circumstances which a change of career would entail. But what makes me mention this matter to you at all is that although I find myself in financial difficulties, I nevertheless have the feeling that there is nothing more solid than a 'handi-craft' in the literal sense of working with one's hands. If you became a painter, one of the things that would surprise you is that painting & everything connected with it is quite hard work in physical terms. Leaving aside the mental exertion, the hard thought, it demands considerable physical effort, and that day after day.

Well, I shall say no more about it now, except to add just this: when you come to Holland, I should like to speak to you alone, not just for half an hour but for, say, a whole morning, about some practical things which I have picked up – either from my own experience or from Mauve and others – just as if I had to explain them to you, teach them to you. I hope you won't have any objection – at worst you will be bored for a morning, but perhaps you won't be bored. I only hope that in the meantime you won't be thinking about the 'selling' of pictures, but about the 'how to <u>do</u> it'.[7] And that you won't consider it being tempted by Satan. Enfin, nous verrons.[8]

If you could send me some money towards the end of this month, it would be very welcome. By then I also hope to have finished the 12 for C. M.! If he pays for them straight away, that will put 30 guilders in my pocket. If something from you were added to that, I would risk buying a few shirts & drawers which I need very, very badly, seeing that the shirts, &c., I own are really getting into a deplorable state and I have only a very few of them.

Since I wrote to you I have been working with the same models the whole time and I must say I'm glad to have found them. I am busy drawing heads, and I urgently need to draw hands and feet as well (but it can't be done all at once). And when summer comes & the cold is no longer a handicap, I must needs in one way or another do some studies of the nude. Not exactly academic poses. But I would, for example, be tremendously pleased to have a nude model for a digger or a seamstress. From the front, from the back, from the side. To learn to see and sense the shape properly through the clothes and to have an idea of the movement. I estimate that about 12 studies, 6 men, 6

7 '"how ... it"': in English.
8 Well, we shall see.

women, would throw a lot of light on the matter. Each study takes a day's work. However, it is difficult to find models for this purpose, and if I can I shall avoid having a nude model hanging about in the studio in case I frighten the other models away.

The fear 'that they will have to strip naked' is usually the first scruple one has to overcome when approaching people about posing. Or at least that has been my experience here already more than once. Actually it even happened with a very old man, who would probably have been very Ribera-like as a nude model. But après tout,[9] I am not looking for a Ribera, still less a Salvator Rosa, I don't see things that way. I am not even enthusiastic about Decamps. I am ill at ease in front of their pictures and cannot visualize them without the feeling that I am missing something and losing sight of something. I'd rather have Goya or Gavarni, although both of them say 'Nada'.[10] As the last word? 'Nada', it seems to me, means precisely the same as Solomon's saying: 'Vanité des vanités, tout est vanité',[11] but that is something on which I cannot lay down my head without having nightmares. So there you are.

However, it's too late to philosophize, seeing that I must be up at half-past five tomorrow morning, because the carpenter is coming round to do a job for me before he goes off to work. So good-night & believe me, I mean it very seriously when I talk about your becoming a painter. Goodbye,

Ever yours,
Vincent

I've done two more small drawings for C. M., a bit of the Scheveningen road and workers in the sand dunes.

Now that I've paid the money back to Tersteeg, I'm afraid that when the landlord comes round at the end of March I shan't have much left for him. So if you can, I do hope you will send me what you can towards the end of March.

9 After all.
10 Nothing.
11 Vanity of vanities, all is vanity.

Theo, on Sunday I went round to De Bock's again – I don't know why, but every time I go and see him I get the same feeling: the fellow's too weak, he'll never make good – unless he changes, unless – unless – I see something weary, something blasé, something insincere in him that oppresses me, there is something consumptive about the atmosphere in his house.

And yet – it doesn't hit you in the eye – and there are probably few among his acquaintance who think of him as I do.

Well, anyway, he does do things that are nice sometimes, or at least not without charm and grace, but, ça suffit-il?[12] So much is demanded nowadays that painting seems like a campaign, a military campaign, a battle or a war.

Van Gogh continued to harp on the theme of Theo's artistic calling, especially in the letters he wrote from Drenthe.

Quite soon after the Kee Vos affair he threw himself into another emotional adventure. The social implications of his befriending the pregnant prostitute Sien Hoornik and her child once again put his good relationship with his brother and his parents at risk. Moreover, the affair led to an abrupt break with Mauve and Tersteeg. It is fascinating to follow the way in which Van Gogh pulled out every emotional stop in his attempts to convince Theo of the rightness of his course of action.

12 Is that enough?

192 [D]

[3–12 May 1882]

Please feel free to tell
Mauve anything you like
about the contents of this
letter, but there's no need for
it to go any further.

My dear Theo,

I met Mauve today and had a most regrettable conversation with
him, which made it clear to me that Mauve and I have parted for
good. Mauve has gone too far to retract, and anyhow he certainly
wouldn't want to.

I invited him to come and see my work, and then to talk
things over. Mauve flatly refused: 'I will certainly not be coming
to see you, that's all over.'

In the end he said, 'You have a vicious character.' I turned
away then – it was in the dunes – and walked home alone.

Mauve takes it amiss that I said, 'I am an artist,' which I won't
take back, because it's self-evident that what that word implies is
looking for something all the time without ever finding it in full.
It is the very opposite of saying, 'I know all about it, I've already
found it.' As far as I am concerned, the word means, 'I am
looking, I am hunting for it, I am deeply involved.'

I have ears, Theo – if somebody says, 'You have a vicious
character,' what am I supposed to do? I turned away and went
home alone, but with a very heavy heart that Mauve should
have been prepared to say that to me. I shall not ask him for an
explanation, nor shall I apologize.

And yet – and yet – and yet. I wish Mauve did feel some
compunction. I am suspected of something . . . it is in the air . . . I
am keeping something back, Vincent is concealing something
that mustn't see the light of day.

Well, gentlemen, I shall say to you, you people who prize

manners and culture, and rightly so, provided it is the genuine article – which is more cultured, more sensitive, more manly: to desert a woman or to concern oneself with one who has been deserted?

Last winter I met a pregnant woman, deserted by the man whose child she was carrying. A pregnant woman who walked the streets in the winter – she had her bread to earn, you'll know how. I took that woman on as a model and have worked with her all winter. I couldn't pay her a model's full daily wages, but I paid her rent all the same, and thus far, thank God, I have been able to save her and her child from hunger and cold by sharing my own bread with her.

When I first came across this woman, she caught my eye because she looked ill. I made her take baths and as many restoratives as I could manage, and she has become much healthier. I have been with her to Leiden, where there is a maternity hospital in which she will be confined.*

It strikes me that any man worth his salt would have done the same in a case like this. I consider what I did so simple and natural that I thought I could keep it to myself. She found posing difficult, yet she has learned, and I have made progress with my drawing because I have had a good model. The woman is now attached to me like a tame dove. For my part, I can only get married once, and when better than now, and to her, because it is the only way to go on helping her and she would otherwise be sent back by want on to the same old path which leads to the abyss. She has no money, but she is helping me to earn money with my work.

I am filled with zest and ambition for my job and my work, and the reason why I have put aside paintings and watercolours for a time is that Mauve's desertion gave me a great shock, and if he sincerely retracted I should start again with renewed courage.

---

* Small wonder she wasn't well, the child was in the wrong position and she needed an operation, that is, the child had to be turned round with forceps. But there is a good chance that she will pull through. <u>She is due to give birth in June.</u>

At the moment I cannot look at a brush, it makes me nervous.

I wrote: Theo, can you enlighten me about Mauve's attitude? – perhaps this letter will help to enlighten you in turn. You are my brother, it is only natural that I should speak to you about private matters, but the moment someone tells me, 'You have a vicious character,' I don't feel like talking to him any more.

I could not do otherwise, I did what was ready to hand, I worked. I thought I would be understood without words. To be sure I thought of another woman for whom my heart was beating – but she was far away and did not want to see me, and this one – there she was, walking about sick, pregnant and hungry – in winter. I could not do otherwise. Mauve, Theo, Tersteeg, you people have my livelihood in your hands, are you going to reduce me to beggary, turn your backs on me? Now I have spoken and wait for whatever else will be said to me.

Vincent

I am sending you a few studies because you may perhaps see from them that she has helped me considerably with her posing. My drawings are 'by my model & me', the one with the white bonnet is her mother. But since in a year's time, when I shall probably be working quite differently, I shall have to base my work on these studies, which I am doing now as conscientiously as I can, I should like to have at least these three back.

You can see that they are done with care. If I need an interior or a waiting room or something of the kind later on, they will prove useful, because I shall be able to look to them for the details. But I thought it would perhaps be a good idea to keep you up to date on how I spend my time. These studies demand a rather dry technique. Had I tried for effect they would have been less useful to me later. But I'm sure you will see this for yourself.

The paper I should really like best is that on which the female figure bending forward is drawn, but if possible the colour of unbleached linen. I don't have any of it left in that thickness. I believe they call it double Ingres. I can't get any more of it here. When you see how that drawing is done, you'll understand that the thin stuff is hardly able to take it. I wanted to send you a small figure in black merino as well, but I can't roll it. The chair near the large figure isn't finished, because I want an old oak chair there.

198 [D]

[14 May 1882]

My dear Theo,

Having received your letter of 13 May, which must have crossed a letter of mine to you, I find it necessary to explain a few things to you without delay.

A great deal of what I read in your letter I certainly appreciate very much, for instance, 'One must be narrow-minded or hypocritical to set one class without question above another.'

The world, however, does not reason like that & never sees or respects man's 'humanity' but only the greater or lesser value of the money or goods he carries with him so long as he is on this side of the grave. The world takes no account at all of what happens beyond the grave. That is why the world goes no further than its feet will take it.

For my part, however, I feel sympathy or antipathy for men just as men, and their circumstances leave me relatively indifferent.

Yet even I take some note (and were my own circumstances to _allow_ me, I should make even further concessions) when you say, 'There are many who maintain a certain social standing in order to avoid attention from others & lest people meddle too much in their affairs.' Very often, indeed, I let things pass, thinking, I'm not going to do or say this or that in case I give offence to somebody or other.

But when it comes to important, serious matters one must act, not in accordance with l'opinion publique, nor according to one's own passions, but following the A.B.C. which is the basis of all morality: 'Love thy neighbour as thyself.' Act in a way you can justify before God. Do the right thing and act loyally.

Now, when it comes to Christien, this is my reasoning: how should I like it if someone first helped me and then left me in the lurch? Wouldn't I think ... someone who behaves like that would have done better to have left me alone. If he doesn't finish what he started – he really has deceived me.

The father of X^{tien}'s[1] child argued in the exact spirit of your letter, Theo, but in my opinion quite wrongly. He was very kind to her, but did <u>not</u> marry her, even when he had made her pregnant, for the sake, he said, of his position and his family, &c. X^{tien} was young at the time & had met him after her father's death, didn't know then what she knows now, and when the man died there she was alone with her child – forsaken, without a penny. A contrecoeur[2] went on the streets, became ill, was taken to hospital, in all sorts of trouble ...

That man's behaviour made him guilty before God, although in the eyes of the world he had kept up his position, 'had paid her off'. But at the moment when he faced death, do you imagine he felt no regret & remorse???

Now, in this world, the characters of people like him come up against characters like, say, mine. I care as little for the world as the aforesaid person cared for what is right. The semblance of doing right was enough for him. As for me, I wouldn't give you tuppence for the world's opinion. What comes first and foremost with me is this: <u>I will not deceive or forsake a woman</u>. If a woman refuses to have anything to do with me, like Kee Vos, I don't try to force her, no matter how strong my passion. I turn away with desolation in my heart the moment my own 'she and no other' is met by her 'certainly not him'.

<u>I will not force & I will not forsake</u>. And I, too, protest when I myself am forced or forsaken.

If I were married to a woman and I realized that that woman was carrying on with another, I wouldn't stand for any nonsense, but even then I wouldn't forsake her before I had tried everything

1 Christien's.
2 Reluctantly.

possible to bring her back. So you see what I think of marriage and that I take it seriously.

Now as you know, when I met X^{tien} she was pregnant, ill, left out in the cold. I was alone, and had just had the experience in Amsterdam I wrote to you about. I started it – though not immediately with marriage in mind. However, when I got to know her better, it became obvious to me that if I wanted to help her I must set about it more seriously.

Then I spoke to her frankly and said, I think about this and that, in such and such a way, I see your position and mine in such and such a way. I am poor – but I am no seducer. Will you be able to put up with me? Otherwise there isn't any point in going on.

At which she said, I want to be with you, no matter how poor you are.

And that is how it all came about. And before very long now she will be going to Leiden and I should like to marry her without any fuss straight after that. Because otherwise there will be something false about her position and mine, which I most decidedly wish to avoid.

I shall be like a workman with a trade in which she is my assistant. My drawings are in your hands and for the first year at least my bread and hers will depend on you and on all those who are willing to help me, because you can see that I am doing my best and that I have the gift of drawing, and I believe of painting as well, which little by little will become more evident.

Now, Theo, I do not think I am disgracing my family by what I have done – and I wish my family would come to terms with it. Otherwise we will remain in opposite camps and I will have to declare: I will not forsake a woman to whom I am attached by a bond of mutual aid and respect in order to oblige anybody. I have come to terms with her past and she has come to terms with my past. If my family disowned me for seducing a woman and I had actually done it, then I should feel like a blackguard, but if I were to be opposed because I remained loyal to a woman to whom I had pledged my troth, I should despise my family.

Not everyone is suited to be a <u>painter's</u> wife – <u>she is willing,</u>

she learns something every day. I understand peculiarities in her character that have repelled others. But H. G. T. would probably think of her what he thinks of me, and say, 'She has a disagreeable nature and there is something unattractive about her,' and there the matter would rest.

But it goes without saying that I have enough knowledge of the world & of human nature to ask for nothing more than that people should not oppose my marriage – and I hope that I will not be wanting for my daily bread as long as I can show that I am doing my best and straining every nerve to become a good painter, or perhaps merely a draughtsman. I shall not be visiting my family or anything of the sort, however, either by myself or with her, but shall remain in the walk of life to which my work has allotted me. And then nobody can take offence, unless 'men of iniquity should deliberately try to find a stumbling block', which I trust will not be the case.

However, you will find me most obliging in everything I am able to do without being disloyal to Christien. I should very much like to have your advice on, for instance, where I should live, and the like. If there is some objection to my remaining in The Hague, then I owe The Hague no loyalty. And I can find somewhere to work wherever you think fit, be it a village or a town. The figures & the landscape that come my way will no doubt always be interesting enough for me to do my best, so you are welcome to speak your mind freely on the subject. But it goes without saying that there must be no question of putting me under guardianship, I made my feelings concerning that perfectly clear during the Gheel affair: that sort of thing would be quite hors de saison.[3]

But as far as being loyal or disloyal to Christien is concerned, my feeling is: 'I must not break a promise of marriage.'

Had Kee Vos been willing to listen to me last summer in Amsterdam, she might not have been so quick to send me packing and then things would have been quite different. At the time, however, as you know, although I followed her all the way,

3 Inopportune.

although I pursued her as far as Amsterdam, all my attempts to speak to her or to establish anything with any certainty – anything I could rely on, that is – proved futile.

Now the very pace of life is driving and urging me on, as well as the work, and the new things that crop up and which I must tackle with a will if I want to hold my own in the bitter struggle. Taking things lying down is what I did in years gone by, taking action and being alert is what I do now, having found my work and my vocation.

So I consider your letter in the main quite mistaken, but perhaps that is because you haven't thought things through, and I credit you with being better than that particular letter this morning suggests.

You mention something that happened to you. I think I am able to recall something about it very faintly in the dim and distant past. If I remember rightly, you were acquainted with a girl from a lower class and ... were fond of her and sl... with her. Now I don't know who the person was, but I do know that you consulted Father about it and also spoke to me about it. And that Father then made you promise something about getting married, I don't know exactly what – but perhaps it was that while you remained a minor you would not do it without his consent. (The rest – what happened to the woman – I don't know.) Since you were a minor, Father had every right to step between the two of you and I can understand why he did it.

Now, the difference between your case & mine is that in the first place you and she were considerably younger than X^{tien} and I, and secondly, your future and mine are different, that is, I for my part ply a humble trade and you hold a position which of necessity requires you to keep up a certain style.

This is all clear enough, it seems to me, and also that being a minor you were right to obey, while I for my part, being of age, am at liberty to say to Father: this is a matter in which you cannot and must not press me.

Now, you say that what has happened between X^n and me does not mean I have to marry her. This is what X^n and I think about it: we both want a very domesticated life, close together, need each other every day for our work and like to be together every day. We want there to be nothing false in our position and consider marriage the only radical means of stopping the world talking and of seeing to it that we are not ... reproached with an illicit relationship. If we do not get married, they could indeed say that something or other is wrong – if we do get married we shall be very poor and give up any social pretences, but our action will be right and honourable. You will understand this, I think.

But if you should now say, 'Vincent, you're going to have a dreadful time and terrible worries,' then what I shall reply is, yes, brother, I'm well aware of that, you are right, but, my dear fellow, what I would find even worse would be the feeling deep down inside of: 'You have treacherously abandoned that woman whom you met in the winter, pregnant and sick, and have thrown her back on to the cruel cobblestones once more.' That is not going to be said about me, and you will realize by now that it isn't 'obstinacy' on my part or 'wantonly having it my own way', but that I must stand by X^{tien}, that I have pledged her my troth & that I shall keep my pledge.

Once again, if my staying in The Hague should bother anyone, please say so frankly, I am only too happy to yield on all matters concerning a home or the like. I need a studio, a living room and a bedroom, and though I am not indifferent as to whether that will be in The Hague or elsewhere, I shall be happy to show willing. However it must all be discussed quite differently from, for example, the way Father did on the Gheel occasion. That was scandalous.

Should it be possible for me to have, say, 150 frs. a month this year (although my work still isn't saleable yet, it is the foundation on which I shall be able to build later on) – then I shall get down to business with a will and in good heart, because I shall at least know then that I shan't be lacking the barest necessities I require for my work – my daily bread, a home, drawing materials – I shall be able to work then.

Were I to be told for certain that you are withdrawing your support, I should be rendered powerless. With the best will in the world my hand would become paralysed – everything would indeed be dreadful then, yes, everything would be terrible. What satisfaction would that give you or anyone else? I should become downhearted and it would go hard with Christien & the child. You may think it's going too far to suppose you capable of doing anything like that, but 'such things can happen'. If this dreadful fate has to befall me – so be it. Though it hangs over my head, I can say nothing other than: I have pledged X^n my troth and she has pledged me hers, and we do not have it in us to break this pledge.

And yet – confound it – what's happening? – and what sort of times do we live in? – wake up, Theo! Don't let them confuse you or sway you with their Jesuitisms. Do I deserve being left in the lurch by you because I have helped a pregnant woman and will not send her back on to the streets? Is that a capital offence???

Goodbye, my dear fellow, but before you strike at me and chop off my head, and X^{tien}'s and the child's as well – sleep on it once more. But again, if it has to be, then in God's name 'off with my head', though preferably not, I still need it for drawing.

Ever yours,
Vincent

P.S. X^n and the child won't be able to pose headless either.

In another letter to Theo, Vincent came to this conclusion: 'Familiar as I am with the prejudices of the world, I know that what I have to do is withdraw from the company of my own class, which cast me out a long time ago as it is.'

Although the child with which Sien was pregnant was not his, he intended to marry her quietly after its birth and to take her into his home: 'I would rather have a crust of bread by my own hearth, however poor, than live without marrying her. [...] we shall risk it despite poverty. Fishermen know that the sea is perilous and the storm fearful, but have never thought the perils reason enough for deciding to take a stroll along the beach instead. They leave that sort of prudence to those who relish it. The storm may come and the night may fall, but which is worse, the danger or the fear of danger? I would sooner have the reality, the danger itself.'

When all was said and done, Van Gogh was afraid of only one thing, namely that even Theo might withdraw his support: '[...] a death sentence from you, to wit, the withholding of your help'. Nevertheless, he was still prepared to forfeit his brother's sympathy by bringing up the embarrassing Kee Vos affair again. Here, according to him, lay the true key to his present situation: 'Then, not all at once, but soon enough, I felt that love die, a void, an infinite void taking its place.'

'I want to taste the joys and sorrows of domestic life in order to be able to portray it from my own experience. When I left Amsterdam I felt that my love, so genuine and strong, had literally been killed stone-dead, but after death one rises from the dead. Resurgam [I shall rise again].' He realized that his proposed marriage to a prostitute down on her luck like Sien, his 'lowering himself', would estrange him even further from his family: 'I keep house like a working man. I am more at ease with it, I wanted to before, but couldn't manage it then [...] I hope you will go on holding your hand out to me across the gulf.'

The Hague, Drenthe and Nuenen

Van Gogh's relationship with his parents deteriorated noticeably and he again began to fear that his father meant to place him under legal guardianship, much as he had previously threatened to have Vincent committed to the mental institution in Gheel. Embittered by his father's mistrust, he wrote, 'Father is capable of doing it, but I must tell you that if he dares to try anything of the sort, I shall resist him for all I'm worth.'

When writing to Theo about Sien, Van Gogh described her as 'an ordinary woman of the people who has something of the sublime for me'. Her profile reminded him of Landelle's *L'ange de la passion*, which he knew from a Goupil print. However, 'She is slightly pockmarked and hence no longer beautiful, but the lines of her figure are simple and not ungraceful.' Her speech might be ugly, but 'she has a good heart'. Sien joined him on his sketching expeditions across the dunes, and on such occasions they felt 'like real Bohemians'. He also thought that her willingness to share his life to the full might have a favourable effect on his painting: 'Because Sien has taken to all the toil and moil of the painter's life and is so willing to pose, I think I shall become a better artist with her than if I had ended up with Kee Vos.' He asked but one thing of his family: 'To leave me to love and care for my poor, weak, overworked little wife as well as my poverty allows, without taking any steps to separate, hinder or distress us'.

204 [D]

[1 or 2 June 1882]

My dear Theo,

Your letter & its enclosure came and I paid the landlord straight away. Since there is a mortgage on the house the rent is collected by somebody else who turned the people downstairs out last month and gave them short shrift. What you say about dividing the month into 3, so that I would get the money on the 1st, 10th and 20th, is extremely welcome news. That will make things much easier for me.

I need not tell you what a relief your letter was.

Did you receive the Dab Drying Shed drawing? I am busy doing a few more of them, so you'll have 2 or 3 done in the same way. C. M. has also got some done like this but I haven't heard from him yet.

I want to tell you something about what you seem to be afraid of, namely the possibility that the family may want to take steps to place me under legal guardianship. If you really think 'a few witnesses (and even then false ones) are all that would be needed to testify that you cannot manage your financial affairs and that would be enough to entitle Father to deprive you of your civil rights and place you under guardianship', if, I say, you really think that this sort of thing is so easy to do these days, then I take the liberty of questioning it.

The legal procedure of guardianship, which has been disgracefully abused so often in order to get rid of individuals considered 'troublesome' or 'unpleasant' (mauvais coucheur[1]), can no longer be applied quite so easily these days. And the law gives the accused the right of appeal and many another remedy.

But you might say: a clever lawyer can twist the law, &c., &c. Que soit,[2] I tell you that it isn't quite so quick & easy to place

1 Awkward customer.
2 Be that as it may.

somebody under guardianship nowadays ... I know of a case in which <u>even the Jesuits</u> failed to have a guardianship order placed on someone they wanted out of the way, for the simple reason that the man said, 'I am positively the last person for whom a guardianship order is even slightly appropriate,' and refused to give in.

Again, there was the case of someone who, placed under supervision somewhere against his will so that he couldn't go where he chose, warned the person under whose supervision he had been placed that he had no right to deprive him of his liberty and that he would have to let him go ... warned him a few times coolly and quite calmly, but was rebuffed. Then bashed his guardian's brains in with a poker and stood there quite calmly and gave himself up. The case was investigated and the result was a complete acquittal, since in certain extreme cases there exists a 'right of self-defence', and when the murder question came up the original case was re-examined and it turned out that the accused was not someone who merited guardianship.

In short, it is far from easy nowadays to place under guardianship someone who protests in a calm, manly and open manner. I really do not believe that the family would do anything like that ... but, you may say, they already tried to do it on the Gheel occasion. Alas, yes, Father is capable of doing it, but I must tell you that if he dares to try anything of the sort again, I shall resist him for all I'm worth. He had best think twice before he starts attacking me, but once again, I doubt they would dare do such a thing. If they do have the will & the temerity, I am not going to say, 'Oh, please don't do that,' but on the contrary will have no hesitation in letting them get on with it so that they incur public disgrace & are saddled with the costs of the case.

Let me tell you, I know of a case where a noble and very rich family tried to place somebody under guardianship and enlisted the services of lawyers and Jesuits – and yet failed with the person in question – although there were <u>two</u> complaints raised against him, in the first place his incompetence in financial affairs & in the second place his being of unsound mind. He protested and the judge let the family know unofficially that they would do well to drop the case. The family had to give up even before the legal proceedings actually started.

Now I would just like to add this – since you are aware that I would always protest against anything of the kind, if at some time or other they should try to take advantage of my being ill or indisposed, by, for instance, 'taking action against me', you will know that it is without my consent. In the event of my being ill, I hope you would object if anyone tried to profit from my helplessness. When my health is good I can take care of myself and am afraid of nothing of that sort. And I simply cannot imagine anyone really taking such a step – but should you ever hear that such moves are afoot, please let me know.

I don't mean if they are <u>talking</u> about it or <u>saying</u> something about it, of course, I take no notice of tittle-tattle, but I do take notice when it is translated into action. If they should <u>do</u> something, then I hope you will warn me. I know the law on guardianship, and <u>I do not believe they can do anything to me.</u>

Once before in my life, though many years ago, I received a letter written in the same vein as your last one. And that was from H. G. T., whom I had consulted about something, and I have regretted ever since that I broached the matter with him. I well remember that I was seized by a kind of panic at the time and that I was frightened of my family. Now, some 10 or 12 years later, I have learned to think differently of my obligations towards & relations with my family.

Father keeps going on about the 'respect & obedience' I am supposed to owe him. I shall not claim that a child does not owe his parents respect & obedience, all I want is to point out that Father has taken undue advantage of it more than once, for instance by immediately labelling as disrespectful any difference of opinion one may have with him. It would be a pretty kettle of fish if I ordered my life the way Father would like me to. My drawing would most certainly come to an end, for I should be unable to do any more. I might be able to come to terms with Father's way of thinking & talk things over with him if he acquired some understanding of art, but that will never happen.

Clergymen often introduce 'things of beauty' into a sermon, but it's dismal stuff & dreadfully stodgy.

Now I am glad that you have given me your frank opinion of Sien, namely that she tricked me and that I allowed myself to be taken in. And I can understand why you should think that, because such things do happen. However, I remember once when a girl did try something like, I shut the door in her face so hard that I rather doubt I am likely to be taken in by such sharp practices.

The way matters stand with Sien is that I am genuinely attached to her & she to me – that she is my loyal helpmate, who goes everywhere with me – and who is becoming more indispensable to me by the day. I feel less passion for her than I did for Kee Vos last year. But the kind of love I have for Sien is the only one I am still capable of after the disappointment of that first passion. She & I are two unhappy people who keep each other company and share a burden, and that is precisely why unhappiness is making way for happiness, and the unbearable is becoming bearable.

Her mother is a little old woman just like the ones Frère paints.

Now you will understand that, given that I remain faithful to her, I should set little store by the formality of marriage were it not that the family does. Father, for one, and I know this for certain, attaches great importance to it, and although he won't approve of my marrying her, he would consider it even worse if I lived with her without marrying. His advice would be to leave her, and he would give that advice in this form: <u>wait</u>, which is cold comfort and quite inappropriate. That is typical of Father ... he puts things off that are urgent and pressing, and this can be absolutely infuriating. So Father had best keep his 'waiting' to himself, for if he came out with it, I should not be able to contain myself.

I am a man of 30 with wrinkles on my forehead & lines on my face that make me look 40 and my hands are full of furrows – yet when Father looks at me through his spectacles he sees me as a little boy (1½ years ago Father wrote to me, 'You are in your first youth'). And that is said with the tuppence-worth of profundity I have heard so often before.

Do you know what I think Father and Uncle Stricker are like? Like 'Les deux augures' by Gérôme. But I am a 'mauvais coucheur' – que soit.

Now you will say, Vincent, you had far better lose yourself in perspective and the Dab Drying Sheds. And then I shall say, you are quite right, brother, and that is why I am getting down to work on the two drawings that go with that first one, and which you will soon be receiving as proof that I like nothing better than losing myself in nature and drawing and not losing myself in such things as being placed under guardianship which seem to me utterly ridiculous. Regards, with my heartfelt thanks for your loyal help,

Ever yours,
Vincent

I kept this letter back because I wanted to send you the small drawings at the same time, but they still need more work. One is finished, though, namely another dab drying shed. Sien and I have been camping in the dunes from morning till night for days on end, like real Bohemians. We took bread along and a small bag of coffee and fetched hot water from a hot-water-&-coals woman in Scheveningen.

That hot-water-and-coals woman and her surroundings are marvellous, charming beyond words, I've called at her little shop as early as 5 o'clock in the morning when the street-sweepers go there for their coffee. My dear fellow, that would really be something to draw!!! Just getting the people I want to pose would cost a pretty penny, but I've a good mind to do it.

Write to me when you get the chance, particularly what you think of these last three drawings. And also if it is really your view that I ought to be more afraid than I am of being placed under guardianship, to my mind an impossible eventuality. Because I should not remain indifferent if steps were actually being taken, that goes without saying. Having to go to Etten would be most inconvenient for me right now, in the first place because

I'm so busy, and 2nd because the trip would cost more than I feel I can afford & I would sooner spend it on Sien.

I think it a delightful prospect that you are coming, I am longing to know what impression Sien will make on you. There is nothing special about her, she is just an ordinary woman of the people who has something of the sublime for me. Whoever loves a plain, ordinary person & has endeared himself to her is happy – despite the dark side of life. Had she not needed help last winter then the bond between her and me would not have been forged in the circumstances, that is after my disappointment and spurned love. As it was, however, it was precisely the feeling of being able to do something useful après tout,[3] despite that disappointment, that brought me to myself again and revived me. Not that I went out looking for it, but I found it, and now there is a warm affection between her and me and it would be quite wrong to give that up.

I might easily have grown disenchanted & sceptical if I had not met Sien – but she and my work now keep me going. And I should like to add this: because Sien has taken to all the toil and moil of the painter's life and is so willing to pose, I think I shall become a better artist with her than if I had ended up with Kee Vos. For though Sien is not as graceful, and her manners are perhaps, or rather certainly, quite different, she is so full of goodwill and dévouement[4] that I am moved by it.

Heyerdahl has seen Sorrow now, but I should be glad if a draughtsman, for instance Henri Pille, could have a look at the last three drawings. I'm sure H. Pille no longer remembers me – though I have been in his company and know that he is someone who can behave very oddly at times – and I don't know whether he would say anything. But all I should want to know is whether the drawings make any impression on him and if they appeal to him. I say this in case you run into Henri Pille from time to time, for it would have to be as if by chance that you let him see them.

3 After all.
4 Devotion.

I must also repeat that I am getting on very well with my collection of woodcuts, which I regard as belonging to you, with me holding a life-interest in them. I now have a good thousand sheets of English (mainly Swains), American and French. And Rappard, for instance, who is also collecting them these days, was greatly taken with them. So that is something which belongs to you though you haven't seen it yet. I only regret that I was unable to buy Doré's London recently, for which the Jew asked 7.50 guilders, which I couldn't afford. And also a Boetzel Album. Anyway, when you come here, you shall have a look at them and, I hope, like them, and perhaps through them become acquainted with some artists of whom you knew little or nothing until now.

Vincent

Van Gogh worked very hard to study and master the laws of perspective. To that end he built a perspective frame, an instrument 'the description of which appears in a book by Albert Dürer and of which the old Dutch masters made use as well. It allows me to compare the proportions of nearby objects with those on a more distant plane, whenever construction by the rules of perspective is not feasible.'

During this period Van Gogh, about whom the myth persists that he sold just one work in his lifetime, received 20 guilders from his uncle C. M. in Prinsenhage for a batch of drawings. He was disappointed, however, that his uncle failed to let him know to what extent he really valued his work.

Early in June Van Gogh was admitted to the municipal hospital in The Hague for treatment of a venereal disease. His colleague George Hendrik Breitner happened to be lying a few wards further along, suffering from a similar complaint. Despite his dreary situation and the painful catheterizations, Van Gogh revelled in Dickens's *Edwin Drood* and Zola's *Une page d'amour*, and he made careful observations of the various 'types' he encountered among nurses and patients as if they were so many potential models. He felt that the hospital was in that respect as good as a third-class waiting room. The doctor had a head like a

Rembrandt and there was 'an old man who would be superb for a St Jerome. A thin, long, sinewy, brown & wrinkled body with joints so marvellously distinct and expressive that it makes one sad not to have him as a model'.

In the meantime, the threat of being placed under legal guardianship continued to haunt Van Gogh until a parcel of clothes from his parents put his mind somewhat at rest, and his father and even Herman Tersteeg came to see him in the hospital. By 1 July, when Van Gogh was discharged, Sien had been admitted to the hospital in Leiden to await her confinement. Van Gogh gave a tender description of the birth of her son, drawing a parallel between the stricken Sien and the burgeoning green of nature.

210 [D]

Sunday afternoon [2 July 1882]

My dear Theo,

As I told you in yesterday's letter, I have been to Leiden. Sien was confined last night, has had a very difficult delivery, but thank God has come out of it alive and with a particularly nice little boy as well.

Her mother and little child and I went there together – you can imagine how very anxious we were, not knowing what we should hear when we asked the orderlies in the hospital about her. And how tremendously glad we were when we heard, 'Confined last night ... but you mustn't talk to her for long ... ' I shall not easily forget that 'you mustn't talk to her for long', for it meant, 'you can still talk to her', when it could easily have been, 'you will never talk to her again'. Theo, I was so happy to see her there, lying close to a window overlooking a garden full of sunshine and greenery, in a sort of drowsy state of exhaustion between sleeping and waking, and then she looked up and saw us all. Ah, my dear fellow, she looked up and was so happy to see us exactly 12 hours after it had happened, as luck would have it, even though there is only 1 hour a week when visits are permitted. And she perked up so, and in a moment she had got her wits about her and asked about everything.

But what I cannot marvel at enough is the child, because although it was delivered by forceps it is not injured in any way and just lay in its cradle with a sort of worldly-wise air. How clever these doctors are! But by all accounts it was a critical case. There were 5 professors standing by when it happened and they put her under with chloroform. Before that, she had suffered a tremendous amount because the child was stuck fast from 9 in the evening until half-past one. And she is still in a lot of pain now. But she forgot everything when she saw us and even managed to convey that we should soon be back drawing again, and I should not mind in the least if her prediction came true. There has been no rupture or anything, which can easily happen in such cases.

Heavens, how grateful I am! Still, the grim shadow goes on threatening, as master Albert Dürer realized only too well when he placed death behind the young couple in that marvellous etching you know. But let us hope that the grim shadow will remain a passing shadow.

Well, Theo, I don't have to tell you that without your help, Sien would probably not be here any longer. One more thing, I had urged Sien to ask the professor to give her a thorough examination, because she often had something they call the whites. And he did that and told her what she must do to get well again. And he says that she had been very close to giving up the ghost more than once, especially when she had had quinsy, during an earlier miscarriage, and again this winter – that she was thoroughly enfeebled by years of worry and agitation, and that now, when she no longer has to lead that sort of life, she will get well by herself if nothing else happens, through rest, through restoratives, by being out in the fresh air a great deal and by not doing any heavy work.

With her earlier misfortune behind her, a completely new period of her life will start, and though she cannot regain her spring, which is past and was but barren, her <u>midsummer growth</u> will be all the greener for it. You will know how in the middle of the summer, when the greatest heat is over, the trees put out fresh young shoots, a new young layer of green over the old, weathered one.

I am writing to you at Sien's mother's, beside a window overlooking a sort of courtyard. I have drawn it twice, once on a large scale and once on a smaller one. C. M. has those two and they were the ones Rappard was pleased with, especially the large one. I should like you to have a look at them if you happen to be at C. M.'s, for I should like to know what you think, especially of the larger one. When are you coming? I look forward to seeing you very much.

Well, brother, you are to blame for my being so happy today that it made me cry. Thanks for everything, my dear fellow, and believe me, with a handshake in my thoughts,

Ever yours,
<u>Vincent</u>

Full of optimism, Van Gogh now prepared himself for his new role of paterfamilias. He moved to 136 Schenkweg, a larger house with a good studio area to which a carpenter had drawn his attention. The simplicity of the accommodation suited him. 'The fact that studio and household merge into each other can be no bad thing as far as the figure is concerned. I clearly remember Ostade's studio interiors, small pen drawings, most likely of corners of his own house, which were enough to show that Ostade's studio probably had little in common with those studios in which Oriental weapons and vases and Persian carpets, &c., may be found.' As for his social position, 'What am I in the eyes of most people – a nonentity or an eccentric or an obnoxious person – someone who has no position in society and never will have, in short the lowest of the low. Well, then – even if that were all absolutely true, I should one day like to show by my work what there is in the heart of such an eccentric, of such a nobody.'

Once again he tried to explain to his brother the difference between the affection he had felt for Kee Vos and his present feelings for Sien. Whereas his passion for Kee had been unrequited, Sien and he had '<u>a</u>

definite need of each other, so that she and I were no longer to be parted, our lives became more and more intertwined, and it was love'. He characterized his new life as 'a new studio, a still young household in full swing. No mystical or mysterious studio, but one rooted in real life. A studio with a cradle and a commode'.

However, an unsolicited visit from Tersteeg 'in policeman-like mood' caused him a great deal of agitation. The art dealer, strongly opposed to Vincent's domestic arrangements, failed to appreciate his new work and seemed about to incite Vincent's family against him. Van Gogh considered responding there and then by marrying Sien, although his financial means were inadequate. But why should that matter, he wrote to Theo: 'There is a promise of marriage between her & me and I would not want you to think that I look upon her as a kept woman or as someone with whom I am having some kind of liaison with no thought to the consequences.' Compassion for Sien set the tone of the extensive correspondence that followed. In one of his letters, he drew Theo's attention to his drawing, given the English title *Sorrow*, of a crouching nude inspired by Albrecht Dürer's *Melancholy*, for which Sien had sat as his model.

Gradually Van Gogh recovered sufficiently to go back to drawing and to painting watercolours and, as he did, art again began to play a dominant role in his letters. The new and larger studio inspired him, not least by the quality of the light.

213 [D]

Thursday
[6 July 1882]

My dear Theo,

It is now the evening before I go back to hospital again, and I don't know what they are going to tell me there – perhaps I'll only be in for a short while, perhaps they'll bring out their probes again and I'll have to keep to my bed for days.

That's why I am writing once again from home. It is so quiet and peaceful here in the studio right now – it is already late –

but it is stormy and rainy outside – and that makes the calm inside even greater.

How I wish I had you here with me during this quiet hour, brother – how much I should have to show you. The studio looks so much like the real thing, or so it seems to me, plain grey-brown wallpaper, scrubbed floorboards, muslin stretched on slats across the windows, everything bright. And, of course, the studies on the wall, an easel on either side and a large unpainted wooden work-table. The studio gives on to a sort of alcove, where the drawing boards, portfolios, boxes, sticks, &c. are kept, as well as all the prints. And in the corner a cupboard with all the pots and bottles and on top of that all my books.

Then the little living room with a table, a few kitchen chairs, an oil stove, a large wicker armchair for the woman in the corner by the window overlooking the yard and the meadows that you know from the drawing, and next to it a small iron cradle with a green cover.

This last piece of furniture is something I cannot look at without emotion – because a man is gripped by a strong and powerful emotion when he sits down next to the woman he loves with a baby in the cradle beside them. And although it was in a hospital that she lay and I sat next to her – it is always that eternal poetry of Christmas night with the infant in the stable, as the old Dutch painters conceived it and Millet and Breton – a light in the darkness, a brightness in the middle of a dark night. And so I hung the large etching after Rembrandt over it, the two women by the cradle, one of them reading from the Bible by candlelight, while the great shadows cast a deep chiaroscuro over the whole room.

I've hung a few other prints there, all of them very beautiful, the Christus Consolator by Scheffer, a phot. after Boughton, Le semeur and Les bêcheurs by Millet, Le buisson by Ruysdael, splendid large wood engravings by Herkomer & Frank Holl, and Le banc des pauvres by De Groux.

Now then, in the small kitchen I have only the barest necessities, but such that if the woman recovers before me she will find all the essentials and be able to get a meal ready in 10 minutes, in short, such as will show her, when she steps into a house which has flowers in the window where she will be sitting, that someone has been giving her a great deal of thought. And upstairs in the large attic, a big bedstead for the two of us and my old one for the child, with all the bedding in good order.

But please don't think I bought all this in one fell swoop. We had already started buying a few bits and pieces here and there during the winter, although at the time I didn't know how things would turn out and where we would finish up. And the result is now, thank God, that this little nest is ready for her after all her pain.

How her mother and I have been exerting ourselves these last few days, especially her. And the most difficult thing was the bedding, everything made or altered by ourselves – we bought straw, sea-grass, coarse linen, &c., and stuffed the mattresses ourselves in the attic. Otherwise it would have been too expensive.

And now, after having paid my old landlord, I still have 40 guilders left out of what you sent me. True, I have to pay 10 guilders of that tomorrow to the hospital, but for that I'll get food and medical treatment there for 14 days. So that this month, although it includes the full cost of moving and settling in and Sien's return after her confinement with all that entails, the cradle, &c., I shall be able to manage without your sending me more than the usual.

On est sûr de périr à part, on ne se sauve qu'ensemble[1] – I believe this saying to be the truth and I base my life on it, might that be a mistake or a miscalculation?

You see, brother, I think of you a very great deal these days, in the first place because everything, all that I have, is really yours, my lust for life and my energy, too, for I am able to get going now with your help and can feel my capacity to work flowing back.

But I think of you so often for another reason, too. I remember that only a short while ago I came back to a house that was not a

1 United we stand, divided we fall.

real home – not full of warmth as it is now – where two great voids stared at me day and night. There was no woman, there was no child, and though I do not believe there was any the less grief, I do believe there was less love. And those two voids kept me company to right and left, in the street, at work, everywhere and always. There was no woman, there was no child.

Look, I don't know if you've ever had that feeling which sometimes forces a sort of sigh or groan from one when one is alone: oh God, where is my wife, oh God, where is my child – is being alone really living? Thinking of you, I'm sure I'm not mistaken in supposing that some of this same melancholy is in you, too, perhaps less passionately and nerve-rackingly than in me, but nevertheless to some extent and at certain moments. And I don't know whether you will approve of it or not, whether you will judge it right or wrong of me, when I tell you that now and then that is how I think of you.

This much, however, I believe about you, and this much I know about myself, notwithstanding my nervousness, that in both our characters there is a foundation of serenity – serenity quand bien même,[2] so that neither of us is unhappy, our serenity being based on the fact that we truly and sincerely love our trade and our work, and that art occupies a large part of our thoughts and makes life interesting. So I most certainly do not want to make you melancholy, but only to explain my conduct and philosophy of life by dint of something in your own temperament.

That brings me to Father – do you think Father would go on being cold and finding fault – beside a cradle? You see, a cradle is not like anything else – there is no trickery about it. And no matter what Sien's past may have been, I know no other Sien than the one from last winter, than that mother in the hospital whose hand pressed mine as we looked with tears in our eyes at the baby for whom we had been toiling all winter.

And look here – entre nous, soit dit[3] – without sermonizing –

2 Despite everything.
3 Just between us.

if there is no God, there is nevertheless one very close by somewhere, and one feels His presence at moments like this. Which is tantamount to saying something for which I would happily substitute the straightforward statement: I believe in a God, and that it is His will that man does not live alone but with a wife and a child, if everything is to be normal.

And it is my hope that you will understand the way I have behaved and take it for what it is, namely natural, and that you will not think of it as tricking myself or being tricked. And, my dear fellow, when you do come – and if you can, come soon to have a look – then please take Sien, just as I do, for a mother and an ordinary housewife and for nothing else. For that is what she really is and in my opinion all the better for having known le revers de la medaille.[4]

The last thing I did was to get a few plates, forks, spoons and knives – for neither Sien nor I had any until now. I thought, 3 people, so 3 sets, but then I had another thought – an extra set for Theo or for Father when they come and have a look. So your little spot by the window and your place at our table are ready and waiting for you ... So, I only want to say – you are definitely coming, aren't you? ... and Father as well?

I thought it sensible and tactful of you not to have spoken about it to Father and Mother as yet – now the confinement is over and the flowers are out again – and it was better for Father and Mother not to be mixed up in it before now. I mean, I thought it best to keep the thorns to myself and to let Father and Mother see nothing but the rose. Thus when the woman is back and I am better, I should like to talk about it in the way I told you, so should they ask you anything now, you could well drop a hint. Goodbye, good-night,

Ever yours,
Vincent

4 The other side of the coin.

218 [D]

[21 July 1882]

Dear brother,

It is already late, but I felt like writing to you again anyway. You are not here – but I need you & sometimes feel we are not far away from each other.

Today I promised myself something, that is, to treat my indisposition, or rather what remains of it, as if it didn't exist. Enough time has been lost, work must go on. So, well or not well, I am going back to drawing regularly from morning till night. I don't want anybody to be able to say to me again, 'Oh, but those are only old drawings.'

I drew a study today of the child's little cradle with some touches of colour in it. I am also at work on one like those meadows I sent you recently.

My hands have become a little too white for my liking, but that's too bad. I'm going to go back outdoors again, a possible relapse matters less to me than staying away from work any longer.

Art is jealous, she doesn't like taking second place to an indisposition. Hence I shall humour her. So you will, I hope, be receiving a few more reasonably acceptable things shortly.

People like me really <u>should</u> not be ill. I would like to make it perfectly clear to you how I look at art. To get to the essence of things one has to work long & hard.

What I want & have as my aim is infernally difficult to achieve, and yet I don't think I am raising my sights too high. I want to do drawings that will <u>touch</u> some people.

Sorrow is a small beginning – perhaps such little landscapes as the Meerdervoort Avenue, the Rijswijk Meadows, and the Dab Drying Shed are also a small beginning. There is at least something straight from my own heart in them. What I want to express, in both figure and landscape, isn't anything sentimental or melancholy, but deep anguish. In short, I want to get to the point where people say of my work: that man feels deeply, that man feels keenly. In spite of my so-called coarseness – do you understand? – perhaps for that very reason. It seems pretentious to talk like that now, but that is the reason why I want to put all my energies into it.

What am I in the eyes of most people – a nonentity, an eccentric, or an unpleasant person – somebody who has no position in society and never will have, in short, the lowest of the low.

All right, then – even if that were absolutely true, then I should one day like to show by my work what such an eccentric, such a nobody, has in his heart.

That is my ambition, based less on resentment than on love malgré tout,[1] based more on a feeling of serenity than on passion.

Though I am often in the depths of misery, there is still calmness, pure harmony and music inside me. I see paintings or drawings in the poorest cottages, in the dirtiest corners. And my mind is driven towards these things with an irresistible momentum.

Other things increasingly lose their hold on me, and the more they do so the more quickly my eye lights on the picturesque. Art demands dogged work, work in spite of everything and continuous observation. By dogged, I mean in the first place incessant labour, but also not abandoning one's views upon the say-so of this person or that.

I am not without hope, brother, that in a few years' time, or perhaps even now, little by little you will be seeing things I have done that will give you some satisfaction after all your sacrifices.

I have had singularly little discourse with painters lately. I haven't been the worse for it. It isn't the language of painters so much as the language of nature that one should heed. I can understand better now than I could a good six months ago why Mauve said: don't talk to me about Dupré, I'd rather you talked

1 In spite of everything.

about the bank of that ditch, or something of the sort. That may sound a bit strong, and yet it is absolutely right. The feeling for things themselves, for reality, is of greater importance than the feeling for painting; anyway it is more productive and more inspiring.

Because I now have such a broad, such an expansive feeling for art and for life itself, of which art is the essence, it sounds so shrill and false when people like Tersteeg do nothing but harry one.

For my own part, I find that many modern pictures have a peculiar charm which the old ones lack. To me, one of the highest and noblest expressions of art will always be that of the English, for instance Millais and Herkomer and Frank Holl. What I would say with respect to the difference between old & present-day art is – perhaps the modern artists are deeper thinkers.

There is a great difference in sentiment between, for instance, Chill October by Millais and Bleaching Ground at Overveen by Ruysdael. And equally between Irish Emigrants by Holl and the women reading from the Bible by Rembrandt. Rembrandt & Ruysdael are sublime, for us as well as for their contemporaries, but there is something in the moderns that seems to us more personal and intimate.

It is the same with Swain's woodcuts & those of the old German masters.

And so it was a mistake when the modern painters thought it all the rage to imitate the old ones a few years ago. That's why I think old Millet is so right to say, 'Il me semble absurde que les hommes veuillent paraître autre chose que ce qu'ils sont.'[2] That may sound trite, and yet it is as unfathomably deep as the ocean, and personally I am all for taking it to heart.

I just wanted to tell you that I am going to get back to working regularly again, and must do so quand même[3] – and I'd

2 It seems absurd to me that people want to seem other than they are.
3 At that.

[218]: enclosed sketch.

just like to add that I look forward so much to a letter – and for the rest, I bid you good-night. Goodbye, with a handshake,

Ever yours,
Vincent

Please remember the <u>thick</u> Ingres if you can, enclosed is another sample. I still have a supply of the thin kind. I can do watercolour washes on the <u>thick Ingres</u>, but on the sans fin,⁴ for instance, it always goes blurry, which isn't entirely my fault.

I hope that by <u>keeping hard at it</u> I shall draw the little cradle another hundred times, besides what I did today.

219 [D] [part]

Sunday morning
[23 July 1882]

My dear Theo,

[...]

I can't tell you how wonderful I find all the space in the studio – now that I have set to work, the effect is immediately apparent. We'll teach them to say of my drawings '<u>they're only the old ones</u>'. After all, I didn't get ill for the fun of it.

So you must picture me sitting at my attic window as early as 4 o'clock in the morning, studying the meadows & the carpenter's yard with my perspective frame just as they're lighting the fires to make coffee in the yard and the first worker comes strolling in. A flock of white pigeons comes soaring over the red tile roofs between the smoking black chimney stacks. Beyond it all lies an infinity of delicate, soft green, miles & miles of flat meadow, and a grey sky, as calm, as peaceful as Corot or Van Goyen.

That view over the ridges of the roofs & the gutters with grass growing in them, very early in the morning, & those first signs of

4 Endless. Van Gogh was probably referring to 'paper on a roll' of a certain standard thickness.

life & awakening – the flying bird, the smoking chimney, the small figure strolling along far below – that is the subject of my watercolour. I hope you will like it.

I'm sure that it depends more on my work than on anything else whether or not I succeed one day. Provided I can just keep going, well then, I shall fight my fight quietly in this way & no other – by calmly looking through my little window at natural things & drawing them faithfully and with love. For the rest, I shall just adopt a defensive attitude against possible molestation, but beyond that I love drawing too much to want to be distracted by anything else. The peculiar effects of perspective intrigue me more than human intrigues.

[...]

Ever yours,
Vincent

Tersteeg's dark shadow looms up frequently in the letters written during this period, but Van Gogh hoped that by 'getting on quietly with my work' he might gradually be able 'to make up for having lost the friendly disposition of Mauve, H. G. T. & others' with 'an entirely new circle of acquaintances'.

Meanwhile, the Muse alone kept Vincent company. He painted watercolours of 'landscapes with a complicated perspective, very hard to draw – but for that very reason there is real Dutch character & sentiment in them'. And much as he tried later, with his *Potato Eaters*, to produce the kind of picture peasants themselves might have painted, so he now drew a depot at Rijnspoor railway station in 'just the way it seems to me the little level-crossing keeper with his smock & his little red flag sees it & must feel when he thinks what dreary weather it is today'.

Although Van Gogh badly needed money, he resolutely refused to compromise, and his reluctance to paint 'saleable' watercolours remained as marked as ever: 'I would just as soon be, say, a hotel waiter as the kind of watercolour manufacturer some of the Italians are.'

He felt certain that the results of his assiduous nature studies would be appreciated in the long run: 'Sooner or later, feeling and love for nature always find a response in people interested in art. The painter's duty is to immerse himself wholly in nature and to use all his intelligence for putting his feelings into his work, so that it becomes intelligible to others. But to my mind, working for the sake of sales is not exactly the way to do it, all it does is pull the wool over art lovers' eyes. And that is something true [artists] have never done, the sympathy they earn sooner or later arriving as the result of their sincerity.'

Life and literature again mirrored each other. Both brothers were immersed in the work of Émile Zola, and wrote to each other about what they felt on reading his *Le ventre de Paris*, Vincent linking the humanity of that work to his own concern for Sien.

By now he was yearning for a reunion with Theo, referring nostalgically to the memorable walks they had taken in their youth and looking forward to recapturing 'the kind of mood we were in in the days of the Rijswijk mill'. He was embarrassed about his increasingly Robinson Crusoe-like appearance, but that evidently did not spoil a successful meeting of the brothers at the beginning of August 1882. This visit gave Vincent, for the first time in many months, the happy feeling of 'again having the prospect of a year of steady work free of calamities. Moreover, because of what you have given me, I have a new horizon in my painting once more.'

Van Gogh was now able to procure decent painting materials and equipment, and although for the time being drawing was still 'the backbone of painting, the skeleton supporting all the rest', he took great pleasure in his first studies in oil.

To his surprise, he was able to achieve a 'pleasing aspect' – and perhaps a more saleable product – in the new medium, with less difficulty and more quickly than he had with laborious drawing.

Van Gogh's first experiences with oil – seven canvases in one week – again gave him cause for enthusiastic descriptions of nature all round The Hague. Much as he would later brave the mistral in Arles while out painting, so he now allowed the sand to whistle round his ears on Scheveningen beach: 'It blew so hard that I could scarcely stay on my feet and could see scarcely anything through the clouds of sand.'

Theo tried gently to persuade Vincent to be a little more tolerant of his parents, and hoped to effect a reconciliation. Van Gogh's parents had meanwhile moved to Nuenen, and it is striking that Theo's account of their picturesque new surroundings should have focused on precisely those same elements Vincent would later choose for his work in the area. 'I should certainly love to do a little old church & churchyard like that,' Vincent replied, 'with sandy graves and old wooden crosses.' Vincent heard about the Brabant weavers from his sister Wil, and even Theo's descriptions of Montmartre seem visionary in the light of Vincent's later work.

227 [D]

Sunday afternoon
[20 August 1882]

My dear Theo,

I have just had a nice letter from home which gave me very real pleasure, and from which it is clear that your visit & the things you said about me & my work have had a reassuring effect on them. This is bound, I think, to have welcome repercussions, and I should like to thank you in particular for the way in which you spoke about me, although it seems to me that you had more good things to say than I deserve as yet.

They seem very taken at home with their new surroundings & are still full of your visit. And so, for that matter, am I, because several things you told me make me think of you even more than before, and certainly not with less affection. In particular, what you told me about your health gives me cause to think of you often.

I am well, it is doing me good just carrying on and not letting things get in my way. But you will understand that I am not completely over it yet, and at times, especially in the evening when I'm exhausted, it does trouble me a little, though luckily it is no longer so bad that I am unable to get on with the work.

This week I painted a couple of fairly large studies in the woods, trying to improve on them and develop them further than the first. The one which I think comes off best is nothing more than a patch of dug-over ground ... white, black and brown sand after a downpour. So that the clods of earth catch the light here & there and stand out more strongly. After I'd been sitting for a while drawing the piece of ground, there was a thunderstorm with a tremendous downpour that went on for a good hour.

I was so keen to get on with it that I stayed at my post and took what shelter I could behind a large tree. When it was finally over and the crows were beginning to fly about again I wasn't sorry I had waited because of the glorious deep tone the woodland soil had taken on after the rain. As I had begun before the storm on my knees, with a low horizon, I now had to kneel in the mud, and it is because of adventures like that, which occur quite often in various forms, that I see nothing odd about wearing an ordinary workman's suit, which is less easily ruined. The result this time was that I could take the piece of ground back with me to the studio, although when we were speaking together once about one of his own studies, Mauve rightly said that it is a hard job to draw those clods of earth and get some perspective into them.

The other study from the woods is of large green beech trunks on a ground with dry leaves and the small figure of a girl in white. The big difficulty there was to keep it bright and to get some space between the trunks standing at various distances, the position and relative thickness of the trunks changing with the perspective. In short, to do it in such a way that one could breathe and walk about in it and smell the wood.

I particularly enjoyed doing these two. As much as something I saw at Scheveningen. A large stretch of dunes in the morning after the rain, the grass a relatively deep green, and on it the black nets spread out in enormous circles, creating deep reddish-black, green and grey tones on the ground. On this sombre ground there sat or stood or walked, like strange dark ghosts, women with white caps and men spreading or repairing the nets. Here nature was as gripping, curious, sombre and severe as the most beautiful Millet, Israëls or De Groux one can imagine. Over the landscape a simple grey sky with a bright streak above the horizon.

Despite the showers of rain, I also made a study of it on a sheet of oiled torchon paper.

There is much still to be gone through before I am able to do it as well as I would like, but in nature it is things such as these that move me most.

How beautiful it is outside when everything is wet from the rain – before, in and after the rain. I really shouldn't let a single shower pass.

This morning I hung all the painted studies up in the studio. I just wish I could talk to you about them.

As I had thought and expected, being so busy has meant buying quite a lot of things, and the money has nearly all been spent on them. For two weeks I've been painting from early morning till late at night, so to speak, and if I carry on like this it will turn out too expensive unless I manage to sell.

If you could see the results, I think it's quite possible you would say that I ought to carry on, not just at times when I particularly feel like it, but regularly, as an absolute priority, even though it might mean more expense. But though I myself enjoy doing it immensely, the heavy expenses will probably prevent me for the time being from doing as much painting as my ambition and inclination demand; still, I don't think I shall lose by spending a great deal of my time on drawing, which I do with no less pleasure.

Even so, I am in two minds. Painting comes easier to me than I imagined, and perhaps the right course would be to put all my effort into it, toiling away at the brush before anything else, but I must confess I'm not sure. At any event, I am sure that charcoal drawing is something I am going to have to study more than ever now. I have enough to do to keep me going, and even if I do have to exercise some restraint with my painting, it won't mean that I shall be working any the less hard.

The reason I have now painted a fairly large number of studies in so short a time is that I keep at it, literally keep at it all day, scarcely taking time off even to eat or to drink.

There are small figures in several of the studies. I have also been working on a larger one and have scraped it all off twice already, something you might have thought rash had you seen the first effect. But it wasn't rashness, it was because I feel that I can do even better by toiling away and trying things out, and I am absolutely determined to do better, no matter how much time or trouble it may take. The landscapes I am doing now definitely call for figures, they are studies for backgrounds which have to be done very thoroughly because the tone of the figure and the effect of the whole depend upon it.

What I find such a pleasant surprise about painting is that you can, with the same effect you put into a drawing, take something home with you that conveys the impression much better and is much more pleasing to look at. And at the same time more accurate, too. In a word, it is more rewarding than drawing. But it is absolutely essential to be able to draw the proportions correctly and to position the objects fairly confidently before you start. If you make a mistake here, it will all come to nothing.

I am looking forward to autumn. By then I must have made sure of a supply of paint and of various other things. I am exceedingly fond of those effects with yellow leaves against which the green beech trunks stand out so beautifully, and the figures no less.

Recently I read part of a rather melancholy book, Letters and Diary by Gerard Bilders. He died at about the age at which I began, and when I read that, I did not regret starting late. He was certainly unhappy and often misunderstood, but at the same time I can see a great weakness in him, something morbid in his character. It is like the story of a plant that sends up shoots too soon, cannot withstand the frost, and one fine night is stricken by it to the roots and withers. At the beginning all is well, he flourishes under his teacher as in a hothouse and makes quick progress, but later, in Amsterdam, he is virtually alone and for all his skill cannot bear it there and finally ends up back home with his father, utterly disheartened, dissatisfied, listless, does a bit of painting and then finally dies of consumption or some other disease in his 28th year.

What I don't like about him is that <u>even as he is painting</u> he complains of terrible boredom and idleness as if it were something he could do nothing about – and that he goes on running around with the same little circle of friends he finds so oppressive, and continues with the diversions and way of life of which he is sick and tired. In short, though I feel sympathy for him, I would sooner read the life of old man Millet or of T. Rousseau or of Daubigny. Reading 1 book by Sensier about Millet buoys one up while Bilders's makes one miserable.

I invariably discover a catalogue of problems in any one of Millet's letters, and yet 'j'ai tout de même fait ceci ou cela'[1] and then he always has other things in prospect which he absolutely must do and in fact does. With G. Bilders I often get the feeling of 'I am in a bad mood this week and making a mess of things – and after going to this or that concert or play, I came away even more miserable than before'.

What strikes me in Millet is that simple 'il faut <u>tout de même</u> que je fasse ceci où ça'.[2] Bilders, for his part, is very witty and can heave droll sighs about Manilas <u>pointus</u>[3] which he likes best but cannot afford to buy, and about tailors' bills, which he sees no chance of settling. He describes his anxiety over financial matters so wittily that he himself and whoever reads about it has to laugh. But no matter how wittily these things may be reported, I find them annoying and have greater respect for the private difficulties of Millet, who says 'il faut tout de même de la soupe pour les enfants',[4] and who doesn't talk about Manilas <u>pointus</u> or about entertainments.

What I'm trying to say is this. G. Bilders's outlook on life was romantic, he was unable to get over his illusions perdues,[5] and I, for my part, consider it something of a privilege not to have started until I had left my romantic illusions behind. I must now

---

1 I did this or that all the same. Vincent actually wrote the Dutch for 'or', *of*, instead of the French *ou*.
2 I must do this or that *all the same*. Vincent wrote *où* [where] instead of *ou*.
3 A type of cigar.
4 There must be soup for the children all the same.
5 Lost illusions.

make up for lost time and work hard, but it is precisely when one has left one's illusions perdues behind one that work becomes a necessity and one of the few pleasures left. And then there ensues much peace and quiet.

I am sorry, though, that it may take a year before you'll be able to see all the things I am painting side by side – even though I might send you something now and then – and before we'll be able to discuss the ins and outs of what to do about it all. I think I can assure you that the things I have painted now will prove to be of use. Perhaps what was unsuccessful in January may succeed now.

Above all, please don't think I don't care about earning money. What I'm trying for is the shortest means to that end – on the understanding that the work is of genuine and lasting merit, which I can only expect if I put something really good into it and make an honest study of nature, not if I work exclusively with an eye to saleability – for which one is bound to suffer later.

Were you to say that my painting is likely to have a better chance, then, of course, I shouldn't refuse to go on with it. But if it will not be saleable for a long time yet, then I should be the first to say: in the meantime we must practise the greatest possible economy, and by <u>drawing</u> one saves much expense and yet makes solid if slow progress.

I can see a change in the things I have painted and I am writing to you about it because you should be able to tell better than I how that might affect their potential sale. It seems to me <u>in any case</u> that painted studies <u>are more pleasing to look at</u> than my drawings.

However, I myself set less store by their more pleasing, less meagre effect, and see as my goal the expression of more severe and more virile things, for which I still have a great deal of hard work to do.

But if you were to say: work on those small wooded views or landscapes or marines, then that needn't stand in the way of my doing bigger and more serious things and I should have no objections. All I would have to know is that they are worth the brushes, the paint and the canvas, that it won't be a waste of money doing a great many of them and that the costs can be recouped.

Supposing that were to, or could, come about, then it might provide the means for tackling more difficult things. I should even work on them most assiduously in that case. I should want to begin by allowing them to mature a bit longer, to put more into them. Then, say in a couple of months' time, I shall send you one and we can see.

I'm sure that most painters have managed to rise to greater heights in just this way.

I shouldn't want to do things that are bad in principle, untrue or misconceived, because I love nature too much. But we are faced with this problem: before I can attain something higher and better, I must produce a great many more studies. Which will turn out to be more profitable: to draw these studies or to paint them?

If the painted ones should be <u>un</u>saleable, then, of course, it would be more profitable to draw with charcoal or something else. But if it were possible to recover the costs of painted studies, then I want you to know that I would have no objections in principle to carrying on with them, now that I can see that they are turning out rather well and may have an outside chance. In principle I am only opposed to wasting paint on things that one could learn just as well in another way and while there is still no chance of selling them.

I don't want to push either of us into unnecessary expense, but it is plain that the painted things have a more pleasing aspect. That makes me unsure about what to do. My money hasn't gone completely yet, but there isn't much left – today is the twentieth, if I am not mistaken, and I have spent less rather than more than usual on household expenses this month. Admittedly I have had to pay a lot out all at once on painting materials, but much of that will last quite a long time. But everything is very expensive. I hope you'll be able to send something soon. Accept a warm handshake in my thoughts, and believe me,

Ever yours,
Vincent

The reason why I myself am very happy with the painting is not its more pleasing aspect, but because it sheds light on other problems of tone and form and material which used to have me floundering but which I can now tackle in this medium. And I can also see, for example, greater opportunity for trying once again to achieve something with charcoal.

I sincerely hope that you won't conclude from this letter that I am presumptuous enough to think that it will be possible to do something straight away with these first studies. C. M. once interpreted certain remarks I made in that way, although I had meant nothing of the sort. Anyway, I used to be able to tell better than I can now what something was worth and if it could be sold or not. Now it is daily brought home to me that I no longer know about that sort of thing and I am more interested in studying nature than the price of pictures.

But I do think I can see that the painted studies have a much more pleasing aspect than either those drawn in black & white or the watercolours you saw recently. And that is why I am not certain if giving painting absolute priority might not turn out to be more profitable despite the greater expense.

I would rather you made such a decision than I, because when it comes to the assessment of financial success I consider you more competent than myself, and because I have complete confidence in your judgement. And if sooner or later I do send you something, it will be to hear whether you have any suggestions to make, not in order to say: I consider this or that item saleable. I no longer know about such things. And I would be sending it to you in any case to show you what I am up to.

You told me to do my best to complete a little drawing as a watercolour – I'm sure painting will actually help me to produce better watercolours than I did before, if I go back to them. But should it not turn out well, you mustn't feel discouraged and neither must I, nor must you hesitate to let me have your comments. I don't throw comments systematically to the winds, though it usually takes longer to change something than to point out what needs changing. For instance, I have only just put into practice things Mauve said to me in January. And I painted that piece of ground, for instance, following a conversation with him about one of his studies.

228 [D]

Sunday morning
[3 September 1882]

My dear Theo,

I have just received your very welcome letter, and as I am taking a bit of a rest today, am answering it right away. Thank you very much for it and for the enclosure, and for the various things you say in it.

And many thanks for your description of that scene with the workmen in Montmartre, which I found very interesting because you convey the colours so well that I can see them. I am glad you are reading the book on Gavarni. I found it very interesting and it made me love G. twice as much.

Paris & its environs may be beautiful, but we have no complaints here either.

This week I did a painting that I think would remind you a little of Scheveningen as we saw it when we walked there together. A large study of sand, sea and sky — a big sky of delicate grey & warm white, with a single small patch of soft blue shimmering through — the sand & the sea light, so that the whole becomes golden, but animated by the boldly and distinctively coloured small figures and fishing smacks, which tend to set the tonal values. The subject of the sketch I made of it is a fishing smack weighing anchor. The horses stand ready for hitching up before pulling the smack into the sea. I am enclosing a small sketch of it.

It was really hard to do, I just wish I'd painted it on panel or on canvas. I tried to get more colour into it, that is, depth, strength of colour.

How strange it is that you & I so often seem to have the same thoughts. Yesterday evening, for instance, I came home from the woods with a study, having been deeply preoccupied with the question of depth of colour the whole week, and particularly at that moment. And I should very much have liked to have talked to you about it, especially with reference to the study I had done – and lo and behold, in this morning's letter you chance to mention that you were struck by the very vivid, yet harmonious, colours of Montmartre. I don't know if it was precisely the same thing that struck the two of us, but I do know that you would most certainly have been affected by what struck me so particularly and would probably have seen it in the same light.

As a start, I am sending you a small sketch of the subject and I shall tell you what the problem was. The woods are becoming thoroughly autumnal, and there are colour effects I don't often see in Dutch paintings.

Yesterday evening I was working on a slightly rising woodland slope covered with dry, mouldering beech leaves. The ground was light and dark reddish-brown, emphasized by the weaker and stronger shadows of trees casting half-obliterated stripes across it. The problem, and I found it a very difficult one, was to get the depth of colour, the enormous power & solidity of that ground – and yet it was only while I was painting it that I noticed how much light there was still in the dusk – to retain the light as well as the glow, the depth of that rich colour, for there is no carpet imaginable as splendid as that deep brownish-red in the glow of an autumn evening sun, however toned down by the trees.

Young beech trees spring from the ground, catching the light to one side, where they are a brilliant green, and the shadow side of the trunks is a warm, intense black-green.

Behind those saplings, behind that brownish-red ground, is a sky of a very delicate blue-grey, warm, hardly blue at all, sparkling. And against it there is a hazy border of greenness and a network of saplings and yellowish leaves. A few figures of wood gatherers are foraging about, dark masses of mysterious shadows. The white bonnet of a woman bending down to pick up a dry branch stands out suddenly against the deep reddish-brown of the ground. A skirt catches the light, a shadow is cast, the dark silhouette of a man appears above the wooded slope. A white bonnet, a cap, a shoulder, the bust of a woman show up against the sky. These figures, which are large and full of poetry, appear in the twilight of the deep shadowy tone like enormous terres cuites[1] taking shape in a studio.

I am describing nature to you – I'm not sure to what extent I reproduced it in my sketch, but I do know that I was struck by the harmony of green, red, black, yellow, blue, brown, grey. It was very De Groux-like, an effect like, say, that sketch of Le départ du conscrit, formerly in the Palais Ducal.

It was a hard job painting it. The ground used up one and a half large tubes of white – even though the ground is very dark – and for the rest red, yellow, brown, ochre, black, sienna, bistre, and the result is a reddish-brown, but one ranging from bistre to deep wine-red and to a pale, golden ruddiness. Then there are still the mosses and a border of fresh grass which catches the light and glitters brightly and is very difficult to capture. So there in the end you have it, a sketch that I maintain has some significance, something to tell, whatever may be said about it.

I said to myself while I was doing it: don't let me leave before there is something of the autumnal evening in it, something mysterious, something important. However – because this effect doesn't last – I had to paint quickly, putting the figures in all at once, with a few forceful strokes of a firm brush. It had struck me how firmly the saplings were planted in the ground – I started on them with the brush, but because the ground was already impasted, brush strokes simply vanished into it. Then I

1 Terracottas.

squeezed roots and trunks in from the tube and modelled them a little with the brush.

Well, they are in there now, springing out of it, standing strongly rooted in it.

In a way I am glad that I never <u>learned</u> painting. In all probability I would then have learned to ignore such effects as this. Now I can say to myself, this is just what I want. If it is impossible, it is impossible, but I'm going to try it even though I don't know how it ought to be done. <u>I don't know myself</u> how I paint it, I just sit down with a white board in front of the spot that appeals to me, I look at what is in front of my eyes, and I say to myself: that white board has got to turn into something – I come back, dissatisfied, I lay it to one side and when I have rested a bit, I go and look at it with a kind of awe. Then I am still dissatisfied, because I have that splendid scenery too much in mind to be satisfied. Yet I can see in my work an echo of what appealed to me, I can see that the scenery has told me something, has spoken to me and that I have taken it down in shorthand. My shorthand may contain words that cannot be deciphered, mistakes or gaps, and yet there is something left of what the wood or the beach or the figure has told me, and it isn't in tame or conventional language derived from a studied manner or from some system, but from nature herself.

Enclosed another little sketch from the dunes. There are small bushes there whose leaves are white on one side, dark green on the other side & are constantly moving & glittering. Beyond them dark trees.

You can see that I am plunging full speed ahead into painting, I am plunging into colour. I have refrained from doing so up till now & am not sorry for it. Had I not already done some drawing, I should be unable to get the feeling of, or be able to tackle, a figure that looks like an unfinished terre cuite. But now that I sense I have gained the open sea, painting must go full speed ahead as fast as we are able.

If I am going to work on panel or canvas, then the expenses will go up again, everything is so expensive, paint is expensive, too, and so quickly used up. Well, these are complaints all painters have, we must see what can be done. I know for certain that I have a feeling for colour and shall acquire more & more, that painting is in the very marrow of my bones.

I value your loyal and effective help more than I can say. I think of you so much; I should so like my work to become vigorous, serious, virile, so that you too may get some pleasure from it as soon as possible.

One thing I should like to bring to your attention as a matter of importance – wouldn't it be possible to obtain paint, panels, brushes, &c., at <u>discount</u> prices? I am having to pay the <u>retail</u> price at the moment. Have you any connection with Paillard or someone like that? If so, I think it would be much more economical to get paints, say, wholesale, for instance white, ochre, sienna, and we could then come to some arrangement about the money. Everything would be cheaper, it goes without saying. Do think it over.

One doesn't paint well by using a lot of paint, but in order to do a ground effectively or to get a sky bright, one must sometimes

[228]: enclosed sketch.

not spare the tube. Sometimes the subject calls for less paint, sometimes the material, the nature of the subjects themselves, demands impasto. Mauve, who paints very frugally in comparison with J. Maris and even more so in comparison with Millet or Jules Dupré, nevertheless has cigar boxes full of the remnants of tubes in the corners of his studio, as plentiful as the empty bottles in the corners of rooms after a soirée or dinner such as Zola describes, for instance.

Well, if there could be a little extra this month, that would be wonderful. If not, then not. I shall work as hard as I can. You ask about my health, but what about yours? I would imagine my remedy would be yours as well: to be out in the open, painting. I am well, I still feel like it even when I'm tired, and that is getting better rather than worse. It's also a good thing, I think, that I live as frugally as possible, but my main remedy is painting.

I sincerely hope that your luck is in and that you will have even more. Please accept a handshake in my thoughts, and believe me,

Ever yours,
<u>Vincent</u>

You will see that there is a soft, golden effect in the little marine sketch and a more sombre, more serious mood in the woods. I am glad that both exist in life.

Much as he had been disappointed with the letters of Gerard Bilders because they lacked the spark of inspiration that made the biographies of Millet or of the illustrator Gavarni so exemplary, so he now was disappointed with his colleagues in The Hague. Looking back over the year 1882, he concluded that nothing had come of his hopes in them: 'I had imagined that the painters here formed a sort of circle or association where warmth and cordiality and a certain solidarity prevailed.' What he had found instead was 'coolness and discord'. From one of Theo's letters, moreover, he gathered that all was not what it might have been in Parisian artists' circles either: 'How many have not become desperate in Paris?' The madness that had struck at the Belgian painter Octave Tassaert was further proof of the martyrdom artists have to face. For all that, Van Gogh never abandoned his dream of setting up a close-knit artists' community.

His estrangement from Mauve in the wake of the Sien affair hurt Van Gogh most of all, but he also felt bitter about him as a teacher: 'I would sooner have had M[auve] speak to me about the <u>use</u> of body colour than tell me, "Whatever you do, you mustn't use body colour," while he himself, and others, use it all the time, so to speak, and to best effect.'

'Finding out for himself' is the only thing the self-taught painter can do, and Van Gogh took comfort from his correspondence with Anthon van Rappard, who was trying to kindle his enthusiasm for a sojourn in Drenthe. Vincent shared his impressions of the Dutch and French paintings he saw at various exhibitions with Van Rappard, and he devoted whole pages to their common passion for the English wood engravers: 'For me, the English draughtsmen are what Dickens is to literature. They have the same sentiment, noble and healthy, and one always returns to them.' With these English illustrations and Daumier as his main sources of inspiration, Van Gogh had meanwhile produced about 100 figure studies, mainly of types he found among ordinary men and women. Among the new subjects he tackled in the autumn of 1882 were studies of seaside visitors strolling along the beach, figures on a small bench under trees, 'orphan' men, 'flocks of orphans with their spiritual shepherds', and autumnal scenes in the Haagse Bos, the wooded park to the east of The Hague. The decline of nature in autumn had a particular appeal for him: 'How beautiful the mud is, and the withering grass.' He even picked his props from rubbish dumps: 'That collection of discarded buckets, baskets, kettles, soldiers' mess kits, oil cans, iron wire, street lamps, stovepipes, might have come from one of Andersen's fairy tales ... I am sure to dream about them tonight,' he wrote to Van Rappard in late October.

A high point from this period was his watercolour of Mooijman's State Lottery office in Spuistraat.

235 [D]

[*c.* 1 October 1882]

My dear Theo,

Just a word to acknowledge the safe receipt of your letter, for the contents of which my hearty thanks.

I have done hardly anything but watercolours these last few days. Enclosed is a small sketch of a large one. You may remember Mooijman's State Lottery office at the top of Spuistraat. I passed it one rainy morning when a crowd of people were standing outside waiting to get their lottery tickets. Most of them were little old women and the sort of people of whom one cannot tell what they do or how they live, but who evidently scrape and struggle to make their way through life.

Of course, superficially a small crowd of people like that so patently interested in 'Today's Draw' is something to make you and me smile, neither of us giving two pins for the lottery.

But I was struck by that small group and their expectant expressions, and while I did the sketch it assumed a greater and deeper significance for me than it had at first sight. It seems to me that it takes on more significance when one views it as: <u>the poor and money</u>. However, that is true of nearly all groups of figures – one must think about them before one can tell what one is looking at. The keen interest in, and the illusions about, the lottery may seem rather childish to us, but are serious indeed when we think of their counterpart, the misery and the sort of efforts de perdus[1] of those poor wretches to find salvation, as they think, through a lottery ticket possibly paid for with their last pennies, money that should have gone on food.

Be that as it may, I am trying my hand at a large watercolour of it. And am also doing one of a pew, which I saw in a small church in the Geest attended by the almshouse people (in these

1 Forlorn efforts.

parts they are called, very expressively, <u>orphan</u> men and women).

Once again hard at work drawing, I sometimes think there is nothing nicer than drawing.

This is a part of that pews piece – there are other heads, of men, in the background. Things like this are difficult, however, and don't always work straight away. When they do work, it's sometimes the end result of a whole series of failures.

Speaking of the orphan men, I was interrupted while writing these lines by the arrival of my model. And I worked with him until dark. He was wearing a large old overcoat (which lends him a curiously broad figure).

I think you may perhaps like this collection of orphan men in their Sunday best & their working clothes.

Then I got him sitting with a short pipe as well. He has a nice bald head, large ears (N.B.) and white side-whiskers.

<u>N.B. Deaf.</u>

I did this sketch at dusk, but perhaps you can just make out the composition. Once it's all together, it's quickly drawn, but it wasn't all that easy to put it together and I wouldn't say that I've put it together as well as I would have liked. I should like to paint it, with the figures about one foot high, or a little less, and the composition a little wider.

But I don't know if I'll do it. It would need a large canvas, and if things go wrong it could mean quite a bit of money wasted. So, much as I should like to do it, I think that if I carry on with my typical figures, these things will come by themselves. They will spring naturally from the studies after the model, be it in this or in another form, but with the same sentiment.

I am beginning to see more and more how useful and essential it is to keep hold of one's studies after the model. Though they have less value for others, the one who made them will recognize the model in them and will be reminded vividly of how things were.

If you get a chance, please try to return some of my old studies. I hope that I shall be able to do better things with them in time.

It goes without saying that in that group of figures, of which I am sending you a quick black sketch, there were many splendid things in colour – blue smocks and brown jackets, white, black and yellowish workmen's trousers, faded shawls, an overcoat that had turned greenish, white bonnets and black top hats, muddy paving stones and boots setting off pale or weather-beaten faces. And it all cries out for watercolour or oils. Well, I am hard at it.

I count on your writing again – you will, won't you? And once more thanks for the timely remittance which is indispensable if I am to carry on working hard. Goodbye, my dear fellow, let me shake your hand warmly in thought, & believe me,

Ever yours,
Vincent

There is a bit more foreground in the watercolour – here, the figures are too prominent and the eye doesn't have enough command of the foreground.

237 [D]

Sunday afternoon
[22 October 1882]

My dear Theo,

I don't need to tell you how delighted I was with your letter & the enclosure, it comes just in time and will be of tremendous help to me.

We are having autumn weather here, rainy & chilly, but full of atmosphere, especially good for figures, which stand out in tone against the wet streets and roads reflecting the sky. It is what Mauve, in particular, does so beautifully time and again. So I have been able to do some work on the large watercolour of the crowd of people in front of the lottery office, and I have also started another one of the beach, of which this is the composition.

I entirely agree with what you say about those times now and then when one feels dull-witted in the face of nature or when nature seems to have stopped speaking to us.

I get the same feeling quite often and it sometimes helps if I then tackle something quite different. When I feel jaded with landscapes or light effects, I tackle figures, and vice versa. Sometimes there is nothing for it but to wait for it to pass, but many a time I manage to do away with the numbness by changing my subject-matter.

However, I am becoming more and more fascinated by the figure. I remember there used to be a time when my feeling for landscape was very strong and I was much more impressed by a painting or drawing which captured a light effect or the atmosphere of a landscape than I was by the figure. Indeed, figure painters in general filled me with a kind of cool respect rather than with warm sympathy.

However, I remember very well being most impressed by a drawing of Daumier's: an old man under the chestnut trees in the Champs Elysées (an illustration for Balzac), though the drawing was not all that important. What impressed me so much at the time was something so stout and manly in Daumier's conception, something that made me think it must be good to think and to feel like that and to overlook or ignore a multitude of things and to concentrate on what makes us sit up and think and what touches us as human beings more directly and personally than meadows or clouds.

That is also why I always feel attracted to the figures of both the English draughtsmen and of the English writers, whose Monday-morning-like soberness and studied restraint and prose and analysis is something solid and substantial to which one can hang on in days when one feels weak. Among French writers the same is true of Balzac & Zola.

I don't know the books by Murger you mention but I hope to become acquainted with them. Did I tell you that I was reading Daudet's Les rois en exil? I thought it rather good.

The titles of those books greatly appeal to me, for instance, La bohème.[1] How far we have strayed these days from la bohème of Gavarni's time! It seems to me that there was definitely something warmer and more light-hearted and alive about those days than there is today. But I cannot be certain, and there is much good nowadays, or there could be much more than in fact there is if there were greater solidarity.

1 Van Gogh was referring to *Scènes de la vie de Bohème*, by Henry Murger.

At the moment I can see a splendid effect out of my studio window. The city, with its towers and roofs and smoking chimneys, is outlined as a dark, sombre silhouette against a horizon of light. This light is, however, no more than a broad streak over which hangs a heavy raincloud, more concentrated below, torn above by the autumn wind into large shreds & lumps that are being chased away. But that streak of light is making the wet roofs glisten here & there in the dark mass of the city (on a drawing one would achieve this with a stroke of body colour), so that although the mass has a single tone one can still distinguish between red tiles & slates. The Schenkweg runs through the foreground like a glistening streak through the wetness, the poplars have yellow leaves, the banks of the ditches & the meadows are a deep green, the little figures are black. I would have drawn it, or rather tried to draw it, had I not been working hard all afternoon on figures of peat-carriers, which are still too much on my mind to allow room for anything new, and should be allowed to linger.

I long for you so often and think of you so much. What you tell me about the character of some artists in Paris, who live with women, are less narrow-minded than others, perhaps trying desperately to preserve something youthful, I think is shrewdly observed indeed. Such people can be found here as well. It may be even more difficult over there than it is here to preserve some freshness in one's daily life, because to do so there means swimming even more against the tide. How many have not become desperate in Paris – calmly, rationally, logically and rightly desperate. I have been reading something of that sort about Tassaert, whom I like very much, and I feel sorry that this was what happened to him.

All the more, all the more do I consider every effort in that direction worthy of respect. I also think it is possible to achieve success without having to start out with despair. Even though one loses out here and there, and even though one sometimes feels a falling off, one must rally and take courage again, even though things should turn out differently from what one originally intended.

Please don't think that I look with contempt on such persons as you describe, just because their lives are not based on serious and well-considered principles. My opinion on the matter is this: what matters is <u>deeds</u>, not some abstract idea. I only approve of principles and think them worth the trouble if they turn into deeds, and I think it is good to reflect and to try to be conscientious, because this concentrates a man's energies and combines his various actions into a whole. The people you describe would, I believe, be more resolute if they thought more clearly about what they were going to do, but for the rest I greatly prefer the likes of them to people who parade their principles without taking the slightest trouble or even thinking about putting them into practice. For the latter gain nothing from the most beautiful principles and the former are precisely the people who, <u>if</u> they come round to living with resolve and thoughtfulness, might do something great. For great things do not just happen by impulse but are a succession of small things linked together.

What is drawing? How does one come to it? It is working through an invisible iron wall that seems to stand between what one <u>feels</u> and what one <u>can do</u>. How is one to get through that wall – since pounding at it is of no use? In my opinion one has to undermine that wall, filing through it steadily and patiently. And there you are – how can one continue such work assidu[2] without being distracted or diverted, unless one reflects and orders one's life by principles? And as it is with art so it is with other things. And great things are not something accidental, they must be distinctly <u>willed</u>.

Whether a man's deeds originate in his principles or his principles in his deeds is something that seems to me as indeterminable (and as little worthy of determination) as the question of which came first, the chicken or the egg. But I consider that trying to develop one's power of thought and will is something positive and of much moment.

I am very curious to know what you will make of the figures I am doing these days, when you eventually see them. That poses another chicken-&-egg question: must one do figures for a previously planned composition, or combine figures that one has done separately so that they give rise to a composition? It seems to me that it probably comes down to the same thing, <u>provided only that one keeps working</u>.

I conclude with the same thing you said at the end of your letter, that we share a liking for peering behind the scenes, or, in other words, we have a tendency to analyse things. Now I believe that this is precisely the quality one has to have in order to paint – the strength one must exert in painting or drawing. It may be that nature has favoured us to some extent (in any case you and I certainly have it – perhaps we owe it to our boyhood in Brabant and to surroundings that taught us to think more than is usual), but it is really and truly not until later that the artistic sensibility develops and matures through work. I cannot tell you <u>how</u> you might become a very good painter, but that you have it in you and can bring it out is something I really do believe. Goodbye, my dear fellow, thank you for what you sent me and an affectionate handshake,

Ever yours,
<u>Vincent</u>

I have already lit my small stove. My dear fellow, how I wish we could just spend an evening together looking at drawings & sketches, and <u>woodcuts</u>, I have some splendid new ones. I hope to get some boys from the orphanage to pose for me this week, I might yet be able to save that drawing of orphans.

Van Gogh was convinced that the art of his day was in decline: 'We have sunk enormously since Millet – the word decadence, now whispered or pronounced in guarded terms [...], will soon ring out like an alarm clock.' His pessimism was increased by the inner emptiness he felt, an emptiness 'I cannot fill with the daily round'. Contemporary art had 'something hectic and hurried that is not at all to my liking, just as if death had passed over it all'. He objected to the attitude of the Hague painter and art collector Hendrik Willem Mesdag, who had eyes for the most up to date only and who despised 'the old style'. With almost religious fervour, Van Gogh stood up for the painters of the last generation, and particularly for Delacroix and Millet: 'There used, in short, to be a body of painters, writers and artists, who were united despite their differences, and they were a force. They did not walk in the dark but in the light of knowing for certain, beyond any doubt, what they wanted.'

Van Gogh's intense study of the figure during this period also coloured his perception of nature as a system of animated figures: 'I see expression in the whole of nature, for instance in trees, and, as it were, a soul. A row of pollard willows sometimes has something of a procession of orphan men about it. The young corn can have an inexpressibly pure and tender air and awaken the same emotions as, say, the expression of a sleeping baby. The trampled grass by the side of the road seems as tired and dusty as people from the backstreets. When it snowed recently, I saw a group of Savoy cabbages standing stiff with cold which reminded me of a group of women I had seen standing in a basement hot-water-and-coals shop early in the morning, in their thin skirts and old shawls.'

In November 1882, inspired by English magazine illustrators and their 'Heads of the People' series, he started on a group of lithographs of working men such as *The Pensioner Drinking Coffee* and *The Digger*. The lithographs were to dominate his correspondence with both Theo and Van Rappard for many months. This work, he felt, would have to culminate in a popular edition, *from the people for the people*. In addition, he hoped that it would bring him in work as a magazine illustrator. The series was to run to thirty sheets, but he failed to produce anything like that number in the end.

In January 1883 it was Theo's turn to make his brother privy to problems of an amorous nature: he had fallen in love with a woman who also happened to be ill. Van Gogh's heart overflowed with warmth at this shared confidence. He sketched their respective situations in graphic terms: 'To you and to me there appeared on a cold, pitiless pavement the downcast, sorrowful figure of a woman, and neither you nor I passed her by, but both of us stopped and followed the dictates of our human heart. Such an encounter is rather like an apparition, at least when one recalls it one sees a pale face, a sorrowful look like an Ecce Homo against a dark background.' It encouraged Vincent to write more often about his life with Sien, whose name had not been mentioned in their correspondence for quite a while.

At about the same time, in early February 1883, Vincent first told Van Rappard about his new life with Sien, which he glowingly described as Bohemian. His often quite light-hearted tone makes a striking contrast with the intense letters about Sien he had exchanged with his brother the summer before. At the time, Van Rappard was recovering from 'brain fever', and Van Gogh did not hesitate on occasion to plead the nerve-racking nature of the artist's life as a mitigating circumstance in his letters to Theo. He also mentioned the fact that as soon as the landscape painter Martinus Boks was admitted to a lunatic asylum, his Hague colleagues' appreciation of his work began to increase. Van Gogh observed this phenomenon with not a little irony. That his own work would be linked to his mental illness by later generations renders these comments particularly poignant. In general, however, Van Gogh's reactions to his colleagues' afflictions were very down to earth. Thus he had nothing positive to say about the effects of Breitner's condition on his work. But even when much later he described his own condition in Saint-Rémy following various attacks, he rarely romanticized the illness, feeling as he did that it had a negative effect on his work. He emphatically gave the word 'healthy' a positive connotation in connection with art.

On the other hand, Van Gogh nourished the conviction that the artist's exceptional calling and position in society sometimes caused him to overstep the bounds of sanity. That placed him in a long, romantic tradition of looking on insanity as an extension, indeed even a prerequisite at times, of genius. In this connection he had mentioned as early as 1873 a painting by the Belgian artist Émile Wauters, whose subject was the madness of the fifteenth-century painter Hugo van der Goes. Later, too, when linking Breitner's work, which he found incomprehensible, to that artist's mental health, he referred to Wauters's painting.

During the first few months of 1883, in addition to indulging his passion for English wood engravings, Van Gogh confined himself largely to the drawing of working people, including fishermen. He also made a series of compositions of scenes in the public soup kitchen. At about the same time, his reading in Dutch of Fritz Reuter's *Ut mine Festungstid*

(From My Time in Prison) gave him the courage to tackle his landlord and to demand improvements to his studio: 'I love my studio in the same way that a sailor loves his ship.'

The painters whose company he kept regularly in The Hague included Herman van der Weele, who followed in Mauve's wake, and Théophile de Bock, whose landscapes were strongly influenced by Corot. Van Gogh wrote: 'There is always something fresh and friendly in them. But there is a certain art, perhaps less flowery and more thorny, that is more after my own heart.' His letters from this time are markedly serene. The appeal of the winter – 'an indescribably beautiful Black & White exhibition' – inspired him once again to poetic descriptions of nature and small vignettes of a Biedermeier-like intimacy.

276 [D]

[c. 21–28 March 1883]

My dear Theo,

You have so often afforded me a glimpse of Paris with your descriptions; this time for a change I am giving you a glimpse out of my window at the snow-covered yard.

I am adding a glimpse into a corner of the house, and they are two impressions of one and the same winter's day.

We are surrounded by poetry on all sides, but putting it on

paper is, alas, not as readily done as looking at it. I made a watercolour of the above, from which this small sketch is taken, but I don't think it is vivid and powerful enough.

I believe I've already written to you that I was able to find some mountain chalk here in the city. I am at work with that, as well.

To my mind the cold spell we had last week was the most perfect part of this winter. It was fantastically beautiful, what with the snow and the curious skies. The thawing of the snow today was almost more beautiful still. But it was typical winter weather, if I may call it that – the kind of weather that awakens old memories and lends the most ordinary things the sort of look one cannot help associating with stories from the age of stage-coaches and post chaises.

Here, for example, is a quick little sketch I made in just such a dream-like state. It shows a gentleman who, having missed a coach or something of the sort, has had to spend the night in a village inn. Now he has risen early, and having ordered a glass of brandy against the cold, he is paying the landlady (a little woman in a peasant's cap). It is still very early in the morning, la piquette du jour[1] – he must catch the post chaise – the moon is still shining and one can see the snow gleaming through the taproom window, and all the objects are casting curious, whimsical shadows. This story is really of no consequence, nor is the little sketch, but one or other may perhaps help you to understand what I mean, that is, that lately everything has a certain je ne sais quoi which makes one feel like getting it down quickly on paper. Still, the whole of nature is an indescribably beautiful Black & White exhibition[2] during such snow effects.

As I am doing small sketches at present anyway, I am adding another, very slight one, of a draw. done in mountain chalk, the girl by the cradle, done like the woman & child you mention. This mountain chalk is truly the strangest material. The other

1 The crack of dawn.
2 'Black ... exhibition': in English.

little sketch of a bargee is after a drawing in which a great deal has been lavis[3] with neutral tint and sepia.

It would not surprise me at all if the few things I sent you recently seem to you rather meagre products. Indeed I believe it could hardly be otherwise. There is something inevitable about the fact that, to appreciate the characteristic nature of work in Black & White,[4] one must take the whole set into account all the time, which cannot always be done. What I mean is that there is a difference between making 10 drawings and making 100 drawings or sketches or studies. Not because of the quantity, to be sure – forget about the quantity – what I am trying to say is this, there is a kind of tolerance to Black & White[5] that enables one to draw a single figure one admires in perhaps 10 different poses, while if one were to do it in, say, watercolour, or to paint it, one would do just one pose.

Now suppose that 9 of those 10 are no good, and I hope in all conscience that this would not be the proportion of good to bad all the time, but just suppose that to be the case. If you were here in the studio yourself, it is my belief that not a week would pass without my being able to show you, not just one, but <u>a whole number</u> of studies, and I should be surprised if you were unable to pick out one from amongst that number that appealed to you every time. Meanwhile the rest would not have been done wholly in vain, since in some respects even unsuccessful studies are likely to prove useful or serviceable one day for some new composition.

And that is why I think that the next time you come, you may well find a few more things about which you can give me a few tips. For instance, it is quite hard, since I am <u>not at all</u> familiar with Lhermitte's drawings (you will remember my asking you about them), but am familiar with Ciceri's watercolours as well as his old lith. drawing examples, though not at all with his current black and white drawings, I repeat, it's quite hard for me

3 Washed.
4 'Black & White': in English.
5 'Black & White': in English.

to grasp your precise meaning when you write with reference to a certain small sketch, 'Couldn't you do something that would somehow fit in with the above-mentioned drawings?' I'm sure that both those artists are infinitely more advanced than I – but your idea could be feasible and I myself will keep learning too, don't you agree? – so it's not beyond the bounds of possibility. And I wanted to emphasize to you again that in my opinion, supposing I do produce something that would fit in, there is a sort of tolerance to Black & White[6] which would allow one to become very productive in that direction, once one has embarked on it. Not without working unremittingly, of course, but I do that anyway.

So if the small drawings in mountain chalk I sent you are not what you intended, although I had your tips in mind when I did them, don't let that put you off and don't hesitate to return to the subject, the more often the better. And bear in mind, too, that as soon as I am sure of what you are after, I shall be ready to do as I said just now, to turn out 10, for example, in order to arrive at one good one. In short, if you do come to the studio one day, I think you would see that I am being fairly energetic, and you would, I hope, go on thinking of me in these terms, wouldn't you, and you would understand as well that even though someone who is fairly energetic may be working hard for himself, or rather without an immediate purpose, it might be twice as stimulating for him if there were a purpose. This is also true of possible work for the illustrated papers.

I immensely enjoyed rereading Fritz Reuter's <u>Gedroogde kruiden</u>[7] recently, it is just like, say, Knaus or Vautier.

Do you know a draughtsman by the name of Regamey? There is a lot of character in his work, I have got some of his woodcuts, including drawings made in prison, and gypsies and Japanese. When you come, you must have another look at the woodcuts, I've acquired a few new ones since last time.

---

6 'Black & White': in English.
7 *Dried Herbs*, the Dutch translation of Reuter's *Sämtliche Werke* (Complete Works).

It may well seem to you that the sun is shining more brightly and that everything has taken on a new charm. That, at any rate, is the inevitable consequence of true love, I believe, and it is a wonderful thing. And I also believe that those who hold that no one thinks clearly when in love are wrong, for it is at just that time that one thinks very clearly indeed and is more energetic than one was before. And love is something eternal, it may change in aspect but not in essence. And there is the same difference between someone who is in love and what he was like before as there is between a lamp that is lit and one that is not. The lamp was there all the time and it was a good lamp, but now it is giving light as well and that is its true function. And one has more peace of mind about many things and so is more likely to do better work.

How beautiful those old almshouses are, I can't find words to describe them. And although Israëls does this sort of thing to perfection, so to speak, I find it strange that so <u>relatively</u> few should have an eye for it. Every day here in The Hague, so to speak, I see a world which very many people pass by and which is very different from what most make of it. And I shouldn't dare to say so if I didn't know from experience that figure painters, too, actually <u>pass it by</u>, and if I didn't remember that whenever I was struck by some figure or other I encountered while out walking with them, I would hear time and again, 'oh, those dirty people', or 'that kind of person' – expressions, in short, one would not expect from a painter.

Yes, that often used to make me think. I remember, for instance, a conversation with Henkes, who frequently saw, and sees, things so clearly, which took me completely by surprise. It is as if they deliberately shun the most serious, the most beautiful things, in short voluntarily muzzle themselves and clip their own wings. And while I am gradually acquiring greater respect for some, I cannot help thinking that others will be reduced to sterility if they go on like that. And the old <u>Bohème</u> was very insistent on this very point, on being productive. And, and 'La Bohème' was no good, according to some, but mind you, there will always be those who want to have their cake and eat it and,

[276]: enclosed sketches.

and, and who will end up with jam on their faces. Snuff out the candle – que soit[8] – but there is no point in applying the snuffer prematurely. Goodbye, with a handshake,

Ever yours,
Vincent

Van Gogh plodded on indefatigably with his series of figures of working men, and although he was short of funds he was able to set enough aside to buy a traditional Scheveningen cloak for his models. His stock of types had grown impressively: 'I have a sower, a mower, a woman at the washtub, a charbonnière [a woman coal miner], a seamstress, a digger, a woman with a shovel, the almshouse fellow, a bénédicité [grace before a meal], a fellow with a barrowload of manure.' Literature was his indispensable companion: 'I cannot understand how one can be a painter of figures and not have a feeling for it [literature] – and I think of the figure-painters' studios that contain no modern writings as bare,' he wrote to Van Rappard. He reread Victor Hugo's *Les misérables*, whose characters – analogous to his own drawings – he considered the 'essence of what one sees in real life. It is the type, of which we meet no more than individual specimens.' In addition, reading Hugo helped him to 'keep some feelings and moods alive. Especially love of mankind and belief in, and awareness of, something higher [. . .]'.

During this period Van Gogh also experimented widely with new types of paper and with such drawing materials as mountain chalk, lithographic chalk and printing ink diluted with turpentine. A visit he paid to Van Rappard in May inspired him to try his hand at more ambitious work. He now combined his separate figure studies into 'more important' compositions, choosing for his charcoal drawings the double square (1 m × 50 cm) – the same format he would use in Auvers for his last paintings. Among the subjects he now tackled were *The Peat Diggers* and *The Manure Heap*.

For company he associated with a young surveyor called Furnée, to whom he also gave drawing lessons. His pupil's father, a pharmacist, in

8 So be it.

turn helped Van Gogh to buy paints cheaply. Van Gogh also saw much more again of his Hague colleagues Van der Weele, De Bock, Blommers and Breitner. His self-confidence regained, he had no difficulty in robustly criticizing their work. Breitner, in particular, came in for some rough handling: 'He is badly off course.' Van Gogh refused to be diverted from his path by the whims of the tastes or fashions of the day, and remained loyal to the painters of Millet's, Daubigny's and Breton's generation. On the other hand, he was open-minded enough to voice his admiration for Michelangelo's *Night*, for a drunkard by Daumier and 'an old horse by Mauve' in a single breath.

299 [D]

[*c.* 11 July 1883]

My dear Theo,

I had been more or less on the lookout for your letter & was very pleased when it came. Many thanks for it.

What you write about the exhibition is very interesting. Which old painting by Dupré was it that you particularly admired? You must tell me when you next write. Your description of the Troyon & the Rousseau, for instance, has enough substance to give me a fair idea of the way in which they were done.

There are other pictures from about the time of Troyon's Pré Communal that had the sort of atmosphere one might call <u>dramatic</u>, although there are no figures in them. Israëls got it quite right when he said of a Jules Dupré (Mesdag's large one), 'It is just like a figure painting,' and it is this dramatic effect that lends it the je ne sais quoi which makes one feel what you say about it: 'It conveys that moment and that place in nature to which one can repair alone, without company.' Ruysdael's Buisson has it very strongly as well.

You must have seen those old Jacques in which it was slightly exaggerated, perhaps done slightly for effect – no, not really – which one used to admire for that very reason, even though the ordinary man in the street didn't rate them among Jacque's finest?

Speaking of Rousseau, do you know the Richard Wallace Rousseau, a lisière de bois[1] in autumn after the rain, a glimpse of meadows stretching endlessly into the distance, marshy, with cattle, the foreground very much in tone. To me that is one of the finest – very much like the one of the red sun in the Luxembourg. The dramatic effect in those paintings is something that, more than anything else in art, makes one understand 'un coin de la nature vu à travers d'un temperament'[2] and 'l'homme ajouté à la nature'.[3] One finds the same thing in, say, portraits by Rembrandt. It is more than nature, something of a revelation. And it seems to me that it is as well to have great respect for it and to hold one's tongue when, as so often, people say it is exaggerated or mannered.

Oh, I must tell you that De Bock has been to see me – rather enjoyable. Breitner, who was totally unexpected because he seemed to have broken contact completely at one time, turned up yesterday. I was pleased, because – when I first moved here – it used to be very agreeable going out with him. I don't mean going out into the country but going out to look for characters and enjoyable experiences in the city itself. There isn't another person here in The Hague with whom I have ever done this, most find the city ugly and give everything in it a miss. And yet the city can be very beautiful at times, too, don't you agree?

Yesterday, for instance, I saw workers in the Noordeinde busy pulling down the section opposite the palace. Men all white with plaster dust, with carts & horses. It was chilly, windy weather, a grey sky, the whole place full of character.

I met V. d. Velden last year – one evening at De Bock's when we were looking at De B.'s etchings. I wrote to you then that he made a very favourable impression on me, although he had little to say and wasn't very good company that evening. But the

1 Edge of a wood.
2 A corner of nature viewed through a temperament.
3 Man added to nature.

immediate impression he made on me was that he is a solid, genuine painter. He has a square, Gothic head – a touch of insolence or boldness and yet gentleness in his look, a sturdy, broad build, in fact the exact opposite of Breitner and De Bock. There is something virile and powerful about him, even though he doesn't say or do anything in particular. I hope to have closer contacts with' him one day – perhaps through V. d. Weele.

I was at V. d. Weele's last Sunday. He was working on a picture of cattle in the milking-yard, for which he's done a number of substantial studies. He is going to the country now for a while.

By way of a change did a few watercolours again in the countryside recently, a little cornfield and a bit of a potato field. And have also drawn a few small landscapes as settings for a couple of figure drawings I am hoping to do.

These are the designs for those figure drawings, very sketchy. The top one is of people burning weeds, the bottom one shows the return from the potato fields. I am seriously thinking of painting a number of figure studies, chiefly with a view to working up the drawings.

What happy news that you plan to come to Holland at the beginning of August; as I've told you often enough, I look forward to seeing you very much.

I'm eager to hear from you how well up your woman is in artistic matters. I imagine in any case that much still remains to be done and encouraged in that direction. Tant mieux.[4] In any case, I hope she will acquire some sort of scrapbook, for which I hope you will be able to find a few sheets from among the smaller studies. Sometimes there are sheets in a sketchbook which, although they are mere scribbles, nevertheless have something to say. I shall put a few things aside against her arrival.

I have talked it over with De Bock and I can store my things at his house when I do my studies in Scheveningen. I also hope to call on Blommers again in the near future. I spoke to De Bock about his painting at the Salon, Novembre, the reproduction of which I admired so much in the catalogue. He must still have a sketch of it, and I should like to see that.

As for my going to London sooner or later, for a longer or shorter period, I agree there would be a better chance of doing something with my work over there. I also think that I could learn quite a lot if I could meet some of the people there. And I assure you I would not be short of subjects. There are bound to be beautiful things to do there at those dockyards on the Thames.

Anyway, there are several matters we must talk over when you come. I hope you won't be in too much of a hurry, there is so much we should discuss.

I really wish I could go to Brabant again in the autumn and do some studies there. I should particularly like to have some

4 So much the better.

studies of a Brabant plough, of a weaver and of the village churchyard at Nuenen. But again, everything costs money.

Well, regards, and many thanks again for your letter and the enclosure. Look after yourself. Are you thinking of bringing your woman along to Holland or isn't that advisable yet? I wish you would. Goodbye, my dear fellow, with a handshake,

Ever yours,
Vincent

I am adding a few lines to tell you some more about Breitner – I have just returned from his temporary studio here (as you know, he lives in Rotterdam at present). You no doubt know Vierge, or Urabietta, who draws for Illustration? Well, at times B. reminds me of Vierge, though not very often.

When he is good, his work looks like something done in a hurry by Vierge, but when he, that is B., does work that is too hurried or unfinished, which is what happens most of the time, then it is hard to say what it looks like, because it doesn't look like anything – unless it is strips of faded old wallpaper from I don't know what period, but anyway a most peculiar and probably very distant one. Just picture the scene, as I step into his garret at Siebenhaar's. It has been furnished in the main with various (empty) matchboxes, and for the rest with a razor or the like and a box with a bed in it. I could see things standing against the chimney, 3 endlessly long strips, which I took at first for sun blinds. But on closer inspection they turned out to be canvases

in
this
format:

As you can see from the above illustration, the first one is a somewhat mystical scene, probably taken from Revelation, or so one might be inclined to think at first sight. But I am told it is artillery manoeuvres in the dunes. My considered opinion is that it is a good 4 metres long by $\frac{3}{4}$ metres.

The second one tells the story of a man leaning against the wall at the extreme left of the painting, while at the extreme right various ghostly female specimens stand gaping at him, care having been taken to leave a fair amount of space between these two groups. And I was also told that the man on the left was meant to represent a drunkard, which might well have been the painter's intention, and I have no wish to call that into question, though it could have been anything else.

The third one is almost better and is a sketch of the market he did last year, which seems, however, to have changed since then to represent a Spanish rather than a Dutch market, at least in so far as anything can be made out in it at all. What sort of wares are being sold in the market, where it may be – I, for my part, doubt it is meant to be on this globe, and to the naïve spectator it would seem rather to represent a scene on one of the planets that Jules Verne's miraculous travellers were in the habit of visiting (by projectile). It is impossible to be specific about the sort of wares actually being sold, though seen from afar it could be enormous quantities of candied fruit or sweetmeats.

Now, you try to imagine something like that, but on ne peut plus absurd[5] and heavy-handed to boot, and you have the work of friend Breitner. From a distance it looks like patches of faded colour on bleached, mouldering and mildewy wallpaper and in that respect it has some qualities, which to me are none the less positively objectionable.

I simply fail to comprehend how it is possible for anyone to produce such things. They are like something seen in a fever, impossible and meaningless as in the most preposterous dream.

I think it just shows that Breitner hasn't yet fully recovered and that he actually did do it while he was feverish, which in view of his illness last year is quite on the cards.

Last year, when I had recovered but couldn't sleep and was feverish myself, I too had moments when I felt like forcing myself to do some work, and I did do a few things, but thank God not too absurdly large, which later I couldn't believe I had done. That's why I believe that B. will be all right again, but I do find this stuff ridiculous.

5 As absurd as can be.

A watercolour study of some small birch trees in the dunes, which was much better and had nothing abnormal about it, lay crumpled in a corner. But his large things are no good.

At V. d. Weele's I saw another very ugly one by him, as well as a very good head, but a portrait of V. d. W. he had started was another bad one. Thus he is hard at it making a fine old mess and on a very large scale. I do at times like the work of Hoffmann and Edgar Poe (Contes fantastiques, Raven, &c.), but I find Breitner's stuff objectionable because the imagination behind it is clumsy and meaningless and has virtually no contact with reality. I think it's terribly ugly. But I look on it as the result of a spell of ill-health. V. d. W. also has two rather curious little watercolours of his, stylishly done, which have a touch, a certain je ne sais quoi, of what the English call 'weird'.[6]

I learned a lesson today thanks to that visit, namely that one is fortunate indeed if in present-day society one can live in fairly normal surroundings and has no need to resort to a coffee-house existence – from which one starts to see things through a growing fog of confusion. For I have no doubt that this is what happened to him. Imperceptibly he has strayed far from a composed and rational view of things, and so long as this nervous exhaustion persists he will be unable to produce a single composed, sensible line or brushstroke.

I wish I could provide him with some company and diversion, I wish I could share his ups and downs more often and perhaps cultivate his friendship a bit more. Do you remember the painting La folie d'Hugues v. d. Goes, by Wauters? In some respects Breitner reminds me a little of V. d. Goes's mental state. I don't want to be the first here to say so, but I believe that people have been talking along these lines about his work for quite some time now.

The cure for him would be to take a good long look at some potato plants, which have lately had such a deep and distinctive colour and tone, instead of driving himself mad looking at pieces of yellow satin and bits of gold leather. Well, we shall have to wait and see. He is intelligent enough, but he persists quand

6 '"Weird"': in English.

même[7] with a sort of eccentric parti pris.[8] If he were merely departing from normality with a rational motive, well and good, but with him it is also a question of no longer taking trouble with his work. I think it is a very bad business and just hope he will come out of it all right, but he has badly lost his way.

Well, I shall be making a start in Scheveningen this week. I could have done with a little extra to buy some painting material.

I am going to have a few drawings photographed in cabinet size[9] or a little larger (to see how they would look on a smaller scale) by a photographer who has taken photographs of drawings by Ter Meulen, Duchatel and Zilcken. He does it for 75 cents, which isn't expensive, is it? I shall have him do the Sower and the Peat Cutters for now, the one with a lot of small figures, the other with 1 large figure. And if those come off, then if I should later have any drawings I shall be able to send you photographs of them, which you could show to, say, Buhot, to see if he thinks he can find buyers. They could reproduce those they want from the actual drawings, or else I could copy them on to their paper.

Regards once again, Theo, all the best. Write again soon. I am having those photographs done because we must keep going after Buhot & C[ie], I must earn a bit of money so that I can start something new and also do some painting, as I am just in the mood for it now.

Mauve has fallen out not just with me but also, to name but one other, with Zilcken. The other day I saw Z.'s etchings and just now at the photographer's I saw photographs of Zilcken's drawings. Leaving myself out of it, I must say that, going by those, it is beyond me what M. has against Z. His drawings were good, not bad at all. It's just capriciousness on Mauve's part.

Après tout,[10] I don't think it's very nice of C. M. not to have sent

7 All the same.
8 Prejudice.
9 A standard size of paper, $6\frac{1}{2} \times 4\frac{1}{2}$ inches (16.5 × 10.5 cm) for photographs.
10 When all's said and done.

one syllable in answer to my letter, when I took the trouble to enclose two croquis[11] of the drawings in question.

Nor do I think it nice of H. G. T., now that I, for my part, have tried to thaw the ice between us, not to come to see me. It's stuff and nonsense to say he's busy, for that isn't the reason, he could easily find the time to come round <u>once</u> a year.

I am adding another half-page to say something about Brabant. Among the figures I've done of working types there are several with what many would call a distinctly old-fashioned character, even in conception, for instance a digger who looks more like those one occasionally comes across on the carved wooden bas-reliefs of Gothic church pews than on a modern drawing. I think of the Brabant figures very often because I find them particularly appealing.

What I should tremendously like to do, and what I feel I could do, too, on the understanding that circumstances made patient posing possible, is the small figure of Father on a path across the heath, the figure rigorously drawn, with character, and as I have said, on a stretch of brown heathland crossed by a narrow white sandy path and a sky applied and suggested with just a touch of passion. In addition, Father and Mother arm in arm, let's say – in autumnal surroundings – or against a small beech hedgerow with shrivelled leaves. I should also like to use Father's figure when I do a peasant funeral, which I fully intend to try, although it won't be easy.

Leaving aside less relevant differences in religious opinion, the figure of a poor village clergyman is for me, in type and character, one of the most sympathetic there is, and I would not be who I am if I did not tackle it some day.

When you come, I should very much like to consult you about arrangements for a trip there. When you see my drawings of orphan men, for instance, you will understand what I want and how I intend to set about it.

11 Sketches.

I want to do a drawing that not quite everybody will understand, the figure simplified to the essentials, with a deliberate disregard of those details that do not belong to the actual character and are merely accidental. That is, it mustn't be, say, a portrait of Father, but rather depict the type of a poor village clergyman on his way to visit the sick. Similarly, the couple arm in arm by the beech hedge will be a typical husband-&-wife who have grown old together in love & fidelity, rather than portraits of Father & Mother, although I hope that they will pose for it. But they will have to understand that it is a serious matter, which they might perhaps not realize if the likeness isn't exact. And so they will have to be gently warned that if it comes off, they will have to adopt the pose I choose and not change it. Anyhow, it should turn out all right, and I don't work so slowly that it need be a big effort for them. And I for my part should set great store by doing it.

The simplification of figures is something that greatly preoccupies me. Anyway, you'll be able to see it for yourself in the figures I'll be showing you. Should I go to Brabant, then I don't think it should be some sort of an outing or a pleasure trip, but a short period of very hard work done at lightning speed.

Speaking of expression in a figure, I am increasingly coming round to the idea that it lies less in the features than in the whole tournure.[12] There are few things I detest more than most of the academic têtes d'expression[13] – I would sooner look at Michelangelo's Night or a drunkard by Daumier or Millet's diggers and that well-known big woodcut of his, La bergère – or at an old horse by Mauve, &c.

A worrying letter from Theo at the end of July 1883 unsettled Van Gogh badly, and financial worries began to surface again more frequently in his letters: 'I am looking on the black side of things right now. If I were still alone, all right, but now there is the thought of the woman and

12 Bearing.
13 Facial expressions.

the children, the poor lambs, whom one would like to keep safe and for whom one feels responsible. [. . .] Working is the only thing one can do, and if that doesn't help, one is at one's wits' end.' In order to demonstrate how much he had been weakened by malnutrition, he described to Theo how, unable to deal with a creditor, he had been floored by the man when they had come to blows.

When Theo pointed out that he had five people to look after in addition to his brother, Vincent retorted, 'The subdivision of my 150 francs among 4 human beings, when all the expenses for models, drawing materials, painting requisites and rent have been taken, makes one sit up and think too, doesn't it?'

His gloomy mood led him, at the beginning of August, to unburden himself abruptly to Theo in a postscript to a letter in which he outlined the course of his career, and, referring to the painter Guillaume Regamey, who had died at the age of thirty-eight, voiced the presentiment that he himself had at most another ten years of life in which to realize his ideals.

309 [D] [postscript]

[*c.* 4–8 August 1883]

[. . .]

For no particular reason, I cannot help adding a thought that often occurs to me. Not only did I start drawing relatively late in life, but it may well be that I shall not be able to count on many more years of life either.

If I think about it dispassionately – as if making calculations for an estimate or a specification – then it is in the nature of things that I cannot possibly know anything definite about it.

But by comparison with various people with whose lives one may be familiar, or by comparison with some with whom one is supposed to have some things in common, one can draw certain conclusions that are not completely without foundation.

So, as to the time I still have ahead of me for work, I think I may safely presume that my body will hold up for a certain number of years quand bien même[1] – a certain number between 6 and 10, say. (I can assume this the more safely as there is for the time being no immediate quand bien même.)

This is the period on which I count firmly. For the rest, it would be speculating far too wildly for me to dare make any definite pronouncements about myself, seeing that it depends precisely on those first, say, 10 years as to whether or not there will be anything after that time.

If one wears oneself out during these years then one won't live beyond 40. If one conserves enough strength to withstand the sort of shocks that tend to befall one, and manages to deal with various more or less complicated physical problems, then by the age of 40 to 50 one is back on a new, relatively normal course.

But such calculations are not relevant at present. Instead, as I started to say, one should plan for a period of between 5 and 10 years. I do not intend to spare myself, to avoid emotions or difficulties – it makes comparatively little difference to me whether I go on living for a shorter or longer time – besides I am not competent to manage my constitution the way, say, a physician is able to. And so I go on like an ignoramus, one who knows just one thing: within a few years I must have done a certain amount of work – I don't need to rush, for there is no point in that, but I must carry on working in complete calm and serenity, as regularly and with as much concentration as possible, as much to the point as possible. The world concerns me only in so far as I owe it a certain debt and duty, so to speak, because I have walked this earth for 30 years, and out of gratitude would like to leave some memento in the form of drawings and paintings – not made to please this school or that, but to express a genuine human feeling. So that work is my aim – and when one concentrates on this notion, everything one does is simplified, in that it isn't muddled but has a single objective. At present the work is going slowly – one reason more not to lose any time.

1 In spite of everything.

Guillaume Regamey was, I think, someone who left behind no particular reputation (you know that there are two Regameys, F. Regamey paints Japanese people and is his brother), but is nevertheless a personality for whom I have great respect. He died at the age of 38, and one period of his life lasting for 6 or 7 years was almost exclusively devoted to drawings with a highly distinctive style, done while he worked under some physical handicap. He is one of many – a very good one among many good ones.

I don't mention him to compare myself with him, I am not as good as he was, but to cite a specific example of self-control and willpower, sustained by one inspiring idea, which in difficult circumstances nevertheless showed him how to do good work with utter serenity.

That is how I regard myself, as having to accomplish in a few years something full of heart and love, and to do it with a will. Should I live longer, tant mieux,[2] but I put that out of my mind. Something must be accomplished in those few years, this thought guides all my plans. You will understand better now why I have a yearning to press on – and at the same time some determination to use simple means. And perhaps you will also be able to understand that as far as I am concerned I do not consider my studies in isolation but always think of my work as a whole.

These last few sentences sum up the crux of a view Van Gogh was to expand upon later, namely that the importance of an artist should not be judged by individual, more or less successful works of art, but by his artistic output as a coherent whole. This concept of the artist's oeuvre was to become an article of faith with Van Gogh. His high opinion of his profession forbade him, in life as in art, to make the slightest compromise, even at the expense of social and family ties. His relationship with Theo also suffered. During the latter part of August 1883, relations between the brothers cooled appreciably following a visit Theo paid to The Hague. Sien was the direct cause, but 'much deeper

2 So much the better.

questions' were at stake. Van Gogh expressed his own point of view tersely and uncompromisingly on 18 August.

313 [D]

[18 August 1883]

Dear brother,

I wish you could understand that there are various things about which I must be consistent.

You know what an 'erreur de point de vue'[1] is in painting, namely something quite different from and much worse than the faulty drawing of some detail or other. A single point determines the inclination and whether the side plane to the left or to the right of the objects is more fully developed throughout the composition.

Well, there is something similar in life. When I say that I am a poor painter and still have years of struggle to face – that I have to arrange my daily life à peu près[2] like a farm labourer or a factory worker, then that is a fixed point from which many things follow, and these things are taken out of context if they are viewed otherwise than as a whole.

There are painters in different circumstances who can and must act differently. Each one has to decide for himself. Of course, if I had other opportunities, were in different circumstances and nothing decisive had happened – that would have influenced my actions. Now, however – and à plus forte raison[3] – if there were the slightest question of my being accused of presuming rights to which I have no claim, even if it turned out that I had such rights après tout,[4] the mere suggestion of it would make me withdraw of my own accord from association

1 Error in viewpoint.
2 More or less.
3 With all the more reason.
4 After all.

with people of a certain standing, even from my family. So we are faced with this fact: my firm resolve to be dead to everything except my work.

However, it is hard for me to speak about things that would really be quite simple were they not unfortunately bound up with much deeper questions. Nothing causes more 'angoisse'[5] than an inner struggle between duty and love, both considered in their highest sense. When I tell you that I choose my duty, everything will be plain to you.

Just a word on the subject during our walk made me realize that nothing in me had changed as far as that was concerned, that it is and remains a wound I have to live with, but one that is buried deep and cannot be healed. Years from now it will be as it was the first day.

I hope you understand what a struggle I have had lately with myself. Still, quoi qu'il en soit[6] (without calling that quoi? into question, for I have no right to inquire into it), I will be on my qui vive to remain a man of honour and doubly attentive to duty.

I have never suspected her, nor do I suspect her now, nor shall I ever suspect her, of having had any but right and proper financial motives. She did no more than was reasonable, other people exaggerated. But you will understand that I make no presumptions about her love for me, and what we said on the walk must not go any further. Still, things have happened since that would not have occurred if I had not been confronted at a certain moment firstly with a flat no, and secondly with a promise that I would not cross her path again.

I respected her sense of duty – I have never suspected her and shall never suspect her of anything mean.

For myself, I know only this, that it is of primary importance not to swerve from one's duty and that one must not compromise with duty. Duty is an absolute. The consequences? We are not responsible for them, but we are for taking the initiative in doing

5 Anguish.
6 Whatever happens.

or _not doing_ our _duty_. Here you have the diametrical opposite of the principle that the end justifies the means. And my own future is a cup that cannot pass from me unless I drain it.

So fiat voluntas.[7]

Regards, have a pleasant journey, write soon – but you know now how I shall face the future, with serenity and without a line on my face to betray the struggle in my very depths,

Ever yours,
Vincent

However, you will also understand that I must avoid everything that might tempt me to hold back, and that I _must_ thus shun whatever might remind me of _her_. This thought has in fact made me more determined this year than I should otherwise have been, and you will see that I shall be able to do this in such a way that nobody will know the real reason.

Van Gogh complained more than once in his letters that the unspoilt character of The Hague and its surroundings was beginning to be eroded by the advance of urban expansion and fashionable seaside-resort life. During a visit, Van Rappard repeated an earlier suggestion that Vincent should move to the lonely and untouched province of Drenthe, where a number of his colleagues had recently gone. Van Gogh now became convinced that he would discover a Dutch Barbizon there and dreamed of realizing his ideal of an artists' community: 'Once there, I think I should stay for good in that region of heath and peat-cutting, to which more and more painters are moving and where a sort of artists' colony may perhaps arise in time.'

A mere look at the map made him wax lyrical: 'I have a small map of Drenthe before me. On it I can see a large white space devoid of any village names. It is crossed by the Hoogeveen canal, which suddenly comes to an end and I can see the words "Peat Moors" written right across the blank space on the map. Around that blank space a number of small black dots with the names of villages and a red dot for the little

7 Thy will be done.

town of Hoogeveen. Near the boundary a lake – the Black Lake – a name to conjure with – I picture all sorts of workmen dredging the banks. Some of the village names, such as Oosterheuvelen [Eastern Hills] and Erica, also exercise the imagination.'

Though life in Drenthe would be much cheaper, Van Gogh was loath to leave Sien and the children behind. He felt responsible for preserving the 'depths' in the 'ruins of her soul and heart and mind' and he was also convinced that without him Sien would fall by the wayside again. However, her lack of steadfastness – and the intrigues of her mother – increasingly irritated him until in the end he tried, as it were in stages, to rid himself of her for good. Though his sense of duty gave him qualms of conscience, step by step he rationalized his decision to go to Drenthe. He declared that he had become discouraged by her failure to gain the slightest insight into her own problems. By shifting an important part of the blame for the hopeless situation on to her tyrannical mother, Van Gogh provided 'the woman' no less than himself with a moral alibi and so justified the impending separation – to himself and to Theo. In Van Gogh's view, his departure for Drenthe was inevitable: ultimately Sien would always listen to the voice of her authoritarian mother, while he hearkened to that of the Muse.

His stay in Drenthe lasted for no more than a few months. The weather was unfavourable and the loneliness unbearable in the end. Moreover, his desertion of Sien and her children filled him with pangs of conscience. Acquaintance with the Drenthe landscape, on the other hand, seemed to exert a magical pull on him, and gave him cause for yet more lyrical descriptions – for instance, of a visit to the small village of Zweeloo.

340 [D]

[probably Friday, 16 November 1883]

Dear brother,

Must just tell you about a trip to Zweeloo, the village where Liebermann stayed for a long time & did studies for his painting at the last Salon, the one with the washerwomen. Where Termeulen and Jules Bakhuyzen spent some time as well.

Imagine a ride across the heath at 3 o'clock in the morning in a small open cart (I went with the man with whom I'm lodging, who had to go to Assen market), along a road, or 'diek' as they call it here, which had been banked up with mud instead of sand. It was even better than the barge.

When it was just starting to get light, and the cocks were starting to crow everywhere round the huts scattered over the heath, everything, the few cottages we passed – surrounded by wispy poplars whose yellow leaves one could hear falling – a stumpy old tower in a little churchyard with an earth bank & a beech hedge, the flat scenery of heath or cornfields, everything was exactly like the most beautiful Corots. A stillness, a mystery, a peace as only he has painted it. When we arrived at Zweeloo at 6 o'clock in the morning it was still quite dark – I had seen the real Corots even earlier in the morning.

The ride into the village was so beautiful. Enormous mossy roofs of houses, stables, covered sheepfolds, barns. The very broad-fronted houses here are set among oaktrees of a superb bronze. Tones in the moss of gold-green, in the ground of reddish or bluish or yellowish dark lilac-greys, tones of inexpressible purity in the green of the little cornfields, tones of black in the wet tree trunks, standing out against the golden rain of swirling, teeming autumn leaves, which hang in loose clumps – as if they had been blown there, loose and with the light filtering through them – from the poplars, the birches, the limes and the apple trees.

The sky smooth and bright, shining, not white but a barely

detectable lilac, white vibrant with red, blue and yellow, reflecting everything and felt everywhere above one, hazy and merging with the thin mist below, fusing everything in a gamut of delicate greys.

I could not find a single painter in Zweeloo, however, and people said that they never turn up in the winter. Whereas I, on the contrary, hope to be there this winter. Since there were no painters, I decided not to wait for my landlord's return, but to walk back instead & do some drawings on the way. So I began to make a sketch of the little apple orchard where Liebermann did his large painting. And then back along the road we had driven down early in the morning. Right now the whole area round Zweeloo is nothing but young corn, sometimes as far as the eye can see, the greenest of greens I know. With a sky above of a delicate lilac-white producing an effect I think cannot be painted, but which, as I see it, is the keynote one must understand in order to find the key to other effects.

A black stretch of earth, flat, unending, a clear sky of delicate lilac-white. The earth sprouts that young corn as if growing a mould of it. That is what the good, fertile lands of Drenthe really are – and all in a misty atmosphere. Think of Brion's Le dernier jour de la création – well, yesterday it felt as if I understood the meaning of that painting. The poor soil of Drenthe is the same, except that the black earth is even blacker – like soot – not lilac-black like the furrows, and overgrown in a melancholy way with perpetually rotting heather & peat.

I notice it everywhere – chance effects on that infinite background: in the peat moors, the turf huts; in the fertile areas, those most primitive hulks of farmhouses & sheepfolds with low, very low little walls and enormous mossy roofs. Oaks all around. Journeying through these parts for hour after hour, one feels that there really is nothing but that infinite earth, that mould of corn or heather, that infinite sky. Horses and men seem as small as fleas. One is unaware of anything else, however large it may be in itself, one knows only that there is earth & sky.

However, in one's capacity of a small speck watching other small specks – leaving the infinite aside – one discovers that every small speck is a Millet. I passed a little old church, exactly, but exactly like L'église de Gréville in Millet's little painting in the Luxembourg. Here, instead of the small peasant with the spade, though, there was a shepherd with a flock of sheep alongside the hedge. In the background was a vista, not of the sea, but of a sea of young corn, a sea of furrows instead of waves. The effet produit[1] was the same. Then I saw ploughmen, hard at work, a sand cart, shepherds, roadmenders, dung carts. In a small roadside inn, I drew a little old woman at her spinning wheel, a small dark silhouette out of a fairy-tale – a small dark silhouette against a bright window through which one saw the bright sky and a little path through the delicate green and a few geese pecking at the grass.

And then, when dusk fell, imagine the silence, the peace!

Imagine <u>then</u> a short avenue of tall poplars with autumn leaves, imagine a wide muddy road, all black mud, with heath stretching to infinity on the right, heath stretching to infinity on the left, a couple of black triangular silhouettes of turf huts, the red glow from small fires shining through the small windows, with a few pools of dirty, yellowish water reflecting the sky, in which fallen trees lie rotting into peat. Imagine that sea of mud at dusk with a whitish sky overhead, thus everything black against white. And in that sea of mud a shaggy figure – the shepherd – and a mass of oval shapes, half wool, half mud, jostling one another, pushing one another out of the way – the flock. You see them coming, you stand in their midst, you turn round and follow them. Laboriously and reluctantly they work their way up the muddy road. The farm beckons in the distance, a few mossy roofs and piles of straw & peat among the poplars. The sheepfold is again like a triangular silhouette, the entrance dark. The door stands wide open like a dark cave. The light of the sky glimmers once more through the chinks in the boards behind it. The whole caravan, masses of wool and mud, disappears into the cave – the shepherd and a little woman with a lantern shut the doors behind them.

1 Overall impression.

That return of the flock in the dusk was the finale of the symphony I heard yesterday. The day passed like a dream, I had been so immersed in that heart-rending music all day that I had literally forgotten to eat & drink – I had had a slice of black bread and a cup of coffee in the little inn where I had drawn the spinning wheel. The day was over and from dawn to dusk, or rather from one night to the next, I had lost myself in that symphony. I came home and as I sat by the fire it occurred to me that I felt hungry, no, I realized I was ravenous.

But now you can see what it is like here. One feels just as if one were at, say, an exhibition des cent chef-d'oeuvres.[2] What does one bring back from such a day? Merely a number of rough sketches. Yet there is something else one brings back – a quiet delight in one's work.

Be sure to write soon. It is Friday today, but your letter has not yet arrived, I'm waiting for it eagerly. It takes time to get it [the money] changed, too, because it has to go back again to Hoogeveen and then here again. We're not sure how it's going to work out, otherwise I should tell you now: perhaps the simplest thing would be to send the money once a month. In any case, write again soon. With a handshake,

Ever yours,
Vincent

324 [D]

[c. 15 September 1883]

My dear Theo,

Now that I have been here for a few days and have done a good deal of walking about in various directions, I can tell you more about the area in which I have ended up. I am enclosing a quick little sketch of the first study I painted here, a cottage on the

2 Of one hundred masterpieces.

heath. A cottage made entirely of turfs and sticks. I have seen the inside of some 6 or so like this, too, and more studies of them will follow.

I can't convey the way they look outside in the dusk or just after sunset better than by reminding you of a certain painting by Jules Dupré, which I think belongs to Mesdag and shows two cottages, their moss-covered roofs standing out surprisingly deep in tone against a misty, hazy evening sky. <u>That could have been here</u>.

Inside, these cottages, dark as a cave, are very beautiful. There are drawings by certain English artists who have worked on the moors in Ireland that portray most realistically what I have found here. Alb. Neuhuys does the same with somewhat more poetry than is apparent at first sight, but he never does anything that is not basically true.

I saw some superb figures in the country – striking in their sobriety. A woman's breast, for instance, has that heaving movement which is the exact opposite of volupté,[1] and sometimes, when the creature is old or ailing, can arouse compassion or respect. And the melancholy which things in general have here is of a healthy kind, as in drawings by Millet. Fortunately, the men here wear short breeches, which show the shape of the leg and give the movements more expression.

To mention one of the many fresh impressions and feelings I have gained on my exploratory outings, let me tell you for instance about the barges drawn by men, women, children, white or black horses, laden with peat, <u>in the middle of the heath</u>, just like the ones you see in Holland, say on the Rijswijk towpath.

The heath is magnificent, I've seen sheepfolds and shepherds more beautiful than those in Brabant. The ovens are more or less as in Th. Rousseau's four communal,[2] and stand in the gardens under old apple trees or among the celery and the cabbages. Beehives, too, in many places.

One sees many individuals who have something wrong with

1 Voluptuousness.
2 Communal oven.

them – I think it can't be very healthy here, perhaps because of foul drinking water. I've seen a few girls of perhaps 17 or even younger with something lovely and youthful about them, whose features were striking, but more often than not they look fané[3] at an early age. Still, this doesn't detract from the fine and noble bearing of some of the figures, even if they do appear quite faded when seen from close to.

There are 4 or 5 canals in the village, to Meppel, to Dedemsvaart, to Coevorden, to Hollands Veld. Following them, one now and then sees a curious old mill, farmhouse, boatyard or lock. And always the bustle of peat barges.

To give you an example of the true character of these parts: as I sat painting that cottage, two sheep and a goat came and started to graze <u>on the roof</u> of the house. The goat climbed up on to the ridge and looked down the chimney. The woman, who had heard something on the roof, rushed out and flung her broom at the said goat, which leapt down like a chamois.

The two hamlets on the heath where I went and where this incident occurred are called Stuifzand and Swartschaap.[4] I've been to various other places too, and you'll have some idea now of how primitive it all still is here – Hoogeveen is après tout[5] a town and yet right next to it one has shepherds, those ovens, those turf huts, &c.

I sometimes think with a great deal of melancholy of the woman and the children. Would that they were provided for – one could say it is the woman's own fault, and it would be true, yet I fear that her adversity will be greater than her fault. I knew from the start that her character was tainted but I had hoped it could be reformed, and now that I no longer see her and can ponder some of the things I saw in her, I am more and more convinced that she was too far gone to be reformed. And that only increases my sense of pity, which gives way to a feeling of melancholy because it is not in my power to help matters.

---

3 Faded.
4 Shifting Sands and Black Sheep.
5 After all.

Theo, when I see a poor woman like that on the heath, with a child on her arm or at her breast, my eyes grow moist. I am reminded of her, and her weakness, her slovenliness, only add to the likeness. I know that she is no good, that I have every right to do as I am doing, that I could not stay with her there, that I really could not take her with me, indeed that what I did was sensible, wise, whatever you like, but that doesn't alter the fact that it cuts right through me when I see a poor little figure like that, feverish and miserable, and it melts my heart.

How much sadness there is in life. Still, it won't do to become depressed, one should turn to other things, and the right thing is work, but there are times when one can only find peace of mind in the realization: I, too, shall not be spared by unhappiness.

Goodbye, write soon and believe me,

Ever yours,
Vincent

330 [D] [part]

[c. 3 October 1883]

My dear Theo,

This time I am writing to you from the remotest corner of Drenthe, where I have arrived following an endless passage by barge through the heathland.

I don't think I shall be able to do justice to the countryside because words fail me, but imagine the banks of the canal as miles and miles of, say, Michels or Th. Rousseaus, Van Goyens or Ph. de Konincks. Level planes or strips, varied in colour, that grow narrower & narrower as they approach the horizon. Accentuated here & there by a turf hut or small farmhouse or a few stunted beeches, poplars, oaks – peat stacked up everywhere and barges constantly passing by with peat or bulrushes from the marshes. Here and there skinny cows, subtle in colour, quite often sheep and pigs.

In general the figures that now & then put in an appearance on the flats are full of character, and sometimes they have an enormous charm. I drew, amongst others, a little woman on the barge, wearing crape round her casque brooches because she was in mourning, and then a mother with a baby – the latter had a purple cloth round its head. There are lots of Ostade types amongst them, physiognomies that put one in mind of pigs or crows, but now and then a little figure who is like a lily among the thorns.

In short, I am very pleased with this trip, for I am full of what I have seen.

This evening the heath was uncommonly lovely. There is a Daubigny in one of the Boetzel Albums which conveys the effect precisely. The sky was of an inexpressibly delicate lilac-white – the clouds not fleecy, for they were joined together more, but in tufts covering the whole sky in tones of more or less lilac-grey-white, with a single small break through which the blue gleamed. Then, at the horizon, a glorious red streak, the surprisingly dark stretch of brown heath underneath and a host of little low-roofed huts against the brilliant red streak.

In the evening this heath often has the kind of effect the English call 'weird'[1] and 'quaint'.[2] The fantastic silhouettes of Don Quixote-like mills or curious monsters of drawbridges are profiled against the vibrant evening sky. Such villages look wonderfully cosy in the evening sometimes, with the reflections of little lighted windows in the water or in the mud & puddles.

[. . .]

In Drenthe Van Gogh regained his old conviction that Theo, too, must become an artist and turn his back on the corrupt world of the art trade. At the time Theo was in dispute with his employers, Messrs Boussod & Valadon, the new owners of Goupil, and Vincent made use of this psychological moment, pressing his brother to abandon 'the world of convention and speculation': 'I see something in you of a person who is

1 '"weird"': in English.
2 '"quaint"': in English.

in conflict with Paris. I don't know how many years in Paris have gone by – but part of your heart is there. I have nothing against that, but something – a je ne sais quoi – is still <u>vierge</u> [untouched]. That is the artistic element. It appears weak now – but that new shoot will sprout, and sprout quickly. I am afraid the old trunk is too deeply split, and I advise you to sprout in an entirely new direction or I fear the old trunk shall yet prove not to be viable.' The 'two brother painters' theme dominated a whole series of letters he wrote from Drenthe.

'In my view it would be an erreur de point de vue [error of judgement] were you to continue in business in Paris. The conclusion then: two brother painters. Would that suit your nature? You may be involved in a difficult and fruitless struggle against it, a struggle that would impede your own liberation, just because you doubt whether you can do it. I know this, alas, from my own experience.

'Après tout [When all is said and done], no matter how much we may be our own enemies, I am beginning to appreciate more and more: "L'homme s'agite, Dieu le mène [Man proposes and God disposes]." An infinitely powerful force prevails over our doing right and wrong. The same is true of your circumstances – be sensible about them – perhaps even sensible enough, in the end, to become a painter. Ultimately I should feel so reassured were you to take up a brush that I should consider the momentary calamity and shipwreck of lesser importance than the certain knowledge that your future is moving in a direction you will never regret.'

We do not know what arguments Theo raised against Vincent's urgent appeals, but one thing is clear: Theo was playing for time.

In late November it became too cold to paint outside. Though Van Gogh had insisted that he would like to settle in Drenthe for good, loneliness made him decide otherwise in the end: 'Taking a house on one's own is so terribly melancholy and bleak.' His brother's uncertain financial position dominated the last letters from Drenthe.

At the beginning of December Van Gogh went to stay with his parents in Nuenen for a few days. His difficult relationship with them, his banishment by his father and his parents' attitude to the Sien affair formed the theme of his first letters from Nuenen. But though he felt that his family had come to look on him as a shaggy dog who might bite in a fit of madness, he decided not to return to Drenthe, and to take up temporary residence with his parents in the village parsonage.

346 [D]

[*c.* 15 December 1883]

Dear brother,

I sense what Father and Mother <u>instinctively</u> (I do not say <u>intelligently</u>) think about me. They shrink from taking me into the house as they might from taking in a large shaggy dog who is sure to come into the room with wet paws – and is so very shaggy. He will get in everyone's way. <u>And his bark is so loud</u>. In short, he is a filthy beast.

Very well, but the beast has a human history, and although he is a dog he has a human soul, and what is more one so sensitive that he can feel what people think about him, which an ordinary dog cannot.

And I, admitting that I am a sort of dog, accept them for what they are.

This house is also far too good for me, and Father and Mother and the family are so exceedingly refined (though not sensitive underneath), and – and – there are clergymen, lots of clergymen.

The dog appreciates that if they do keep him, they are only putting up with him, only just tolerating his presence 'in this house', so he will try to track down a kennel elsewhere.

In fact this dog used to be Father's son once upon a time, and it was Father who left him out in the streets a little too long, so he was bound to become rougher, but seeing that Father forgot this many years ago and has never thought <u>deeply</u> about what the bond between father and son means, we had best say nothing about it.

And then – the dog could easily bite – he could easily become rabid – and the village policeman would have to come round and shoot him.

Oh yes, all that is perfectly true, no doubt about it.

On the other hand, dogs can also be guard dogs. But there's no need for that, they say, it's peaceful here, there's no question of any danger. So I shall say no more about that idea.

The only thing the dog regrets is that he came back, because it wasn't as lonely on the heath as it is in this house – despite all the kindness. The poor beast's visit was a weakness, which I hope will be forgotten, and which he will avoid repeating in the future.

Because I have had no expenses since I have been here and because I have twice received money from you, I paid for the journey myself and also for the clothes Father bought me because mine weren't good enough, and at the same time I have repaid the 25 guilders to friend Rappard. I'm sure you'll be pleased about this, everything was such a mess.

Dear Theo, enclosed is the letter I was writing when I received yours. Which I shall now answer, having carefully read what you say.

I shall start by saying I think it noble of you that, believing that I am making things difficult for Father, you take his part and give me a brisk dressing-down. I value this in you, although you are taking up arms against one who is neither Father's enemy nor yours but who would nevertheless like to present a few serious questions for Father's consideration and yours, who tells you what I am telling you because that is the way I feel, and who asks: why is this so?

In many respects, your answers to various passages in my letter bring out certain aspects of the matter with which I am not unfamiliar myself. Your objections are partly my own objections, but they are not sufficient. So once again I appreciate your goodwill and likewise your desire for reconciliation and peace – which, indeed, I have never doubted.

Even so, brother, I could easily raise a great many objections to your suggestions, except that I think that would be tedious and there is a shorter way. There is a desire for peace and reconciliation in Father and in you and in me. And yet we do not seem able to bring peace about.

Well, it is my belief that I am the stumbling block, and so it is up to me to find a way of not 'making things difficult' for you or for Father any longer. And I am now prepared to make things as easy as possible and as peaceful as possible, for both of you.

So you are also of the opinion that I am the one who is making things difficult for Father and that I am a coward. So . . .

Well, I shall do my best in future to keep everything from you and from Father, I shan't visit Father again and, if you approve, shall stick to my proposal that (for the sake of our mutual freedom of thought, and for the sake of not making things difficult for you as well, a view I fear you are inadvertently beginning to take) we put an end to our financial arrangement by March. I ask for a little grace for the sake of order and to allow myself time to take a few steps which, though they have very little chance of success, my conscience does not allow me to put off in the circumstances.

You must take this calmly and in good heart, brother – it is not an ultimatum to you. But if our feelings differ too greatly, well then, we must not rush to sweep everything under the carpet. Isn't that more or less your opinion as well?

You do realize, don't you, that I'm sure you have saved my life and I shall never forget that. Even after we have put an end to relations which, I fear, would place us in a false position, I shall still not only be your brother, your friend, but I shall also owe you an infinite debt of loyalty because you held out your hand to me and because you have gone on helping me . . .

Money can be repaid, not kindness such as yours.[1]

So leave me to carry on by myself – I am only sorry that a complete reconciliation has not proved possible, and wish it might still come about, but you people do not understand me, and I am afraid you never will.

Please send me the usual by return, if you can, then I shan't have to ask Father for anything when I leave, which I ought to do as soon as possible.

I gave all the 23.80 guilders you sent on 1 Dec. to Father, for 14 guilders borrowed and 9 guilders for shoes and trousers. I gave all the 25 guilders you sent on 10 December to Rappard. I still have a quarter and a few cents in my pocket. So that is the financial position, which you will understand if you also take

1 'Money . . . yours': in English.

into account that I paid for the expenses in Drenthe over a long period out of the money from 20 November, which arrived on 1 Dec., because of some hitch that was later put right, and that I paid for my journey, etc., out of the 14 guilders (which I borrowed from Father and have since returned).

From here I shall go to Rappard's. And from Rappard's perhaps to Mauve's. My intention is thus to try to do everything in a calm and orderly fashion.

There is too much in my candidly expressed opinion of Father which I cannot take back in the circumstances. I appreciate your objections, but many of them do not convince me, others I have already thought of myself, even though I write as I do. I have put my feelings in strong terms, and they have naturally been modified by my appreciation that there is much good in Father − that modification has been substantial, of course.

Allow me to tell you that I never knew that someone of 30 was 'a boy', particularly when he has probably had more experience than most during those 30 years. But do think of my words as the words of a boy if you want. I am not responsible for how you view what I say, am I? That's _your_ business.

And as far as Father is concerned, I shall take the liberty of putting what he thinks of me from my mind the moment we part.

It may be politic to keep what one feels to oneself, but it has always seemed to me that sincerity is a duty, especially for a painter − whether people understand what I say, whether they judge me rightly or wrongly, is neither here nor there as far as I am concerned, as you yourself once pointed out to me.

Well, brother, even if there is a separation in whatever way, know that I am your friend, perhaps much more than you realize or understand − and even Father's friend. With a handshake,

Ever yours,
Vincent

In any event I am neither Father's enemy nor yours, nor shall I ever be.

347 [D] [part]

[*c.* 17 December 1883]

My dear Theo,

Mauve once told me, 'You will find yourself if you persist at your art, if you go more deeply into it than you have been doing up to now.' He said that 2 years ago.

Lately I have been thinking a lot about those words of his. I have found myself – I am that dog. The notion may be a bit overstated – real[ity] may have less pronounced, less starkly dramatic, contrasts – but I believe that fundamentally the rough character-sketch applies.

The shaggy sheepdog I tried to portray for you in yesterday's letter is my character, and the animal's life is my life, if, that is, one omits the details and merely states the essentials. That may seem exaggerated to you – but I do not take it back.

Personalities aside, just as an impartial character study – as if I were talking about strangers and not about you and me and Father – for the sake of analysis I draw your attention once more to last summer. I see two brothers walking in The Hague (look upon them as <u>strangers</u>, as <u>other people</u>, do not think of yourself or of me or Father).

One of them says, 'I am getting more & more like Father – I have to maintain a certain social position – a certain affluence (very moderate both in your case and in Father's) – I must stay in business. I don't think I'm going to become a painter.'

The other says, 'I am getting [less and less] like Father – I am turning into a dog, I feel that the future will probably make me uglier and rougher still and I foresee "a degree of <u>poverty</u>" as my lot – but, but, <u>man</u> or <u>dog</u>, I shall be a painter, in short a creature with feeling.'

So, for the one, a certain position or affluence, and a dealer. For the other, a degree of poverty and exclusion, and a painter.

And I see those same two brothers in earlier years – when you had just entered the art world, had just begun to read, &c., &c. –

near the Rijswijk mill, or, for example, on a winter outing to Chaam across the snow-covered heath early one morning! <u>Feeling, thinking and believing the same</u> to such an extent – that I wonder: can those be the same two? Wonder: what will the outcome be – will they separate for ever or will they take the same path once and for all?

I tell you, <u>I am choosing the said dog's path</u>, I am remaining a <u>dog</u>, I shall be <u>poor</u>, I shall be a <u>painter</u>, I want to remain <u>human</u>, <u>in</u> nature. To my mind anyone who turns away from nature, whose head is forever filled with thoughts of keeping up this and keeping up that, even if that should remove him from nature to such an extent that he cannot help admitting it – oh, going on like that, one so easily arrives at a point where one can no longer tell white from black – and, and one becomes the precise opposite of what one is taken for or believes oneself to be.

For instance: at present you still have a manly fear of mediocrity in the worst sense of that word. Why then, in spite of that, are you going to kill, to extinguish the best in your soul? <u>Then</u>, yes, <u>then</u> your fear might well come true. How does one become mediocre? By complying with and conforming to one thing today and another tomorrow, as the world dictates, by never contradicting the world and by heeding public opinion!

Do not misunderstand me, what I am trying to say is just that basically you are better than that – I see this when, for example, you take Father's part once you think I have made things difficult for Father. If I may say so, to my mind your opposition in that case is misdirected. I do appreciate what you are doing, and I say, do be more sensible, direct your anger elsewhere and fight with the same strength against other influences than, of all things, mine, and, and then you will probably be less upset.

I don't mind Father when I consider him on his own, but I do mind him when I compare him with the great Father Millet, for instance. His doctrine is so great that Father's way of thinking looks extremely petty by comparison. Now you will think this is terrible of me – I can't help that – it is my deep conviction and I confess it freely, because <u>you</u> confuse <u>Father's</u> character with Corot's, for instance. How do I see Father? As someone with the same kind of character as <u>Corot's father</u> – but Father has nothing of Corot himself. Anyway, Corot loved his father, <u>but did not follow him</u>. I love Father, too, so long as my path is not made too difficult by differences of opinion. I do <u>not</u> love Father at the moment, when a certain petty-minded pride stands in the way of the generous and satisfactory accomplishment of a complete, permanent and most desirable reconciliation.

I had no intention whatever of putting you or Father to expense by the steps I had in mind when I came back home. On the contrary, I wanted to use the money to better advantage so that we should lose less, that is, less time, less money and less energy.

Am I to be blamed when I point to the Rappards who, although richer than Father or you or I, manage things more sensibly and get better results from acting in concord, though it is probably not always very easy for them either?

Am I to be blamed for wanting to put an end to the discord in the family with a 'thus far but no further'? In what respect am I wrong for wanting this to be brought about <u>thoroughly</u> and conclusively and for <u>not being content</u> with a <u>sham</u> or a too <u>half-hearted</u> reconciliation? Reconciliation with mental reservations, conditions, etc., bah! It just won't do. <u>Readily</u> or <u>not at all</u> – with empressement,[1] otherwise it is absolutely useless and worse may be expected.

You say you think it <u>cowardly</u> of me to rebel against Father. In the first place this is a verbal rebellion – no violence is involved. On the other hand it might be argued that I am all the sadder and more disappointed and speak all the more gravely and resolutely precisely because Father's grey hairs make it evident to me that the time left to us for reconciliation is perhaps, in truth, not very long. I do not much care for deathbed reconciliations, I prefer to see them <u>during life</u>.

I am quite prepared to grant that Father means well, but I should far rather it didn't stop at meaning well but might, <u>for once</u>, lead to a mutual understanding, though it has been left

[1] Eagerness.

very late. But I fear it will never happen! If you knew how sad I think that is, if you knew how much I grieve over it!

You say: Father has other things to think about – oh, really, well, to my mind those things preventing Father from thinking matters through, year in, year out, are quite <u>unimportant</u>. And that is just the point – Father doesn't feel that there is anything to be reconciled about or to be made up, Father has other things to think about – very well – leave him to his other things, I am beginning to tell myself. Are you, too, sticking to <u>your</u> 'other things'? Father says, 'We have always been good to you,' &c., and I say, 'Oh, really, you may be satisfied, I am not.'

Something better than the days of the Rijswijk mill – namely the same thing but for good and all – two poor brother artists – bound up in one and the same feeling, for one and the same nature and art – will it ever come to that? Or will the certain social position, the certain affluence, win the day? Oh, let them win it – but I foresee that it will only be for a while, that you will grow disillusioned with them before you are 30. And if not, well, if not – then, then, then – <u>tant pis</u>.[2] With a handshake,

Ever yours,
<u>Vincent</u>

[...]

[enclosed in letter 347]

Since writing the enclosed letter, I have thought some more about your remarks and have spoken to Father again. I had as good as made up my mind not to stay on here – regardless of how they might take it or what the result might be. But then the conversation took a fresh turn when I said, I have been here now for 14 days and feel I have got no further than during the first half hour, had we understood each other better we should have settled all sorts of things by now – I have no time to waste and

2 Too bad.

must reach a decision. A door has to be either open or shut, I cannot see how there can be anything in between, and in fact there cannot.

It all ended with the little room at home where the mangle now stands being put at my disposal for storing my bits and pieces and if need be for use as a studio too. And a start has been made with clearing the room, which had not been done while things were still in the air.

I want to tell you something that I appreciate better now than when I wrote to you what I thought about Father. My opinion has softened, not least because I can see that Father (and one of your hints seems to bear this out to some extent) is genuinely unable to follow me when I try to explain things to him. He hangs on to a <u>part</u> of what I say, and that makes no sense when it is taken out of context. This may all be due to more than one cause, but old age must bear most of the blame. Well, I respect old age and its weaknesses as much as <u>you</u> do, <u>even though</u> it may not seem so to you or you may not credit me with it. What I mean is that some of the things I should take amiss in a man in full possession of his mental powers, I shall probably put up with in Father's case – for the above-mentioned reasons.

I also thought of Michelet's saying (who had it from a zoologist), 'Le mâle est très sauvage'.[3] And because at this time of my life I know myself to have strong passions and believe that I should have them, I grant that I may well be 'très sauvage' myself. And yet my passion subsides when I face someone weaker than myself, and then I don't fight. Although, mark you, taking issue in <u>words</u> or over principles with a man who holds a position in society, and please note, as a guide to man's spiritual life, is not only permissible but cannot possibly be cowardly. After all, our weapons are equal.

Do please think it over, the more so as I tell you that for many reasons I want to give up even the verbal struggle, because it occasionally occurs to me that Father no longer has the full mental power it takes to concentrate one's thoughts on a single

3 The male is very savage.

point. Yet in some cases a man's age grants him additional power.

Getting to the heart of the matter, I take this opportunity of telling you that, in my view, it was Father's influence that made you concentrate on business more than is in your nature. And that I believe, no matter how certain you may now feel that you must remain a businessman, that a certain something in your original nature will <u>endure</u> and may well produce a stronger reaction than you bargain for.

Since I know that our thoughts coincided during our early days at G. & Cie, that is, that both you and I then thought of becoming painters but so deep down that we didn't dare tell even each other straight out, it might well happen, in these latter years, that we draw more closely together. The more so because of circumstances and conditions in the trade itself, which has undergone a change since our early years and in my view will change even more.

At the time I did violence to myself, and was moreover so oppressed by the preconception that I was no painter, that <u>even after I had left</u> G. & Cie, I never thought of becoming one but turned to something else (which was a second mistake on top of the first), feeling discouraged about my prospects because my timid, very timid, approaches to a few painters were not even acknowledged. I am telling you this, not because I want to <u>force</u> you to think as I do – I do not force anybody – but only out of a sense of fraternal and friendly concern.

My views may sometimes be incongruous, that may well be so, but I do believe that there must be some truth in them and in their action and direction.

It was not primarily for selfish reasons that I tried to get them to open up the house to me again, even to give me a studio. What I do feel is that, though we do not see eye to eye in many things, Father, you and I have the will to pull together, either all the time or by fits and starts. Our estrangement having already lasted so long, it can do no harm to place some weight on the other side, so that to the eyes of the world, too, we do not look more divided than we actually are, so that to the eyes of the world we do not seem to have gone to extremes.

Rappard said to me, 'A human being is not a lump of peat, since a human being cannot bear being flung into an attic to be forgotten there.' And he pointed out that he considered it a great misfortune for me not to be able to live at home. Do please give that some thought.

I believe a little too much emphasis has been laid on the charge that I acted wilfully or recklessly – well, you know that better than I do – when in fact I was forced to do certain things and could not act differently from the way they saw me act or wanted to see me act. And it was their biased view that my objectives were base, &c., which made me grow cold and feel quite indifferent towards many people.

One more thing, brother – at this time of your life you would do well to reflect deeply on this: I believe you are in danger of taking a distorted view of a great many things, and I think you will have to examine your perspective on life very carefully and that your <u>life will improve</u> as a result. I am not saying this as if it were something I know and you do not, I am saying it because I am coming to see more and more how terribly hard it is to tell where one goes right and where one goes wrong.

Partly under the influence of a letter from Anthon van Rappard, Van Gogh decided to remain in Nuenen, where he concentrated on painting weavers at work in their little cottages. At a time of growing industrialization, cottage weavers were becoming a dying race, and it was typical of Van Gogh's hankering after the authentic and original country life *à la* Millet that he should single out those old-fashioned 'contraptions of looms with their rather complicated machinery, and the small figure sitting in the middle'. Although the subject had been used by seventeenth-century painters and by contemporaries of Van Gogh's such as Liebermann and Sérusier, Van Gogh felt convinced that he was tackling an original theme. At the same time, he was worried about his mother, who had fractured her femur.

The mangle room in the parsonage at Nuenen, rather unfortunately placed between the sewer and the manure heap, was being converted into a studio. During a brief visit to The Hague, where Van Gogh saw to the removal of his prints, studies and other possessions, he found time for a final meeting with Sien: 'Now that we are separated, we shall remain separated, but in retrospect we regret not having chosen a middle path, and even now there is still a mutual attachment which has roots or foundations that are too deep to be transitory.'

Although Theo had helped him support Sien during the Hague period, it began to dawn on Vincent that his brother had also played a significant role in the breakup of the relationship. He now held Theo partly responsible for his departure for Drenthe. Finding Sien living 'in great misery', he came to realize how much power Theo exerted over him with his financial support.

In early March 1884, Vincent broached another delicate subject: how much effort had Theo really put into selling his work? And did Theo's remittances give him the right to make Vincent feel from time to time that he was calling the tune? Worse still, Vincent was gradually coming to think that there was a lack of even the slightest spark of warmth in their relationship: 'Now everything is getting grimmer and colder and more dreary around me.'

358 [D]

[*c.* 1 March 1884]

My dear Theo,

Thanks for your letter – Mother is doing well – at first the doctor said it would take half a year for the leg to heal – now he speaks of a good 3 months – and he told Mother, 'But we have your daughter to thank for that, for I have rarely, very rarely, come across care as good as she gives.' What Wil does is exemplary, exemplary, I shan't easily forget it.

Almost everything fell on her shoulders from the beginning and she has spared Mother a great deal of misery. To give just one example, it is undoubtedly thanks to her that Mother has so few bedsores (which had been absolutely dreadful in the beginning and in quite an advanced condition). And I assure you that the chores she has to do are not always pleasant.

Now look, when I read your letter about the drawings I immediately sent you a new watercolour of a weaver and five pen drawings. I must also tell you frankly that for my part I'm sure you're right to say that my work must improve a great deal, but at the same time I also think that your efforts to do something with it could become a bit more determined. You have never yet sold a single thing I have done – whether for a lot or a little – in fact, you haven't even tried.

Look, I'm not angry about it, but we need to speak our minds now for once. I could certainly not put up with it in the long run. You, for your part, can also continue to speak frankly.

As far as saleability or unsaleability is concerned, that's a dead horse I don't intend to go on flogging. Anyway, as you can see, my answer is to send you some new ones – and I shall be very happy to go on doing so – I should like nothing better. Only be unsparing for once with your candour – which is what I much prefer – about whether you intend to bother with them or whether your dignity will not allow you. Leaving the past aside, I have to face the future, and regardless of what you think about them I shall definitely try to do something with them.

The other day you told me yourself that you are a dealer – all right – one does not indulge in sentimentality with a dealer, one says, 'Sir, if I give you some drawings on commission, may I then count on your showing them?' The dealer must know for himself whether his answer will be yes, no, or something in between. But the painter would be mad to send them on commission if he could tell that the dealer looked on his work as something that ought not to see the light of day.

Well, my dear fellow, we both live in the real world, and precisely because we do not want to put a spoke in each other's wheel we must speak candidly. If you say, 'I can't be bothered with them' – all right, I won't be angry, but I'm not obliged to take you for an infallible oracle either, am I? You say the public will take offence at this little smudge or that, &c., &c. Now listen, that may well be true, but you, the dealer, are even more upset by that sort of thing than the public in question, as I have observed so often, and you <u>set out</u> with that idea.

I, too, must make my way somehow or other, Theo, and with you I am still in precisely – precisely – the same position I was a few years ago. What you say about my current work – 'it is <u>almost</u> saleable, <u>but</u>' – is <u>literally the same thing you wrote to me when I sent you my first Brabant sketches from Etten</u>.

That's why I tell you – it's a dead horse. And I have to conclude that you'll go on saying the same thing for ever – and that I, who have been consistently chary of going to the dealers up to now, am going to have to change my tactics and try my very best to get my work sold.

It's become very clear to me by this time that you couldn't care less about my doings, but while you couldn't care less, I cannot help thinking it is rather wretched of you, and I dread certain things that are bound to occur – namely that people will say, how strange, don't you do any business with your brother or with Goupil? Well, what I'll say then, is – it is beneath the dignity of Ces Messieurs[1] G. & Cie, Van Gogh & Cie. That may well give them a bad impression of me – for which I am quite prepared by now – but I also foresee that I shall grow cooler and cooler towards you.

I have now painted the little old church, and another weaver. Are those studies from Drenthe as bad as all that? I don't feel disposed to send you the painted studies I have done here, no, we won't start with them – you can see them if you come here in the spring.

What you write about Marie is quite understandable – if a woman isn't all milk & water, I can well imagine her not showing much enthusiasm for moping about in the company of cantankerous fathers as well as spiritual sisters. In any event, a woman no less than a man would feel sorely tempted to end the stagnation quand même[2] – stagnation which may start out as splendid resignation, but which, alas, one will generally be made

1 Those Messrs.
2 For all that.

to regret as soon as one feels one is going to freeze solid in the end. Once I read a passage by Daudet about spiritual women. 'Ces deux visages se regardèrent – elles échangèrent un regard méchant froid fermé – qu'a-t-il? Toujours la même chose – elle.'³ There you have it, that singular look of Pharisees and devout ladies. Yes, and as for us – what's always the matter with us, too, is – la même chose.

So, what am I to make of what you say about my work – say, the studies from Drenthe. Some of them are very superficial, and I said as much myself. But why do I get chided for those painted out of doors, quietly, calmly and simply, in which I was trying <u>to express nothing but what I saw</u>? What I get is: aren't you too obsessed with Michel?*

You would no doubt say exactly the same thing about the old churchyard. And yet, faced neither by the churchyard nor by the turf huts did I think of Michel, I was thinking of the subject I had before me. A subject that I believe would indeed have stopped Michel short, and touched him, had he passed by.

As far as I am concerned, in no way do I put myself on a par with Master Michel – and I most certainly do not <u>imitate</u> Michel either.

Well, perhaps I shall try to sell something in Antwerp, and I'm going to put a few of those very same Drenthe studies in a black wooden frame – I'm approaching a carpenter here about it – I prefer to see my work in a deep black frame, and he makes them cheaply enough.

Don't take offence at my mentioning it, brother. I am trying to put something quiet and calm into my work. You see, I approve <u>just as little</u> of it lying about unseen as I would of seeing it displayed in fluted frames in the leading shops.

* I am referring here to the study of the cottage at dusk and to the largest of the turf huts, namely the one with the small green field in the foreground.

3 Those two faces looked at each other – they exchanged a spiteful, cold, secretive glance – what is the matter? Always the same thing – she is.

Now is the time to start taking that middle course, in my view, so I must know fairly definitely how I stand with you, or rather I must tell you again that, although you are still evading the question, I'm sure that you are <u>not</u>, in fact, going to show the work, and I don't think you'll be changing your mind for the time being either. I won't enter into whether or not you are right about this.

You will tell me that other dealers will treat me in just the same way, except that you, although you cannot be bothered yourself with my work, nevertheless provide me with money, and other dealers will certainly not do that, and that without money I shall be completely stuck. I shall reply that things are not as cut and dried as that in real life, and that I shall try to get by, living from day to day.

I told you beforehand that I wanted to settle matters this month, and so I must. Anyway, seeing that you may already be planning to come here in the spring, I am not going to insist that you take a final decision <u>immediately</u>, but I must tell you that as far as I am concerned, I cannot leave matters as they are. Everywhere I go, and especially at home, a constant watch is being kept on what I do with my work, whether I get anything for it, &c. In our society virtually everybody looks out all the time for that sort of thing, trying to find out everything about it. And that's quite understandable. But being permanently in a false position is a wretched business for me. Allons[4] – things cannot be allowed to remain as they are. Why not? Because they can't, that's why.

Seeing that I am as cool as can be towards Father, towards C. M. – why should I act any differently towards you, once I've noticed that you use the same tactics of never speaking your mind? Do I consider myself better than Father or you? Most probably not, most probably I distinguish less and less between good and bad – but I do know that this tactic does not behove a painter, and as a painter one should speak one's mind and cut through a few knots. Well, I believe qu'une porte doit être ouverte ou fermée.[5]

4 Come now.
5 That a door must be either open or closed.

Anyway, I'm sure you do understand that a dealer <u>cannot</u> be neutral towards painters – that it makes <u>absolutely</u> no difference whether you say no with or without beating about the bush, and that it's probably even more annoying when you dress it all up in compliments.

This may be something you'll understand better later on than you do at the moment. I pity dealers when they grow old – though they may feather their own nest, that isn't any cure-all, at least it won't be by then. Tout se paye,[6] and things can often turn out to be an icy-cold wasteland <u>then</u>.

But you may perhaps have different ideas about this. You may point out that it's a bit sad as well when a painter dies miserably in hospital and is buried alongside the whores in the fosse commune,[7] where many lie, après tout[8] – especially when one bears in mind that dying is perhaps not as difficult as living.

Anyway, a dealer can't be blamed for not always having the money to help out, but in my opinion a certain worthy dealer can indeed be blamed if he's all kind words but is ashamed of me in his heart and ignores my work altogether.

So, frankly, I shall not blame you for telling me candidly that you don't think my work is good enough, or perhaps that there are other reasons why you cannot be bothered with it, but if you put it away in a corner somewhere and do not show it, it isn't kind to couple that with the assurance – <u>which is not accepted</u> – that you yourself see something in it. I don't believe it – you mean hardly one word of it. And from the very fact that you yourself say that you know my work better than anyone else, I am entitled to conclude that you must have a very poor opinion of it indeed if you won't soil your hands with it. Why should I force myself upon you? Well, regards.

Ever yours,
<u>Vincent</u>

6 Everything has its price.
7 Common grave.
8 After all.

Apart from a few years which I can scarcely comprehend myself, when I was confused by religious ideas, by some kind of mysticism – that period aside, I have always lived with a certain warmth. Now everything is getting grimmer and colder and more dreary around me. And when I tell you that in the first place I <u>will</u> not stand it, quite apart from the question of whether or not I <u>can</u>, I am referring to what I told you at the very beginning of our relationship.

What I have had against you this past year is a kind of relapse into cold respectability which seems to me sterile and futile – the diametrical opposite of everything that is active, and of everything that is artistic in particular.

I am putting this to you bluntly, not in order to make you miserable, but so that you can see, and if possible feel, what has gone wrong, why I can no longer think of you as a brother and a friend with the same pleasure as before.

There needs to be more gusto in my life if I am to get more brio into my brush – exercising patience will not get me a hair's breadth further. If you, for your part, do relapse into the above-mentioned state, don't blame me for not being the same towards you as I was during, say, the first year.

As to my drawings – at this moment it seems to me that the watercolours, the pen-and-ink drawings of weavers, the latest pen-and-ink drawings on which I am working now, are not on the whole so boring as to be utterly worthless. But <u>if</u> I should come to the conclusion myself that they are no good and Theo is right not to show them to anybody – then, then, it will be <u>one proof more</u> to me that I am right to object to our present false position, and I shall try all the harder to make a change quand même, for better or for worse, just as long as things don't remain the same ...

Now supposing I realized that you, in the belief that I had not yet made enough progress, were trying to do something to further that progress – for instance, Mauve having fallen by the wayside, to put me in touch with some other able painter – or, anyway, <u>something</u>, some sign or other that would prove to me that you really believed in my progress or had it at heart. But instead there is – the money, yes – but for the rest nothing but 'just carry on working', 'have patience', as cold, as dead, as arid and as insufferable as if Father, for instance, had said it. I cannot live on that, it is getting too lonely, too cold, too empty and too dull for me.

I am no better than the next man, inasmuch as I have the same needs and desires as everyone else, and it is perfectly natural for one to kick when one <u>knows for certain</u> that one is being kept dangling, being kept in the dark. If one goes from bad to worse – which is not impossible in my case – what difference does that make? If one is badly off, one simply must take the chance to better one's lot.

Brother, let me remind you once more how things stood with us when we first started together. I even felt free to draw your attention to the problem of women. I still remember taking you to Roosendaal station that first year and telling you then that I was so set against being alone that I would sooner be with a bad whore than be alone. You may perhaps remember that.

At first the idea that our relationship might not last was all but intolerable to me. And I would have been tremendously pleased if it had been a simple matter to change things. But I <u>cannot</u> keep flying in the face of the evidence and fooling myself that it <u>is</u>. The resulting depression was one of the causes for my writing from Drenthe and urging you so strongly to become a painter. And it subsided the moment I saw that your dissatisfaction with business had disappeared, that you were once again on a better footing with Goupil. At first I thought that less than sincere of you – then later, and even now, I find it entirely understandable and consider it more a mistake on my part to have written, 'become a painter', than a mistake on your part to have resumed your business with gusto once things had become more acceptable and the machinations to make things impossible for you had ceased.

It remains a fact, however, that I do feel depressed about the falseness of the position between us. At this moment it is of greater importance to me to sell for 5 guilders than to receive 10 guilders by way of patronage.

Now you have repeatedly written, very firmly, that neither in the first place as a dealer (I shall leave it at that for the moment and do not at any rate hold it against you), nor in the second place in your private capacity (which I do hold against you a little), have you taken, are you taking, or do you think you will be able to take for some time to come, the very slightest, smallest possible, step to further my work.

I mustn't be supine or spineless about this, so, to be blunt: <u>if you do nothing with my work, I do not want your patronage</u>. I state the reason plainly, the more so as I can hardly avoid giving you some explanation for it. So it is not that I am overlooking the help you have given me since the beginning or wish to belittle it. The fact is that I see more good in the most miserable, most wretched drudgery than in <u>patronage</u>, into which matters are degenerating. In the very, very beginning one cannot do without it, but for heaven's sake, it is time for me to try and muddle along, God knows how, rather than acquiesce in something that, after all, will get us <u>no further</u>.

Whether brotherly or otherwise, if you can do absolutely nothing except give financial assistance, you might as well keep that to yourself too. As matters are now, and have been during the past <u>year</u>, they have, if I may say so, been exclusively confined to money. And though you say you leave me completely free, it seems to me that ultimately, for example, if I keep company with a woman of whom you and others do not approve, perhaps rightly, though <u>sometimes</u> I don't give a damn about that, there is a small tug at the purse strings to make me feel that it is 'in my own interests' to defer to your opinion.

When it came to that business with the woman, you also had your way, and it came to an end, but ... I'm damned if I'll practise morality in order to get a little bit of money. Yet in itself I don't think it was absurd of you to disapprove when I wanted to go through with it last summer. But I can foresee the following in the future: I shall again have a relationship with someone from what you people call the lower orders – and, should I still have a relationship with you, meet with the same opposition. Opposition from all of you that might have some semblance of justification if I were given enough money to live differently. Which is what you do not, cannot or will not give, après tout – neither you nor Father nor C. M. nor any of the others who are in the forefront when it comes to disapproving of this or that, and which I don't want from you, après tout, seeing that I don't give a great deal of thought to the question of lower or upper orders.

Do you see why I wasn't being foolhardy, and wouldn't be if I tried the same thing again? Firstly, because I have no pretensions, <u>do not feel the slightest</u> urge to maintain any sort of position in society or whatever you call it, and secondly because, as I do not receive the necessary means from anyone, nor do I earn them, I consider myself absolutely free to consort with the so-called lower orders if the opportunity should arise.

We should be perpetually coming back to the same problem. Now, just ask yourself if I am alone among those in my trade who most resolutely refuse the kind of patronage that entails being obliged to keep up some sort of position while the money is below the requisite level, so that they incur debts instead of making progress. Could it be done on the money, I might perhaps knuckle under like so many others. But we have certainly not reached that point yet – as you said yourself, I still have a good many years to get through during which my work will have precious little commercial value. All right – then I would rather end up having to eke out a living and manger de la vache enragée[9] than fall into the hands of Messrs van Gogh.

My only regret about quarrelling with Father at the time is that I didn't do it 10 years earlier. If you continue to follow in the footsteps of Father, &c., you will find yourself gradually getting bored – and becoming boring to certain people. But those are 'mauvais coucheurs'[10] you will say, people who carry no weight.

Just think it over, my dear fellow – I do not hide my innermost thoughts from you – I weigh the pros and cons on

9 To go through hard times.
10 Awkward customers.

both sides. A <u>wife</u> you cannot give me, a <u>child</u> you cannot give me, <u>work</u> you cannot give me. Money, yes – but what good is that to me? If I have to forgo the rest, your money remains sterile, because it is not used in the way I have always told you it should be – a working man's household if needs be, but if one doesn't make sure of having a home of one's own, then art cannot flourish.

And as for me – I told you plainly enough, to be sure, in my younger days: if I cannot get a good woman, I shall take a bad one, better a bad one than none at all. I know enough people who profess the exact opposite and who are as frightened of 'children' as I am of 'no children'.

And as for me – just because something often goes wrong – I do not give a principle up lightly. And the reason why I have few fears for the future is because I know how and why I have acted in the past. And because I know that there are others who feel the way I do.

You say that you are suspicious – but why, of what, and what good will it do you or me? Do you grow wiser by being suspicious? I hope you realize that the contrary is true – but again, it is loyal of you to admit that you are suspicious – and that is why I reply, something that would otherwise have been beneath me. And my reply is very short: I mean neither you, nor Father nor anyone else any harm, but I am very seriously thinking of deciding to part company with you and of seeking a new relationship, precisely with a view to preventing further harm. Sooner or later we would clash as Father and I have clashed <u>and then I could not allow myself to yield</u>. Voilà tout,[11] on the one hand my duty commands me to love my father and my brother – <u>which I do</u> – but we are living in an age of renewal and reform and many things have become completely outmoded, and consequently I see, I feel, I believe differently from Father, differently from you. And because I try to distinguish between the good as an abstract ideal and my own imperfect self, I do not come out with big words, but simply say, the way to stay good

11 That's all.

friends is – to part company. It is a hard thing for me to say, but I am reconciled to it.

You will probably gather that though I may be unclear about the future, I am not afraid. And am even in a very tranquil frame of mind. And yet, there is a great deal going on inside me, in part from a keen sense of obligation, which is certain to persist – and on the other hand from a feeling of disappointment, seeing that the reasons why my career must be broken off as it began, namely with your help and support, strike me as being utterly absurd.

Still, it would be wrong to carry on, since – if we did – we should most probably have a violent quarrel in a few years' time, and it might end in hatred. Now I still have time to look around – and if I should be forced to do battle elsewhere, then at least it will not be with my brother. And – isn't that looking at things coolly and weighing up the pros and cons?

I shan't be depressed as a result, believe me, but neither am I being reckless. I have found peace of mind now that I have resolved on a separation, because I am convinced that if we went on as before, we should later become a hindrance to each other rather than a help.

Rappard said, don't go to Antwerp before you are sure of finding something there – but how can one tell in ad ...nce what one may come across? And if I keep my studio here as a bolthole, then now is the time to make a start. It will always be there, so it is certainly not my immediate intention to turn my back on these parts completely.

You probably realize, Theo, that on my long walks I have thought things over at length and often. I don't want to get embroiled in a second series of quarrels, of the kind I had with Father I, with Father II – Father II being yourself. One is enough. That phrase is planted fair and square at the centre of my thoughts – draw your own conclusions.

What's more, let me also tell you that I never behaved aggressively towards Father, nor do I want to be aggressive towards you, my brother. I have often restrained myself – when with strangers I would have fought quite differently and more fiercely.

But this is just what ties my hands in the circumstances. There is a new field over there for me and one where I can do as I please, as a stranger among strangers – over there, I shall have neither rights nor duties. And shall be able to be more offhand – bonne volonté d'être inoffensif, certitude de résister,[12] that is my goal and I am in search of it with all there is in me.

But taking everything lying down has to be paid for later – so – one has to act. Working here and looking for new contacts is the way forward. Unfortunately money is needed for both and the prospects for making a breakthrough are poor. And – time is money, too – and by carrying on as I am now I shall not get any richer.

But now you know my motives – if I should go on, you would become Father II in my life, and although I know that you mean well – you don't understand me at all and so no headway can be made.

While his relationship with his brother remained under great strain and Van Gogh ranked the associated emotions among 'things without pith', his letters to Van Rappard increasingly served as a vehicle for his thoughts on art. He sent his friend drawings and copied out innumerable poems by François Coppée and Jules Breton. They exchanged ideas on art criticism and above all on the relativity of the concept of 'technique'. Central to an understanding of Van Gogh's views is the passage in which he states that 'art is something which, though produced by human hands, is not wrought by hands alone, but wells up from a deeper source, from man's soul [...].' It was that dimension in a work of art that caused Van Gogh, in addition to his purely factual account, to give this description of a weaver at his loom: 'Whenever that black monster of grimy oak, with all its slats, stands out starkly against the greyness in which it is set, then right in the very middle of it there sits a black ape or hobgoblin or spook making a clatter with those slats from early morning till late at night.'

---

12 Willingness not to cause offence, confidence to stand firm.

R43 [D] [letter from Vincent to Anthon van Rappard]

[second half of March 1884]

Dear friend Rappard,

Many thanks for your letter, which I was pleased to get. I was very glad to hear that you saw something in my drawings.

I shan't enter into generalities concerning technique, but I certainly foresee that as I gain more of what I shall call expressive force, people will say not <u>less</u> but <u>even</u> more than they do now that I have <u>no</u> technique.

Hence I absolutely agree with you that what I am saying in my present work will have to be said more <u>forcefully</u>, and I am working hard to strengthen that aspect, but – that the general public will understand me better <u>when I do</u> – no.

That doesn't alter the fact that, in my view, the reasoning of the artless fellow who asked of your work, 'Does he paint for money?', is the reasoning of a bloody idiot, since this intelligent creature evidently considers it axiomatic that originality prevents one from making money with one's work. Trying to pass this off as an <u>axiom</u>, <u>because</u> it can decidedly <u>not</u> be proved as a <u>proposition</u>, is, as I said, a common trick of bloody idiots and idle little Jesuits.

Do you really think I don't care about technique or that I don't try for it? Oh, but I do, although only inasmuch as it allows me to say what I want to say (and if I cannot do that yet, or not yet perfectly, I am working hard to improve), but I don't give a damn whether my language matches that of the rhetoricians (you remember making the comparison: if someone had something useful, true and necessary to say but said it in terms that were hard to understand, what good would that be to the speaker or to his audience?).

Let me just hold on to this point – the more so as I have often come across a rather peculiar historical phenomenon. Don't misunderstand me: it goes without saying that one must speak in the mother tongue of one's audience, if that audience knows one language only, and it would be absurd not to take that for granted.

But now for the second part of the question. Suppose a man has something to say and says it in a language in which his audience, too, is at home. Time and again we shall find that the speaker of truth lacks oratorical style and does not appeal to the greater part of his audience, indeed, is scorned as a man 'slow of tongue' and despised as such. He can count himself lucky if he can edify just one, or at best a very few, with what he says, because those few are not interested in oratorical tirades, but positively listen out for the true, useful, necessary content of the words, which enlighten them, broaden their minds, make them freer or more intelligent.

And now for the painters – is it the object and the 'non plus ultra' of art to produce those peculiar smudges of colour, that waywardness in the drawing – that are known as the refinement of technique? Certainly not. Take a Corot, a Daubigny, a Dupré, a Millet or an Israëls – men who are certainly the great forerunners – well, their work goes beyond the paint, standing out from that of the fashionable crowd as much as an oratorical tirade by, say, a Numa Roumestan differs from a prayer or a good poem.

So the reason why one must work on one's technique is simply to express better, more accurately, more profoundly what one feels, and the less verbiage the better. As for the rest, one need not bother with it.

Why I say this is because I think I have noticed that you sometimes disapprove of things in your own work which in my opinion are rather good. In my view, your technique is better than, say, Haverman's, because your brushstroke often has an individual, distinctive, reasoned and deliberate touch, while what one invariably gets with Haverman is convention, redolent at all times of the studio, and never of nature.

For instance, those sketches of yours I saw, the little weaver and the Terschelling women, appeal to me, they are a stab at the core of things. All I get with Haverman is a feeling of malaise and boredom, little else.

I am afraid that you – and I congratulate you on it – are going to hear the same remarks about your technique in the future <u>as well</u>, and about your subjects and ... about everything, in fact, even when that brushstroke of yours, which has so much character already, acquires still more of it. <u>Yet there are</u> art lovers who, après tout,[1] appreciate most what has been painted with emotion. Although we no longer live in the days of Thoré and Théophile Gautier, alas.

Just consider whether it is sensible to talk a great deal about technique nowadays. You will say that I myself am doing just that – as a matter of fact, I regret it. But as far as I am concerned, I am determined, <u>even</u> when I shall be much more master of my brush than I am now – to go on telling people methodically <u>that I cannot paint</u>. Do you understand? <u>Even when</u> I have achieved a solid manner of my own, more complete and concise than the present one.

I liked what Herkomer said when he opened up his own art school to a number of people <u>who already knew how to paint</u> – he urged his students to be kind enough <u>not</u> to paint the way he did but in their own way. 'My aim,' he said, 'is to set original forms free, not to recruit disciples for Herkomer's <u>doctrine</u>.' Entre lions on ne singe pas.[2]

Anyway, I've been painting quite a bit lately, a seated girl winding shuttles for the weavers and a weaver on his own. I'm rather anxious that you should see my painted studies one of these days – not because I'm satisfied with them but because I think they'll convince you that I really am keeping my hand in, and that when I say that I set relatively little store by technique, it's not because I'm trying to save myself trouble or to avoid problems, for that is not my way.

Apart from that, I am looking forward to your getting to know this corner of Brabant some day – in my opinion it is much more beautiful than the Breda side.

These last few days it has been delightful. There is a village here, <u>Son en Breugel</u>, which bears an amazing resemblance to

1 When all is said and done.
2 Lions do not ape one another.

Courrières, where the Bretons live – though the figures are even more beautiful over there. As one's love for the <u>form</u> grows, one may well come to dislike 'the Dutch national costume', as it's called in the photograph albums they sell to foreigners.

I detest writing or talking about <u>technique</u> in general, Rappard – though I may occasionally get the urge none the less to discuss how to execute some idea or other of mine, be it with you or with someone else, and I never make light of the practical value of such discussions. But that doesn't gainsay my first thought – which I may not have expressed properly.

That thought, I can't find the right words, is based not on something negative but on something positive. On the positive awareness that art is something greater and higher than our own skill or knowledge or learning. That art is something which, though produced by human hands, is not wrought by hands alone, but wells up from a deeper source, from man's soul, while much of the proficiency and technical expertise associated with art reminds me of what would be called self-righteousness in religion.

My strongest sympathies in the literary as well as in the artistic field are with those artists in whom I see the soul at work most strongly – Israëls, for example, is clever as a technician, but so is Vollon – but I like Israëls more than Vollon because I see something more in Israëls, something quite different from the masterly reproduction of the materials, something quite different from light and brown, something quite different from the colour – yet that something quite different is achieved by the precise rendering of the light effect, the material, the colour.

This something different of which I find so much more in Israëls than in Vollon is pronounced in Eliot, and Dickens has it as well. Does it lie in their choice of subjects? <u>No</u>, for that, too, is only an <u>effect</u>.

What I am driving at, among other things, is that while Eliot is masterly in her execution, above and beyond that she also has a genius all of her own, about which I would say, perhaps one improves through reading these books, or perhaps these books have the power to make one sit up and take notice.

In spite of myself I keep writing about exhibitions, though actually I give them precious little thought. Now that by chance I do happen to be thinking about them, I am examining my thoughts with some surprise. I should not be expressing them fully enough if I didn't add that in some pictures there is something so thoroughly honest and good that no matter what is done with them – whether they end up in good or in bad, in honest or dishonest hands – something good emanates from them. 'Let your light shine before men,' is, I believe, the duty of every painter, but in my view does not mean that letting the light shine before men must be done through exhibitions. Believe me, I just wish there were <u>more</u> and <u>better</u> opportunities than exhibitions to bring art to the people. Far from wanting to hide the light under a bushel, I would sooner let it be seen. Well, enough of this.

I have recently been reading Eliot's Felix Holt, the Radical. This book has been very well translated into Dutch. I hope you know it. If you don't, see if you can get hold of it. It somewhere contains certain views of life that I find outstandingly good – profound things expressed in a droll way. It is a book written with great verve, and various scenes are described as Frank Holl or someone similar might have drawn them. The way of thinking and the outlook are similar. There are not many writers as utterly sincere and good as Eliot. This book, The Radical, is not as well known in Holland as, say, her Adam Bede, and her Scenes from Clerical Life are not all that well known either – more's the pity, much as it's a great pity that not everyone knows Israëls's work.

I am enclosing a little booklet on Corot, which I believe you will read with pleasure if you don't know it already. It contains a number of accurate biographical details. I saw the exhibition at the time for which this is the catalogue.

It's remarkable, I think, that this man should have taken so long to settle down and mature. Just look what he did at different periods of his life. I saw things in the first of his <u>real</u> contributions – the result of years of study – that were as honest as the day is long, thoroughly sound – but how people must have despised them! For me Corot's <u>studies</u> were a lesson when I saw them, and I was even then struck by the difference between them and the studies of many other landscape painters. I would compare <u>your</u> little country churchyard with them, if I didn't find <u>more technique</u> in it than in Corot's studies. The sentiment is identical, an endeavour to render only what is intimate and essential.

The gist of what I am saying in this letter is this. Let us try to grasp the secrets of technique so well that people will be taken in and swear by all that is holy that we have no technique. Let our work be so savant[3] that it <u>seems</u> naïve and does not reek of our cleverness. I do <u>not</u> believe that <u>I</u> have reached this desirable point, and I do not believe that even <u>you</u>, who are more advanced than I, have reached it yet.

I hope you'll see something more than verbal nitpicking in this letter.

I believe that the more contact one has with nature herself, the more deeply one delves into her, the less attracted one is by all the trucs d'atelier[4] and yet I do want to give them their due and <u>watch</u> them painting. I often look forward to visiting studios myself.

'Not in books have I found it. And from the "learned", ah, but little have I learned,' says De Genestet, as you know. By way of a variation one might say, 'Not in the studio have I found it, and from painters/connoisseurs, ah, but little have I learned.' Perhaps you are shocked to find me putting in painters or connoisseurs indiscriminately.

But to change the subject, it is fiendishly difficult not to feel anything, not to be affected when those bloody idiots say 'does he paint for money?' One hears that drivel day in, day out, and one gets angry with oneself later for having taken it to heart. That's how it is with me – and I think it must be much the same with you. One doesn't really care a rap, but it gets on one's nerves all the same, just like listening to off-key singing or being

3 Skilful.
4 Tricks of the studio.

pursued by a malicious barrel organ. Don't you find that to be true of the barrel organ, and that it always seems to have picked on you in particular? For wherever one goes, it's the same old tune.

As for me, I'm going to do what I tell you: when people say something or other to me, I shall finish their sentences even before they are out – in the same way as I treat someone I know to be in the habit of extending his finger to me instead of his hand (I tried the trick on a venerable colleague of my father's yesterday) – I too have a single finger ready and, with an absolutely straight face, carefully touch his with it when we shake hands, in such a way that the man cannot take exception, yet realizes that I am giving as good as I damned well got. The other day I put a fellow's back up with something similar. Does one lose anything as a result? No, for to be sure, such people are sent to try us, and when I write to you about certain expressions of yours I do so only in order to ask you: are you certain that those who are so loud in their praises of technique are de bonne foi?[5] I'm only asking because I know that your aim is to avoid studio chic.

Van Gogh remained dissatisfied with his brother's ineffectual attempts to sell his work. For the time being he resigned himself to the situation, but in early April 1884, he managed to wring a form of contract out of Theo. They agreed that what money Theo sent his brother would no longer be considered 'a handout to a poor beggar' but a business transaction, namely payment for the work Vincent would be sending Theo month by month. Vincent, for his part, stated: 'That work will then be your property, as you say – and I completely agree with you that you will then be fully entitled to put it to one side – indeed, I should not even be able to object if you saw fit to tear it up.'

Van Gogh spent the summer of 1884 recording the landscape all round Nuenen. 'And reality sometimes comes very close to the Brabant of our dreams.' In the middle of May the Protestant pastor's son

5 Of good faith.

abandoned the little mangle room and rented two adjoining rooms in the Roman Catholic presbytery, there to set up a somewhat more spacious studio.

Van Gogh had a keen eye not only for the weavers but also for the beauty of nature in his immediate surroundings. He painted the presbytery garden and the little church in which his father preached, and made short excursions to paint the striking water-mills in the neighbourhood. During this first part of his stay in Brabant, he again immersed himself in Sensier's biography of Millet, which strengthened his resolve to become a painter of peasant life. In addition, he read a great deal on the theory of colours: 'The colour <u>laws</u> are unutterably beautiful, precisely because they are <u>not accidental</u>. Just as people have ceased to believe in arbitrary <u>miracles</u>, in a God who capriciously and despotically changes his mind, but are beginning to be filled with greater respect and admiration for, and faith in, nature, so also, & for the same reasons, I think that the old-fashioned ideas in art of innate genius, inspiration, &c., must be, I would not say discarded, but re-examined closely, verified and – modified very considerably.'

In August he met 'someone in Eindhoven who wants to decorate a dining room'. Van Gogh was now able to put his experience to practical use and suggested to the man, one Antoon Hermans, that he choose six representations from peasant life in the Meijerij (the area around 's-Hertogenbosch). Van Gogh himself designed the compositions and made the preliminary oil sketches, but his client, who was an amateur painter, insisted on painting the final panels himself.

Having read about Van Gogh's final meeting with Sien, in the late summer of 1884, we are quite unprepared for the new sentimental attachment he had meanwhile formed, and its dramatic denouement. Though the relationship between Vincent and Margot Begemann, his next-door neighbour in Nuenen, had become quite a close one, her sisters fiercely opposed any possible marriage.

Margot sought a way out of this dilemma by taking poison. The suicide attempt was unsuccessful, however, and she was placed under the care of a doctor in Utrecht, where Van Gogh visited her. From his response to a letter from Theo which has been lost, it seems that he felt fate had once again driven him into a corner, from which he now defended his worship of 'the love which they, the theologians, call <u>sin</u>'.

Even in these dramatic circumstances, Van Gogh could not contemplate his situation without drawing parallels with famous passages in literature. In reply to a letter in which Theo had obviously identified himself with the art dealer Octave Mouret, the eponymous hero of Zola's novel, Vincent compared Margot Begemann's attempted suicide with that of Madame Bovary. His next few letters to Theo were full of indignation at what 'present-day Christianity' was doing to man's talents, 'though its founder was sublime'. Van Gogh also continued to voice his regrets about his dependence and his inability to do anything to change his financial situation.

378 [D]

[October 1884]

My dear Theo,

Thanks for your letter, thanks for the enclosure.

Now look here. What you say is all very well and good, but as for scandal, I'm somewhat better prepared now than I used to be to nip it in the bud. No fear that Father and Mother might leave, for example. Although they have only just received a new call. (Father and Mother could, if anything, consolidate their position here, if they managed things properly.)

Now, there are people saying to me, 'Why did you have anything to do with her?' – that's one fact. And there are people saying to her, 'Why did you have anything to do with him?' – that's another fact.

Apart from that, both she and I have grief enough and trouble enough, but as for regrets – neither of us has any. Look here – I believe without question, or have the certain knowledge, that she loves me. I believe without question, or have the certain knowledge, that I love her. It has been sincerely meant. But has it also been foolish, etc.?

Perhaps, if you like – but aren't the wise ones, those who never do anything foolish, even more foolish in my eyes than I am in theirs? That's my reply to your argument and to other people's arguments. I say all this simply by way of explanation, not out of ill-will or spite.

You say that you like Octave Mouret, you say that you are like him. I've read the second volume too, since last year, and like him much better in that than I did in the first. The other day I heard it said that 'Au bonheur des dames' would not add greatly to Zola's reputation. I consider it contains some of his greatest and best things. I have just looked it up and am copying out a few of Octave Mouret's words for you.

Don't you think you've been moving in Bourdoncle's direction during the last 1½ years or so? You would have done better to stick to 'Mouret', that was and still is my opinion. Save for the enormous difference in circumstances, indeed, the diametrically opposed circumstances, I actually lean more in the direction of Mouret than you might think – when it comes to belief in women and the realization that one needs them, must love them. Mouret says, 'Chez nous on aime la clientèle.'[1] Do give this some thought – and remember my regret when you said you had 'cooled off'.

I now repeat more emphatically than ever everything I said by way of bitter warning against the influence of what I called Guizot-esqueness. Why? It leads to mediocrity. And I don't want to see you among the mediocrities, because I have loved you too much, indeed still do, to bear watching you petrify. I know things are difficult, I know that I know too little about you, I know that I may be mistaken. But anyway, do read your Mouret again.

I mentioned the difference and yet the parallels between Mouret and what I should like. Now look. Mouret worships the modern Parisian woman – fine. But Millet and Breton [worship] the peasant woman with the same passion. The two passions are one and the same.

Read Zola's description of women in a room in the twilight – most of the women aged between 30 to 50 – such a sombre, mysterious place. I find it splendid, indeed sublime.

1 At our place we love the clients.

But to me, Millet's Angélus is just as sublime, with that same twilight, that same boundless emotion – or that single figure of Breton's in the Luxembourg, or his Source.

You will say that I am not a success – vaincre or être vaincu,[2] it doesn't matter to me, one has feeling and movement in any event, and they are more akin than they may seem to be or than can be put into words.

As for this particular woman, it remains a mystery how it will turn out, but neither she nor I will do anything stupid. I am afraid that the old religion will once again benumb her and freeze her with that damnable icy coldness that broke her once before, many years ago, to the point of death.

Oh, I am no friend of present-day Christianity, though its founder was sublime – I have seen through present-day Christianity only too well. That icy coldness mesmerized even me, in my youth – but I have taken my revenge since then. How? By worshipping the love which they, the theologians, call sin, by respecting a whore, etc., and not too many would be[3] respectable, pious ladies. To some, woman is heresy and diabolical. To me she is the opposite.

Regards,

Ever yours,
Vincent

Here you are, from Octave Mouret.

Mouret dit: 'Si tu te crois fort, parce que tu refuses d'être bête et de souffrir! Eh bien – alors tu n'es qu'une dupe, pas davantage.'

'Tu t'amuses?'

Mouret ne parut pas comprendre tout de suite, mais lorsqu'il se fut rappelé leurs conversations anciennes sur la bêtise vide et l'inutile torture de la vie, il répondit: 'Sans doute – jamais je n'ai tant vécu … Ah! mon vieux – ne te moques pas! Ce sont les heures les plus courtes où l'on meurt de souffrance.'

---

2 To conquer [or] to be conquered.
3 'would be': in English.

Je la veux, je l'aurai!... et – s'il [*sic*] elle m'échappe tu verras les choses que je ferai pour m'en guérir – Tu n'entends pas cette langue, mon vieux; autrement tu saurais que l'action contient en elle sa récompense – agir, créer. Se battre contre les faits, les vaincre ou être vaincu par eux, toute la joie et toute la santé humaines sont là!

Simple façon de s'étourdir – murmura l'autre: 'Eh bien: j'aime mieux m'étourdir – crever pour crever – je préfère crever de passion que de crever d'ennui.'[4]

It is not only I who say this quand même,[5] but she, too, and instinctively so, quand même. That is why I saw something grand in her from the outset. Only it's a confounded pity that she allowed herself to be overwhelmed by disappointments in her youth, overwhelmed in the sense that her old-fashioned religious family felt they had to suppress the active, indeed, highly gifted element in her and so rendered her passive for evermore. If only they had not broken her in her youth! Or if they had left it at that instead of once again driving her to distraction, and this time with 5 or 6 or even more women fighting against her alone. Just read Daudet's L'évangeliste about those women's intrigues – those here were different, yet of the same sort.

Oh, Theo, why should I change – I used to be very passive and very gentle and quiet – I'm that no longer, but then I'm

4 Mouret says, 'If you think you are strong because you refuse to be stupid and to suffer, well, then you're just a fool, that's all.'

'Are you enjoying yourself?'

Mouret did not seem to understand immediately, but when he remembered their earlier conversation about the empty stupidity and the pointless torture of life, he replied, 'Of course – I have never lived so intensely... Ah, my dear fellow, don't scoff! The hours in which one dies of suffering are the shortest.'

I want her, I shall have her!... and – if she escapes me then you'll see what I do to be cured of it all – You don't understand this language, my dear fellow, otherwise you'd know that action is its own reward – to act, to create. To fight against the facts, to conquer them or be conquered by them, therein lies all human health and happiness!

That's just acting in order to forget – muttered the other, 'Well, I prefer such action – if perish we must – I would sooner perish of passion than be bored to death.' (Emile Zola, *Au bonheur des dames*)

5 In spite of everything.

no longer a child either now – sometimes I feel my own man.

Take Mauve, why is he quick-tempered and <u>difficult to get on with at times</u>? I haven't come as far as he has, but I, too, shall go further than I am now.

I tell you, if one wants to be active, one must not be afraid of going wrong, must not be afraid of making mistakes now and then. Many people think that they will become good just by doing <u>no harm</u> – but that's a lie, and you yourself used to call it that. That way lies stagnation, mediocrity.

<u>Just slap anything on</u> when you see a blank canvas staring at you like some imbecile. You don't know how <u>paralysing</u> that is, that <u>stare</u> of a blank canvas, which says to the painter: <u>you can't do a thing</u>. The canvas has an <u>idiotic</u> stare and mesmerises some painters so much that they turn into idiots themselves. Many painters <u>are afraid</u> in front of the blank <u>canvas</u>, but the blank canvas <u>is</u> afraid of the real, passionate painter who dares and who has broken the spell of 'you can't' once and for all.

Life itself, too, is forever turning an infinitely vacant, disheartening, dispiriting blank side towards man on which <u>nothing</u> appears, any more than it does on a blank canvas. But no matter <u>how</u> vacant and vain, how <u>dead</u> life may appear to be, the man of faith, of energy, of warmth, who knows something, will not be put off so easily. He wades in and <u>does something</u> and stays with it, in short, he <u>violates</u>, 'defiles' – they say. Let them talk, those cold theologians.

Theo, I feel so much confounded pity for this woman, just because her age and just <u>possibly</u> a liver and gallbladder complaint hang so threateningly over her head. And this is aggravated by emotions. For all that, we shall find out what can or what, fatally, cannot be done. However I shall do nothing without a <u>very good</u> doctor, so <u>I</u> shall do her no <u>harm</u>.

Just because I anticipate that, <u>if</u> our roads should lead us to one and the same place, we might have rather strong differences of opinion – for that very reason I don't want you to be able to hold my dependence on you against me. I am still in two minds about what I should try to do, but in all probability I shall not be staying on here – and the question will then be, where to?

I don't think you'll be pleased about my coming to Paris – but what am I meant to do about that, since you refuse point blank to look after my interests – all right, but for my part I can't possibly leave things as they are. Had you written less peremptorily that it was beneath you, I should never have given it a thought, but now – well, now, I must go my own way.

In brief, I have no wish to barter the <u>chance</u> (be it no more than a <u>chance</u>) of making my own way for the certainty of a patronage that is, après tout,[6] somewhat confining. Since I can see that I am forfeiting my chance of selling by continuing to take money from you, we shall just have to go our separate ways.

Don't you think it eminently reasonable that, hearing you say that you won't be able to do anything with my work for the next few years, I get the feeling that there is a marked contrast here, that while you stand on your dignity, I – precisely because I don't sell, no matter how hard I work – am forced to say, 'Theo, I am 25 guilders short, couldn't you see your way to letting me have a little bit extra?' which then proves to be impossible.

What is so very contrary about you is that when one sends you something or one asks, please try to find me an opening with the illustrated papers so that I can earn something – one hears nothing in reply and <u>you do not lift a finger</u> – but one is not allowed to say, I can't manage on the money. Up to now, at any rate – but things can't go on like this.

And I should like to add that I shan't be asking you whether you approve or disapprove of anything I do or don't do – I shall have no scruples, and if I should feel like going to Paris, for example, I shan't ask whether or not you have any objections.

Although Vincent wrote to his brother shortly afterwards that he was 'still badly upset about it all', Margot Begemann's name soon vanished from their correspondence. In 1887, writing from Paris, he asked his sister Wil about Margot's health once more and two years later, in

6 After all.

1889, he again wrote to Wil from Saint-Rémy, saying that he would like Margot to be given one of his paintings.

The relationship between the two brothers remained extremely tense for some time to come. Referring to pictures by Delacroix and Daumier of the revolution of 1848, Vincent compared his brother and himself to two soldiers on different sides of a barricade, firing at each other for the sake of their respective ideals: 'But since we are brothers, let us, for instance, rule out killing each other (in a figurative sense). Even so, we cannot help each other as much as two people who are standing side by side in the same camp [...]. My gibes are not bullets aimed at you, who are my brother, but more generally at the side [the art trade] to which you happen to belong.'

In the letters he wrote during the autumn of 1884, Van Gogh mooted the idea of going to Antwerp for further training. When Theo wrote to tell him how hard it was to sell Vincent's dark pictures in Paris, where modern painters were currently using a much brighter palette, Van Gogh realized how little he really knew about the latest developments in art. He could barely fathom what Theo meant when he wrote about 'impressionism', something Vincent himself had never come across: 'Here in Holland, it is hard to make any sense out of what impressionism really means. But both he [Van Rappard] and I are very interested in finding out what the present-day trend is.'

None the less, Van Gogh's tone during this period had a slightly more self-confident ring. For instance, he seemed to have acquired no fewer than three pupils, whom he taught to paint still lifes against payment in tubes of paint. In addition he had great plans for an ambitious interior with figures in which he hoped to emulate his beloved Millet and De Groux in realism, character and 'serious senti-ment'. He described it as 'a piece showing these peasants round a dish of potatoes in the evening'. He produced a long series of studies of Brabant types, the heads of peasants and of peasant women, for it, and, as a first step, completed a large sketch of the proposed composition. At times, however, his ambition seemed not to stretch beyond becoming an illustrator for a leading magazine, such as *Le chat noir*. He sent a lithograph based on the sketch to Van Rappard, as well as to his brother in Paris, asking Theo to show the print to the art dealer Alphonse Portier.

In the end there emerged, painted from memory, the fruit of the well-nigh endless series of studies, Van Gogh's first genuine 'painting', the definitive version of *The Potato Eaters*.

Anticipating his later use of coloured woollen threads to test colour combinations, Van Gogh compared his efforts to combine the right colours with the way in which a weaver composes his patterns. The heads of the peasants had 'the colour of a good dusty potato', and the whole was done in 'copper and green-soap-like tones'.

400 [D]

[*c.* 13 April 1885]

My dear Theo,

Many thanks for your regist. letter of yesterday & the enclosure. I am writing at once in reply & enclose a small sketch, based more closely on my last study than the one before. I haven't been able to get as far with it as I would have liked. I worked on it continually for 3 days from morning to night, and by Saturday night the paint had begun to get into a state which prevented further work until it had dried out completely.

I went to Eindhoven today to order a small stone, as this is to become the first of a series of lithographs, on which I intend to start again. When you were here I asked you about the costs of reproduction by the G. & Cie process. I think you said it would be 100 frs. Well, the old, now so little thought of, ordinary lithographic process is quite a lot cheaper – especially in Eindhoven, perhaps. I get the use of the stone, graining, paper, & the printing of 50 copies for 3 guilders.

Anyway, I intend to do a series of subjects from peasant life – les paysans chez eux.[1]

Today I went for a splendid walk for a few hours with an acquaintance of mine whose first watercolour of a figure I showed you.

1 Peasants at home.

I don't say that the scenery isn't <u>even more</u> stirring and more dramatic, say in Brittany, in Katwijk or in the Borinage – yes indeed, but even so, the heath and the villages here are <u>very</u> beautiful as well, and once there, I find an inexhaustible source of subjects from peasant life – and the only thing that matters is to get down to it, to work.

I've a great mind to do some watercolours & drawings again as well – and when I'm in my studio, I'll be able to make time for that in the evenings.

I was <u>tremendously</u> pleased that you sent me the 100 frs. As I said, it was absolutely essential that I pay several things off – and that was on my mind. Not that people were bothering me for it, but I knew they needed the money. And that is why I wrote that I might have to keep something back when the estate is settled.[2] But that won't be necessary now – although I can tell you that this year is bound to be very grim. But I keep thinking of what Millet said, 'Je ne veux point supprimer la souffrance, car souvent c'est elle, qui fait s'exprimer le plus énergiquement les artistes.'[3]

I think I'll be moving by 1 May – although I'm getting on well of course with Mother and our sisters, I can still see and sense it is pour le mieux[4] this way – since in the long run it would hardly be feasible to live together. Which I can put down neither to them personally nor to myself personally so much as to the incompatibility of the ideas of people who seek to maintain a certain social standing and a painter of peasant life who gives the matter no thought.

When I say that I am a painter of peasant life, that is a fact, and it will become increasingly apparent to you in the future that I feel at ease as one. It was not for nothing that I spent so many evenings musing by the fire in their homes with the miners and the peat cutters and the weavers & the peasants – unless I was working too hard for that.

2 Pastor Theodorus van Gogh had unexpectedly died of a heart attack on 26 March 1885.
3 I would never do away with suffering, for it is often what makes artists express themselves most forcefully.
4 For the best.

By continually observing peasant life, at all hours of the day, I have become so involved in it that I rarely think of anything else.

You write that the public attitude – that is, indifference to Millet's work, as you have just had occasion to observe at the exhibition – is not encouraging, either for artists or for those who have to sell paintings. I quite agree – but Millet himself felt & knew this – and on reading Sensier I was very struck by something he said at the beginning of his career, which I don't remember word for word, only the purport of it, namely, 'that (i.e. that indifference) would be bad enough if I had need of fine shoes and the life of a gentleman, but – puisque j'y vais en sabots – je m'en tirerai'.[5] And so it turned out.

What I hope never to forget is that 'il s'agit d'y aller en sabots',[6] that is, being content with the kind of food, drink, clothes and sleeping arrangements with which peasants are content.

That is what Millet did and indeed he wanted nothing else – and to my mind this means that he set an example to painters as a human being, which Israëls and Mauve, for instance, who live rather luxurious lives, have not, and I repeat, Millet is father Millet, that is, counsellor and mentor in everything to the younger painters. Most of those whom I know, but then I don't know all that many, would not subscribe to this view. For my part, I do, and fully believe in what he says.

I'm talking at some length about this dictum of Millet's because you write that when city-dwellers paint peasants, their figures, splendidly done though they may be, cannot but remind one of the faubourgs[7] of Paris. I used to have the same impression too (although in my opinion B. Lepage's woman digging potatoes is certainly no exception), but isn't this because the painters have so often failed to immerse themselves personally in peasant life? Millet said on another occasion, Dans l'art il faut y mettre sa peau.[8]

5 As I go about in clogs, I'll manage.
6 What matters is going about in clogs.
7 Suburbs.
8 One has to put one's all into art.

De Groux – this is one of his qualities – painted <u>peasants</u> properly. (And they, the State, demanded historical pictures from him! Which he also did well, but how much better he was when he was allowed to be <u>himself</u>.) It will always be a shame and disgrace that De Groux is not yet as fully appreciated by the Belgians as he deserves. De Groux is one of the <u>best Millet-like masters</u>. But although he neither was nor is acknowledged by the public at large, and although, like Daumier and Tassaert, he remains in obscurity, there are people, <u>Mellery</u>, for example, to name but one, who are working along his lines again today.

I saw something by Mellery recently in an illustrated paper, a <u>bargee's</u> family in the little cabin of their boat – husband, wife, children – round a table.

As far as <u>popular</u> support is concerned – years ago I read something on the subject in Renan which I have always remembered and which I shall always continue to believe – that anyone who wishes to accomplish something good or useful must not count on or seek the approval or appreciation of the general public, but, on the contrary, must expect only a very few warm hearts to sympathize and go along with him – and then only <u>perhaps</u>.

If you come across the 'Chat noir' people, you might show them this small sketch <u>to be going on with, but I can do a better one if they like, for this one was done in a great rush</u> and is simply meant to give you a clearer idea of the effect and the composition than the first one. Regards & thanks, with a handshake,

Ever yours,
<u>Vincent</u>

You needn't tell the 'Chat noir' that I also intend to make a lith. of this subject for myself. That lith. won't be for publication, anyway, but is entirely a private affair. For that matter, I don't much care if they <u>don't</u> want to have it – because I shall certainly make lithographs myself of whatever I want to have lithographed.

404 [D]

[c. 30 April 1885]

My dear Theo,

My warmest good wishes for good health & peace of mind on your birthday. I should have liked to send the painting of the Potato Eaters for this day, but although it's coming along well, it isn't quite finished yet.

Though the actual painting will have been completed in a comparatively short time, and largely from memory, it has taken a whole winter of painting studies of heads & hands.

And as for the few days in which I have painted it now – it's been a tremendous battle, but one for which I was filled with great enthusiasm. Even though at times I was afraid it would never come off. But painting, too, is 'agir-créer'.[1]

When weavers weave that cloth which I think they call cheviot, or those curious multicoloured Scottish tartan fabrics, then they try, as you know, to get strange broken colours and greys into the cheviot – and to get the most vivid colours to balance each other in the multicoloured chequered cloth – so that instead of the fabric being a jumble, the effet produit[2] of the pattern looks harmonious from a distance.

A grey woven from red, blue, yellow, off-white & black threads – a blue broken by a green and an orange, red or yellow thread – are quite unlike plain colours, that is, they are more vibrant, and primary colours seem hard, cold and lifeless beside them.

Yet the weaver, or rather the designer, of the pattern or the colour combination does not always find it easy to make an exact estimate of the number of threads and their direction – no more than it is easy to weave brush strokes into a harmonious whole.

1 Acting-creating.
2 Overall effect.

If you could see the first painted studies I did on my arrival here in Nuenen side by side with the canvas I am doing now, I think you would agree that things are livening up a bit as far as colour is concerned.

I feel certain that you too will get involved in the question of colour analysis one day. For as an art connoisseur and critic, it seems to me, one must also <u>be sure</u> of one's ground and have firm <u>convictions</u> – for one's own pleasure at least, and in order to <u>substantiate one's opinion</u>. And one should also be able to explain it in a few words to others who sometimes turn to someone like yourself for information when they want to know a little more about art.

But now I have something to say about Portier. Of course I am not wholly indifferent to his private opinion and I also appreciate his saying that he does not take back anything of what he has said. Nor do I mind that he apparently failed to hang these first <u>studies</u>. But – if he wants me to send him a painting intended for him, <u>then he can only have it on condition that he shows it</u>.

As for the Potato Eaters – it is a painting <u>that will do well in gold</u> – of that I am <u>certain</u>. But it would do just as well on a wall papered in a deep shade of ripe corn. However, it <u>simply mustn't be seen</u> without being <u>set off</u> in this way. It will <u>not</u> appear to full advantage against a <u>dark</u> background and especially not against a <u>dull</u> background. And that is because it is a glimpse into a very grey interior. In <u>real life</u> it is also set in a gold frame, as it were, because the hearth and the light from the fire on the white walls would be nearer the spectator – they are situated outside the painting, but in its natural state the whole thing is projected backwards.

Once again, it must be <u>set off</u> by putting something coloured a deep gold or copper round it. Please bear that in mind if you want to see it as it should be seen. Associating it with a gold tone lends brightness to <u>areas where you would least expect it</u>, and at the same time does away with the <u>marbled</u> aspect it assumes if it is unfortunately placed against a dull or black background. The shadows are painted with blue and the gold colour sets this off.

Yesterday, I took it to a friend of mine in Eindhoven who is doing some painting. In about 3 days' time I'll go back over there and give it some egg-white and finish off a few details.

This man, who is trying very hard himself to learn how to paint and to handle colour, was particularly taken with it. He had already seen the study on which I had based the lithograph and said that he would never have believed I could improve the colour and the drawing to such an extent. As he, too, paints from the model, he is well aware of what there is to a peasant's head or fist, and as for the hands, he said that he now had a quite different understanding of how to do them.

The point is that I've tried to bring out the idea that these people eating potatoes by the light of their lamp have dug the earth with the self-same hands they are now putting into the dish, and it thus suggests <u>manual labour</u> and – a meal honestly <u>earned</u>. I wanted to convey a picture of a way of life quite different from ours, from that of civilized people. So the last thing I would want is for people to admire or approve of it without knowing why.

I've held the threads of this fabric in my hands all winter long and searched for the definitive pattern – and although it is now a fabric of rough and coarse appearance, the threads have none the less been chosen with care and according to certain rules. And it might just turn out to be a <u>genuine peasant painting</u>. <u>I know that it is</u>. But anyone who prefers to have his peasants looking namby-pamby had best suit himself. Personally, I am convinced that in the long run one gets better results from painting them in all their coarseness than from introducing a conventional sweetness.

A peasant girl, in her patched and dusty blue skirt & bodice which have acquired the most delicate shades from the weather, wind and sun, is better looking – in my opinion – than a lady. But if she dons a lady's clothes, then her authenticity is gone. A peasant in his fustian clothes out in the fields [is] better looking than when he goes to church on Sundays in a kind of gentleman's coat.

And similarly, in my opinion, it would be wrong to give a

painting of peasant life a conventional polish. If a peasant painting smells of bacon, smoke, potato steam, fine – that's not unhealthy – if a stable reeks of manure – all right, that's what a stable is all about – if a field has the smell of ripe corn or potatoes or of guano & manure – that's properly healthy, especially for city dwellers. Such pictures might prove <u>helpful to them</u>. But a painting of peasant life should not be perfumed.

I am eager to know whether you will find something in it to please you – I hope so.

I'm glad that just as Mr Portier has said that he'll handle my work, I've got something more important for him than studies. As for Durand Ruel – though he didn't consider the drawings worth bothering with, do show him this painting. Let him think it ugly, I don't mind – but let him have a look at it all the same, let people see that we put some effort into our endeavours. No doubt you'll hear 'quelle croûte!'³ Be prepared for that, as I am prepared myself. Yet we must go on providing something <u>genuine</u> and <u>honest</u>.

Painting peasant life is a serious business, and I for one would blame myself if I didn't try to make pictures that give rise to serious reflection in those who think seriously about art and life.

Millet, De Groux, so many others, have set an example of <u>character</u> by turning a deaf ear to such taunts as 'sale, grossier, boueux, puant',⁴ &c., &c., so it would be a disgrace should one so much as waver. No, one must paint peasants as if one were one of them, as if one felt and thought as they do. Being unable to help what one actually is. I very often think that peasants are a world apart, in many respects one so much better than the civilized world. Not in all respects, for what do they know of art and many other things?

I still have a few smaller studies – but you will appreciate that I'm being kept so busy by the larger one that I've been able to do little else. As soon as it is completely finished and dry, I shall forward you the canvas in a small packing case, adding a few

3 What a daub!
4 nasty, crude, filthy, stinking.

smaller items. I think it would be as well not to delay the dispatch too long, which is why I'll make haste with it. The second lithograph of it will probably have to be abandoned in that case, though I realize that Mr Portier, for instance, must have his opinion endorsed if we are to count on him once and for all as a friend. It is my sincere hope that we may.

I have been so absorbed in the painting that I almost forgot that I am moving house, something that has to be attended to as well. My worries won't be any the less, but the lives of all painters in this genre have been so full of cares that I shouldn't want to have things any easier than they did. And since they managed to get their paintings done anyway, I, too, may be <u>held back</u> by material difficulties, but not <u>destroyed</u> or <u>undermined</u> by them. So there you are.

I believe that <u>The Potato Eaters</u> will turn out well – as you know, the last few days are always tricky with a painting because before it's completely dry one can't use a large brush without running a real risk of spoiling it. And changes must be made very coolly and calmly with a small brush. That's why I took it to my friend and asked him to make certain I didn't spoil it, and why I'll be going to his place to apply those finishing touches.

You'll certainly see that it has originality. Regards, I'm sorry it wasn't ready for today – best wishes once again for your health and peace of mind, believe me, with a handshake,

Ever yours,
<u>Vincent</u>

I'm still working on some smaller studies that will go off at the same time. Did you ever send that copy of the Salon issue?

No matter how profoundly his painting technique and use of colour were to develop under the influence of Impressionism, Van Gogh never disowned his first 'masterpiece'. An attempt in Saint-Rémy to return to the same theme with a new technique came to no more than a few sketches.

In homage to Pastor van Gogh, Vincent painted his father's tobacco pouch and pipe in the foreground of a still life with honesty. Touchily, he returned a letter of condolence from Van Rappard, who had made slighting remarks about the lithograph of *The Potato Eaters*. The letter had indeed been very tactless – Van Rappard's suggestion that 'such work can't be meant seriously' and his view that the peasant woman in the background had a 'coquettish' little hand, were bound to go down badly with the deadly serious Van Gogh. Van Rappard's final thrust, 'And after working like that you still dare to invoke the names of Millet and Breton', must have been particularly galling. To Van Gogh, the letter was 'so supercilious and so full of insults [...] that I am as good as certain that I have lost him as a friend for ever'. The art dealer Portier and the painter Serret, upon seeing the lithograph in Paris, had had criticisms to make, too, but they had also shown some appreciation.

At the beginning of June, Van Gogh sent a small packing case to Paris with two new and important paintings: *The Cottage* and *Country Churchyard with Old Church Tower*. He likened the cottages in which the Brabant peasants lived to the bird's-nests he was collecting at the time, and said of the *Country Churchyard*: 'I have left out some details – I wanted to express by those ruins that the peasants have been laid to rest for centuries among the very fields in which they toiled when they were alive. I wanted to express how very simple death & burial are, just as easy as the falling of an autumn leaf – nothing but a bit of earth turned over, a small wooden cross. Where the grass of the churchyard ends, over the little wall, the fields around it form a last line against the horizon – like the horizon of a sea. And now the ruins tell me how faith and religion moulder away, no matter how firmly grounded they are – but that the lives & deaths of the peasants are always the same, steadily sprouting and withering like the grass and the little flowers that grow in that churchyard there. "Les religions passent, Dieu demeure [Religions pass, God remains]," is a saying of Victor Hugo's, whom they have also just buried.' How much Van Gogh was attached to the French tradition in all things may also be gathered from the fact that he provided both these works with official French titles, namely *La chaumière* and *Cimetière de paysans*. His output at this time also included several watercolours and twelve painted studies, amongst them a head inspired by Zola's *Germinal*.

During the second half of June he decided to send Van Rappard a strongly worded reply to his criticism of the lithograph of *The Potato Eaters*.

R52 [D] [letter from Vincent to Anthon van Rappard]

[second half of June 1885]

Dear friend Rappard,

One or two things have happened to cause me to write to you, more to explain myself than because I enjoy doing it.

With regard to the abrupt return by me of your last letter, there were two reasons for that, each of which I considered well founded.

In the first place, supposing your remarks about the lithograph that I sent you were correct, supposing I could raise no objections to them – even then you wouldn't have been justified in condemning all my work in such an insulting [manner], or rather, in dismissing it in the way you did.

And secondly – seeing that you have received more friendship, not only from me but from my family, than you have given, you certainly cannot <u>claim as of right</u> that, on an occasion such as my father's death, we were <u>obliged</u> to send you anything other than a circular letter. Least of all <u>myself</u>, seeing that, even before that, you had failed to reply to a letter of mine. Least of all <u>myself</u>, seeing that on the occasion of my father's death, though you did express your sympathy in a letter addressed to my mother – it was such that, when it arrived, it made the family wonder why you had not written to me instead! I wasn't looking for a letter from you then, nor am I now.

You know that I haven't been on the best of terms with my family for years. During the first few days following my father's death I <u>had</u> to correspond with the nearest relatives. But as soon as other members of the family arrived, I withdrew completely. So any possible omissions must be blamed on my family, not on me. And I must tell you that you are still an exception, because I especially asked the family whether they had sent you a notification, only to be told that they had forgotten. Enough of this now, more than enough.

The reason I am writing to you again has nothing to do with

answering your criticisms on that subject. Nor is it to repeat my comments on what you said about painting – you might care to reread your letter. If you still think you were right, if you really mean that 'when you set your mind to it, you express yourself damned well', well, then, the best thing is simply to leave you to your delusions.

To get to the point, the reason I am writing to you – though it was not I who insulted you in the first place but you who insulted me – is just that I've known you too long to believe this to be a reason for breaking off all contact. What I have to say to you is as one painter to another, and that will be so for as long as you and I go on painting – whether we keep up our acquaintance or not.

There was mention of Millet. All right, my friend, I shall answer you. You wrote, 'And someone like that dares invoke Millet and Breton.' My answer is simply that I advise you in all seriousness not to fight with me. As far as I am concerned, I suit myself – understand? – but I have no desire to pick a quarrel with anyone right now, not even you. You can say whatever you like – but were you to have any more such observations they would be like so much water off a duck's back. Let's leave it at that for the moment.

As for what you have said more than once – that I care nothing for the shape of the figure – it is beneath me to take it seriously, and, my dear fellow, it is beneath you to say anything as uncalled for as that. You have known me for years – have you ever seen me work otherwise than after the model, shouldering the often very heavy expenses, when I am poor enough in all conscience? What you wrote, not in your last letter, but repeatedly and ad nauseam in previous ones, was about 'technique', and was the reason for my writing the letter to which you did not reply. What I said then and say once more, is that there is the conventional meaning increasingly assigned to the word technique, and there is the real meaning, knowledge. Well, Meissonier himself says, 'la science – nul ne l'a'.[1] Now, to start

---

1 Knowledge – no one has that.

with, la science is not the same as 'de la science',[2] and that you will not deny. But not even that is the crux of the matter.

Take Haverman, for instance, of whom they say – you too – that he has such a lot of <u>technique</u>. But not just Haverman – how many others don't have the sort of knowledge of art that H. has? Jacquet among the French painters, perhaps, and he is <u>better</u>.

My contention is simply this, that drawing an academically correct figure, and having a steady, well-judged brushstroke, has little to do, or at least less than is generally supposed, with the needs – the pressing needs – of contemporary painting.

If instead of saying, H. has a lot of 'technique', you said, H. has a lot of 'métier',[3] I should agree with you for once. You will probably know what I mean when I say that, when Haverman sits down in front of a beautiful lady's or young girl's head, he will make it more beautiful than almost anyone else, but sit him in front of a peasant and he won't have even the faintest idea where to start. His art, or what I know of it, seems especially suited to subjects one can easily dispense with – especially suited to subjects that are almost the precise opposite of Millet's and Lhermitte's, and more in line with Cabanel – who for all his 'métier', as I call it, has achieved little that will last or take us forward.

And, I implore you, do not <u>confuse</u> this with the style of a Millet or Lhermitte. What I said and will go on saying is this – the word technique is being applied far too often in a conventional sense, and used far too often in bad faith. The <u>technique</u> of all those Italians and Spaniards is praised, and they are people who are more conventional, and more stuck in routine, than most. And I'm afraid that with people like Haverman, 'métier' all too quickly turns into 'routine'. And then, what is it worth then?

What I should like now to ask you is – what is your real motive for breaking with me? The reason I am writing to you again is precisely because I love Millet, Breton and <u>all those</u> who paint <u>peasants</u> and the <u>people</u>, and I count you among them. I

2 A little knowledge.
3 Professional expertise.

don't say this because I gained much from our friendship, for, my friend, I got precious little out of it – and, forgive me for telling you bluntly for the first and last time, I know no more arid friendship than yours.

But firstly I am not doing it <u>for that reason</u>, and, secondly, that, too, might have improved. But having created my own opportunity now for finding models, &c., I am not so petty-minded as to keep it to myself. On the contrary, if any painter, no matter who, should come to these parts, I should be happy to invite him in and to show him the ropes – precisely because it isn't always that easy to find models prepared to pose, and because not everyone thinks that having a pied-à-terre some-where is a matter of indifference. And I'm telling you this because, if you would like to come and paint here, there's no need for you to feel embarrassed because we have fallen out. And even though I'm living in this studio on my own now, you could come here as well.

Perhaps, though, you will tell me condescendingly that you don't care one way or the other – well, then, so be it. I am so used to insults that they really run off me like water off a duck's back, so someone like you will probably find it hard to under-stand, for instance, how completely cold a letter like yours leaves me. And since I couldn't care less about it, I have no hard feelings either. But more than enough clear-headedness and calmness of mind to answer you as I do now. If you want to break with me – that's all right with me. If you want to stay here and paint – you can ignore this spot of bother in our correspond-ence. What you produced the last time you were here had and still has my full support, and, friend Rappard, it is because you worked so damned well the last time and because I think you may perhaps be anxious for the opportunity here to remain open, that I am writing to you.

It's up to you – I'm putting it plainly – and while fully appreciating your painting, I do worry that you may not be able to stay the course in the <u>future</u>. I sometimes fear that because of the influences to which you cannot help being exposed by virtue of your social position and station in life, you may not remain as good in the long run as you are at present – in your work as a painter, that is, the rest is no business of mine.

So as one painter to another, I say to you that if you would like to come and look for subjects here, <u>things will be just as they used to be</u>. You can come here and, even though I'm on my own, you can stay here just as before. I thought that perhaps you'd got some satisfaction out of it, you see, and might again, and I just wanted to tell you so. If you can do equally well elsewhere, so be it, I shall have no reason to grieve, and then farewell.

You write nothing about <u>your</u> work, nor I about <u>mine</u>. Take it from me, there's no point in arguing with me about Millet. Millet is someone I will not argue about, although I do not refuse to discuss him. Regards,

<u>Vincent</u>

Letters went back and forth, until Van Gogh decided in late July to put an end to their 'ridiculous' quarrel. The disagreement now struck him as resembling 'the dispute between some pair of God-fearing preachers'. He accepted that Van Rappard had not acted from malice, but had felt compelled in all conscience to voice his opinions.

Meanwhile another four pictures of small cottages were ready to be dispatched to Paris. Van Gogh sent them 'just as they come, off the heath'. He also composed several still lifes with bird's-nests chosen from a small collection he had built up: 'My whole heart is in <u>la nichée</u> et <u>les nids</u> [the brood and the nests], especially those <u>human</u> nests, those cottages on the heath and their inhabitants.'

He wanted above all to paint the figure again, but had no money to pay models. Basing his position on Courbet's saying that he could not paint angels because he had never seen one, Van Gogh set his face against the Salon artists who thought nothing of painting exotic and historical subjects quite outside their own experience. The portrayal of working people was to his mind one of the most important thematic innovations of contemporary art, the 'essential modern' aspect. Even 'the old Dutch masters, who depicted so many conventional actions', fell short in this respect: the figures portrayed by Terborch and Ostade, or Velásquez's water carrier, did not actually *work*. He did not care for academic accuracy in the presentation of the figure. On the contrary, he preferred painting such 'aberrations, reworkings, transformations of reality, as may turn it into, well – lies, if you like – but truer than the literal truth'.

418 [D]

[July 1885]

My dear Theo,

I wish the 4 canvases I wrote to you about had gone. If I keep them here for much longer, I might paint them over again and I think it's better if you get them just as they come, off the heath. The reason I haven't sent them is that I don't want to send them to you carriage forward at a time when you say that you yourself might be short of cash, and I cannot afford the carriage myself.

I have never seen the little house in which Millet lived – but I imagine that these 4 little human nests are of the same sort. One is the residence of a gentleman popularly known as 'the mourning peasant' – the other is inhabited by a worthy soul who, when I went there, was up to nothing more mysterious than digging her potato-clamp, but who must be capable of practising witchcraft – she goes by the name of 'the witch's head', anyway.

You'll remember that Gigoux's book tells how it came about that 17 of Delacroix's pictures were turned down all at the same time. That shows – to me at least – that he and others of that period were faced with connoisseurs and non-connoisseurs alike, who neither understood them nor wanted to buy anything by them – but that they, who are rightly called 'les vaillants'[1] in the book, didn't talk of fighting a losing battle but went on painting.

What I wanted to say again is that if we take that story about Delacroix as our starting point, we still have a lot of painting to do.

1 The brave.

I find myself faced with the necessity of being that most disagreeable of people, in other words of having to ask for money. And since I don't think that sales will pick up in the next few days, the situation seems rather dire. But I put it to you, isn't it better for both of us, après tout,[2] to work hard, no matter what problems that may entail, than to sit around philosophizing at a time like this?

I can't foretell the future, Theo – but I do know the eternal law that all things change. Think back 10 years, and things were different, the circumstances, the mood of the people, in short everything. And 10 years hence much is bound to have changed again. But what one does remains – and one does not easily regret having done it. The more active one is, the better, and I would sooner have a failure than sit idle and do nothing.

Whether or not Portier is the right man to do something with my work – we need him now at any rate. And this is what I have in mind. After, say, a year's work, we shall have put together more than we have now, and I know for sure that my work will fare better the more I can add to it. People who show some liking for it now, who speak of it as he does, and show it from time to time are useful, because if I work for, let's say, another year and they are able to add a few more things to their collection, that will speak for itself even if the collectors themselves have nothing at all to say.

If you happen to see Portier, tell him that, far from giving up, I intend sending him much more. You, too, must go on showing my work if you meet people. It won't be all that long before we have more important things to show.

You yourself will have seen – and it is something that pleases me enormously – that 1-man shows, or shows by just a few who belong together, are becoming increasingly popular. I'm sure that in the art world this has more avenir[3] than other ventures.

It's a good thing people are beginning to realize that a Bouguereau does not do well next to a Jacque – or a figure by

2 After all.
3 Future.

Beyle or Lhermitte next to a Schelfhout or Koekkoek. Scatter Raffaëlli's drawings about and judge for yourself if it's still possible to get a good idea of that singular artist. He – Raffaëlli – is different from Regamey, but I think he has just as much personality.

If I kept my work with me, I am sure I should go on repainting it. Sending it to you and Portier just as it comes from the countryside or from the cottages, I may well include an example that isn't any good – but some things will have been saved that would not have been improved by frequent repainting.

Now supposing you had these 4 canvases and a few smaller studies of cottages, someone who saw nothing else of mine would be bound to think that I painted nothing but cottages. And likewise with the series of heads. But peasant life involves so many different things, that when Millet speaks of 'travailler comme plusieurs nègres',[4] this is truly what has to be done if one wants to assemble a body of work.

One may laugh at Courbet's saying, 'Peindre des anges! qui est-ce qui a vu des anges?'[5] But to that I should like to add, 'des justices au harem, qui est-ce qui a vu des justices au harem?'[6] And Benjamin Constant's painting, Des combats de taureaux, 'qui est-ce qui en a vu?'[7] And so many other Moorish and Spanish things, cardinals, and then all those historical paintings they keep on doing yards high and yards wide! What is the use of it all and what are they doing it for? Within a few years most of it looks dull and dreary and more & more boring. But still, perhaps they are well painted, they could be that.

Nowadays, when connoisseurs stand in front of a painting like the one by Benj. Constant, or like some reception given by some cardinal by I don't know which Spaniard – it's the custom to say, with a meaningful air, something about 'clever technique'. But as

4 Working like several slaves.
5 Painting angels! Who has ever seen angels?
6 Justice in the harem, who has ever seen justice in the harem?
7 Bullfights, who has ever seen those?

soon as those same connoisseurs are confronted by a subject from peasant life or a drawing by, say, Raffaëlli, they criticize the technique with the same knowing air – à la C. M.

You may think I'm wrong to comment on this, but I'm so struck by the fact that all these exotic pictures were painted in the studio. Just try going outside and painting things on the spot! All sorts of things happen then. I had to pick off a good hundred or more flies from the 4 canvases you're about to receive, not to mention dust and sand, &c., not to mention the fact that if one carries them through heath and hedgerows for a couple of hours, a branch or two is likely to scratch them, &c. Not to mention the fact that when one arrives on the heath, one feels tired and hot after a couple of hours' walk in this weather. Not to mention the fact that the figures don't stand still like professional models, and that the effects one wants to capture change as the day wears on.

I don't know how it is with you – but as far as I am concerned, the more I work at it, the more absorbed I get in peasant life. And the less I care for Cabanel-like things, among which I would include Jacquet, and the present-day Benj. Constant – or the highly praised but inexpressibly, hopelessly dry technique of the Italians & Spaniards. 'Imagiers!'[8] I often think of that term of Jacque's.

Yet I do have parti pris,[9] I respond to Raffaëlli, who paints something quite other than peasants – I respond to Alfred Stevens, to Tissot, to mention something completely different from peasants – I respond to a beautiful portrait.

Zola, who otherwise, in my opinion, makes some colossal blunders when he judges pictures, says something beautiful about art in general in Mes haines: 'Dans le tableau (l'oeuvre d'art), je cherche, j'aime l'homme – l'artiste.'[10]

There you have it; I think that's absolutely true. I ask you, what kind of man, what kind of visionary, or thinker, observer, what kind of human character is there behind certain canvases

8 Makers of popular prints!
9 Prejudice.
10 In the picture (the work of art), I look for, I love the man – the artist.

extolled for their technique – often <u>no kind at all</u>, as you know. But a Raffaëlli is somebody, a Lhermitte is <u>somebody</u>, and with many pictures by almost unknown people one has the feeling that they were made with a <u>will</u>, with <u>feeling</u>, with <u>passion</u>, with <u>love</u>.

The <u>technique</u> of a painting from peasant life or – in Raffaëlli's case – from the heart of urban workers, introduces problems quite other than those of the smooth painting and portrayal of actions of a Jacquet or Benjamin Constant. Namely, living in cottages day in and day out, being out in the fields just like the peasants – in the heat of the sun in summer, enduring snow and frost in winter, not indoors but out in the open, and not just while taking a walk but day in, day out, like the peasants themselves.

And I ask you, all things considered, am I really so wrong to object to the criticisms of those experts, who more than ever before bandy this so <u>often</u> irrelevant word 'technique' about (giving it an increasingly conventional relevance)? Considering all the traipsing and trudging it takes to paint 'the mourning peasant' in his cottage, I dare say this work involves a longer, more tiring journey than the one so many painters of exotic subjects – whether 'la justice au harem' or 'reception at a cardinal's' – have to go on to produce their choicest eccentric subjects – since Arabic or Spanish or Moorish models are readily available, against payment, in Paris. But anyone who, like Raffaëlli, paints the ragpickers of Paris <u>in their own quarter</u>, has greater problems and his work is more serious.

<u>Nothing seems simpler than painting peasants or ragpickers and other workers, but – there are no subjects in painting as difficult as those everyday figures</u>! As far as I know, not a single academy exists in which one can learn to draw and to paint a digger, a sower, a woman hanging a pot over the fire, or a seamstress. But every city of any importance has an academy with a choice of models for historical, Arabic, Louis XV – in a nutshell, <u>every sort of figure, provided they do not exist in reality</u>.

When I send you & Serret a few studies of diggers or peasant women weeding, gleaning corn, &c., <u>as the first</u> of a whole series on all kinds of work in the fields, you or Serret may discover flaws in them, which it will be helpful for me to know about and which I shall in all probability acknowledge.

But I should like to point out something perhaps worthy of consideration. All academic figures are put together in the same way, and, let us admit, 'on ne peut mieux'[11] – impeccably – <u>faultlessly</u>. You will have gathered what I am driving at – they do not lead us to <u>any new discoveries</u>.

Not so the figures of a Millet, a Lhermitte, a Regamey, a Lhermitte [*sic*], a Daumier. They are also well put together – but <u>après tout, not the way the academy teaches</u>. I believe that no matter how academically correct a figure may be, it is superfluous, though it were by Ingres himself (with the exception of his Source, because that <u>surely</u> was, is and always shall be, something new), once it lacks that essential modern aspect, the intimate character, the real <u>action</u>.

You may ask, when will the figure <u>not</u> be superfluous, for all its faults, and grave faults to my way of thinking? When the digger digs, when the peasant is a peasant and the peasant woman is a peasant woman, is this anything new? Yes, even the little figures by Ostade and Terborch don't work as people do today.

I could say much more on the subject, and I should like to say how much I myself want to improve what I have begun – and how much more highly I value the work of some others than I do my own. I ask you – do you know of a single digger, a single sower, in the old Dutch school? Did they ever try to do 'a worker'? Did Velásquez look for one in his water carrier or his types from the people? No. <u>Work</u>, that's what the figures in the old pictures don't do.

I've been plodding away the last few days at a woman whom I saw pulling carrots in the snow last winter. Look – Millet has done it, Lhermitte, and by and large the painters of peasants from this century – say an Israëls – they consider it more

11 It cannot be done better.

beautiful than anything else. But even in this century, how relatively few among the legion of artists paint the figure – yes, for the figure's sake avant tout,[12] i.e. for the sake of form and modelé,[13] yet cannot imagine it otherwise than in action, and want – what the old masters and even the old Dutch masters who depicted so many conventional actions avoided – want, as I say, to paint the action for the action's sake. So that the painting or the drawing has to be a figure drawing for the sake of the figure and of the unutterably harmonious form of the human body – but at the same time a pulling of carrots in the snow. Do I make myself clear? I hope so, and you might mention it to Serret.

I can put it more succinctly – a nude by Cabanel, a lady by Jacquet, and a peasant woman not by Bastien Lepage but by a Parisian who has learned his drawing at the academy, will always convey the limbs and the structure of the body in the same way – sometimes charming, accurate in proportion and anatomical detail. But when Israëls, or, say, Daumier or Lhermitte, draw a figure, one gets much more of a sense of the shape of the body, and yet – and that's the very reason I'm pleased to include Daumier – the proportions will sometimes be almost arbitrary, the anatomy and structure often anything but correct in the eyes of the academicians. But it will live. And Delacroix too, in particular.

It still isn't well put. Tell Serret that I should be in despair if my figures were good, tell him that I don't want them to be academically correct, tell him that what I'm trying to say is that if one were to photograph a digger, he would certainly not be digging then. Tell him that I think Michelangelo's figures are splendid, although the legs are unquestionably too long, the hips and buttocks too broad. Tell him that, to my mind, Millet and Lhermitte are the true artists, because they do not paint things as they are, examined in a dry analytical manner, but as they, Millet, Lhermitte, Michelangelo, feel them to be. Tell him that I

12 Above all.
13 Modelling.

long most of all to learn how to produce those very inaccuracies, those very aberrations, reworkings, transformations of reality, as may turn it into, well – a lie if you like – but truer than the literal truth.

And now it's nearly time to close – but I felt the need to say once more that those who paint peasant life or the life of the people, though they may not be counted among the 'hommes du monde',[14] may well stay the course better in the long run than the creators of exotic harems and cardinals' receptions, painted in Paris.

I know that it is disagreeable of one to ask for money at awkward moments – but my excuse is that painting what appear to be the most commonplace things is sometimes the most difficult and expensive. The expenses that <u>I must incur if I want to work</u>, are at times considerable when compared with my means. I assure you that had my constitution not become virtually like that of a peasant, through exposure to the elements, I should not have been able to endure it, for there is simply nothing left over for my personal comfort. But then I don't seek that for myself either, any more than many peasants seek anything other than to live as they do. But what I do ask for is paint, and above all models.

From what I write about the figure drawings you will no doubt have gathered that I am particularly keen on going ahead with them. You wrote not long ago that Serret had spoken to you 'with conviction' about certain faults in the structure of the figures in the Potato Eaters. But you will have seen from my answer that I found fault on that score myself as well, though I did point out that this was my impression after I had seen the cottage many evenings in the dim lamplight, after I had painted 40 heads, from which it follows that I set out from a different point of view.

However, now that we have started to discuss the figure, I have a great deal more to say. I find Raffaëlli's perception of 'character', that is, the words he uses to describe it, good and well chosen and exemplified by the drawings. But those who, like Raffaëlli, move in artistic and literary circles in Paris, have, après tout, different ideas from, for instance, mine, out here in the country among the peasants. My point is that they are looking for a single word that will sum up all their ideas – he suggests the word 'character' for the figures of the future. I agree with that, with what I think is the meaning – but I believe as little in the accuracy of the word as in the accuracy of other words – as little as in the accuracy or effectiveness of my own expressions.

Rather than say, 'there must be character in a digger', I would put it like this: the peasant must be a peasant, the digger must dig, and then there will be something essentially modern in them. But I feel that even these words may give rise to misconceptions – even were I to add a whole string of them.

Far from cutting down on the expenses for models – which is a fairly heavy burden on me now as it is – I think spending a little more is called for, very much called for. For what I am aiming at is quite different from doing 'a little figure' drawing. To show the <u>peasant figure in action</u>, that – I repeat – is what an essentially modern figure painting really does, it is the very essence of modern art, something neither the Greeks nor the Renaissance nor the old Dutch school have done.

This is a question I ponder every day. The difference between the great, or the lesser, masters of today (the great, e.g. Millet, Lhermitte, Breton, Herkomer; the lesser, e.g. Raffaëlli and Regamey) and the old schools is, however, something I have rarely seen frankly expressed in articles about art. Just think about it and see if you don't agree. They started doing peasants' and workmen's figures as a 'genre' – but nowadays, with Millet, the perennial master, in the lead, these figures have become the very essence of modern art and so they will remain.

People like Daumier – one must respect them, for they are among the pioneers. The simple <u>but modern nude</u> – as revived by Henner and Lefèvre – ranks high. Baudry, and above all such sculptors as Mercier and Dalou, are also amongst the very soundest. But the fact is that peasants and ouvriers[15] are not nudes, nor does one need to imagine them in the nude. The more that people begin to do workers' and peasants' figures, the better I shall like it. And for myself, I can think of nothing I like as much.

This is a long letter and I'm not even sure if I've made myself entirely clear. Perhaps I'll write a few lines to Serret too. If I do, I'll send the letter to you to read, for I do want to make plain how much importance I attach to the figure issue.

During the summer months Van Gogh was busy with scenes of the wheat harvest and 'little women among the potatoes'. At the beginning of September, he informed Theo that the 'reverend gentlemen of the [Roman Catholic] clergy' were beginning to make his life difficult by advising the people of Nuenen ('God-fearing natives') not to pose for him any longer because he was thought to be responsible for the pregnancy of a local girl: 'These last two weeks, I have had a lot of trouble with the reverend gentlemen of the clergy, who gave me to understand, albeit with the best intentions and believing like so many others that they were obliged to intervene – that I ought not to be too familiar with people below me in station. But while they put the matter to me in these terms, they used quite a different tone with the "people of lower station", namely threatening them if they allowed themselves to be painted. This time, I went straight to the burgomaster and told him all about it, pointing out that it was no business of the priests, and that they ought to stick to their own sphere of more abstract concerns. In any case, for the moment I am having no more opposition from them and I hope it will stay like that.

'A girl I had frequently painted was about to have a baby and they suspected me, though I had nothing to do with it. But I heard what had really happened from the girl herself, namely that a member of the priest's own congregation in Nuenen had played a particularly ugly part in the affair, and so they could not get at me, at least not on that occasion. But you can see that it isn't easy to paint people in their own home or to draw them going about their business.'

15 Workers.

At the beginning of October 1885, longing once again to feast his eyes on the old Dutch masters, Van Gogh travelled to Amsterdam for a few days, accompanied by his friend and pupil, Anton Kerssemakers. The new Rijksmuseum had just been opened with great ceremony, and there he admired not only the work of great seventeenth-century painters but also Jozef Israëls's *Zandvoortse visser* and the Dutch and French Romantic painters in the Fodor Collection. Van Gogh looked to his predecessors for support of his own working method, and he was pleasantly surprised to discover that the old Dutch paintings, for example the work of Frans Hals, had 'for the most part been done quickly'. Moreover, his short excursion to Amsterdam convinced him that the old masters, too, had considered 'drawing and colour as one'.

Observations on the theory of colours filled many pages of the letters he wrote during this period. Delacroix was his great exemplar, and he considered the Barbizon painter Jules Dupré to be Delacroix's peer when it came to landscape. Much as would happen later in his Paris period, the painting of still lifes helped Van Gogh to apply the colour theory he was learning at the time from Bracquemond's book *Du dessin et de la couleur*. He responded to Theo's analysis of the use of colour in Manet's painting of a dead bullfighter by sending his brother his own *Still Life with Open Bible*, which he had dedicated to his late father as a second act of homage and a *memento mori*.

Despite his profound interest in technique, he felt that other considerations were of still greater importance: 'Let people talk rot as much as they like about technique in pharisaical, hollow, hypocritical terms – true painters are guided by that conscience which is called sentiment. Their soul, their brains, are not there for the sake of the brush but the brush for their brains. Furthermore, it is the canvas which is frightened of the real painter, not the painter who is frightened of the canvas.'

From Nuenen to Antwerp

During the first weeks of November 1885 Van Gogh still managed to produce several glorious autumn landscapes. In the middle of the month, his old intention of going to Antwerp surfaced once again, and he decided to terminate his tenancy of the studio in Nuenen as from May 1886. The antagonism of the sexton and the priest had continued to thwart his search for a model, and there could be no question of drawing nudes in Brabant. Antwerp now beckoned as a welcome release from banishment. The recent trip to Amsterdam had shown him that a painter must keep in constant touch with the work of his predecessors, and he felt that, in Antwerp, he could learn much from the work of Rubens, in his view the greatest of all Baroque painters of the figure.

He arrived in Antwerp at the end of November and rented a small room above a paint-merchant's shop at 194 rue des Images – a fittingly named street. For the first time we read that the reproductions pinned to his walls included a 'lot of small Japanese prints'. When and how Van Gogh first became interested in Japanese woodcuts remains somewhat obscure – at the end of the nineteenth century they were to be found in various Dutch collections, but there is no mention of these in Van Gogh's letters. It would seem that his recent perusal of the de Goncourts' book on eighteenth-century art, and their battle cry 'Japonaiserie for ever', had kindled his interest in 'fanciful, peculiar, unheard of' Japanese art. During the second half of his Parisian period in particular and again in Arles, the influence of Japanese prints would be clearly reflected in his work, and though that influence is hard to detect in the Antwerp period, we have his own word that it already coloured his experience of that city significantly.

Brought face to face with heads by Rubens and Jordaens, Hals and Rembrandt, in Antwerp, Van Gogh decided to concentrate on portraits himself. In this field, he resolved to surpass photography, which, he felt, remained lifeless at all times, while 'painted portraits have a life of their own, which springs straight from the painter's soul and which no machine can approach'. However, when acute lack of cash forced him to forgo hot meals, he was prepared to compromise and to consider earning some money with portraits painted from photographs.

In the hope of finding customers eager to acquire a view of Antwerp as a souvenir, he also painted the Steen, the city's famous castle, and made studies of the Cathedral of Our Lady. 'Still, I would sooner paint people's eyes than cathedrals, for there is something in the eyes that is lacking in a cathedral – however solemn and impressive it may be. To my mind a man's soul, be it that of a poor beggar or of a streetwalker, is more interesting.'

He found his model, a woman typifying urban life, in a sympathetic Antwerp barmaid. Using Rembrandt's head of a whore as his reference, he tried to achieve the same effect as he had earlier produced with the heads of peasant women in Brabant. He found other models in the lively dockside quarter and at the 'bals populaires', dance halls, but continued to feel depressed at his failure to sell his work. Even Theo's promising contacts with the Parisian dealer Portier seemed to be leading nowhere.

437 [D]

[28 November 1885]

My dear Theo,

I just wanted to send you a few more impressions of Antwerp. This morning I took a good long walk in the pouring rain, the object of the outing being to fetch my things from the custom house. The various warehouses and storage sheds on the quays look quite splendid.

I've walked in many different directions along the docks & quays several times already. The contrast is particularly marked for one who has just arrived from the sand and the heath & the tranquillity of a country village and has been in quiet surroundings for a long time. It's all an impenetrable confusion.

One of de Goncourt's sayings was, 'Japonaiserie for ever.'[1] Well, those docks are one huge Japonaiserie, fantastic, peculiar, unheard of – or at any rate, that's one way of looking at them. I would love to take a walk there in your company some day, just to find out if we see things in the same way.

Everything could be done there, townscapes, figures of the most diverse character, ships as the main subject with water & the sky a delicate grey – but, above all – Japonaiseries. The point I'm trying to make is that there are always figures in motion there, one sees them in the strangest setting, everything looks fantastic, with interesting contrasts at every turn. A white horse in the mud in a corner where piles of merchandise lie covered with a tarpaulin – against the old, black, smoke-stained walls of the warehouse. Perfectly simple, but with a Black & White[2] effect.

Through the window of a very elegant English public house one can look out on the filthiest mud and on a ship from which, say, such pleasing wares as hides and buffalo horns are being unloaded by docker types as ugly as sin, or by exotic sailors, while a very fair, very delicate English girl stands at the window looking out at this or at something else. The interior with figure wholly in tone, and for light – the silvery sky above the mud and the buffalo horns – again a series of fairly strong contrasts.

Flemish sailors with excessively ruddy faces and broad shoulders, lusty and tipsy, Antwerpers through & through, are to be seen eating mussels or drinking beer with a great deal of noise and commotion. In contrast – there goes a tiny little figure in black, small hands clasped close to her body, scuttling noiselessly past the grey walls. In an encadrement[3] of jet-black hair, a small oval face. Brown? Orange-yellow? I'm not sure. For a moment she looks up and gives a slanting glance from a pair of jet-black eyes. She is a Chinese girl, quiet as a mouse, stealthy, small, naturally bedbug-like. What a contrast to the group of Flemish mussel-eaters!

1 'for ever': in English.
2 'Black & White': in English.
3 Frame.

Another contrast – one walks down a very narrow street between tremendously tall buildings, warehouses and storehouses. But at ground level in the street – alehouses for every nationality, with males and females to match, shops for food, for seamen's clothing, colourful and bustling. The street is long, at every turn one sees a typical scene, a commotion, perhaps, more intense than usual, as a squabble breaks out. For example, there you are walking along, just looking around – and suddenly cheers go up and there's a lot of yelling. A sailor is being thrown out of a brothel by the girls in broad daylight and is being pursued by a furious fellow and a string of prostitutes, of whom he seems to be terrified – anyway, I see him clamber over a pile of sacks and disappear through a window into a warehouse.

When one has had enough of this hullaballoo – with the city behind one at the end of the landing stages where the Harwich and Havre steamers lie, there is nothing, absolutely nothing to be seen in front except for an infinite expanse of flat, half-flooded pasture, immensely melancholy and wet, with undulating dry reeds, and mud – the river with a single small black boat, water in the foreground grey, sky misty and cold, grey – still as the desert.

As to the overall impression of the harbour, or of one of the docks – at one moment it is more tangled and fantastic than a thorn hedge, so chaotic that one finds no rest for the eye, grows giddy, and is forced by the 'papillot-ering'[4] of colours and lines to look first here, then there, unable to distinguish one thing from another – even after looking at the same point for a long time. But if one moves on to a certain spot with an undefined stretch of land in the foreground, then one again encounters the most beautiful, most peaceful lines and those effects which Mols, for instance, so often achieves.

Here one may see a splendidly healthy-looking girl, who is, or at least seems, wholly honest and unaffectedly cheerful; there a face so slyly vicious, like a hyena's, that it frightens one. Not to forget faces ravaged by smallpox, the colour of boiled shrimps,

4 Flickering. Van Gogh 'Dutchified' the French *papillotement*.

with dull, grey little eyes, no eyebrows and sparse, greasy, thinning hair the colour of pure hog bristle, or a bit yellower – Swedish or Danish types.

I'd like to do some work round there, but how and where, for one would get into trouble exceedingly quickly. All the same I've roamed through quite a number of streets & alleyways without mishap, have even sat down to talk in a very friendly way with various girls, who seemed to take me for a bargee.

I think it not unlikely that painting portraits may help me to come by some good models. I got my gear today, and some materials, to which I'd been looking forward very eagerly. So now my studio is all ready. If I could come by a good model for a song, I'd be afraid of nothing. Nor do I mind very much that I haven't enough money to force the pace. Perhaps the idea of doing portraits and getting the subjects to pay for them by posing is a safer method. You see, in the city things aren't the same as when one deals with peasants.

Well, one thing is certain, Antwerp is a splendid and very remarkable place for a painter.

My studio isn't at all bad, especially now that I've pinned up a lot of small Japanese prints which I enjoy very much. You know, those small female figures in gardens or on the beach, horsemen, flowers, gnarled thorn branches.

I'm glad I came here – and hope not to sit still and do nothing this winter. Anyway, it's a relief to have a small hideaway where I can work when the weather is bad. It goes without saying that I won't be living in the lap of luxury.

Try to send your letter off on the first, for while I've enough to live on until then, I shall be getting the wind up after that.

My little room has turned out better than I expected and certainly doesn't look dreary.

Now that I have the 3 studies I took along with me here, I shall try to make contact with the marchands de tableaux,[5] who seem, however, to live for the most part in private houses, with no display windows giving on to the street.

5 Picture dealers.

The park is beautiful too. I sat there one morning and did some drawing.

Well – I've had no setbacks so far, and I'm well off as far as accommodation is concerned, for by sacrificing another few francs I've acquired a stove and a lamp. I shan't easily get bored, believe me.

I've also found Lhermitte's Octobre, women in a potato field in the evening, splendid, but not his Novembre yet. Have you kept track of that by any chance? I've also seen that there's a Figaro illustré with a beautiful drawing by Raffaëlli.

My address, as you know, is 194 Rue des images, so please send your letter there, and the second de Goncourt volume when you've finished with it. Regards,

Ever yours,
Vincent

It's odd that my painted studies look darker here in the city than in the country. Is that because the light isn't as bright in the city? I'm not sure, but it might matter more than one might think at first sight. I was struck by it and can imagine that some of the things that are with you now also look darker than I thought they were in the country. Yet those I brought along with me don't seem the worse for it – the mill, avenue with autumn trees, a still life, as well as a few small things.

442 [D]

[28 December 1885]

My dear Theo,

It's more than time I thanked you for the 50 fr. you sent, which enabled me to get through the month, although from today onwards things will be more or less back to normal.

But – a few more studies have been done and the more I paint the more progress I think I make. The moment I received the money I took on a beautiful model and did a life-size painting of her head. It's all quite light, except for the black hair. Yet the head itself stands out in tone against a background into which I have tried to put a golden glimmer of light.

Anyway, here is the colour range: a flesh colour full of tonal values, with more bronze in the neck, jet-black hair – black which I had to do with carmine and Prussian blue – off-white for the little jacket, light yellow, much lighter than the white, for the background. A touch of flame red in the jet-black hair and again a flame-coloured bow in the off-white.

She's a girl from a café-chantant[1] and yet the expression I was looking for was somewhat 'ecce homo-like'. But that was because I was aiming for the truth, especially in the expression, though I also wanted to put my own thoughts into it. When the model arrived, it was obvious she had had quite a few busy nights – and she said something that was fairly characteristic: 'Pour moi le champagne ne m'égaye pas, il me rend tout triste.'[2] Then I knew how matters stood and tried to produce something voluptuous and at the same time heart-rending.

I've started a second study of the same subject in profile.

Apart from that I've done the portrait about which, as I told you, I'd been negotiating, and a study of the same head for myself. And now, during these last few days of the month, I'm hoping to paint another head of a man. I feel very cheerful, especially as far as work is concerned, and being here is doing me good.

I imagine that no matter what the girls may be, one can make money painting them, sooner than anything else. There's no denying that they can be damned beautiful, and that it is in keeping with the times that just that kind of painting should be gaining ground. Nor can there be any objections to that from even the highest artistic standpoint – painting <u>human beings</u>, that was the old Italian art, that was Millet and that is Breton.

The only question is whether one should start from the soul or from the clothes, and whether one allows the form to serve as

1 Café providing a cabaret or musical entertainment.
2 For my part, champagne doesn't cheer me up, it makes me very sad.

a peg for hanging ribbons and bows from, or if one looks upon the form as a means of conveying an impression, a sentiment – or again, if one does modelling for the sake of modelling because it is such an infinitely beautiful thing to do. Only the first is ephemeral, the other two are high art.

What rather pleased me was that the girl who posed for me wanted to have one of the portraits for herself, preferably just like the one I'd done. And that she's promised to let me paint a study of her in a dancer's costume at her room, as soon as possible. It can't be done right away because the man who runs the café where she stays objects to her posing, but she's about to take lodgings with another girl, and both she and the other girl would like to have their portraits done. And I really very much hope that I'll get her back, for she has a remarkable head, and she's witty.

However, I must first get into practice because it certainly takes a special knack – they don't have much time or patience. Actually, the work needn't be the worse for being done fairly quickly, and one must be able to paint even if the model doesn't sit stock-still.

Well, you can see that I am working with a will. If I could sell something so that I could earn a bit more, I should work even harder.

As for Portier – I haven't lost heart yet – but poverty is dogging my steps and at present all dealers are suffering a little from the same defect, that of being more or less 'une nation retirée du monde'³ – they are so much sunk in gloom that how is one really to feel inspired to go grubbing about in all that indifference and apathy – the more so as the disease is catching.

For it's just a lot of nonsense that business is slack, one has to work quand bien même⁴ with self-confidence and enthusiasm, in short with some zeal.

And as for Portier – you wrote to me yourself that he was the first to show the impressionists & that he was overwhelmed by

3 A people withdrawn from society.
4 Even so.

Durand-Ruel – well, one is bound to conclude from this that he has the initiative not just to say things but also to <u>do</u> them. It could be put down to his 60 years, however – and anyway, perhaps it was just one of those many cases when, at the time when paintings were all the rage, and trade was doing well, a great many intelligent people were being wantonly brushed aside, as if they were incompetent and of no importance, simply because they couldn't bring themselves to believe that the sudden rage for paintings and the enormous rise in prices would last. <u>Now</u> that business is hanging fire, one sees those same dealers who were so very entreprenant[5] a few years ago – let's say about 10 years ago – turning more or less into 'une nation retirée du monde'. And we haven't yet seen the end of it.

Personal initiative with little or no capital is perhaps the seed corn for the future. We shall see.

Yesterday I saw a large phot. of a Rembrandt I didn't know – I was tremendously impressed by it – it was the head of a woman, the light falling on breast, throat, chin, the tip of the nose and the lower jaw. Forehead and eyes in the shadow of a large hat, with feathers that are probably red. Probably more red or yellow in the low-necked jacket. Dark background. The expression a mysterious smile like that of Rembrandt himself in his self-portrait with Saskia on his knee and a glass of wine in his hand.

My thoughts are full of Rembrandt and Hals these days, not because I see many of their paintings but because I see so many types amongst the people here that remind me of that period. I still keep going to those bals populaires[6] to look at the heads of the women and of the sailors and soldiers. One pays an entrance fee of 20 or 30 centimes and drinks a glass of beer – for there isn't much hard drinking and one can have a first-rate time all evening, or at least I can, just watching the people's en-train.[7]

I must do a lot of work from the model, it's the only way to ensure real progress.

5 Enterprising.
6 Dance halls.
7 High spirits.

I've discovered that my appetite has been held in check a bit too long and when I received your money I couldn't stomach any food. But I shall certainly do my best to remedy that. It doesn't take away from the fact that I have all my wits and energy about me when I'm painting. But when I'm out of doors, work in the open air is too much for me and I come over all weak.

Well, painting is something that wears one out. However, Van der Loo[8] said, when I consulted him shortly before I came here, that I am reasonably strong après tout.[9] That I needn't despair of reaching the requisite age to produce a complete body of work. I told him that I knew several painters who, for all their nervousness, etc., had reached the age of 60, or even 70, fortunately for themselves, and that I should like to do the same.

I also believe that if one aims for serenity, and retains one's zest for living, one's state of mind helps a great deal. And in that respect I have gained by coming here, for I've new ideas and new means of expressing what I want; the better brushes are going to prove a great help, and I'm very excited by those two colours carmine & cobalt.

Cobalt — is a divine colour and there is nothing as fine for putting an atmosphere round things. Carmine is the red of wine and is warm and lively like wine. The same goes for emerald green too. It's false economy to dispense with them, with those colours. Cadmium as well.

Something about my constitution that has pleased me a great deal is that a doctor in Amsterdam, with whom I once discussed a few things that sometimes made me think that I wasn't long for this world, and whose opinion I didn't ask for directly, wanting simply to gauge the first impression of someone who didn't know me at all and availing myself of a small upset I had at the time to bring the conversation round to my general constitution — I was absolutely delighted that this doctor took me for an ordinary worker, saying, 'I daresay you're an ironworker by

8 Van Gogh's doctor in Brabant.
9 After all.

trade.' That's exactly what I'd been trying to achieve – when I was younger you could tell that my mind was overwrought, and now I look like a bargee or an ironworker.

And changing one's constitution so that one gets 'le cuir dur'[10] is no easy matter. However, I must go on being careful, try to hold on to what I have and to improve on it still.

Above all, I should like you to tell me if you think it absurd of me to suggest that now might be a good time for us to sow the seeds of a future business. As far as my present work is concerned, I feel I can do better – however, I do need more air and space, in other words I must be able to spread my wings a little. Above all, above all, I still haven't enough models. I could soon produce work of higher quality, but my expenses would be heavier. Still, one should aim at something lofty, genuine, something distinguished, shouldn't one?

The female figures I see among the people here impress me enormously – far more for the purpose of painting them than of having them, though if the truth be told I should like both.

I am again rereading de Goncourt's book, it is first-rate. In the preface to Chérie, which you should read, there is an account of what the de Goncourts went through – and of how, at the end of their lives, they were pessimistic, yes – but also sure of themselves, knowing that they had <u>done something</u>, that their work would last. What fellows they were! If only we got on together better than we do now, if only we too could be in complete accord – we could be the same, couldn't we?

By the way, since, après tout, I've been virtually fasting for 4 or 5 days at this year's end – send your letter no later than 1 January.

You may well find it difficult to imagine, but it is a fact – when I receive the money my greatest craving will not be for food, though I shall have been fasting, but even more so for painting – and I shall immediately go on a hunt for models and continue until all the money is gone. Meanwhile what will be keeping me going is my breakfast with the people where I live,

10 A tough hide.

and a cup of coffee and some bread in the crêmerie[11] in the evening. Supplemented, when I can, by a second cup of coffee and bread in the crêmerie for my supper or else some rye bread I keep in my trunk. As long as I am painting that is more than enough, but when my models have left, a feeling of weakness does come over me.

The models here appeal to me because they're so completely unlike the models in the country. And more especially because their character is completely different. And the contrast has given me some new ideas for the flesh colours in particular. And though I'm still not satisfied with what I've achieved with my last head, it does differ from the earlier ones.

I think you value the truth enough for me to speak freely to you. For much the same reasons that if I paint peasant women I want them to be peasant women – so I want to get a whore's expression when I paint whores.

That is precisely why a whore's head by Rembrandt struck me so forcefully. Because he had caught that mysterious smile in such an infinitely beautiful way, with a sérieux[12] of his very own – the magician of magicians.

This is something new for me, and I want to achieve it at all costs. Manet has done it and Courbet – well, sacrebleu,[13] I've the same ambition too, the more so as I've felt the infinite beauty of the study of women by the giants of literature – Zola, Daudet, de Goncourt, Balzac – in the very marrow of my bones.

Even Stevens fails to satisfy me, because his women are not like any I know personally. And those he chooses are not the most interesting there are, I find.

Well, be that as it may – I want to get on à tout prix,[14] and – I want to be myself. I am feeling obstinate, too, and no longer care what people say about me or about my work.

It seems more difficult to get a nude model here – the girl I

11 Teashop.
12 Gravity.
13 Confound it.
14 At all costs.

used wouldn't do it, at any rate. Of course, that 'wouldn't' is probably relative, but you certainly can't take it for granted. Still, the fact is she would be splendid.

From a business point of view I can only say that we are in what people have already begun to call 'la fin d'un siècle'[15] – that the women have the same charm as at a time of revolution – and just as much to say – and that one would be 'retiré du monde' if one worked without them. It is the same everywhere, in the country as much as in the city – one has to take women into account if one wants to be up to date.

Goodbye, have a happy New Year, with a handshake,

Ever yours,
<u>Vincent</u>

On 18 January Van Gogh enrolled in the painting class of Charles Verlat, director of the Antwerp Academy. He also attended the evening course in drawing from classical plaster casts. He told Theo that he had been thinking of moving on to Paris to seek inspiration in the Louvre and from the modern paintings in the Musée du Luxembourg. He also wanted to take further lessons there. Theo suggested in reply that he try to get into Fernand Cormon's studio in Paris.

Vincent was chronically short of money and his health, too, was suffering. To make matters worse, he had large dentist's bills to pay. His lamentations alternated with philosophical and political diatribes that sounded as if he had only just picked them up in artistic circles. They included reflections on life during the *fin-de-siècle*, that interesting period in which they lived: '... we are in the last, 4th quarter of a century that will again end in a tremendous revolution. But let us suppose that we are both there to witness its beginning at the end of our lives. We shall certainly <u>not</u> live to see the better times when the air is cleared and all society refreshed <u>after</u> those great storms [...] we may be stifling now, but generations to come will be able to breathe more freely.' His reading of Zola, the de Goncourts, Turgenev and Daudet strengthened him further in this belief.

15 The end of the century.

Meanwhile, he was continually at loggerheads with his teachers at the Antwerp Academy, who felt that he was a bad influence on his fellow students, and he decided to stop attending the classes there. The brothers Van Gogh then discussed the date on which Vincent should move to Paris, where they would be able to cut costs by sharing an apartment. Theo was not immediately enthusiastic about this proposed move at such short notice and would have preferred Vincent to come after July. Vincent, for his part, assured Theo 'that I'll be very pleased if I could have a year to work at Cormon's [...] The ancients won't interfere with our being realists, far from it. I also can't wait, of course, to see the French paintings.' Vincent was not in favour of a temporary return to Nuenen and, to bring further speculation and discussion to an end, he faced his brother with a *fait accompli*: at the beginning of March he unexpectedly turned up in Paris.

459 [F]

[*c.* 1 March 1886]

My dear Theo,

Don't be angry with me for arriving out of the blue. I've given it so much thought and I'm sure we'll gain time this way. Shall be at the Louvre from midday onwards, or earlier if you like.

Please let me know what time you can get to the Salle Carrée. As far as expenses are concerned, I repeat that it won't make much difference. I still have some money left, of course, and I want to talk to you before spending any of it. We'll sort everything out, you'll see.

So come as soon as you can. I shake your hand.

Ever yours,
<u>Vincent</u>

Paris

During the period that the brothers shared an apartment – from March 1886 to February 1888 – they had no need to continue the correspondence from which we have been able to glean so many details of Van Gogh's life. The lack of letters from just these years is especially unfortunate because the period was so turbulent. Thus we have nothing more than scanty and indirect knowledge of Van Gogh's time in Cormon's studio, of his introduction to Impressionist and Neo-Impressionist circles, of his friendship with his new comrades – Henri de Toulouse-Lautrec, Paul Signac, Émile Bernard and Louis Anquetin (the so-called Impressionists of the Petit Boulevard) – of his café life, and of his painting expeditions to the new suburbs of Paris. All we have to go by for this period are the statements of others, and the few reminiscences Van Gogh himself devoted to this period during his stay in Provence. By contrast, the works painted in Paris provide a very good insight into his artistic development.

That development was tempestuous. Van Gogh eagerly absorbed the new impressions gained from his visits to exhibitions and from close association with artists of his generation. In this, he benefited at first from Theo's connections, but he in turn seems to have put Theo in touch with such modernists as Lautrec and Bernard, whom Vincent had met at Cormon's studio and who were to change the face of French painting in their day.

It was thanks to Theo that Vincent first became acquainted with the work of Claude Monet and other Impressionists. Although Impressionism had by then ceased to be a novelty confined to avant-garde circles, only a few of the artists Van Gogh characterized as 'les impressionistes du Grand Boulevard' were able to live by their work.

The year 1886 was a turning point in the history of art. It not only saw the eighth and last group exhibition by the Impressionists but also witnessed the launching of the Neo-Impressionist movement by Seurat and Signac. The last Impressionist group exhibition had already included work by some of the younger artists with whom Van Gogh was to form links, among them Paul Signac and Lucien Pissarro. That exhibition also presented for the first time a number of masterpieces by Georges Seurat, painted in the revolutionary, quasi-scientific technique of divisionism.

Van Gogh assimilated all these influences in his own way. Having clung for some time to the dark palette associated with his Nuenen days, he made a rapid change to the use of brighter colours. We can follow this development with the help of some twenty self-portraits he painted in Paris at different times. In a series of still lifes with flowers he also experimented with various colour combinations, and in his land-scapes he tried now an impressionist, now a pointillist, approach, or at times both methods side by side or mixed up together. Van Gogh's highly original interpretation of Seurat's pointillism, the use of separate dots of unmixed colour, gradually paved the way for a strikingly individual and expressive method of applying colour in streaks and dashes, which would henceforth typify Van Gogh's brushstroke no less than his drawing style.

In Paris, both brothers also became involved in building up an art collection of their own. In a letter Theo wrote to his mother in June 1886, he told her that though Vincent had not yet sold anything, he had started to exchange work with fellow artists and that an art dealer had taken four of his pictures on consignment. The two brothers acquired paintings by Adolphe Monticelli, an artist from Marseilles, and at the same time Vincent added appreciably to his collection of Japanese prints with purchases from the print dealer Siegfried Bing. The influence of these woodcuts on his own work may be gathered not only from the copies he painted after them but also from his increasingly daring compositions, from his stylized contours and from his expressive use of colour.

Although Van Gogh had come to Paris with the aim of learning what he could from Cormon, he must have been amazed to discover how out of touch his own method of working was with that of his leading contemporaries. And though he would later turn his back on much in their art that struck him as being modish and superficial, for the time being he changed course drastically. As a result, his Parisian period became a new term of apprenticeship, much more so than he could have anticipated. He not only embraced the new colour theories and other technical and theoretical insights of the Impressionists but also changed his subject-matter radically. In Paris he seems for the first time to have broken free of the hold of Millet and the painters of rural life, flinging himself into the portrayal of urban scenes, of the cafés and boulevards, and of life in the new suburbs of Paris such as Asnières.

Until the end of June 1886, the brothers lived in an apartment in the rue de Laval, from where they moved to more spacious quarters in Montmartre, at 54 rue Lepic. A letter written – in English – by Van Gogh to the English painter Horace M. Livens, whom he had met in Antwerp, painted a favourable picture of his first few months in the French capital, but also included a warning about the high cost of living there.

'My dear Mr. Levens [sic],

Since I am here in Paris I have very often thought of yourself and work. You will remember that I liked your colour, your ideas on art and literature and I add, most of all your personality. I have already before now thought that I ought to let you know what I was doing where I was. But what refrained me was that I find living in Paris is much dearer than in Antwerp and not knowing what your circumstances are I dare not say come over to Paris from Antwerp without warning you that it costs one dearer, and that if poor, one has to suffer many things – as you may imagine –. But on the other hand there is more chance of selling. There is also a good chance of exchanging pictures with other artists.

In one word, with much energy, with a sincere personal feeling of colour in nature I would say an artist can get on here notwithstanding the many obstructions. And I intend remaining here still longer.

There is much to be seen here – for instance Delacroix, to name only one master. In Antwerp I did not even know what the impressionists were, now I have seen them and though <u>not</u> being one of the club yet I have much admired certain impressionists' pictures – <u>Degas</u> nude figure – <u>Claude Monet</u> landscape.

And now for what regards what I myself have been doing, I have lacked money for paying models else I had entirely given myself to figure painting. But I have made a series of colour studies in painting, simply flowers, red poppies, blue corn flowers and myosotys, white and red roses, yellow chrysanthemums – seeking oppositions of blue with orange, red and green, yellow and violet seeking les tons rompus et neutres [broken and neutral tones] to harmonise brutal extremes. Trying to render intense colour and not a grey harmony.

Now after these gymnastics I lately did two heads which I dare say are better in light and colour than those I did before.

So as we said at the time: in colour seeking life the true drawing is modelling with colour.

I did a dozen landscapes too, frankly green frankly blue.

And so I am struggling for life and progress in art.

[. . .]'

He gave a vivid, amusing and warm account of his early days in Paris to his sister Wil, responding most affectionately to a description of nature she had sent him, and saying that people in love were 'perhaps more serious and saintly than those who sacrifice their love and their hearts to an idea'. He told her something of his ambition to become a portrait painter and disclosed his plan to travel to the south. The letter to Wil also contains an ironic self-portrait in words that bear out some of the painted self-portraits we know from the Paris period.

The few letters preserved from the Paris period suggest that the brothers' love-life continued to be eventful. A letter Vincent wrote to Theo, who was then in the Netherlands, in August 1886, makes it clear that Theo was attempting to break with a sick mistress. A recently discovered letter from Vincent's sister Wil, written to a Dutch girlfriend, Line Kruysse, on 26 August 1886, comments on this visit by Theo to the Netherlands. It is an interesting document because it reveals how sympathetic the family in Holland was towards Vincent's career, and how optimistically Theo viewed the future in the summer of 1886.

'My second brother, Theo, from Paris, left yesterday; he really is a dear boy. He told us so many good things about Vincent, the eldest, who is living with him. His paintings are getting so much better and he is beginning to exchange them for those of other painters, so everything's sure to come right in time. According to Theo, he is definitely making a name for himself. But we are under no illusions, and are only too grateful that he is having some slight success. You don't know what a hard life he has had, and who can say what is still in store for him. His disappointments have often made him feel bitter and have turned him into an unusual person. That was difficult for my parents, who could not always follow him and often misunderstood him. My father was strict, and attached to all sorts of conventions of which my brother never took any particular notice; needless to say, that often led to clashes and to words spoken in anger, which neither party was quick to forget. So during the past eight years Vincent has been a bone of contention with many, and all too often one tended to forget all the good there was in him, the appearances to the contrary. During the past few years he has been working at home with us; after my father's death, Anna thought it would be more peaceful for Mother if he stopped living at home, and saw to it that he left us. He took that so badly that from then on he has not been in touch with us, and it is only through Theo that we have news of him.'

One year later, Theo was again in the Netherlands, and now it was Vincent himself who was involved in the aftermath of an affair, with the Italian artists' model Agostina Segatori. He calmly noted that his desire for family life was dwindling. La Segatori was the proprietress of the Café Le Tambourin, and his comment, 'I still feel affection for her and I hope that she, too, still feels some for me', alludes to a relationship with her. Vincent organized an exhibition of Japanese prints at her café which made a great impression on many of his friends. In the portrait he did of her, seated at one of the small tambourine-shaped tables from which her establishment took its name, the Japanese prints may be seen in the background.

Japanese prints also form the setting for two fine portraits of Père Tanguy, the generous art and paint dealer who supported so many young Impressionists and who, in his shop, was one of the first to offer Van Gogh's work for sale. His name, too, crops up in these letters.

461 [F]

[summer 1887]

My dear friend,

Enclosed is a letter which arrived yesterday, but which the concierge didn't give me straight away.

I've been to the Tambourin, since if I hadn't gone, they would have thought I was afraid.

And I told la Segatori that I wouldn't pass judgement on her in this matter, but that it was for her to judge herself.

That I had torn up the receipt for the pictures – but that she had to return <u>everything</u>.

That if she had not had a hand in what had happened to me, she would have seen me the next day.

That as she didn't come to see me, my feeling was that she knew they were trying to pick a quarrel with me, but that she had tried to warn me by saying, 'Go away,' which I hadn't understood, and furthermore, perhaps didn't want to understand.

To which she replied that the pictures, & all the rest, were at my disposal. She maintained that it was I who had tried to pick a quarrel – which doesn't surprise me – knowing that if she sided with me they would take it out on her. I also saw the waiter when I went in, but he made himself scarce. I didn't want to take the pictures immediately, but I said that when you returned we would discuss the matter because these pictures belong to you as much as to me, and in the meantime I advised her to think about what had happened again. She didn't look well and was white as a sheet, which isn't a good sign. She didn't know that the waiter had gone up to your place. If that's true, I would be more inclined to believe she had tried to warn me they were trying to pick a quarrel with me than that she had plotted the whole thing herself. She cannot do as she likes. I'm awaiting your return now before taking any action.

I've done two pictures since you left. Have only got two louis[1]

1 A 20-franc piece.

left and I'm afraid I don't know how I'm going to manage from now until your return.

Don't forget that when I started working at Asnières I had plenty of canvases and Tanguy was very good to me. In fact he still is, but his old witch of a wife realized what was going on and complained. So I gave Tanguy's wife a piece of my mind and told her that it was her fault if I didn't buy anything more from them. Old man Tanguy is sensible enough to keep quiet, and will do whatever I want anyway. But with all this, work isn't easy.

I saw Lautrec today, he's sold a picture, through Portier I think. A watercolour of Mme Mesdag's has arrived which I find very beautiful.[2]

Now I hope you'll enjoy your trip over there, remember me to my mother, to Cor & to Wil. And if you could manage, by sending me something again, to ensure that I don't have too hard a time from now until you get back, then I shall try to do some more pictures for you – as I'm really very happy as far as my work goes. What worried me a little about this business was that it looked a little cowardly not going there, to the Tambourin. And my peace of mind has been restored by my going there.

I shake your hand,
Vincent

462 [F]

Paris [summer 1887]

My dear friend,

Thank you for your letter, and for what it contained. It saddens me to think that even successful paintings do not cover their costs.

I was touched by what you wrote about the family. 'They are fairly well but even so it's sad to see them.' Twelve years ago one would have sworn that, come what may, the family would always get on and do well. It would give Mother much pleasure

2 Probably *Grapes and Pears*.

if your marriage came off, and you also ought not to stay single for the sake of your health and business. As for me – I feel the desire for marriage and children dwindling and now and then I'm rather depressed that I should be like that as I approach 35, when I ought to be feeling quite the opposite. And sometimes I blame it all on this rotten painting. It was Richepin who said somewhere: the love of art is the undoing of true love. I think that's absolutely right, but on the other hand true love makes one weary of art. And although I already feel old and broken, I can still be amorous enough at times to feel less passionate about painting. One must have ambition to succeed, and ambition seems to me absurd. I wish above all I were less of a burden to you – and that needn't be impossible from now on, for I hope to make such progress that you'll be able to show what I do in full confidence without compromising yourself. And then I'll retire somewhere down south and get away from the sight of so many painters who fill me with disgust as human beings.

You can be sure of one thing – I shan't be trying to do any more work for the Tambourin. Anyway, I think it's about to change hands, and I most certainly won't raise any objections to that. As for la Segatori, that is quite a different matter. I still feel affection for her and I hope that she, too, still feels some for me. But at the moment she is in a difficult situation, she is neither a free agent nor mistress in her own house, on top of which she's in pain and unwell. Although I wouldn't say so openly – I'm convinced she's had an abortion (unless, that is, she did have a miscarriage) – anyway, in her case I don't hold it against her.

She'll be better in about two months' time, I hope, and then she may well be grateful to me for not having bothered her. Mind you, once she's well again, if she refuses in cold blood to return what is mine, or does me down in any way, I shan't pull my punches – but it won't come to that. After all, I know her well enough to trust her still. And mind you, if she does manage to hang on to her establishment, then from a business point of view I shouldn't blame her for choosing to fleece rather than be fleeced. If that means she has to tread on my toes a bit – all right – she can get on with it. When I saw her last, she didn't tread all over my heart, which she would have done had she been as nasty as people say.

I saw Tanguy yesterday and he has put a canvas I've just done in the window. I've done four since you left and I've got a big one under way. I realize that these big, long canvases are hard to sell, but later on people will see that there's fresh air and good humour in them. The whole lot would do well as decoration for a dining room or a country house. And if you were to fall properly in love and were to get married, then it doesn't seem impossible to me that you might manage to acquire a country house like so many other art dealers. If one lives well, one spends more, but also gains more ground, and perhaps nowadays one does better looking rich than looking hard up. It's better to enjoy life than to do away with oneself. Regards to all at home.

Ever yours,
Vincent

W I [D] [letter from Vincent to Wil]

[summer or autumn 1887]

My dear little sister,

Thank you very much for your letter, but for my part I hate writing these days. Still, there are some questions in your letter which I should like to answer.

To begin with, I must disagree with you when you say you thought Theo looked 'so wretched' this summer. Personally, I think that on the contrary Theo's appearance has become a great deal more distinguished during the past year. One has to be strong to stand life in Paris for as many years as he has done.

But might it have been that Theo's family and friends in Amsterdam and The Hague didn't treat him, or even receive him, with the cordiality he deserved from them and was entitled to expect? On that score, I can tell you that he may have felt hurt but is otherwise not at all bothered; after all, he is doing business even in these particularly bad times for the picture trade, so may it not be that his Dutch friends were somewhat affected by jalousie de métier?[1]

Now, what shall I say about your little piece on the plants & the rain? You can see yourself that in nature many flowers are trampled underfoot, frozen or scorched, and for that matter that not every grain of corn returns to the soil after ripening to germinate & grow into a blade of corn – indeed, that by far the greatest number of grains of corn do not develop fully but end up at the mill – isn't that so? To compare human beings with grains of corn, now – in every human being who is healthy and natural there is a germinating force, just as there is in a grain of corn. And so natural life is germination. What the germinating force is to the grain, love is to us.

Now we tend to stand about pulling a long face and at a loss for words, I think, when, thwarted in our natural development, we find that germination has been foiled and we ourselves placed in circumstances as hopeless as they must be for a grain between the millstones.

When that happens to us and we are utterly bewildered by the loss of our natural life, there are some amongst us who, though ready to bow to the inevitable, are yet unwilling to relinquish their self-confidence, and determine to discover what is the matter with them and what is really happening.

And if, full of good intentions, we search in the books of which it said that they illuminate the darkness, with the best will in the world we find precious little that is certain, and not always the satisfaction of personal consolation.

And the diseases from which we civilized people suffer most are melancholy and pessimism. So I, for instance, who can count so many years of my life during which I lost any inclination to laugh – leaving aside whether or not this was my own fault – I, for one, feel the need for a really good laugh above all else. I've found it in Guy de Maupassant, and there are others – Rabelais among the older writers, Henri Rochefort among the present-day ones – who provide it as well – and Voltaire in Candide.

1 Professional jealousy.

If, on the other hand, one wants the truth, life as it is, then there are, for instance, de Goncourt in Germinie Lacerteux,[2] La fille Eliza, Zola in La joie de vivre and L'assommoir, and so many other masterpieces, all portraying life as we feel it ourselves, thus satisfying our need for being told the truth.

The work of the French naturalists, Zola, Flaubert, Guy de Maupassant, de Goncourt, Richepin, Daudet, Huysmans, is magnificent, and one can scarcely be said to be of one's time if one is not acquainted with them. Maupassant's masterpiece is Bel-ami. I hope to be able to get it for you.

Is the Bible enough for us? These days I think Jesus himself would say again to those who sit down in melancholy, 'It is not here, it is risen. Why seek ye the living among the dead?' If the spoken or written word is to remain the light of the world, then we have the right and duty to acknowledge that we live in an age when it should be written and spoken in such a way that, if it is to be just as great and just as good and just as original and just as potent as ever to transform the whole of society, then its effect must be comparable to that of the revolution wrought by the old Christians.

I, for my part, am always glad that I have read the Bible more carefully than many people do nowadays, just because it gives me some peace of mind to know that there used to be such lofty ideals.

But precisely because I find the old beautiful, I find the new beautiful à plus forte raison[3] because we are able to take action in our own time while the past and the future concern us but indirectly.

My own adventures are confined above all to making swift progress towards growing into a little old man – you know, with wrinkles, a tough beard, a certain number of false teeth, &c. But what does all that matter? I have a dirty and difficult trade, painting, and if I were not as I am, I should not paint, but being as I am, I often work with pleasure and can visualize the vague

2 A novel by the de Goncourts.
3 With greater reason.

possibility of one day doing paintings with some youth and freshness in them, even though my own youth is one of the things I have lost.

If I didn't have Theo, I should not be able to do justice to my work, but having him for a friend, I'm sure I shall make progress and things will fall into place. As soon as possible I plan to spend some time in the south, where there is even more colour and even more sun.

But what I really hope to do is to paint a good portrait. So there.

To get back to your little piece, I have qualms about adopting for my own use, or about advising others to do so for theirs, the belief that there are powers above us that interfere personally in order to help or console us. Providence is such a strange thing, and I must confess that I haven't the slightest idea what to make of it. And well, there is still a degree of sentimentality in your little piece, and its form is reminiscent above all of tales about the above-mentioned providence, or let us say the providence under consideration. Tales that so often do not hold water, and to which a great many objections might be made.

And above all I find it alarming that you believe you must study in order to write. No, my dear little sister, learn how to dance, or fall in love with one or more notary's clerks, officers, in short, any within your reach – rather, much rather commit any number of follies than study in Holland. It serves absolutely no purpose than to make people slow-witted, so I won't hear of it.

For my part, I still continue to have the most impossible and highly unsuitable love affairs, from which as a rule I come away with little more than shame and disgrace. And in my own opinion I'm absolutely right to do this, since, as I keep telling myself, in years gone by, when I ought to have been in love, I gave myself up to religious and socialist affairs, and considered art holier than I do now.

Why are religion or justice or art so sacred? People who do nothing but fall in love are perhaps more serious and saintly than those who sacrifice their love and their hearts to an idea. Be that as it may, in order to write a book, do a deed, make a picture with some life in it, one has to be alive oneself. And so, unless you never want to progress, study is a matter of very minor importance for you. Enjoy yourself as much as you can, have as many amusements as you can, and remember that what people demand in art nowadays is something very much alive, with strong colour and great intensity. So intensify your own health and strength and life, that's the best study.

I should be most obliged if you could let me know how Margot Begemann is and how things are with the De Groots, how did that business turn out? Did Sien de Groot marry her cousin? And did her child live?

Of my own work I think that the picture of peasants eating potatoes I did in Nuenen is après tout[4] the best I've done. But since then I've had no chance of getting models, though on the other hand I did have the chance to study the colour question. And if I should find models again for my figures later, then I would hope to be able to show that I am after something other than little green landscapes or flowers.

Last year I painted almost nothing but flowers so as to get used to colours other than grey, viz. pink, soft or bright green, light blue, violet, yellow, orange, glorious red.

And when I was painting landscapes at Asnières this summer, I saw more colour in them than I did before. Now I'm going to try it with a portrait. And I must say that I'm not painting any the worse for it, perhaps because I could tell you a very great deal that's wrong with both painters and paintings if I wanted to, quite as easily as I could tell you something that's good about them ...

I don't want to be included among the melancholy or those who turn sour and bitter and bilious. 'Tout comprendre, c'est tout pardonner',[5] and I believe that if we knew everything we should attain some serenity. Now, having as much of that serenity as possible, even when one knows little or nothing for

4 After all.
5 To understand everything is to forgive everything.

certain, is perhaps a better remedy for all ills than what is sold in the pharmacy. Much of it comes by itself, one grows and develops of one's own accord.

So don't study and swot too much, for that makes one sterile. Enjoy yourself too much rather than too little, and don't take art or love too seriously – there is very little one can do about it, it is chiefly a question of temperament.

If I were living near you, I should try to drive home to you that it might be more practical for you to paint with me than to write, and that you might be able to express your feelings more easily that way. In any case, I could do something personally about your painting, but I am not in the writing profession.

Anyway, it's not a bad idea for you to become an artist, for when one has fire within and a soul, one cannot keep bottling them up – better to burn than to burst, what is in will out. For me, for instance, it's a relief to do a painting, and without that I should be unhappier than I am.

> Give Mother much love from me,
> Vincent

I was deeply moved by A la recherche du bonheur. I've just read Mont-Oriol by Guy de Maupassant.

Art often seems very exalted and, as you say, sacred. But the same can be said of love. And the only problem is that not everyone thinks about it this way, and that those who do feel something of it and allow themselves to be carried away by it have to suffer a great deal, firstly because they are misunderstood, but quite as often because their inspiration is so often inadequate or their work frustrated by circumstance. One ought to be able to do two or even more things at once. And there are certainly times when it is far from clear to us that art should be something sacred or good.

Anyway, do weigh up carefully if those with a feeling for art, and trying to work at it, wouldn't do better to declare that they are doing it because they were born with that feeling, cannot help themselves and are following their nature, than make out they are doing it for some noble purpose. Doesn't it say in A la recherche du bonheur that evil lies in our own nature – which we have not created ourselves? I think it so admirable of the moderns that they do not moralize like the old. Thus many people are appalled and scandalized by 'Le vice et la vertu sont des produits chimiques, comme le sucre et le vitriol'.[6]

6 Vice and virtue are chemical products, like sugar and vitriol.

Arles

In the letter to Wil just quoted, Van Gogh was already talking of his wish to go south, ostensibly in search of more light and colour. There has been much speculation about the precise reason why Van Gogh left Paris for Provence. He himself gave somewhat conflicting explanations in his letters.

Frequently recurring tensions between the two brothers cannot, of course, be ruled out. In March 1887, Theo had been very frank about this matter in a letter to Wil. At the time there was already talk of Vincent leaving in order to live on his own, but within a month the 'intolerable' situation had been repaired. That the brothers' relationship improved markedly during the rest of 1887 may be gathered from Theo's great sense of emptiness once Vincent had left for Arles: 'When he came here two years ago, I did not think we would grow so attached to each other, for I certainly feel an emptiness now that I am alone in the apartment once again. If I can find somebody, then I shall take him in, but someone like Vincent is not easy to replace.'

Vincent himself cited the severe Parisian winter and his indifferent health to Wil as reasons for his departure for the south, and in the letter he sent Theo on 21 February 1888, after his arrival in Arles, he declared: 'It appears to me to be almost impossible to work in Paris, unless you have a retreat where you can go to recover your peace of mind and self-confidence. Otherwise you become irrevocably dulled.' He described himself as a worn-out Paris cab horse about to be put out to pasture.

An incontestable fact is that Van Gogh arrived in Arles, the capital of Provence, on Monday, 20 February 1888. Taking temporary lodgings at the Restaurant Carrel, he found to his amazement that the little town ('no bigger than Breda') lay under a thick blanket of snow: 'And the landscapes in the snow, with the white peaks against a sky as bright as the snow, were just like the winter landscapes the Japanese do.' For all that, the almond trees were already in blossom.

Although Van Gogh barely devoted one stroke of his brush to the countless relics of Roman antiquity during his stay in Arles, he does not seem to have been entirely insensitive to the local architecture: 'There is a Gothic portico here which I am beginning to marvel at, the portico of St. Trophîme. But it is so brutal, so monstrous, so like a Chinese nightmare, that even this splendid monument in so grand a style seems to belong to another world, to which I fortunately belong no more than to the glorious world of the Roman Emperor, Nero. In all honesty, I have to add that the Zouaves, the brothels, the charming little Arlésiennes on their way to their first Communion, the priest in his surplice, who resembles a dangerous rhinoceros, and the absinthe drinkers, also strike me as beings from another world.'

From Arles, Van Gogh kept in touch by letter – for the most part through Theo – with the young painter and poet Émile Bernard, with whom he had explored the suburbs of Paris and who shared his love of Japanese art, incorporating it systematically into his own stylized paintings.

Bernard, for his part, had close ties with Paul Gauguin, who was having problems with his health at the time and was seriously short of money. Van Gogh then had the idea of establishing a sort of painters' cooperative with the aim of achieving better prices for his own and for that of his fellow artists' work. This seemingly strange combination of a cloistered fellowship of painters *à la japonaise* with a pragmatic financial arrangement, reveals that during his stay in Paris Vincent must have absorbed something of his brother's business acumen. Indeed, his plans even included a role for Herman Tersteeg, the head of Goupil's Hague branch.

468 [F]

[10 March 1888]

My dear Theo,

Thank you for your letter and the enclosed 100 fr. note. I very much hope that Tersteeg will be coming to Paris soon, as you seem to expect. It would be most welcome with things in the state you say they're in, everyone with their backs to the wall and in such financial straits. I'm very interested in what you write about the Lançon sale and the painter's mistress. He's done work of much individuality, his drawing often reminds me of Mauve's. I'm sorry not to have seen the exhibition of his studies, just as I also very much regret not having seen the Willette exhibition.

What do you think of the news that Kaiser Wilhelm has died? Will that speed things up in France, and will Paris stay calm? It seems unlikely. And what effect will all this have on the picture trade? I read that there seems to be some talk of abolishing import duties on pictures in America, is that true?

It might be easier to get a few dealers and art lovers to agree to buy the impressionist pictures than to get the artists to agree to equal shares in the price of the pictures sold.

Even so, the artists could not do better than combine forces, give their pictures to the association, and share the proceeds of any sales, the society thus guaranteeing that its members can go on living and working. If Degas, Claude Monet, Renoir, Sisley and C. Pissarro would take the initiative and say, Look here, the five of us will each hand over 10 pictures (or rather, we'll each hand over work to the value of 10,000 fr., estimated by expert members co-opted by the society such as Tersteeg and yourself, the said experts also investing capital in the form of pictures), and we furthermore undertake to hand pictures over every year to the value of ... And we invite the rest of you, Guillaumin,[1]

---

1 Armand Guillaumin (1841–1927), early Impressionist, some of whose work the brothers Van Gogh had acquired.

Seurat, Gauguin, &c., &c., to join us (your pictures subjected to the same expert valuation).

Thus the great impressionists of the Grand Boulevard, by giving pictures that would become general property, would preserve their prestige, and the others would no longer be able to reproach them for keeping to themselves the advantages of a reputation no doubt acquired in the first place by their personal efforts and their individual talent – but in the second place also enhanced, consolidated and maintained by the paintings of a whole battalion of artists who have been working in unremitting poverty.

Be that as it may, it is to be hoped that this will come off and that Tersteeg and you will become the society's expert members (perhaps together with Portier?).

I've got two more landscape studies. I hope the work will go on steadily from now on and that I'll be able to send you a first batch in a month – I say in a month, because I want to send you only the best, and because I want them to be dry, and because I want to send at least a dozen of them at a time, on account of the freight charges.

I congratulate you on the purchase of the Seurat[2] – with what I'm going to send you, you might try to arrange another exchange with Seurat as well.

You do realize that if Tersteeg joins you in this business, the two of you could easily persuade Boussod & Valadon to grant a sizeable credit for the necessary purchases. But it is urgent, or else other dealers will pull the carpet from under your feet.

I've made the acquaintance of a Danish artist[3] who talks about Heyerdahl and other people from the north, Kroyer, &c. What he does is dry, but very conscientious, and he is still young. He saw the impressionist exhibition in the Rue Lafitte some time ago. He'll probably come to Paris for the Salon, and wants to do a tour of Holland to see the museums.

I approve of your exhibiting the Books with the Indépendants – you should give this study the title 'Romans parisiens'.

2 The drawing *L'Eden Concert.*
3 Christian Vilhelm Mourier-Petersen.

I would be so glad to learn that you had managed to persuade Tersteeg – do be patient with him, anyway.

I had to get 50 frs.' worth of bits and pieces when your letter arrived. I'll be starting this week on 4 or 5 things.

I think every day about this artists' association, and the plan has developed further in my mind, but Tersteeg must be in on it, and much depends on that. Right now the painters would probably let themselves be persuaded by us, but we can get no further until we have Tersteeg's help. Without that we'd have to listen to the lamentations of one and all from morning to night and each one would be forever coming round individually demanding explanations and axioms, &c. I shouldn't be a bit surprised if Tersteeg took the view that one could not do without the artists of the Grand Boulevard – and that he will advise you to persuade them to take the initiative in the association by handing in pictures which would then become common property and cease to belong to them alone. A proposal which, in my opinion, the Petit Boulevard would be morally obliged to support.

And these gentlemen of the Grand Boulevard will only hold on to their present high reputation by forestalling the not unfounded criticisms of the lesser impressionists who will say, 'Everything goes into your own pocket.' To that they may well reply, 'Not at all, on the contrary, we are the first to say our pictures belong to the artists.' If Degas, Monet, Renoir and Pissarro were to say that – (even leaving plenty of latitude for their personal views on how best to implement the scheme) – they would be doing better than by saying nothing at all and letting things slide.

Yours,
Vincent

At the end of March, spring arrived in all its splendour. While for the first time his work was being shown in Paris at the exhibition of the Indépendants, together with that of his Impressionist colleagues, Van Gogh was at work on a series of six fruit trees in blossom.

Theo sent his brother regular supplies of paint and canvas. Vincent had realized that the colours the Impressionists had introduced tended to fade, 'one more reason for simply making them too bright – in time they will just lose colour'. The grey palette of the Hague School had definitely made way for the more powerful and expressive use of colour associated with Delacroix and Monticelli.

Much as Claude Monet was working on a coherent series of paintings at the end of the 1880s, so Van Gogh, too, did not conceive his canvases of orchards as individual pictures, but as elements of a larger set. A small sketch of one such triptych conveyed a good idea of what he had in mind. He called one of the orchards *Souvenir de Mauve*, in memory of his cousin and teacher, who had died in February. Vincent felt sure of himself and was full of plans to make Holland sit up and take notice of his work. He proposed to send studies to Breitner and Tersteeg and to 'give the 2 landscapes of Montmartre hung at the Indépendants to the Modern Museum in The Hague, since we have so many memories of The Hague'. He also wanted to exchange several canvases with colleagues. In the event, however, none of these paintings reached the Netherlands in Vincent's lifetime – with the exception of *Souvenir de Mauve*, which went to Mauve's widow.

His collection of Japanese prints continued to be an enduring inspiration, and among the new subjects he planned to tackle was 'a starry night with cypresses', an idea he was not to implement until 1889, in Saint-Rémy.

474 [F]

[9 April 1888]

My dear Theo,

Thank you for your letter and the enclosed 100 fr. note. I have sent you some sketches of the pictures intended for Holland. It goes without saying that the painted studies are more vivid in colour. Am hard at work again, still on orchards in bloom.

The air here is definitely doing me good, I wish you could fill your lungs with it. One of its effects on me is quite amusing, a single small glass of cognac here goes to my head, so without my having to use stimulants to make my blood circulate, my constitution is under less strain. The only thing is, I've had a terribly weak stomach ever since I arrived, but that's probably just a question of being patient.

I hope to make real progress this year which, to be sure, I badly need to do. I've got a new orchard which is as good as the pink peach trees – apricot trees of a very pale pink. At the moment I'm working on some plum trees, yellowy white, with thousands of black branches. I am using up an enormous amount of canvases and paints, but I hope it's not a waste of money for all that. Out of 4 canvases there'll be perhaps one at the most which will make a <u>picture</u>, like Tersteeg's or Mauve's, but the studies might come in useful as exchanges, I hope. When can I send you something? I'm very keen to do two of the one I did for Tersteeg, as it's better than the Asnières studies.

I saw another bullfight yesterday, where 5 men played the bull with banderillas and cockades. A toreador crushed one of his balls jumping the barricade. He was a fair man with grey eyes who showed great sang froid – they said he'll be laid up for a long time. He was dressed in sky blue and gold, exactly like the little horsemen in our Monticelli with the 3 figures in a wood. The bullrings are quite beautiful when there is sunshine and a crowd.

Good for Pissarro, I'm sure he's right. I hope he'll do an exchange with us one day. The same goes for Seurat. It would be a good deal getting a painted study by him. Anyway, I'm working hard, hoping we can bring something like this off.

It's going to be a hard month for you and me, but if you can possibly manage, it would be to our advantage to make the most of the orchards in bloom. I am into my stride at the moment and could do with another 10, I think, of the same subject.

You know I chop and change in my work, and this passion for painting orchards won't last for ever. After this it could be bullrings. Then I also have an <u>enormous</u> number of drawings to do, as I want to do some in the manner of Japanese prints. There's nothing like striking while the iron is hot. Shall be exhausted after the orchards, as the canvases are sizes 25 & 30 &

20. We could never have too many of them, even if I turned out double the amount. It seems to me that this may well break the ice in Holland once and for all. Mauve's death was a severe blow to me. You will see that the pink peach trees were painted with some passion. I must also do a starry night with cypresses or – perhaps over a field of ripe corn. There are some extremely beautiful nights here. I am in a constant fever of work.

Am very curious to know what the result will be by the end of a year. I hope that by then I'll be less dogged by ill-health. At present I suffer quite a lot on some days, but am not in the least worried as it is merely a reaction to last winter, which was out of the ordinary. And my blood is coming right, that's the main thing.

We must get to the point where the value of my pictures covers my expenditure, and even exceeds it, in view of how much has already been spent. Oh well, it will come. I don't bring everything off, naturally, but the work is coming along. You haven't complained about what I've laid out so far, but I warn you that if I continue to work at the same rate I shall find it very hard to make ends meet. It's just that there is an inordinate amount of work.

If there is a month or a fortnight when you feel hard pressed, let me know – I'll immediately get down to some drawings, and that will cost us less. Just to tell you that you mustn't put yourself out without good reason – there is so much to do here, all kinds of studies, not as in Paris, where you can't even sit down where you want to.

If you could possibly manage to spare a bit extra for one month, so much the better, because orchards in bloom are the sort of thing that stand some chance of selling or exchanging. But I haven't forgotten that you have your rent to pay, that's why you must warn me if things get too tight.

I'm still going around all the time with the Danish painter, but he'll be leaving soon. He's an intelligent fellow, very dependable and well mannered, but his painting is still not up to much. You'll probably see him when he passes through Paris.

It was good of you to go to Bernard's. If he does his service in

Algeria, who knows, perhaps I'll go there to keep him company. Is winter in Paris over at last?

I think what Kahn says is perfectly true, that I haven't taken tonal values into account enough, but they'll be saying something very different later on – no less true. It's impossible to deal with tonal values and colour. Th. Rousseau did it better than anyone else, but because of the mixing of the colours, the darkening with time has increased, and his pictures are now unrecognizable. One cannot be at the pole and the equator at the same time. One has to choose, which I hope I do, and it will probably be colour. Good-bye for now. A handshake to you, Koning and our friends,

Vincent

By the end of April the fruit trees had finished flowering and Van Gogh had no choice but to abandon this series. One year later he was to pick up the theme again. Because painting was proving too costly, he confined himself to drawings for a time. He experimented with a new technique which he associated with his beloved Japan – using the reed pen.

By now he had also decided to move – he had found a house in the place Lamartine and had rented its right wing, 'which contains 4 rooms, or rather two with two small box rooms. It is painted yellow outside, whitewashed within, and in the full sun.' In this 'Yellow House', not far from the Rhône, he dreamed of setting up a 'studio of the south'. 'If need be I could share this new studio with someone else and I wouldn't mind that. Perhaps Gauguin will come south,' he wrote on 1 May 1888.

Meanwhile, he had just two colleagues in the neighbourhood, the American artist Dodge MacKnight, who lived in nearby Fontvieille, and the Danish painter Christian Vilhelm Mourier-Petersen. His first priority, though, was to do something about his poor health, the result of immoderate drinking in Paris and of his 'rather too artistic way of life'. That involved furnishing his house and studio decently, at a cost he estimated at about 1,000 francs. However, money was scarce, it seemed furniture was not available for hire, and so he asked Theo if he could have his old bed from their Paris apartment, once the Dutch painter Arnold Koning, who had moved in with Theo, had left again. In an interesting passage, he voiced his belief that he bore an hereditary taint and belonged to a generation of weaklings.

'My friend, though our neurosis, &c., is certainly due to our rather too artistic way of life, it is also part of an inescapable heritage, since in our civilization people grow weaker from one generation to the next. Take our sister Wil, she has never been given to drinking, or led a loose life, and yet we know a portrait of her in which she has the facial expression of a lunatic. Isn't that proof enough that, if we face up to our true state of mind, we have to acknowledge that we are among those who suffer from a mental illness rooted quite a long way back in the past? I think Gruby got hold of the right end of the stick here: good food, healthy living, not taking much notice of women, in short living as if one were already in the throes of a disease of the brain or the spine, over and above the mental illness which is undeniably present. One would, of course, be taking the bull by the horns like this, not a bad policy. Degas is doing just that, and successfully, too. But don't you agree that it's a terribly hard business? And, all in all, doesn't it do one an enormous amount of good to heed the wise counsel of Rivet and Pangloss, those distinguished optimists of the real and so jovial Gallic race, who leave your self-respect intact? If we want to live and work we must be very careful and look after ourselves. Cold water, fresh air, simple, good food, decent clothing, a good night's sleep and no worries. And no womanizing or living the good life whenever you feel the urge.'

482 [F] [part]

[*c.* 4 May 1888]

My dear Theo,

I'm dropping you another line to tell you that on reflection I think it would be better for me just to take a rug & a mattress and make a bed on the floor in the studio. It will be so hot all summer that this will be more than enough. When winter comes we can see whether we need to get a bed.

As for the bed at your place, I think that as far as conversation and company are concerned, having a painter to stay with you is good for both you and the painter. So that even when Koning leaves there may well be someone to take his place. Anyway, why don't you keep the bed with you?

It's quite possible that as far as the house is concerned, I might find something better either at Martigues, by the sea, or somewhere else. Only, what is so delightful about this studio is the garden opposite. But we'd do well to wait before doing any repairs to it or furnishing it halfway decently – it would be wiser – especially as, if we should get cholera here in the summer, I might up and go to the country. This is a filthy town with all its old streets!

The women of Arles about whom people talk so much, don't they – you know what I really think of them? They are indeed truly charming, but no longer what they must once must have been. They are more often like a Mignard than a Mantegna, because they're now in decline. That doesn't stop them from being beautiful, very beautiful, and I'm talking here only of the Roman type – a bit boring & run of the mill – but what exceptions there are! There are women like Fragonards and – like Renoirs. And some that one cannot pigeonhole as anything done in painting so far.

The best thing one could do here, from every point of view, would be portraits of women and children. Only I don't think that I am the man to do it, I'm not enough of a M. Bel Ami for that.

But I should be extremely happy if this Bel Ami of the south, which Monticelli was not, but tried to be – who, I'm sure, is on his way, though I realize it isn't to be me – I should be extremely happy, as I say, if a kind of Guy de Maupassant of painting turned up to make happy pictures of all these beautiful people and things round here.

As for me, I shall carry on working, and here and there something of my work will prove of lasting value – but who will there be to achieve for figure painting what Claude Monet has achieved for landscape? However, you must feel, as I do, that someone like that is on the way – Rodin? – he doesn't use colour – it won't be him. But the painter of the future will be a <u>colourist the like of which has never yet been seen</u>. Manet was getting there but, as you know, the impressionists have already made use of stronger colour than Manet.

I can't imagine the painter of the future living in small restaurants, setting to work with a lot of false teeth, and going to the Zouaves' brothels as I do.

But I'm sure I'm right to think that it will come in a later generation, and it is up to us to do all we can to encourage it, without question or complaint. [...]

The names of Drs Gruby and Rivet recur in a letter written during the third week of May 1888, when Theo's severe listlessness was causing Vincent concern. The letter may well have been referring to a depression, one of the symptoms of the neurosyphilis that was to cause Theo's death. Vincent's advice to his brother – 'to have nothing to do with women if you can help it' – may be read in that light.

An unexpected passage refers to previously unmentioned Parisian acquaintances of Vincent, the Comtesse de la Boissière and her daughter in Asnières, to whom he seems to have given two small pictures the year before.

The feeling of being 'a link in the chain of artists' reconciled Vincent with his mortality and helped him to sublimate his instincts: 'I no longer feel so much need for diversion, I am less plagued by passions and am able to work more calmly.' The art of the future, 'so lovely and so young that [...] we can only gain in serenity by it', was well worth the sacrifice of youth and health.

489 [F] [part]

[*c.* 20 May 1888]

My dear Theo,

What you write about your visit to Gruby has upset me, but all the same I'm relieved you went.

Has it occurred to you that the lethargy – the feeling of extreme lassitude – might be due to your heart condition, in which case the potassium iodide would have nothing to do with your exhaustion? Remember how exhausted I was last winter myself, to the point of being completely incapable of doing anything, apart from a little painting, and yet I was taking no potassium iodide at all. So if I were you, I would have it out with Rivet if Gruby tells you not to take any. After all, I'm sure you intend to keep on friendly terms with both.

I often think of Gruby <u>here</u> and <u>now</u>, and generally speaking I feel quite well, but it is the pure air and the warmth here which makes that possible. What with all the troubles & the poor air of Paris, Rivet takes things as he finds them, without trying to create a paradise, and without attempting in any way to make us perfect. But he forges a suit of armour, or rather he arms us against illness and keeps up one's morale, I think, by making light of any illness one has.

So, if you could spend just one year of your life now in the country and with nature, it would make Gruby's cure much easier. And he may well advise you to have nothing to do with women if you can help it, but in any case as little as possible. As for me, I'm doing very well, but that's because I have work and nature <u>here</u>. If I didn't have that, I should turn melancholy. So long as the work has some attraction for you and the impressionists are doing well, there is much to be gained by staying on. For what is really wretched is loneliness, worries, problems, and the unfulfilled need for kindness and sympathy. Feelings of sadness or disappointment undermine us more than dissipation – those of us, I say, who find ourselves the happy owners of irregular hearts.

I'm sure potassium iodide purifies the blood & the whole system, don't you think? Can you get along without it? Anyway, you must talk it over frankly with Rivet, he's not likely to be jealous.

I wish you had people around you more rudely alive, warmer than the Dutch. Although Koning, for all his whims, is a pleasant exception. Anyway, it's always a good thing to have someone, though I wish you had a few more friends among the French.

Would you do me a great favour? My friend the Dane, who is leaving for Paris on Tuesday, will give you 2 little pictures – nothing special – which I should like to present to Mme la Comtesse de la Boissière in Asnières. She lives in the Boulevard

Voltaire, on the first floor of the first house, at the end of the Pont de Clichy. Old Perruchot's restaurant is on the ground floor. Would you take them there in person for me, and say that I had hoped to see her again this spring, and that even here I have not forgotten her? I gave them 2 small ones last year, too, her and her daughter. I'm sure you won't regret making the acquaintance of these ladies – they are a real <u>family</u>.

The countess is far from young, but she is a countess first, then a <u>lady</u>, the daughter the same. And it makes sense for you to go, because I can't be sure that the family is staying at the same place this year (though they've been going there for several years, and Perruchot should know their address in town). Perhaps I'm deceiving myself, but – I can't help thinking about it, and it might give them some pleasure, and you too, if you met them.

[...]

I've done two still lifes this week.

A blue enamelled coffee pot, a cup (on the left), royal blue and gold, a pale blue & white checked milk jug, a cup – on the right – white with a blue & orange pattern, on a greyish-yellow earthenware plate, a blue barbotine or majolica jug, with a pattern of reds, greens and browns, and lastly 2 oranges and 3 lemons. The table is covered with a blue cloth. The background is greenish-yellow, so there are 6 different blues and 4 or 5 yellows & oranges. The other still life is the majolica jug with wild flowers.

Thank you very much for your letter and the 50 fr. note. I hope the packing case will arrive within a day or so. Next time, I think I'll take the canvases off the stretchers so they can be rolled up and sent by express train.

[...]

I haven't yet managed to do any business with the furniture dealer. I've seen a bed, but it is dearer than I thought it would be. I feel I ought to get a lot more work done before spending more on furniture. My lodging is 1 fr. per night. I've bought some more linen and also some paint. I got very hard-wearing linen.

As my blood is gradually coming right, thoughts of success are also reviving. It wouldn't surprise me at all if your illness, too, were a reaction to that awful winter, which lasted an eternity. And so it will be the same story as mine. Take as much spring air as possible, go to bed very early, because you must have sleep, and as for food, plenty of fresh vegetables, and no bad wine or bad alcohol. And very few women, and lots of patience.

If it doesn't clear up immediately, no matter. Gruby will prescribe a high meat diet for you there. I couldn't take much of that here – and here there's no need for it.

That mental exhaustion of mine is disappearing, I no longer feel so much need for diversion, I am less plagued by passions, and am able to work more calmly. I could be alone without getting bored. I have come out of this feeling a little older, but no sadder.

I shall not believe you if you tell me in your next letter that there's nothing wrong with you any longer. There may well be a radical change, though, and I wouldn't be surprised if you were a little despondent during the time it takes for you to recover. At the height of artistic life there is, and remains, and returns time and again, a hankering after real life – ideal and unattainable.

And sometimes one lacks the will to throw oneself back

wholeheartedly into art, and to regain one's capacity for it. One knows one is a cab horse, and that one is going to be hitched up to the same old cab again – and that one would rather not, and would prefer to live in a meadow, with sunshine, a river, other horses for company as free as oneself, and the act of procreation.

And perhaps, in the end, the heart complaint is caused by that. I shouldn't be at all surprised if it is to some extent. One no longer rebels against things, but neither is one resigned – one is ill and does not get better – and one cannot find a precise cure.

I'm not sure who called this condition 'being stricken by death and immortality'. The cab one is pulling along must be of some use to people one doesn't know. And so, if we believe in the new art, in the artists of the future, our presentiment will not play us false.

When good old Corot said a few days before his death, 'Last night in a dream, I saw landscapes with skies all pink,' well, they've arrived, haven't they, those pink skies, and yellow and green ones into the bargain, in the impressionist landscape? Which means that some things one can foresee in the future do indeed come about.

And those of us who are, as I am led to believe, still fairly far from death, nevertheless feel that these things are bigger than we are and will outlive us.

We do not feel we are dying, but we do feel that in reality we count for little, and that to be a link in the chain of artists we are paying a high price in health, in youth, in liberty, none of which we enjoy, any more than does the cab horse pulling a coachload of people out enjoying themselves in spring.

Anyway – what I wish you, as well as myself, is success in regaining our health, because we are going to need it. That Espérance by Puvis de Chavannes is so very true. There is an art of the future, and it will be so lovely and so young that even if we do give up our youth for it, we can only gain in serenity by it.

It may be very silly to write all this down, but that is how I feel. It seemed to me that you were suffering, like me, from seeing our youth go up in smoke – but if it throws out new growth in one's work then nothing is lost, for the capacity to work is another form of youth. So take a bit of trouble over getting better, because we shall need our health. A warm hand-shake for you, and for Koning,

Ever yours,
Vincent

Early in June 1888 Van Gogh visited the little port of Les-Saintes-Maries-de-la-Mer on the Mediterranean. Here he produced some mag-nificent seascapes and the delightful *Fishing Boats on the Beach*. Besides painting 'marines' he hoped also to draw inspiration for 'a furious onslaught on the figure', as he wrote to his Dutch colleague Arnold Koning. He planned, in addition, to combine various drawings into albums as the Japanese do and to present these to Gauguin and Bernard.

Japanese influences continued to dominate his philosophy: 'We like Japanese painting, we are influenced by it – all impressionists have that in common.' A stay in the south was bound to bring an artist very close to Japan: 'In time, your outlook changes, you look on things with a more Japanese eye, you experience colours differently. [. . .] So I'm convinced that my personality will develop if I live here for a long time.' To emphasize his identification with Japanese art, he sent Gauguin a portrait of himself as a 'bonze' (a Japanese priest).

Van Gogh grew impatient at the lack of news about Gauguin's departure for the south. To expedite his plans for sharing a house with Gauguin, he sent Theo a draft letter of proposals he had written for Gauguin towards the end of May 1888: 'If my brother were to send us 250 francs a month for the two of us, would you be prepared to come then? We'd be able to share things. If we do that, however, we shall have to make up our minds to eat at home as often as possible. We can take on a cleaning woman or the like for a few hours a day and so save on all hotel expenses. And you would give my brother one painting a month and do what you like with the rest.'

His ambition to set up a community of artists was reinforced when he read a book on Richard Wagner, whose ideas on 'total' and 'communal' art had found an echo at the time in many French artists. Wagner was then considered a revolutionary artist *par excellence*, thanks to his artistic no less than to his political beliefs. 'What an artist! A man like him in painting would be quite something, and <u>one will come</u>,' Van Gogh wrote to Theo.

Summer inspired him, as it had done earlier in Nuenen, to depict harvest scenes. The landscape of the Camargue and the Crau was 'beautiful and infinite like the sea', and the cicadas carried on 'like Dutch frogs'. After some pen sketches of the plain of the Crau, he did one of his most important works, the magnificent *Harvest Landscape*, with a painting of haystacks as the pendant. The immense stretch of flat land reminded him of paintings by such seventeenth-century Dutch artists as Ruysdael and Philips Koninck. Van Gogh was captivated by the variety of motifs he discovered in Provence. This very profusion enabled him to distinguish himself from his colleagues and to choose quite different subjects from Monet and even from Cézanne, still the pre-eminent painter of Provence. In a letter to Theo, he dwelt on the contrast between his own portrayal of the harvest and Cézanne's.

497 [F]

[12–13 June 1888]

My dear Theo,

I'm dropping you another line as your letter hasn't come yet. But I take it you thought I would probably be in S^tes Maries.

Since the rent of the house and the painting of the doors & windows and the purchases of canvases all came at the same time, I've run out, and you would be doing me a very great service if you could send me the money a few days earlier.

I'm working on a landscape with wheat fields which, I think, is as good as, say, the white orchard. It is in the same genre as the two Butte Montmartre landscapes which were at the Indépendants, but I think it's more robust and rather more stylish.

And I've another subject, a farm and some haystacks, which will probably be the pendant.

I'm very curious to know what Gauguin plans to do. I hope

he'll be able to come. You'll tell me it's pointless to think of the future, but the painting is progressing slowly and where that's concerned you do have to plan ahead. If I sold no more than a few canvases, that would be neither Gauguin's salvation nor mine. To be able to work one has to order one's life as best one can, and to secure one's existence one needs a fairly solid basis. If he and I stay here for a <u>long</u> time, our pictures will become more and more individual, precisely because we shall have made a more thorough study of subjects in this region.

Now that I have made a start in the south, I can hardly conceive of going anywhere else. Better not to do any more moving – just to keep going out into the countryside.

I'm sure I should have a greater chance of success if I tackled subjects – and even business matters – on a somewhat bigger scale, instead of confining myself to one that is too small.

And for that very reason I'm thinking of working on larger canvases and going over boldly to the 30 square. These cost me 4 francs apiece here, and taking carriage into account that isn't expensive.

The latest canvas completely slays all the rest – it's only a still life with coffee pots and cups and plates in blue & yellow, but it's in a different class. It must be due to the drawing.

I can't help recalling what I've seen of Cézanne's work, because – as in the harvest which we saw at Portier's – he has brought out the harsh side of Provence so much.

It has changed entirely from what it was in the spring, but certainly [my love for] the countryside, which is already beginning to appear scorched, has grown no less. You could say that everything has old gold, bronze and copper in it, and this, together with the green-azure of the white-hot sky, imparts a delicious, exceptionally harmonious colour, with broken tones à la Delacroix.

If Gauguin were willing to join us it would be, I think, a step forward for us. It would establish us firmly as openers-up of the south, and no one could argue with that.

I must try to achieve the solidity of colour I got in that picture which slays all the rest. I remember Portier used to say that his Cézannes, seen on their own, looked like nothing on earth, but that when placed next to other canvases they wiped the colour out of all the rest. And also that the Cézannes looked good in gold, which implies a brilliant palette.

Perhaps, perhaps, I am therefore on the right track and am getting an eye for the countryside here.

We'll have to wait and see.

This latest picture stands up well to the red surroundings of the bricks with which the studio is paved. When I put it on the floor, on this brick-red, <u>deep red</u>, ground, the colour of the picture does not look washed-out or blanched.

The countryside near Aix – where Cézanne works – is just the same as here, it is still the Crau. When I get back home with my canvas and say to myself, hallo, I've got old Cézanne's very tones, all I mean is that since Cézanne, just like Zola, is <u>so at home in these parts</u> and hence knows them so intimately, one must be making the same mental calculation to arrive at the same tones. It goes without saying that seen side by side they would go together, but not look alike. With a handshake, I hope you'll be able to write one of these days,

Ever yours,
Vincent

In Parisian art circles, Theo gradually emerged as champion of the Impressionists, who were still fighting for recognition. He even sent their work to Goupil's in The Hague, hoping to open a market for them in the Netherlands. In particular, he supported Camille Pissarro, who had found himself in dire financial straits. Theo also organized an 'absolutely beautiful' Monet exhibition at about this time. When he wrote to his brother that the naturalist writer Guy de Maupassant, whom Vincent admired, had come to see the exhibition, Vincent replied that, for him, Maupassant was to Zola what Vermeer was to Rembrandt.

In Arles, Vincent worked steadily on, adding to his oeuvre as a painter of peasant life. Writing to Émile Bernard in the middle of June 1888, he explained how his ambitious painting of *The Sower* had come about and how he had handled the colours. In it, Van Gogh had tried to match his distinguished model, Millet, whose work by the same name he had already copied and imitated in his earliest drawings. For him the new picture was the embodiment of a hankering after 'the eternal, of which the sower and the sheaf of corn are the symbols'; it gave him the chance to realize his greatest ambition: '[...] what still remains to be done after Millet and Lhermitte is ... the sower in colour and large-sized'.

At the same time, he was working on a number of portraits. A young soldier, a Zouave, about to go off to Africa, at long last provided him with a decent model: '[...] a young man with a small face, a bull neck, the eyes of a tiger'. He was consciously aiming for an 'ugly' effect – 'a rough combination of incongruous colours [...] very harsh, and yet I'd be happy if I could always work on such vulgar and even garish portraits as this'. At the same time he was still thinking of producing a painting of the starry sky.

B7 [F] [letter from Vincent to Émile Bernard]

[c. 18 June 1888]

My dear Bernard,

Forgive me for writing in haste, I'm afraid my letter will be illegible, but I did want to reply at once.

Do you realize that we have been very stupid, Gauguin, you and I, in not going to the same place? But when Gauguin left, I still wasn't sure if I could get away, and when you left, that awful money business, and the bad reports I sent you about the cost of living here, stopped you from coming.

It wouldn't have been such a stupid thing to do if we had all gone to Arles together, for with three of us here, we could have done our own housekeeping. And now that I have found my bearings a bit more, I am beginning to discover the advantages. For my part, I'm getting on better here than I did in the north. I even work right in the middle of the day, in the full sun, with no shade at all, out in the wheat fields, and lo and behold, I am as happy as a cicada. My God, if only I had known this country at 25 instead of coming here at 35! At that time I was fascinated by grey, or rather lack of colour. I kept dreaming of Millet, and then I also had such acquaintances among the Dutch painters as Mauve, Israëls, etc.

Here is a sketch of a sower: a large piece of land with clods of ploughed earth, for the most part a definite purple. A field of ripe wheat, in yellow ochre with a little carmine.

The sky chrome yellow, almost as bright as the sun itself, which is chrome yellow 1 with a little white, while the rest of the sky is chrome yellow 1 and 2 mixed. Thus very yellow.

The Sower's smock is blue and his trousers white.

Size 25 canvas, square.

There are many touches of yellow in the soil, neutral tones produced by mixing purple with the yellow, but I couldn't care less what the colours are in <u>reality</u>. I'd sooner do those naïve pictures out of old almanacs, old farmers' almanacs where hail, snow, rain or fine weather are depicted in a wholly primitive manner, like the one Anquetin used so successfully in his

Moisson.[1] To be honest with you, I have absolutely no objection to the countryside, since I grew up in it – I am still enchanted by snatches of the past, have a hankering after the eternal, of which the sower and the sheaf of corn are the symbols. But when shall I ever get round to doing the <u>starry sky</u>, that picture which is always in my mind?

Alas, alas, it is just as the excellent fellow Cyprien says in J. K. Huysman's 'En ménage': the most beautiful paintings are those which you dream about when you lie in bed smoking a pipe, but which you never paint.

Yet you have to make a start, no matter how incompetent you feel in the face of inexpressible perfection, of the overwhelming beauty of nature.

How I should like to see the study you have done of the brothel!

I am always reproaching myself for not having done any figures here yet.

Herewith another landscape. Setting sun? Rising moon?

A summer sun, anyway.

Town purple, celestial body yellow, sky green-blue. The wheat has all the hues of old gold, copper, green-gold or red-gold, yellow-gold, yellow-bronze, red-green. Size 30 canvas, square.

I painted it at the height of the mistral. My easel was fixed in the ground with iron pegs, a method I recommend to you. You push the legs of the easel deep into the ground, then drive iron pegs fifty centimetres long into the ground beside them. You tie the whole lot together with rope. This way you can work in the wind.

This is what I wanted to say about black and white. Take the Sower. The picture is divided in two; one half is yellow, the upper part, the lower part is purple. Well, the white trousers help rest the eye and distract it just as the excessive contrast of yellow and purple starts to jar. There you are, that's what I wanted to say.

1 Louis Anquetin, *Harvest*, 1887.

quand donc serai je le ciel étoilé ce tableau
...jours me préoccupe — helas helas c'est bien
...t l'excellent copain Cyprien dans ... en ménage ...
...mans : les plus beaux tableaux sont ceux que l'on rêve
...et des pipes dans son lit mais qu'on ne fait pas. S'agit
...de les attaquer quelqu'incompétent qu'on se sente ...
...s perfections de splendeurs glorieuses de la nature.
...me je voudrais voir ... l'étude que tu as fait au bordel
...de reproches à m'en passant de ne pas encore avoir fait

...toile de 30 carrée
...t en plein mistral. mon chevalet était fixé en ... avec
...de fer ... procédé que je te recommande
...fout les pieds du chevalet et puis on ... enfonce
...piquet de fer long de 50 centimètres
...ainsi travailler dans le vent—

ce que j'ai voulu dire pour le blanc et le noir
...ns le Semeur le tableau est coupé en deux
...oitié est jaune le haut, le bas est violet.
...en le pantalon blanc repose l'oeil
...e distrait au moment où le contraste simultané
...de jaune et de violet l'agacerait. Voilà
...que j'ai voulu dire

I know a second lieutenant in the Zouaves here; his name is Milliet. I give him drawing lessons – with my perspective frame – and he is beginning to do some drawings and, honestly, I've seen far worse. He is keen to learn, has been in Tonkin, etc ... He is leaving for Africa in October. If you were to join the Zouaves, he would take you along and guarantee you a fairly large measure of freedom to paint, at least if you were willing to help him with his artistic plans. Might this be of any use to you? If so, let me know as soon as possible.

One reason for working is that the canvases are worth money. Since you doubt that, you may call this reason fairly prosaic. But it is true. One reason for not working is that canvases and paint simply swallow up our money while they are waiting to be sold.

Drawings, on the other hand, don't cost a lot.

Gauguin too is bored at Pont-Aven, complains just like you of his isolation. If only you could go and see him! But I haven't any idea whether he means to stay, and I'm inclined to think he's planning to go to Paris. He told me he thought you would come to Pont-Aven. My God, if only all three of us were here! You will say that it's too out of the way. All right, <u>but think of the winter</u>, for here you can work all year round. The reason why I love this country is that I have less to fear from the cold, which, because it stops my blood circulating properly, makes it impossible for me to think or even do anything at all.

You will see that for yourself when you are a soldier. Then your melancholy will be gone, which could easily be the result of your having too little or the wrong blood, which I don't really think is the case.

It's the fault of that damned foul wine in Paris and those foul greasy steaks.

My God, I had reached the point where my blood was no longer circulating at all, literally no longer at all. But after four weeks it has started to circulate again. However, my dear friend, at the same time I have had, just like you, a fit of melancholy, from which I would have suffered as much as you, had I not welcomed it with great pleasure as a sign that I was recovering – which is indeed what happened.

So, don't go back to Paris but stay in the countryside, for you will need your strength to come through the trial of serving in Africa. Well then, the more blood you produce beforehand, good blood, the better it will be, for over there in the heat you may not be able to do it quite so easily.

Painting and fucking a lot don't go together, it softens the brain. Which is a bloody nuisance.

The symbol of St. Luke, the patron saint of painters, is, as you know, an ox. So you just be patient as an ox if you want to work in the artistic field. Still, bulls are lucky not to have to work at that foul business of painting.

But what I wanted to say is this: after the period of melancholy is over you will be stronger than before, you will recover your health, and you will find the scenery round you so beautiful that you will want to do nothing but paint.

I think that your poetry will change in the same way as your painting. After a few eccentric things, you have succeeded in doing some with Egyptian calm and a great simplicity.

> 'Que l'heure est donc brève
> Qu'on passe en aimant,
> C'est moins qu'un instant,
> Un peu plus qu'un rêve.
> Le temps nous enlève
> Notre enchantement.'[2]

That's not by Baudelaire, I don't know who wrote it. They're the words of a song found in Daudet's Nabab – that's where I took it from – but doesn't it express the idea just like a shrug of the shoulders from a real lady?

The other day I read Loti's Madame Chrysanthème, it includes interesting details about Japan.

My brother is holding a Claude Monet exhibition at the moment which I should very much like to see. Guy de Maupassant

---

2 'How short, then, the hour/One spends in loving, /It is less than an instant, /Little more than a dream. /Time strips us of/Our enchantment.'

among others came to have a look, and said that he'll be coming often to the Boulevard Montmartre in the future.

I must go and paint, so I'll stop; I'll probably write again soon. A thousand apologies for my not putting enough stamps on that letter, even though I stuck them on at the post office, nor is this the first time that it has happened here that, being in doubt and enquiring at the counter, I have been given the wrong information about the postage. You have no idea of the indifference, the unconcern of the people here. Anyway, you'll soon be seeing all that with your own eyes, in Africa. Thanks for your letter, I hope to write again soon, at a moment when I'm in less of a rush. With a handshake,

Vincent

The plan to set up a painters' cooperative with some twelve Impressionists was continually on Van Gogh's mind. He broached the subject frequently in letters to Theo or to fellow painters, as well as to his sister Wil, to whom he aired his dissatisfaction with the artist's social status: 'We live in an unspeakably awful and miserable world for artists. The exhibitions, the shops selling pictures, everything, everything is in the hands of people who grab all the money.' Patronage or a rich wife seemed to be the artist's only means of escape: 'Painting is like keeping a mistress of ill-repute who does nothing but spend money and more money and never has enough.'

Vincent was sorry to hear that Theo's attempt to introduce the work of the Impressionists in Holland had failed. Apparently the Dutch public had been 'bitterly, bitterly disappointed, finding it slapdash, ugly, badly painted, badly drawn, badly coloured, altogether miserable'. But Vincent could understand their reaction: 'That had also been my impression when I first arrived in Paris, my head full of Mauve, Israëls and other accomplished painters.' But though the Impressionists were still being rejected by the Salon, Van Gogh was convinced that in the long run his French friends would turn the tables on official art, which had outlived its usefulness and was 'slow-witted and mouldering, like religion'. Salvation would come from 'those twenty or so painters who are called impressionists – though a few of them have become fairly rich and quite big names in the world, the majority are poor devils, who hang about in coffee houses, lodge in cheap taverns and live from hand to mouth'.

While a letter to Wil written in Paris and quoted earlier (see page 333) contained a somewhat ironic self-portrait in words, the letter to her from Arles mentioned above included an interesting account of his famous *Self-Portrait in Front of the Easel*. This ambitious canvas was one of the last works he had painted in Paris and had been hanging in Theo's apartment ever since. Johanna van Gogh was later to refer to it as the best likeness in a self-portrait that she knew. It shows the artist with a 'pinkish-grey face and green eyes, ash-coloured hair, wrinkles on his forehead and around the mouth, stiff, wooden, a very red beard, fairly untidy and sad-looking, but the lips are full, a blue smock of coarse linen and a palette with lemon yellow, vermilion, Veronese green, cobalt blue, in short, a palette with all the colours save the orange of the beard, though unbroken colours only. The figure is against a greyish-white wall.

'You'll say that it has a slight resemblance to, for instance, the face of – Death, in Van Eeden's book, or something of the sort, all right, but it's still a figure – and it isn't easy to paint oneself – not, at any rate, if it is to be <u>something</u> other than a photograph. And you see – in my opinion this is just what impressionism has over the rest – it is not banal, and aims at a deeper likeness than the photographer's.'

After that description of this impressive if sombre portrait, Van Gogh went on to give an account of his looks at the time, after several months in the south of France: 'Well, nowadays I look different as I have neither hair nor beard, both being kept close-shaved. Apart from that my complexion has changed from greenish-grey-pink to greyish-orange, and I am wearing a white suit instead of a blue one. I'm always covered with dust and invariably loaded up like a porcupine with sticks, an easel, canvases and other articles. Only the green eyes have stayed the same [...].'

In a letter to his friend Bernard, dated 23 June 1888, Van Gogh attacked the prevailing views about the representation of religious subjects in contemporary art. He was alarmed at the turn Bernard's own work appeared to be taking, and contended that the only nineteenth-century painters who seemed to have truly grasped the message of the

Bible and to have produced religious art in the real sense of the word were Delacroix, Millet and Puvis de Chavannes. No one should try to paint the figure of Christ without a proper model, as Bernard and Gauguin had done. In the Bible, Christ was the pivot round whom, in Van Gogh's view, everything revolved – 'an artist greater than all other artists, scorning marble and clay and paint, working in the living flesh'. The painter's role, he concluded laconically, was that of 'a monk who goes to the brothel every two weeks'.

B8 [F] [letter from Vincent to Émile Bernard] [postscript omitted]

[23 June 1888]

My dear Bernard,

You do very well to be reading the Bible. I begin with that, because I have always refrained from advising you to do so. As I read the many sayings of Moses, Luke, etc., I couldn't help thinking, you know, that's all he needs – and now it has come to pass ... the artistic neurosis. For that is what the study of Christ inevitably leads to, especially in my case, where it is aggravated by the smoking of innumerable pipes.

The Bible is Christ, for the Old Testament leads to that culmination. Paul and the evangelists stand on the other slope of the holy mountain.

How small-minded the old story really is! My God! Does the world consist solely of Jews, who declare from the very start that all those who are different from them are impure?

Why didn't the other nations under the great sun over there, the Egyptians, the Indians, the Ethiopians, Babylon and Nineveh, record their annals with the same care? Well, anyway, the study of it is beautiful, and, after all, being able to read everything would be tantamount to not being able to read at all.

But the consolation of that deeply saddening Bible, which arouses our despair and indignation, which seriously offends us and thoroughly confuses us with its pettiness and infectious foolishness – the consolation it contains like a stone inside a hard rind and bitter pulp, is Christ.

Only Delacroix and Rembrandt have painted the face of Christ in such a way that I can feel him ... and then Millet painted ... the teachings of Christ.

The rest rather makes me laugh, the rest of religious painting – from the religious point of view, not from the point of view of painting. And the Italian primitives – Botticelli, or let's say the Flemish primitives, Van Eyck, the German, Cranach – they are no more than heathens who only interest me for the same reason as do the Greeks, Velásquez and so many other naturalists.

Christ alone, of all the philosophers, magicians, etc., has affirmed eternal life as the most important certainty, the infinity of time, the futility of death, the necessity and purpose of serenity and devotion. He lived serenely, <u>as an artist greater than all other artists</u>, scorning marble and clay and paint, working in the living flesh. In other words, this peerless artist, scarcely conceivable with the blunt instrument of our modern, nervous and obtuse brains, made neither statues nor paintings nor books. He maintained in no uncertain terms that he made ... <u>living men</u>, immortals.

That is a profoundly serious matter, the more so as it is the truth.

Nor did this great artist write books. Christian literature as a whole would undoubtedly have aroused his ire, and includes very few literary works beyond Luke's Gospel or Paul's epistles – so simple in their austere and militant form – that would have found favour in his eyes.

This great artist – Christ – although he did not concern himself with writing books on ideas (sensations), felt considerably less disdain for the spoken word, and for parables in particular (what a sower, what a harvest, what a fig tree! etc.).

And who would dare claim that he lied on that day when, scornfully predicting the destruction of Rome, he said, 'Heaven and earth shall pass away, but my words shall not pass away.'

These spoken words – which, like a prodigal grand seigneur, he did not even deign to write down – form one of the pinnacles, the highest pinnacle, reached by art, which at that point becomes creative force, pure creative force.

These thoughts, Bernard, dear friend, lead us far, very far, afield, they raise us above art itself. They give us a glimpse of the art of life-creation, the art of being immortal and alive. They are bound up with painting. The patron saint of painters – Luke, physician, painter, evangelist – who has as a symbol, alas, nothing more than an ox, gives us hope.

Yet our own life is a modest one indeed, our life as painters, languishing under the back-breaking yoke of the problems of a calling that is almost too hard to practise on this ungrateful planet, where 'love of art drives out true love'.

However, since nothing confutes the assumption that lines and forms and colours exist on innumerable other planets and suns as well, we are at liberty to feel fairly serene about the possibilities of painting in a better and different existence, an existence altered by a phenomenon that is perhaps no more ingenious and no more surprising than the transformation of a caterpillar into a butterfly or of a grub into a maybug.

The existence of a painter-butterfly would be played out on the countless celestial bodies which, after death, should be no more inaccessible to us than the black dots on maps that symbol-ize towns and villages are in our earthly lives.

Science – scientific reasoning – strikes me as being an instru-ment that will go a very long way in the future.

For look: people used to think that the earth was flat. That was true, and still is today, of, say, Paris to Asnières.

But that does not alter the fact that science demonstrates that the earth as a whole is round, something nobody nowadays disputes.

For all that, people still persist in thinking that life is flat and runs from birth to death.

But life, too, is probably round, and much greater in scope and possibilities than the hemisphere we now know.

Future generations will probably be able to enlighten us on this very interesting subject, and then science itself – with all due respect – may reach conclusions that are more or less in keeping with Christ's sayings about the other half of our life.

Be that as it may, the fact is that we are painters in real life, and it's a matter of continuing to draw breath while one has breath left in one's body.

Oh, what a beautiful picture that is by Eug. Delacroix, Christ in the Boat on the Sea of Gennesaret! He – with his pale lemon-yellow aureole, sleeping, luminous in the dramatic purple, dark-blue, blood-red patch of the group of bewildered disciples – on that terrible emerald-green sea, rising, rising, right to the top of the frame. Ah, what an inspired conception! I would do a sketch of it for you, but because I've been drawing and painting a model – a Zouave – for three or four days now, I am all in. Writing, on the other hand, calms and diverts me.

What I've been doing looks very ugly – a drawing of a seated Zouave, a painted sketch of the Zouave against a completely white wall, and finally his portrait against a green door and some orange bricks in a wall. It is harsh, and taking it all in all, ugly and unsuccessful. Yet, because I was tackling a real difficulty with it, it may pave the way for the future.

Nearly all the figures I do look abominable in my own eyes, let alone the eyes of others. Yet the study of the figure is the most useful of all, provided one does it in a different way from that taught at, for instance, Monsieur Benjamin Constant's.

Your letter pleased me very much, the sketch[1] is very, very interesting, and I thank you very much for it. One of these days I shall be sending you a drawing of mine. Tonight I am too exhausted, my eyes are tired even if my mind is not.

Tell me, do you remember the John the Baptist by Puvis? I find it staggeringly beautiful and as magical as Eugène Delacroix.

The passage about John the Baptist you tracked down in the Gospel means exactly what you have read in it ... people crowding round a man: 'Are you the Christ? Are you Elias?' As would happen today if you were to ask of impressionism or of one of its questing representatives, 'Have you found it yet?' Exactly the same.

1 *Brothel Scene.*

My brother is holding an exhibition of Claude Monets, 10 paintings done in Antibes from February to May, apparently it's all very beautiful.

Have you ever read the life of Luther? Because Cranach, Dürer, Holbein belong with him. He – his personality – is the shining light of the Middle Ages.

I don't like the Sun King any more than you do – that Louis XIV was rather a killjoy, it seems to me – my God, what an utter bore that Methodist Solomon was. I don't like Solomon either and Methodists not at all. Solomon strikes me as a hypocritical heathen. I have really no respect for his architecture, an imitation of other styles, and none at all for his writings, for the heathens have done better.

Do tell me how things are going with your military service. Do you want me to speak to that second lieutenant in the Zouaves or not? Are you going to Africa or not? Do the years in Africa count double in your case or not? Try to make sure above all that your blood is all right – anaemia doesn't get you very far and your painting slows right down. You must try to acquire an iron constitution, a constitution that will allow you to grow old, you ought to live like a monk who goes to the brothel every two weeks – that's what I do myself, it isn't very poetic, but I feel it's my duty to subordinate my life to painting.

If I were at the Louvre with you, what I should very much like would be to go and see the primitives in your company. I still go, full of love, to look at the Dutch in the Louvre, Rembrandt first, Rembrandt, whom I used to study so much – and then, say, Potter, who paints a white stallion alone in a meadow on a size 4 or 6 panel – a stallion neighing and aroused – forlorn under a heavy thundery sky, inconsolable in the soft green immensity of the damp meadow. In short, there are marvels among the old Dutchmen which cannot be compared to anything else.

With a handshake, and once again thanks for your letter and your sketch,

Ever yours,
Vincent

[. . .]

When Van Gogh nevertheless tried to paint a religious subject soon afterwards, he was so dissatisfied that he destroyed it, informing Theo in early July, 'I have scraped off a large painted study, an olive garden, with a figure of Christ in blue and orange, a yellow angel, a red stretch of earth, green and blue hills, olive trees with purple and carmine trunks and grey-green and blue-green foliage, lemon yellow sky. I have scraped it off because I don't think one should do figures of this importance without a model.' In a few portraits and the olive gardens he was to do later in Saint-Rémy, he did, however, manage to translate these religious subjects into paint.

At the end of June 1888, Theo reported that Gauguin had agreed to share a house with Vincent, but it was not until later – in October – that he actually arrived in Arles.

In the meantime, Van Gogh regularly followed in the footsteps of his most important predecessors in Provence. His own struggle with the mistral, he felt, had helped him to understand and forgive the 'clumsy touch' Cézanne had shown in some of his studies: it was the wind which had made the easel wobble. He had also begun to wonder whether the intensity of a painter's feelings and thoughts was not worth more than perfect brushwork. Although Van Gogh held relatively traditional views of what constituted a good painting worthy of the name, and did not grant that status to many of his own outdoor studies, he gradually became convinced that work he painted quickly, in a single long session, was often among his best. He explained this paradox with the conclusion, 'quickly done, but given a great deal of thought beforehand'.

In his use of colour he felt some affinity with Adolphe Monticelli, the painter from nearby Marseilles who had died in 1886 and whose work he and Theo had collected in Paris. As so often with artists he admired, he allied respect for the technical quality of the work with personal identification with the artist. True, he wrote, his 'colour philosophy [is] a maze from which you cannot easily escape unscathed [but] I think very, very often of that excellent painter, Monticelli, who – they said – was such a drunkard and a bit soft in the head, when I myself come back home after the mental exertion of having had to balance the six primary colours – red, blue, yellow, orange, lilac, green – a labour of cool calculation in which the mind is strained to the utmost, like an actor on the stage playing a difficult role – with a thousand and one things to think of simultaneously in one half hour'.

That summer, the dominant colour was yellow: the colour of the fierce sun and of the sunflowers. The other seasons, too, had their characteristic colours, however, and Van Gogh eagerly looked forward to the autumn: 'The wheat fields offered as great an opportunity to work as the orchards in bloom. And I only just have time to prepare for the next campaign, the grape harvest. And in between I should also like to do some seascapes. The orchards stand for pink and white, the wheat fields for yellow, the seascapes for blue. Perhaps I shall now go in search of greens a bit more. Well, autumn provides the entire spectrum.'

For lack of willing models among the local population, he turned to his friends, the family of the postman, Joseph Roulin, and Madame Ginoux, the wife of the owner of the Café de la Gare, where he lived before moving to the Yellow House, and remained a regular customer.

He got on well with the Zouave lieutenant and particularly with Joseph Roulin, in his blue uniform and gold trimmings, and heavily bearded, whom he compared, as he had done earlier with Tanguy, to Socrates. The painter Dodge MacKnight had been joined by the Belgian painter Eugène Boch, but until Gauguin turned up, the painters' muse remained Van Gogh's chief companion: 'Far from complaining, it is just at times like these that I feel almost as happy living the artist's life – though it isn't real life – as I might be living the ideal, the real, life.'

His failure to master the Provençal dialect stood in the way of his befriending the locals: 'So far, I have made not the slightest headway in people's affection [. . .]. Whole days go by without my speaking a single word to anyone, except to order my meals or a coffee. And so it has been from the beginning. But up to now the loneliness hasn't troubled me much because I've been held in thrall by the fiercer sun and its effect upon nature.' More than company, he needed 'feverish hard work', and 'if the storm within grows too violent, I take a glass too many to seek diversion'. Just like Delacroix, he had 'un soleil dans la tête et un orage dans le coeur [a sun in the head and a storm in the heart]'.

And then, of course, there were his letters to his friends. He discussed Cézanne with Bernard, while repeatedly enjoining him to model himself on the seventeenth-century Dutch masters, Rembrandt in particular, of course.

B11 [F] [letter from Vincent to Émile Bernard]

[*c.* 17 July 1888]

My dear friend Bernard,

I've just sent you another 9 sketches after painted studies. So you'll see subjects from the scenery that inspires old man Cézanne, because the Crau near Aix is almost the same as the countryside round Tarascon or the Crau here. The Camargue is even plainer, for often there is nothing, nothing, other than poor soil and tamarisk bushes and the coarse grass that is to these bare pastures what esparto grass is to the desert.

Knowing how keen you are on Cézanne, I thought you might like these sketches of Provence; not that a drawing of mine and one by Cézanne have much in common. No, indeed, any more than Monticelli and I! But I too love the countryside they have loved so much, and for the same reasons, the colour and the logical composition.

My dear friend Bernard, by <u>collaboration</u> I did not mean to say that I think two or more painters would have to work on the same pictures. What I was driving at was paintings that differ from one another yet go together and complement one another.

Just take the Italian primitives or the German primitives or the Dutch school or the real Italians, in short, take the whole of the art of painting!

Whether they want it or not, their work forms a 'group', a 'series'.

Well, now, at present the impressionists also form a group, despite all their disastrous civil wars, in which both sides have been trying to get at each other's throats with a dedication they would have done better to reserve for other ends.

In our northern school, you have Rembrandt, who heads that school because his influence may be seen in anyone who comes to know him more closely. Thus we find Paulus Potter painting rutting and excited animals in equally exciting landscapes – in a thunderstorm, in the sunshine, in the melancholy of autumn –

while that selfsame Paulus Potter, before he came to know Rembrandt, was rather dry and over-fussy.

Here are two people, Rembrandt and Potter, who belong together like brothers, and even though Rembrandt probably never touched a picture by Potter with his brush, that doesn't alter the fact that Potter and Ruysdael owe him all that is best in them – the thing that moves us so deeply when we have learned how to look at a corner of old Holland as if through their temperament.

Moreover, the material problems of the painter's life make it desirable that painters should collaborate and unite (much as they did in the days of the Guilds of St. Luke). If only they would ensure their material well-being, and love one another like friends instead of making one another's life hell, painters would be happier, and in any case less ridiculous, less foolish and less culpable.

However, I shan't labour the point, because I realize that life carries us along so fast that we haven't the time to talk and to work as well. That is the reason why, with unity still a long way off, we are now sailing the trackless deep in our frail little boats, all alone on the high seas of our time.

Is it a renaissance? Is it a decline? We cannot judge, because we are too close to it not to be deceived by distorted perspectives. Contemporary events, our setbacks and successes, probably assume exaggerated proportions in our eyes.

A hearty handshake from me and I hope to hear something from you soon.

Ever yours,
Vincent

B12 [F] [letter from Vincent to Émile Bernard]

[*c.* 23 July 1888]

My dear friend Bernard,

Many, many thanks for the drawings you sent me. I very much like the avenue of plane trees along the seashore with the two women talking in the foreground and people strolling about. And the woman under the apple tree, the woman with the umbrella. Then the four drawings of nude women, especially the one who is washing herself, a grey effect, enhanced with black, white, yellow, brown. It's charming.

Ah, Rembrandt! . . . With all due admiration for Baudelaire, I venture to presume, especially going by those verses, that he knew virtually nothing about Rembrandt. Not long ago I found and bought a small etching after Rembrandt here, a study of a male nude, realistic and simple. He stands, leaning against a door or a pillar, in a dark interior, a shaft of light from above glancing across his bent head and thick red hair. A Degas, you would say, because the animality of the body is real and intensely felt. But listen, have you ever taken a <u>good</u> look at the 'Ox' or the 'Interior of a Butcher's Shop' in the Louvre? You haven't taken a really good look at them, have you, and Baudelaire infinitely less so. It would be a real treat for me to spend a morning with you in the Dutch Gallery. All those things are almost impossible to describe, but standing in front of the paintings I should be able to point out the miracles and mysteries which are the reason why the primitives do not necessarily take first place in my admiration.

But then, I am scarcely an eccentric; a Greek statue, a peasant by Millet, a Dutch portrait, a female nude by Courbet or Degas, these calm and perfectly modelled representations are the reason why very many other things, the primitives no less than the Japanese, give me the impression of having been <u>composed with the pen</u>. I find that immensely interesting, but anything complete and perfect renders infinity tangible, and the enjoyment of any beautiful thing is like coitus, a moment of infinity.

Do you, for instance, know a painter called Vermeer, who, among other things, painted a very beautiful and pregnant Dutch lady? The palette of this remarkable painter is blue, lemon yellow, pearl grey, black, white. Of course, all the riches of a full palette are there too, in his rarely encountered pictures, but the combination of lemon yellow, pale blue and pearl grey is as characteristic of him as black, white, grey and pink are of Velásquez.

Anyway, I know perfectly well that Rembrandt and the Dutch painters are scattered widely over museums and collections, and it isn't very easy to get an overall idea of them if you only know the Louvre. Yet it is the French, Charles Blanc, Thoré, Fromentin and several others, who have written about their art better than the Dutch have.

Those Dutch painters had hardly any imagination or fantasy, but an enormous amount of taste and a feeling for composition. They did no paintings of Christ, Our Lord, etc. – Rembrandt did, of course, but he was the only one (and biblical subjects are relatively rare in his work). He was the only one who, exceptionally, painted figures of Christ, etc. And with him, they look quite unlike anything done by other religious painters, it is all metaphysical magic.

This is how Rembrandt painted angels. He does a self-portrait, old, toothless, wrinkled, wearing a cotton cap, a picture from life, in a mirror. He is dreaming, dreaming, and his brush takes up his self-portrait again, but this time from memory, and the expression on the face becomes sadder and more saddening. He dreams, dreams on, and why or how I cannot tell, but just as Socrates and Mohammed had their guardian spirits, so Rembrandt paints a supernatural angel with a da Vinci smile behind that old man who resembles himself.

I am showing you a painter who dreams and paints from the imagination, and I started by contending that it is characteristic of the Dutch that they do not invent anything, that they have neither imagination nor fantasy.

Am I being illogical? No.

Rembrandt did not invent anything, and that angel and that

strange Christ came about because he knew them, felt that they were there.

Delacroix paints a Christ using the unexpected note of bright lemon yellow in such a way that the colourful and radiant note in the picture assumes the inexpressible strangeness and charm of a star in a corner of the firmament. Rembrandt works with tonal values in the same way that Delacroix works with colours.

Well now, there is a world of difference between the method used by Delacroix and Rembrandt and that of all other religious painters.

I'll write again soon. This is to thank you for the drawings, which have given me enormous pleasure. I have just finished a portrait of a girl of 12, brown eyes, black hair and black eyebrows, yellowish-grey flesh, white background, strongly tinged with Veronese green, a blood-red bodice with violet stripes. Blue skirt with large orange polka dots, an oleander flower·in the sweet little hand. It has exhausted me so much that I am hardly in a fit state to write. Goodbye for now, and once more many thanks,

Ever yours,
Vincent

During the second half of July, Van Gogh painted some splendid 'studies' of flower gardens: 'This really is a subject for a painting, just as in other studies I have. And I really can't tell if I shall ever again do paintings that are calmly and quietly worked out, because I have the feeling that they will always be incoherent.' It was at this time that he began to work on his famous *Night Café*: 'I shall probably make a start today on the interior of the café where I live – at night, by gaslight. It is what they call a "night café" (they are fairly common here), which stays open all night. "Night owls" can take refuge there if they haven't enough money to pay for lodgings or are too drunk to be taken in anywhere.'

At the same time, he tried to put heart into Theo, who was clearly still bowed down by depression, insisting that, as an art dealer, Theo was an inspiration to artists, playing an essential role in their lives and indirectly participating in their creative work.

When his sister Wil wrote to tell him of the death of their uncle Vincent in Prinsenhage, he replied on 31 July 1888, adding an account of the most important works he had produced during the summer.

In his despair about ever making his mark as a painter, he sometimes placed a very low value on his work: 'A canvas painted by me is worth more than a blank canvas. I can claim no more than that.'

514 [F] [part]

[*c.* 25 July 1888]

My dear Theo,

Thank you for your kind letter. If you remember, mine ended with 'we are getting old, that is the <u>fact of the matter</u>, and all the rest is <u>imagination</u> and simply does not exist'. Well, I said that more for myself than for you. And I said it because I feel it is absolutely essential for me to take action accordingly, not perhaps by working harder but with greater seriousness.

You mention the emptiness you sometimes feel, and that's exactly what I feel myself.

Consider, if you will, the times in which we live to be a true and great renaissance of art, the worm-ridden official tradition still holding sway yet ultimately impotent and idle, the new painters still isolated, poor, treated as madmen, and because of this treatment actually going insane, at least as far as their social life is concerned – then remember that you are doing exactly the same job as these primitive painters, since you provide them with money and sell their canvases, which enables them to produce others.

If a painter ruins himself emotionally by working hard at his painting, and renders himself unfit for so much else, for family life, &c., &c., if, consequently, he paints not only with colour but with self-sacrifice and self-denial and a broken heart, then your own work is not only no better paid, but costs you, in exactly the same way as a painter, this half-deliberate, half-accidental eclipse of your personality.

What I mean is that though you are <u>indirectly</u> involved in painting, you are more productive than I am, for instance. The more completely you are involved in dealing, the more of an artist you become. And so I hope the same thing for myself ... the more wasted and sick I become, a broken pitcher, the more I may also become a creative artist in this great renaissance of art of which we speak.

All this is certainly so, but eternally continuing art, and this renaissance – this green shoot sprung from the roots of the old sawn-off trunk, these are matters so spiritual that we can't help but feel rather melancholy when we reflect that we could have created life for less than the cost of creating art.

You will be doing well if you can make me feel that art is alive, you who love art perhaps more than I do.

I tell myself that it isn't the fault of art, but my own, that the only means of regaining my confidence and peace of mind is to <u>do better</u>.

And that brings us back again to the end of my last letter – I myself may be getting old, but it would be sheer fantasy to think that art has had its day.

Now, if you know what a 'mousmé' is (you will find out when you read Loti's Madame Chrysanthème), I have just painted one. It took me a whole week, and I haven't been able to do anything else, because I still haven't been too well. That is what annoys me – had I felt well, I would have been able to run off some more landscapes in the meantime, but to do justice to my mousmé I had to conserve my mental energies. A mousmé is a Japanese girl – Provençal in this case – 12 to 14 years old.

That makes 2 figures I've got now, the Zouave and her.

Look after your health, take baths, especially <u>if Gruby has advised you to</u>, for in 4 years' time – which is how much older I am than you – you will realize that reasonably good health is essential for anyone who wants to work. Now, for those of us who work with our brains, our one and only hope of not running out of steam too soon is to prolong our lives artificially by observing an up-to-date health regime as rigorously as we can. I, for one, do not do all I ought to. And a little good humour is worth more than all the medicines in the world.

[. . .]

Bernard has sent me 10 sketches including his brothel. Three of them are in the style of Redon, for whom he feels an enthusiasm I myself do not really share. But there is a woman washing herself, very Rembrandtesque or à la Goya, and a landscape with figures, very strange. He expressly forbade me to send them to you – however you will be receiving them by the same post.

I'm sure Russell will take other things of Bernard's.

I've seen some work by this <u>Boch</u> now, it's strictly impressionist, but not strong, he's still too preoccupied with the new technique to be himself. He will gain in strength and his personality will come out, I think. But MacKnight does watercolours to match those by <u>Destrée</u> – you remember, that revolting Dutchman we used to know. However, he has washed a few small still lifes, a yellow pot on a purple foreground, a red pot on green, an orange pot on blue – better, but still pretty poor.

The village where they are staying is <u>pure Millet</u>, poor peasants, nothing more, absolutely <u>rustic</u> and homely. This feature completely escapes them. I believe that MacKnight has civilized his brute of a landlord, converting him to civilized Christianity. At any rate, this scoundrel and his worthy spouse shake your hand when you go there – it's a café, of course – and when you order a drink they have a way of refusing money, 'Oh, I couldn't take money from an artisst,' with two s's. Anyway, it's their own fault it's so dreadful round there, and this Boch must have become quite stupid in MacKnight's company.

I think MacKnight must have some money, but not much. That's how they contaminate the village. If it weren't for that, I'd go over there quite often to work. What they should not be doing there is passing the time of day with polite society – well, the only people they know are the station master and a score of bores, and that's the main reason why they are getting no-where. I've already said all this to Mourier, who at one time thought MacKnight had great feeling for 'the man of the soil'.

Naturally, these simple and naïve country folk make fun of them and despise them. Whereas, if they went about their work instead of clinging to these village layabouts with their detachable collars, then they'd be welcome in the peasants' homes and let their owners earn a few coppers. Then this blessed Fontvieille would be a treasure-trove for them, for the natives are – like Zola's humble peasants – innocent and gentle beings, as we know.

No doubt MacKnight will soon be doing little landscapes with sheep, for chocolate boxes.

Not just my pictures but I myself have become especially haggard of late, almost like Hugo van der Goes in the painting by Émile Wauters. Except that, having had all my beard carefully shaved off, I think I'm as much the very placid abbot in that picture as the mad painter so cleverly portrayed in it. And I'm not displeased at falling somewhere between the two, for one must live, especially as there is no getting away from the fact that there may be a crisis one of these days if your situation with the Boussods were to change. All the more reason for keeping up contacts with artists, on my part as much as on yours.

For the rest, I think I have spoken the truth: that I would be doing no more than my duty should I ever manage to pay back in kind the money you have laid out. And in practice that means doing portraits.

As for drinking too much . . . I have no idea if it's a bad thing. Take Bismarck, who, think what you like, is very practical and very intelligent – his good doctor told him that he drank too much and that he'd been putting a severe strain on his stomach and his brain all his life. B. stopped drinking at once. He has gone downhill ever since and is still getting no better. He must be laughing up his sleeve at his doctor, whom, luckily for him, he did not consult sooner.

So there we are. With a hearty handshake,

Ever yours,
Vincent

The portrait of the young girl is on a white background strongly tinged with Veronese green, the bodice is striped blood-red and violet. The skirt is royal blue with large yellow-orange dots. The matt flesh tints are yellowish-grey, the hair purplish-blue, the eyebrows and the eyelashes black, the eyes orange and Prussian blue, & an oleander branch between her fingers, for the 2 hands are in the picture.

Bear in mind that we don't have to change our minds about helping Gauguin if the proposal is acceptable as it is, <u>but we do not need him</u>. So don't think that working by myself worries me, and <u>be sure</u> not to press the matter on my account.

W5 [D] [letter from Vincent to Wil]

[31 July 1888]

Dear sister,

I want to answer your letter of this morning straight away.

I shall probably learn from Paris by tomorrow what Theo is going to do, whether or not he can get away. I have no doubt he'll go to you if he can. It is always a shock when somebody one knows sets out on the great journey to that other hemisphere of life, whose existence we surmise. And it goes without saying that my best wishes accompany today's traveller.

I am hard at work here – for me, the summer here is extremely beautiful, more beautiful than any I ever experienced in the north, and yet the people here complain loudly that it is not the same as usual. Now and then it rains in the morning or the afternoon, but infinitely less than in our part of the world. The harvest has long since been brought in. There is a lot of wind here, though, a very spiteful, whining wind – le mistral – a great nuisance most of the time if I have to paint in it, when I lay my canvas flat on the ground and work on my knees. Because the easel won't keep steady.

I've done a study of a garden, almost three feet across, poppies & other red flowers set in green in the foreground, then a bed of blue campanula, then a bed of orange and yellow African marigolds, then white and yellow flowers, and finally, in the background, pink and lilac and dark violet scabious, and red geraniums and sunflowers, and a fig tree and a laurier rose[1] and a vine. Right at the back, black cypresses against low white cottages with orange roofs – and a delicate green-blue strip of sky. Now I'm well aware that not one of the flowers has been properly drawn, that they are only small dabs of colour, red, yellow, orange, green, blue, violet, but the impression of all those colours next to one another is there – in the painting as in nature. Still, I imagine you might be disappointed and find it ugly if you saw it. You can tell that the subject is fairly summery, though.

Uncle Cor has seen work of mine more than once, and he thinks it's hideous.

Right now I'm working on the portrait of a postman in his uniform of dark blue with yellow. A head a bit like Socrates, almost no nose, a high forehead, bald crown, small grey eyes, highly coloured plump cheeks, a big pepper-and-salt beard, large ears. The man is a well-known republican and socialist, argues quite well and knows a great deal. His wife gave birth to a child today, so he's in fine fettle and beaming with satisfaction.

Actually, I much prefer painting this sort of thing to doing flowers. But seeing that one can do the one without forgoing the other, I take my chances as they come.

I've also done a portrait of a 12-year-old girl, brown eyes, black hair & eyebrows, yellowish matt complexion. She is sitting in a cane chair, has a blood-red and violet striped bodice, a deep blue skirt with orange polka-dots, and a branch of laurier rose in her hand. The background is light green, almost white.

And I'm always on the lookout for the same thing – a portrait, a landscape, a landscape and a portrait. I hope I shall get the chance to paint the baby born today, too.

I've also done a garden without flowers, or rather a stretch of grass, just mown, very green with the grey hay spread out in

1 Oleander.

long rows, a weeping ash and some cedars and cypresses, the cedars yellowish and spherical, the cypresses tall, blue-green, and at the back, laurier rose and a corner of green-blue sky. The blue shadows of the shrubs on the grass.

Also a portrait bust of a Zouave, blue uniform with red and yellow trimmings, sky-blue sash, blood-red cap with blue tassel, sunburnt, black hair cut short, eyes like a cat's, missing nothing, orange & green, a small head on a bull-like neck. In this one the background is a bright green door and some orange bricks in the wall & the white plaster.

As to your question about whether it's true that I'm going to be sharing with somebody else, it seems quite likely, and with a first-rate painter, too, but one who, like the other impressionists, has a life full of care and is the proud owner of a liver complaint.[2] Theo bought a large painting of his some time ago, of negresses in pink, blue, orange and yellow cotton clothes under tamarind, coconut and banana trees, with the sea in the distance.[3] Like the description of Otaheite in Loti's Le mariage. He's been in Martinique, you see, working in the tropical scenery there.

We've got a second painting of his, too, which he exchanged for one of my studies, a dried-up river with purple mud and puddles of water reflecting the pure cobalt blue of the sky, green grass.[4] A negro boy with a white and red cow, a negress in blue, and some green forest. He works like one possessed and paints all sorts of things. At present he's in Brittany.

We shall be living together in order to economize and to keep each other company. Should either of us sell anything in the next few days, so that his journey can be paid for, he'll come. It's not impossible that something will still intervene, but it is looking quite on the cards. And even if it doesn't happen and I have to go on working by myself, my doing work in the same direction as other people, albeit each in his own way, will ensure

2 Paul Gauguin.
3 *Négresses*.
4 *By the Shore, Martinique.*

that there is some comradeship and might well give rise to interesting correspondence.

How is your health? Good, I hope. Try above all to go out in the open air as much as possible. I still suffer odd bouts of not being able to take food, more or less as you used to. But by and large I muddle along steering clear of the rocks. 'If you can't be strong, be clever', is a motto you and I, with our constitutions, should take to heart. Incidentally, work, when it does go well, helps a great deal.

I find it tremendously beautiful here in the summer, the green is very deep and rich, the air thin and amazingly clear. And yet, the wide plain often reminds one of Holland – here, where there are hardly any mountains & rocks – if the colour were not so different. I particularly enjoy the colourful clothes, the women and girls dress in cheap, simple material, green, red, pink, yellow, havana brown, purple, blue, polka-dots, stripes. White scarves, red, green and yellow parasols. A strong sulphurous sun which shines down on it all, the great blue sky – it is all as tremendously cheerful as Holland is gloomy. What a pity everybody can't have these two extremes.

Now I must stop. Uncle's death is an important event for you and for Mother, and especially for our aunt. The impression it has left on me is very strange, because, of course, my image of the man is made up of memories from so long ago, from much earlier years, and it seems most peculiar that someone one knew so intimately should have become such a stranger. No doubt you will understand that. Viewed in this way, life is very dream-like, and from the moment it becomes simpler again and the sick man sets out on his great journey, one regains a better understanding of it – no doubt my feelings about it all are similar to yours. Theo, too, will feel it very much, for he had much more to do with Uncle than I did.

How is Mother right now? I think of you both often and wish you all the best from the bottom of my heart.

Vincent

I am up to my ears in work, and can seldom think of anything else. My address is

> 2 Place Lamartine
> Arles
> B. d. Rh.

If you <u>can</u>, do bear in mind those books and prints of mine I mentioned.

The uncertainty about Gauguin's arrival continued. Impatiently, Van Gogh considered going to Brittany himself. His plans for equipping and decorating the Yellow House suggest, however, that he had not yet given up all hope. On the contrary, he was painting away 'with the enthusiasm of a Marseillais sitting down to his bouillabaisse'. In a letter to Bernard, who had meanwhile joined Gauguin at Pont-Aven, we read for the first time how Vincent intended to set off the place before Gauguin's arrival: '[...] some six paintings of sunflowers, a decor in which the vivid or broken chrome yellows will stand out sharply against various blue backgrounds, from the palest Veronese green to <u>royal blue</u>, in a frame of thin slats painted in <u>red lead</u>'. Writing to Theo, he went into further details about his project, which was rapidly expanding in both size and ambition.

The tension between artistic and 'real' life was an important element of Vincent's letters to Bernard in August. It was largely reflected in Van Gogh's sexual preoccupations, the artist revealing himself as a new Pygmalion. To him, a beautiful woman was 'a living miracle, while the pictures by da Vinci and Correggio only exist for other reasons. Why am I so little an artist that I keep regretting that the statue and the picture are not alive? Why do I understand the musician better, why do I appreciate the reasons for his abstractions better?' The discussion then concentrates on their older colleague Edgar Degas, the master of the female nude, whose own appearance was in such contrast with the world from which he took his subjects. 'Why,' Van Gogh asked Bernard, 'do you say Degas can't get it up properly? Degas lives like some petty lawyer and doesn't like women, knowing very well that if he did like them and bedded them frequently, he'd go to seed and be in no position to paint any longer. The very reason why Degas's painting is virile and impersonal is that he has resigned himself to being nothing more than a petty lawyer with a horror of kicking over the traces. He observes human animals who are stronger than himself screwing and fucking away and he paints them so well for the very reason he isn't all that keen on it himself.' At a time when Van Gogh was in such financial straits that he had to content himself with 'the kind of 2-franc women who were originally intended for the Zouaves', there was nothing for it but to 'live like monks or hermits, with work as our overriding passion, and renouncing prosperity'. Had not the old Dutch masters, and Cézanne as well, led respectable lives, and had Balzac not claimed that 'relative chastity is beneficial to the modern artist'?

While his landscapes were piling up against the walls of his studio, Vincent's real ambition was still to become a portrait painter: 'Taking it all in all, that is the only thing in painting that moves me to the depths, and it makes me feel closer to infinity than anything else.' In portraiture lay 'the great simplicity'. Both as an 'obstinate colourist' and also in pursuit of his humanitarian ideals, he felt that he might still be able to make a valuable contribution to art in that genre. He was thinking of painting a symbolic portrait 'of an artist friend who dreams great dreams' with a mysterious, starry night in the background. He quickly discovered the perfect model in the Belgian painter Eugène Boch, whom he saw, moreover, as a suitable marriage partner for his sister Wil.

The pleasant warmth of the south and his satisfaction with his portrait of the peasant Patience Escalier made him forget that 'things are extremely grim these days, materially speaking'.

520 [F]

[11 August 1888]

My dear Theo,

Before long you will be making the acquaintance of Mr Patience Escalier – a typical 'man of the hoe', a former Camargue herdsman, now a gardener at a farmhouse in the Crau.

I shall be sending you this very day the drawing I did after that painting, just like the drawing I did after the portrait of the postman, Roulin.

The colouring of this peasant portrait isn't as dark as the Nuenen potato eaters, but our so civilized Parisian Portier[1] – presumably so called because he chucks the pictures out through the door – will find himself once more faced with the same problem. You have changed since then, but you will find that he has not. It really is a pity that there are not more pictures with clogs in Paris. I don't think my peasant will do any harm, for instance, to your Lautrec,[2] and I even make so bold as to imagine that the Lautrec would appear still more distinguished by the contrast, and that mine would gain by the odd association, because that sunlit, sunburned quality, weatherbeaten by the full sun and open air, would come even more into its own alongside the face powder and the fashionable clothes.

How wrong the Parisians are in not acquiring a taste for things that are out of the ordinary, for Monticellis, for barbotine. Still, one shouldn't be discouraged because Utopia isn't round the corner. It is just that what I learned in Paris is deserting me and that I am going back to the ideas I had in the country before I knew the impressionists. And I shouldn't be very surprised if before very long the impressionists were to find fault with my way of working, which has been enriched by the ideas of Delacroix rather than theirs.

For instead of trying to reproduce exactly what I see before me, I make more arbitrary use of colour to express myself more forcefully. Well, so much for theory, but let me give you an example of what I mean.

I should like to paint the portrait of an artist friend who dreams great dreams, who works as the nightingale sings, because it is his nature. This man will be fair-haired. I should like to put my appreciation, the love I have for him, into the picture. So I will paint him as he is, as faithfully as I can – to begin with.

1 Doorman.
2 Henri de Toulouse-Lautrec, *Young Woman at a Table, 'Poudre de Riz* [Face powder]'.

But that is not the end of the picture. To finish it, I shall be an obstinate colourist. I shall exaggerate the fairness of the hair, arrive at tones of orange, chrome, pale yellow. Behind the head – instead of painting the ordinary wall of the shabby apartment, I shall paint infinity, I shall do a simple background of the richest, most intense blue that I can contrive, and by this simple combination, the shining fair head against this rich blue background, I shall obtain a mysterious effect, like a star in the deep blue sky.

I used the same approach in the portrait of the peasant. Without wanting in this case, however, to conjure up the mysterious brilliance of a pale star in the blue of infinity. But by imagining the marvellous man that I was about to paint right in the middle of the sweltering midday heat of harvest, I arrived at the flashing orange colours like red-hot iron and the luminous tones of old gold in the shadows.

Ah, my dear brother – and the worthies will see only caricature in this exaggeration. But what does that matter to us? We have read La terre and Germinal, and if we paint a peasant we want to show that what we have read has, in the end, become a small part of us.

I don't know if I can convey the postman as I feel him. This man is a revolutionary like old Tanguy. He is probably considered a good republican, because he heartily detests the republic which we now enjoy, and because all in all he is somewhat doubtful and a little disillusioned with the republican idea itself. But one day I saw him singing the Marseillaise, and I thought I was watching '89, not next year, but the one 99 years ago. It was a Delacroix, a Daumier, straight out of old Holland. Unfortunately he cannot pose, and a painting demands an intelligent model.

I must now tell you that things are extremely grim these days, materially speaking. Whatever I do, life is very expensive here, almost like Paris, where you don't get much for 5 or 6 francs a day.

When I have models, I have to make great sacrifices as a consequence. No matter, I shall continue. And if by chance you should happen to send me a little more money sometimes, I assure you it would benefit the pictures, not me. The only choice I have myself is between being a good painter or a bad one. I choose the first. But the needs of painting are like those of a ruinously expensive mistress, one can do nothing without money, and one never has enough of it. Painting should thus be done at public expense instead of overburdening the artist.

But there, we should keep our own counsel, because <u>no one is forcing us to work</u>, indifference towards painting being inevitably pretty general, pretty well permanent.

Fortunately, my stomach has recovered so much that I have lived 3 weeks of the month on ship's biscuits with milk and eggs. The pleasant heat is restoring my strength. I certainly did the right thing coming south <u>now</u> instead of waiting until my complaint was past curing. Yes, I am as well as other men now, which I have been no more than briefly in the past, in Nuenen for instance – and it is not unpleasant. By 'other men' I mean something like those labourers on strike, or old Tanguy, old Millet, the peasants. When you are in good health you should be able to live on a piece of bread while doing a full day's work and have enough strength left over to smoke and have a drink, because <u>you need that</u> under those conditions. And yet be clearly aware of the stars and infinity on high. Then life seems almost enchanted after all. Ah, those who don't believe in the sun here are quite godless.

Unfortunately, along with the good god sun, there is the devil <u>mistral</u> 3 quarters of the time.

Saturday's post has been, damn it, and I was quite sure that your letter would come, but you can see I'm not getting in a state about it. With a handshake,

Ever yours,
Vincent

531 [F] [postscript omitted]

[3 September 1888]

My dear Theo,

I spent the day with the Belgian again yesterday – he has a sister who belongs to the Vingtistes too[1] – it wasn't good weather, but it was a very good day for talking. We went for a walk anyway, and saw some very beautiful sights at the bullfights and outside the town. We talked more seriously about the idea of my keeping my lodgings in the south while he set up some sort of base among the collieries. Then Gauguin and I and he, supposing the importance of a picture justified the journey, could change places – sometimes being up north, but in a familiar area where there would be a friend, and sometimes down south.

You'll see him soon, this young man with the Dantesque appearance, because he is coming to Paris, and you'd do him a good turn by putting him up, if the room is free. He looks very distinguished, and I'm sure he'll become so as far as his pictures are concerned. He likes Delacroix, we talked a lot about Delacroix yesterday, and what do you think, he knew that tempestuous sketch of La Barque du Christ.

Well, thanks to him, I've finally got a first sketch for that picture I've dreamed of for so long – the poet. He posed for me. His fine head with that green gaze stands out in my portrait against a starry sky of deep ultramarine. The clothing consists of a short yellow jacket, a collar of unbleached linen, gaily coloured tie. He gave me two sittings in one day.

I had a letter yesterday from our sister, who has seen all sorts of things. Ah, if she could marry an artist, it would be no bad thing. In fact, we must continue to urge her to sort out her personality rather than her artistic talents.

I've finished Daudet's L'Immortel. I rather like the sculptor Védrine's saying that achieving glory is something like shoving

1 The avant-garde group of Brussels artists, also called Les XX or Les Vingt.

the lighted end of a cigar into one's mouth while smoking. Now I like L'Immortel decidedly less, far less than Tartarin.[2]

It seems to me, you see, that L'Immortel isn't as wonderfully colourful as Tartarin, because, for all that mass of finely drawn, exact observation, it reminds me of the dreary pictures by Jean Béraud, so dry, so cold. Now Tartarin is _truly_ great, with the greatness of a masterpiece, just like Candide.

I would especially ask you to air my studies of this place as much as possible, as they are still not completely dry. If they remain shut away or in the dark, the colours will pay for it.

It wouldn't be a bad idea if you could put the portrait of the _young girl_, _the harvest_ (the large landscape with the ruin in the background and the range of mountains), the small seascape, and the garden with the weeping tree and the conifer shrubs, on stretchers. I am rather attached to those. You can tell by the drawing of the small seascape that it has the most detail.

I am having 2 oak frames made for my new peasant's head and for my poet study. Ah, my dear brother, sometimes I know so well what I want. I can well do without God in both my life and also in my painting, but, suffering as I am, I cannot do without something greater than myself, something which is my life – the power to create.

And if, deprived of the physical power, one tries to create thoughts instead of children, one is still very much part of humanity. And in my pictures I want to say something consoling, as music does. I want to paint men and women with a touch of the eternal, whose symbol was once the halo, which we try to convey by the very radiance and vibrancy of our colouring.

Portraits conceived in this way do not turn into Ary Scheffers just because there is a blue sky in the background, as in the Saint Augustine, and Ary Scheffer is scarcely a colourist.

Instead, they would be more in tune with what Eug. Delacroix tried and managed to do in his Tasso in Prison, and in so many other pictures representing a _real_ man. Ah, portraiture, portraiture

2 A series of books by Alphonse Daudet.

with the mind, the soul of the model – that is what really must come, it seems to me.

We talked a lot yesterday, the Belgian and I, about the advantages and disadvantages of this place. We are very much in agreement about both. And about how important it is for us to be able to <u>travel</u>, sometimes north, sometimes south.

He is going to stay with MacKnight again, so as to live more cheaply. That does, however, have one disadvantage for him, I think, because living with an idler makes one idle.

I'm sure you would enjoy meeting him. He is still young. I think he'll be asking your advice about buying Japanese prints and Daumier lithographs. So far as the latter are concerned, the Daumiers, it would be a good thing to get some more of them, because we might not be able to get them later on.

The Belgian was saying that he paid 80 francs for board and lodging with MacKnight. So what a difference living together makes – I have to pay 45 a month just for my lodging. And then I always come back to the same calculation, that living with Gauguin, I should spend no more than living on my own, and be no worse off for it. But we have to bear in mind that their accommodation was very poor, not so much in terms of sleeping arrangements as in opportunities for working at home.

So, I am always caught between two currents of thought, firstly, material difficulties, turning this way and that to make a living, and then, the study of colour. I keep hoping that I'll come up with something. To express the love of two lovers by the marriage of two complementary colours, their blending and their contrast, the mysterious vibrations of related tones. To express the thought of a brow by the radiance of a light tone against a dark background. To express hope by some star. Someone's passion by the radiance of the setting sun. That's certainly no realistic trompe l'oeil, but something that really exists, isn't it?

Goodbye for now. I'll let you know <u>another time</u> when the Belgian may call, because I'll be seeing him again tomorrow. With a handshake,

Ever yours,
Vincent

[...]

With undiminished fervour, Van Gogh pursued his dream of setting up an 'atelier du Midi', an artists' house in the south. Following a 'cry for help' from Gauguin in the second week of September he urged Theo anew to conclude the financial arrangement with Gauguin and so speed his departure for Arles. But as Gauguin continued to vacillate, Van Gogh's thoughts turned to Bernard as a possible alternative. Meanwhile the furnishing of the Yellow House proved a heavy drain on his funds.

Van Gogh was in great form, though, painting away 'without giving thought to a single rule', full of self-confidence: 'I am rushing ahead like a painting locomotive.' He found a new subject in the small public park in front of his house, which not only reminded him of similar themes in Manet's work but into which he projected a world of ideas going back to the Renaissance poets Petrarch and Boccaccio. The south had taught him, moreover, that night can often be more colourful than day, and during three nights in September he completed his reproduction of the refuge of the 'night owls', the *Night Café*, where he had been living since May. He had first mentioned the subject to Theo at the beginning of August, and as happened so often when he was engaged on a special painting assignment, he described the result as 'ugly': '[...] the painting is one of the ugliest I have done. It is similar to the Potato Eaters and yet different. I have tried to depict man's terrible passions with red and green.' In his choice of colour, he based himself – despite his respect for such pointillists as Seurat and Signac – on the school he had tried to emulate before he came to Paris, with Delacroix and Monticelli as his mentors. He identified himself more and more emphatically with the second of these two: 'I sometimes really think that I am continuing in the footsteps of this man.'

At the end of September the weather changed. An article on Tolstoy filled him with thoughts of a 'consoling' inner revolution. For the time being, however, the philosophical appeal of Japanese art seemed to be stronger still. His ideal now was to live and to work as a Japanese painter might, 'close to nature, like the ordinary man in the street'. He delighted in a new consignment of Japanese prints his brother had sent him and with which he decorated his studio. Much as Japanese artists were in the habit of exchanging their work with one another, so Van Gogh suggested to Gauguin and Bernard that they exchange portraits: 'I should very much like to have the portrait of Bernard by Gauguin here, as well as the one of Gauguin by Bernard.' His painter friends went along with this, inasmuch as each decided to paint a self-portrait, with a portrait of the other pictured in the background.

534 [F]

[9 September 1888]

My dear Theo,

I have just put the sketch of the new picture, the Night Café, in the post, as well as another that I did some time ago. I might finish by doing a few Japanese prints one day.

Now, yesterday I was busy with the furnishing of the house. Just as the postman & his wife had told me, the two beds will come to 150 fr. each if one wants them to be sturdily made. I found that everything they'd said about prices was true. So I had to change tack, and this is what I've done: I've bought one bed in walnut, and another in deal, which will be mine, and which I shall decorate later. Then I bought bedding for one of the beds, and <u>two</u> mattresses. If Gauguin, or someone else, comes, his bed will be ready in a minute. From the start I wanted to arrange the house, not just for me, but so that I'll be able to put someone up.

Naturally, that swallowed up the greater part of the money. With the rest I bought 12 chairs, a mirror, and a few small necessities. Which means, in short, that I'll be able to move in by next week.

For visitors, there'll be the prettiest room upstairs, which I shall do my best to turn into something like the boudoir of a really artistic woman.

Then there will be my own bedroom, which I want to keep extremely simple, but with large, solid furniture, bed, chairs, table, all in deal.

Downstairs the studio and another room, also a studio, but a kitchen at the same time.

One day you'll see a picture of the little house itself, in bright sunshine, or else with the window lit up and the starry sky.

From now on you can consider yourself the owner of a country house here in Arles. Because I'm very eager to arrange it so that you'll be happy in it, and to turn it into a studio clearly designed as such. If, say, you came for a holiday here in Marseilles in a year's time, it would be ready – and I intend the house to be filled with pictures from top to bottom by then.

The room you'll stay in then, or which will be Gauguin's if Gauguin comes, will have white walls hung with large yellow sunflowers.

In the morning, when you open the window, you'll see the green of the gardens and the rising sun and the road into town.

And you'll see these big pictures of bunches of 12 or 14 sunflowers crammed into this tiny boudoir with its pretty bed and everything else elegantly done. It will be something special.

And the studio – the red tiles on the floor, the walls and ceiling white, the rustic chairs, the deal table – hung, I hope, with portraits. There will be a feeling of Daumier about it – and I'll go so far as to predict that it will be something very special.

Now please would you look out for some Daumier lithographs for the studio, and some Japanese things, but there is absolutely no hurry, and only when you happen to get duplicates of them. And also some Delacroixs, and some ordinary lithographs by modern artists. There is no hurry whatever, but I have it all planned. I really do want to make it – an artist's house, but not affected, on the contrary, nothing affected, but everything from the chairs to the pictures full of character.

As for the beds, I got the sort of beds they have here, large double beds instead of iron bedsteads. They have an air of solidity, permanence and calm, and if that takes a little more bedding, it's too bad, but they must have character. Most luckily, I have a housemaid whom I can rely on, otherwise I shouldn't have dared to start living here. She is quite old and has many varied offspring, and she keeps my tiles nice and red and clean.

I can't tell you how much pleasure it gives me to be tackling such a big and important task. For I hope that what I am doing here will turn out to be one great decoration.

Thus, as I've already told you, I'm going to paint my own bed.

There will be 3 subjects on it. Perhaps a nude woman, I haven't decided, perhaps a cradle with a child, I don't know, but I'm going to take my time.

I no longer feel any hesitation at all about staying here, as I have a wealth of ideas for work. I intend to buy something for the house every month now. And given patience, the house will be worth something because of the furniture and the decorations.

I must warn you that very soon I shall be needing a large consignment of paints for the autumn – which I think is going to be absolutely stunning. On second thoughts I am enclosing the order with this.

In my picture of the Night Café, I have tried to express the idea that the café is a place where one can destroy oneself, go mad or commit a crime. In short, I have tried, by contrasting soft pink with blood-red and wine-red, soft Louis XV-green and Veronese green with yellow-greens and harsh blue-greens, all this in an atmosphere of an infernal furnace in pale sulphur, to express the powers of darkness in a common tavern. And yet under an outward show of Japanese gaiety and Tartarin's good nature.

But what would Mr Tersteeg say about this picture, a man who, faced with a Sisley, Sisley mind you, the most unassuming and sensitive of the impressionists, said, 'I can't help thinking that the artist who painted this was a bit tipsy.' Faced with my picture he'd say it was a raging case of delirium tremens.

I can find absolutely nothing to object to in your idea of exhibiting at the Revue Indépendante, provided, that is, I don't make it difficult for those who usually exhibit there.

Except that we must then tell them that I should like to reserve a second exhibition for myself, after this first one, of what are really studies. Then next year I will give them the pictures from the house to exhibit, when the set is complete. Not that I'm all that keen, but I want to make sure that these studies are not taken for compositions, and to convey in advance that the first showing will be one of <u>studies</u>.

For the Sower and the Night Café are the only attempts at finished paintings.

As I write, the poor peasant who resembles a caricature of our father has just come into the café. The resemblance really is striking. Particularly the air of evasiveness and weariness and the vagueness of the mouth. It still seems a pity to me that I haven't been able to do it.

I am adding to this letter the order for paints, which is not exactly urgent, only I am so full of plans, and then autumn promises so many splendid subjects, that I simply don't know if I'll be starting 5 or 10 canvases. It will be just as it was in the spring with the orchards in bloom, the subjects will be endless. If you entrusted old Tanguy with the cruder colour, he would probably make a good job of it.

His other, delicate, colours are really inferior, especially the blues.

I hope to improve the quality a little while preparing the next batch. I am doing relatively less work, and spending longer going back over it. I have kept back 50 francs for the week, the furniture having swallowed up 250 already. Still, I'll be recouping the money. And from today you can tell yourself that you have a kind of country house, unfortunately a little far away. But it would stop being too far away if there were a permanent exhibition in Marseilles. In a year's time that's something we may well see. With a handshake,

Ever yours,
Vincent

539 [F] [part]

[*c.* 17 September 1888]

My dear Theo,

I wrote to you earlier this morning, then I went and did some more work on a picture of a sunny garden. Then I brought it back in – and went out again with a blank canvas, and that, too, has been finished. And now I want to write to you again.

You see, I have never had such luck before, nature here is extraordinarily beautiful. Everything and everywhere. The dome of the sky is a wonderful blue, the sun has rays of a pale sulphur, and it is as soft and delightful as the combination of heavenly blues and yellows in Vermeer of Delft. I cannot paint as beautifully, but it absorbs me so much that I let myself go without giving thought to a single rule.

That makes 3 pictures of the gardens opposite my house. Then the two cafés. Then the sunflowers. Then the portrait of Boch and myself. Then the red sun over the factory, and the men unloading sand, and the old mill. Leaving the other studies aside, you can see that there's been some work done.

But my paint, my canvas, my purse, are completely exhausted today. The last picture, done with the last tubes of paint on the last canvas, is of a garden, green by nature, but painted without any actual green, nothing but Prussian blue and chrome yellow. I am beginning to feel completely different from the way I did when I came here. I no longer have doubts, I no longer hesitate to tackle things, and this feeling could well grow.

But what scenery! Where I am there's a public garden right next to the street with the girls of easy virtue, and Mourier, for instance, hardly ever went there even though we go for a walk in the gardens almost every day, on the far side (there are 3 of them). But you see, it's just that which lends a touch of Boccaccio to the place.

That side of the garden, by the way, is for reasons of chastity or morality bare of flowering shrubs such as oleanders. There are ordinary plane trees, groves of stiff pine, a weeping tree and green grass. But it has such intimacy! There are gardens by Manet like that.

For as long as you can bear the burden of all the paint and canvas and all the money that I have to spend, carry on sending it to me, because what I am getting ready will be better than the last batch, and I'm sure we'll make a profit out of it instead of losing, provided I can manage to produce a decent set. Which is what I am trying to do.

But is it absolutely impossible for Thomas to lend me two or three hundred francs against my studies? That would mean I'd earn more than a thousand on them, and I can't tell you how thrilled, thrilled, thrilled I am by what I see. And that fills one with expectations for the autumn, an enthusiasm which makes the time pass without one's feeling it – beware the morning after the night before, and the winter mistrals!

Today, working all the while, I thought a lot about Bernard. His letter is full of veneration for Gauguin's talent – he says that he thinks him so great an artist that he is almost afraid of him, and that he finds everything that he, Bernard, does inadequate in comparison with Gauguin. And you know that last winter Bernard was still picking quarrels with Gauguin. In the long run, be that as it may and whatever happens, it's very comforting that these artists are our friends, and I like to think they'll remain so, no matter how things turn out.

I am so happy with the house – with work – that I even dare to think that this happiness will not remain confined to me, but that you, too, will share in it and have some good luck as well!

Some time ago I read an article on Dante, Petrarch, Boccaccio, Giotto and Botticelli. My God, that made an impression on me, reading the letters of those men! Now Petrarch lived very near here, at Avignon, and I see the same cypresses and oleanders. I have tried to put something of that into one of the Gardens, painted in a thick impasto of lemon yellow and lime green. I was most of all touched by Giotto – <u>always suffering</u>, and always full of benevolence and zeal, as though he were already living in another world.

Giotto is extraordinary, anyway, and I understand him better than I do the poets Dante, Petrarch and Boccaccio. It always seems to me that poetry is more <u>terrible</u> than painting, although painting is dirtier and ultimately more tedious. And the painter on the whole says nothing, he holds his tongue, and I prefer that too.

My dear Theo, when you have seen the cypresses, the oleanders and the sun here – and that day will come, rest assured – then you will think even more often of the beautiful works of Puvis de Chavannes, of Doux pays, and so many others.

There is so much that is Greek throughout both the Tartarin side and the Daumier side of this strange country, where the good people have the accent with which you are familiar, and there is a Venus of Arles just like the Lesbos one, and despite everything, one is still aware of the youth of it all.

I haven't the slightest doubt that one day you too will know the south. Perhaps you'll go and see Claude Monet when he is in Antibes, or you'll find some opportunity, anyway.

When the mistral blows, however, it is just the opposite of a <u>pleasant</u> country, because the mistral gets on one's nerves badly. But what compensation, what compensation when there is a day without wind. What intensity of colours, what pure air, what vibrant serenity.

Tomorrow I am going to draw until the paint arrives. But I am now resolved not to draw any more pictures with charcoal. It serves no purpose, you must tackle drawings with colour if you want to draw well.

Oh – the exhibition at the Revue Indépendante – good – but once and for all, we have smoked too much to put the wrong end of the cigar in our mouths. We must try to sell if we want to do the things we have sold all over again, but better. It's because we are in a bad trade – but don't let's play to the gallery and suffer for it at home.

This afternoon I had a select audience ... 4 or 5 pimps and a dozen urchins, who found it extremely interesting watching the paint come out of the tubes. Well, that audience – there's fame for you, or rather, I firmly intend to be as unconcerned about ambition and fame as those urchins and layabouts along the Rhône and the rue du Bout d'Arles.

I went to Milliet's today. He is coming tomorrow, having prolonged his stay by 4 days.

I wish Bernard would do his military service in Africa, because he would do some good things there, and I still don't know what to say to him. He told me that he would exchange his portrait for one of my studies.

But he says he <u>daren't</u> do Gauguin as I asked him to, because he feels too shy in front of Gauguin. Bernard is basically so temperamental!! He can be silly and unpleasant sometimes, but I certainly haven't any right to reproach him, because I myself am only too familiar with that nervous disorder, and I'm sure he would not reproach me either. If he went to Africa to stay with Milliet, Milliet would certainly befriend him, for Milliet is a very loyal friend, and makes love so easily that he almost holds love in contempt.

What is Seurat doing? I wouldn't dare show him the studies I've sent you, but the ones of the sunflowers, and the taverns, and the gardens, I wouldn't mind him seeing those – I often think about his method, and yet I don't follow it at all, but he is an original colourist, and so is Signac, but to a different degree. The pointillists have discovered something new, and anyway I like them a lot. But as far as I am concerned – I tell you frankly – I am going back more to what I was trying to do before I went to Paris, and I don't know if anyone before me has spoken of suggestive colour, but Delacroix and Monticelli did it without talking about it.

But I am the way I was at Nuenen again, when I made a vain effort to learn music – I was keenly aware even then of the relationship between colour and Wagner's music.

Now, it is true that I see in impressionism a resurrection of Eugène Delacroix, but as the interpretations are both divergent and also rather irreconcilable, impressionism cannot yet formulate a doctrine. That is why I am staying with the impressionists, because it means nothing, and commits you to nothing, and as one of them I do not have to take up any position. My God, you have to play the fool in this life. I ask only for time to study, and you, do you ask for anything other than that? I know that you, like me, must love having the peace one needs for objective study.

And I am so afraid of depriving you of it by my demands for money.

And yet, I budget so carefully, but found today again that with the ten metres of canvas I had budgeted accurately for all the colours except one, the fundamental one of yellow. If all my colours are used up at the same time, isn't that proof that I can sense the relative amounts in my sleep? It's the same with drawing, I take hardly any measurements, and in that I differ quite radically from Cormon, who says that if he didn't measure he would draw like a pig.

[...]

It's a comfort that we are always engrossed in our raw materials, not speculating but wanting only to produce. And so we cannot go wrong.

I hope it will go on being like that, and if I am doomed to exhaust my paint, my canvas and my purse, not even that will be our undoing, of that you may be sure. Even supposing you exhaust your own purse and everything in it yourself, that would be a serious matter, of course, but just say to me calmly, there is nothing left – and there will still be something left, because of what I have done with your money.

But you will then quite naturally say to me – and in the meantime? In the meantime – I'll do some drawing, since doing nothing but drawing is easier than painting.

A warm handshake. What days these are, not because of what is happening, but because I feel so strongly that you and I are not in decline, nor done for yet, nor are we going to be. But you know, I won't argue with the critics who will say that my pictures are not – finished.

With a handshake, and for now,

Ever yours,
Vincent

I too have read Richepin's Césarine – I very much like what the woman says about that fool: the whole of life is just a matter of the right equations.

542 [F] [part]

[24 September 1888]

My dear Theo,

The lovely weather of the last few days has gone, to be replaced by mud and rain. But it's sure to come back again before winter. Only one must make the most of it, as the fine days are short.

Especially for painting. This winter I intend to do a lot of drawing. If only I could draw figures from memory, I should always have something to do. But if you take a figure by the most skilful of all the artists who sketch from life – Hokusai, or Daumier – in my opinion that figure will never compare to a figure painted from the model by those same masters or other master portrait painters.

Anyway – if we are so often fated to go short of models, and especially of intelligent models, we mustn't despair or tire of the struggle.

I have arranged all the Japanese prints in the studio, and the Daumiers, and the Delacroixs, and the Géricaults. If you come across Delacroix's Pietà again, or the Géricault, I urge you to get as many of them as you can.

What I should really love to have in the studio as well is Millet's Les Travaux des champs – and Lerat's etching of his Semeur, which Durand-Ruel sells for 1.25 fr. And lastly the little etching by Jacquemart after Meissonier, Le liseur, a Meissonier I've always admired. I cannot help liking Meissonier's work.

I am reading an article on Tolstoy in the Revue des Deux Mondes – it appears that Tolstoy is enormously interested in the religion of his people. Like George Eliot in England. I believe there is a book on religion by Tolstoy, I think it's called My Religion, it's sure to be very good. In it he goes in search, or so I gather from the article, of what remains eternally true in the Christian religion and what all religions have in common. It seems that he admits neither the resurrection of the body, nor even that of the soul, but says, like the nihilists, that after death there is nothing else. Though man dies, and dies completely, living humanity endures for ever.

Anyhow, not having read the book itself, I'm not able to say exactly what his conception is, but I don't imagine that his religion is a cruel one which increases our suffering, but must be, on the contrary, a very comforting one, inspiring one with peace of mind, and energy, and the courage to live, and many other things.

I think the drawing of the <u>blade of grass</u> and the carnations and the Hokusai in Bing's reproductions are <u>admirable</u>.

But whatever they say, the most ordinary Japanese prints, coloured in flat tones, seem admirable to me for the same reason as Rubens and Veronese. I know perfectly well that they are not primitive art. But just because the primitives are so admirable, there is absolutely no reason for me to say, as is becoming the <u>custom</u>, 'When I go to the Louvre I cannot get any further than the primitives.'

If I said to a <u>serious</u> collector of Japanese art – to Lévy himself – Sir, I cannot help admiring these Japanese prints at 5 sous apiece, it is more than probable that he would be a little shocked, and would pity my ignorance and bad taste. Just as at one time it was considered bad taste to admire Rubens, Jordaens and Veronese.

I'm sure I shan't end up feeling lonely in the house, and that during bad winter days, and the long evenings, I shall find something absorbing to do.

A weaver or a basket maker often spends whole seasons alone, or almost alone, with his craft as his only distraction. And what makes these people stay in one place is precisely the feeling of being at home, <u>the reassuring and familiar look of things</u>. Of course I'd welcome company, but it won't make me unhappy if I don't have it, and anyway, the time will come when I will have someone, I have little doubt of that.

I'm sure that if you were willing to put people up in your house too, you'd find plenty of artists for whom the question of lodgings is a very serious problem.

[. . .]

As for the pictures done in fairly thick impasto, I think they need longer to dry out <u>here</u>. I've read that the works of Rubens in Spain have remained infinitely richer in colour than those in the north. Even the <u>ruins</u> here exposed to the open air remain white, whereas in the north they turn grey, dirty, black, &c. You may be sure that if the Monticellis had dried in Paris, they would be very much duller by now.

I am beginning to appreciate the beauty of the women here better, so my thoughts return to Monticelli over and over again. Colour plays a tremendous part in the beauty of these women – I'm not saying that their figures are not beautiful, but that is not the native charm. That is to be found in the grand lines of the colourful costume, worn just right, and in the tone of the flesh rather than the shape. It won't be easy doing them the way I'm beginning to feel about them. But what I am sure of is that by staying here I shall make progress. And in order to do a picture which is really of the south, a little skill is not enough. It is observing things for a long time that gives you greater maturity and a deeper understanding.

I didn't think when I left Paris that I should ever find Monticelli and Delacroix so <u>true</u>. It is only now, after months and months, that I am beginning to realize that they didn't dream it all up. And next year I think you'll see the same subjects again, orchards, the harvest, but – with a different colouring, and above all, a change in treatment. And these changes and variations will go on.

My feeling is that I must work at a leisurely pace. Indeed, what about practising the old saying, One should study for ten years or so, and then produce a few figures? That is what Monticelli did, after all. Hundreds of his pictures should be considered as nothing more than studies. But still, figures like the woman in yellow, or the woman with the parasol, the little one you have, or the lovers that Reid had, those are complete figures and one can only admire the way they were drawn. For in them Monticelli achieves drawing as rich and magnificent as that of Daumier and Delacroix. Certainly, at the price Monticellis are fetching, it would be an excellent speculation to buy some.

The day will come when his beautiful <u>drawn</u> figures will be considered very great art.

As for the beauty of the women and their costume, I'm sure the town of Arles was infinitely more glorious in the past. Everything has a blighted, faded quality about it now. Still, if you look at it for a long time, the old charm re-emerges.

And that is why I can see that I will lose absolutely nothing by staying where I am and contenting myself with watching things go by, like a spider in its web waiting for flies.

I can't force things, and now that I'm settled in, I'll be able to profit from all the fine days and all the opportunities for catching a real picture now and then.

Milliet is lucky, he has as many Arlésiennes as he wants, but then, he can't paint them, and if he were a painter, he wouldn't have them. I shall just have to bide my time without rushing things.

I've read another article on Wagner – Love in Music – I think by the same author who wrote the book on Wagner. How we need the same thing in painting!

It seems that in the book My Religion, Tolstoy implies that whatever happens in a violent revolution, there will also be an inner and hidden revolution in the people, out of which a new religion will be born, or rather, something completely new which will be nameless, but which will have the same effect of consoling, of making life possible, as the Christian religion used to.

The book must be a very interesting one, it seems to me. In the end, we shall have had enough of cynicism, scepticism and humbug, and will want to live – more musically. How will this come about, and what will we discover? It would be nice to be able to prophesy, but it is even better to be forewarned, instead of seeing absolutely nothing in the future other than the disasters that are bound to strike the modern world and civilization like so many thunderbolts, through revolution, or war, or the bankruptcy of worm-eaten states.

If we study Japanese art, we discover a man who is undeniably wise, philosophical and intelligent, who spends his time – doing what? Studying the distance from the earth to the moon? No! Studying the politics of Bismarck? No! He studies ... a single blade of grass. But this blade of grass leads him to draw all the plants – then the seasons, the grand spectacle of landscapes, finally animals, then the human figure. That is how he spends his life, and life is too short to do everything.

So come, isn't what we are taught by these simple Japanese, who live in nature as if they themselves were flowers, almost a true religion?

And one cannot study Japanese art, it seems to me, without becoming merrier and happier, and we should turn back to nature in spite of our education and our work in a conventional world.

Isn't it sad that the Monticellis have never been reproduced in beautiful lithographs or vibrant etchings? I should love to see what artists would say if an engraver like the one who engraved Velásquez's work made a fine etching of them. Be that as it may, I think it rather more our duty to try to admire and know things for ourselves than to teach them to others. But the two can go hand in hand.

I envy the Japanese the extreme clarity of everything in their work. It is never dull and it never seems to be done in too much of a hurry. Their work is as simple as breathing, and they do a figure in a few sure strokes as if it were as easy as doing up your waistcoat.

Oh, I still have to learn to do a figure in a few strokes. That will keep me busy all winter. Once I can do that, I shall be able to do people promenading along the boulevards, in the streets, masses of new subjects. While I've been writing this letter to you, I've already drawn a dozen. I'm on the right track, but it's very complicated, as what I am trying to do in a few strokes is to provide the figure of a man, a woman, a child, a horse or a dog, with a head, a body, legs and arms that all fit together.

For the moment, and with a hearty handshake,

Ever yours,
Vincent

One day Madame de Larebey Laroquette said to me, Monticelli, Monticelli, now he was a man who should have been at the head of a great studio in the south.

I wrote to our sister the other day, and to you, you remember, that sometimes I felt I was continuing Monticelli's work here. Well, now you can see we are setting up that studio in question.

What Gauguin will be doing, what I shall be doing as well, will be in keeping with Monticelli's fine work, and we shall try to prove to the good people that Monticelli did not die slumped across the café tables of the Canebière, but that the little fellow is still alive.

And the thing won't end with us, we shall merely start it off on a fairly solid basis.

Not only Monticelli but Corot, too, seemed to provide Van Gogh with a precedent for his plan to share a house with a fellow artist – Corot, that amiable artist, 'on finding Daumier on the verge of despair, made such good provision for him that the other approved of everything'. Although Van Gogh had met Gauguin no more than fleetingly during his stay in Paris, he felt it his duty to help him. He considered him 'a very great master and a most superior person as to character and intelligence'.

At the beginning of October 1888, Gauguin wrote to say that he and Bernard had finished their self-portraits for Van Gogh. Gauguin had given his portrait a symbolic dimension by depicting himself as Jean Valjean, the main character in Victor Hugo's *Les misérables*. He described the portrait to Vincent as the 'mask of a shabbily dressed and accomplished rogue like Jean Valjean [. . .] disowned by society, outlawed, yet with all his love and strength – isn't that also the picture of the contemporary impressionist? And because I have lent him my features, you have a portrait not just of myself, but of all of us, poor victims of society who take revenge by doing good.'

In his reply to Gauguin, Van Gogh expressed his diffidence at receiving so important a work as a present and added that he had finished his own self-portrait as a 'bonze' and proposed to give it to Gauguin in return. He also gave detailed descriptions of the other works he had completed in this period as decorations for the Yellow House, namely *The Green Vineyard* and *The Poet's Garden*. In passing, the letter also throws interesting light on Van Gogh's last days in Paris.

[F] [letter from Vincent to Paul Gauguin][1]

[3 October 1888]

My dear Gauguin,

This morning I received your excellent letter, which I have again sent on to my brother. Your view of impressionism in general, of which your portrait is a symbol, is striking. No one could be more anxious than I am to see it – but I am sure even now that this work is too important for me to take in exchange. But if you would like to keep it for us, my brother will, if you agree, buy it at the first opportunity – and I immediately asked him to do so – so let's hope it happens before long.

For we are trying once more to make it as easy as possible for you to come here soon.

I must tell you that even while working I think continually about the plan of setting up a studio in which you and I will be permanent residents, but which both of us want to turn into a shelter and refuge for friends, against the times when they find that the struggle is getting too much for them.

When you left Paris, my brother and I stayed on together for a time, which will always remain an unforgettable memory for me. The discussions ranged further and wider – with Guillaumin, with the Pissarros, father and son, and with Seurat, whom I had not met before (I visited his studio just a few hours before my departure).

These discussions often dealt with something so near to my brother's heart and to mine, namely what steps to take in order

[1] This letter was sent by Gauguin to Émile Schuffenecker on 8 October 1888 with the observation, 'I am sending you this letter from Vincent to let you know how things stand between us and with all our present plans.'

to safeguard the material existence of painters, to safeguard their means of production (paints, canvases) and to safeguard their true share in the price their pictures fetch these days – though not until long after they have left the artists' possession.

When you're here, we can mull over all these discussions.

Anyway, when I left Paris I was in a sorry state, quite ill and almost an alcoholic after driving myself on even while my strength was failing – and then withdrawing into myself, still bereft of hope.

Now, hope is vaguely beckoning on the horizon again, that flickering hope which used sometimes to console my solitary life.

I should so much like to imbue you with a large share of my faith that we shall succeed in starting something that will endure.

When we have had a talk about those strange days spent in discussion in run-down studios and the cafés of the Petit Boulevard, you will understand the full scope of this idea of my brother's and mine – as yet unrealized when it comes to setting up a society.

Still, you will appreciate that in order to remedy the terrible situation of the last few years something is needed, either along the precise lines we proposed or else very much like them. That much we have taken for our unshakeable foundation, as you will gather when you have the full explanation. And you will agree that we have gone a good way beyond the plan we have already communicated to you. That we have gone beyond it is no more than our duty as picture dealers, for you probably know that I, too, spent several years in the trade and do not despise a profession in which I used to earn my living. Suffice it to say that I'm sure that, although you have apparently cut yourself off from Paris, you haven't stopped feeling a fairly close rapport with Paris.

I am having an extraordinary spell of feverish activity these days. Right now I am tackling a landscape with a blue sky above an immense green, purple and yellow vineyard, with black and orange vines. Little figures of ladies with red parasols and little figures of grape pickers with their small cart make it even gayer. Grey sand in the foreground. Another size 30 square canvas to decorate the house.

I've a portrait of myself, all ash grey. The ashen colour – which has been obtained by mixing Veronese green with orange lead – on a pale Veronese background, all in harmony with the reddish-brown clothes. Not wishing to inflate my own personality, however, I aimed rather for the character of a bonze, a simple worshipper of the eternal Buddha. Though I have taken rather a lot of trouble with it, I shall have to go over it again if I want to express the idea properly, and I shall have to recover even further from the stultifying effect of our so-called state of civilization if I am to have a better model for a better picture.

One thing that gives me enormous pleasure is the letter I received yesterday from Boch (his sister is one of the Belgian Vingtistes), who writes that he has settled down in the Borinage to paint miners and coal mines there. He nevertheless intends to return to the south – to vary his impressions – and if he does he is certain to come to Arles.

I consider my views of art excessively run of the mill compared with yours.

I have always had coarse animal tastes.

I neglect everything for the external beauty of things, <u>which I cannot reproduce</u> because I render it so ugly and coarse in my pictures, albeit nature seems so perfect to me.

At present, however, my bony carcass is so full of energy that it makes straight for its objective. The result is a degree of sincerity, perhaps original at times, about what I feel, but only if the subject lends itself to my crude and clumsy touch.

I feel sure that if from now on you were to consider yourself the head of this studio, which we shall try to ensure will become a refuge for many – little by little, as our unremitting labour provides us with the means of completing it – I'm sure that you would then feel more or less consoled for the present ordeals of penury and ill-health, seeing that we shall probably be devoting our lives to a generation of painters that will last a long while to come.

This part of the country has already seen the cult of Venus – in Greece, primarily artistic – followed by the poets and artists of the Renaissance. Where these things could flourish, impressionism can as well.

I have made a special decoration, the <u>Poet's Garden</u>, for the room you will have (there is a first draft of it among the sketches in Bernard's possession – it was later simplified). The ordinary public garden contains plants and shrubs that conjure up landscapes in which one can readily imagine Botticelli, Giotto, Petrarch, Dante and Boccaccio. I have tried to distil in the decoration the essence of what constitutes the immutable character of this country.

And I set out to paint that garden in such a way that one is put in mind of the old poet from these parts (or rather from Avignon), Petrarch, and of the new poet from these parts – Paul Gauguin –

However clumsy this attempt may be, it may show you perhaps that I have been thinking of you with very great emotion as I prepared your studio.

Let us be of good heart about the success of our venture, and please keep thinking of this as your home, for I feel very sure that all this will last for a very long time.

A warm handshake, and believe me,

Ever yours,
Vincent

I am only afraid that you will think Brittany more beautiful, indeed, that you will find nothing more beautiful here than Daumier, the figures here are often pure Daumier. It shouldn't take you long to discover that antiquity and the Renaissance lie dormant under all this modernity. Well, you are free to revive them.

Bernard tells me that he, Morel, Laval and somebody else will be making exchanges with me. In principle I am very much in favour of the system of exchanges between artists because I have seen the important part it played in the life of the Japanese painters. Accordingly, one of these days I shall be sending you what studies I have that are dry and that I can spare, so that you may have first pick. But I shall make no exchanges at all with you if it means that on your side it costs you something as important as your portrait, which is sure to be too beautiful. Truly, I wouldn't dare, because my brother would gladly buy it from you for a whole month's money.

Following this bout of frantic activity Van Gogh was forced to take a rest for a few days. The painting campaigns of the summer and autumn had exhausted him to such an extent that he felt he was 'reduced once more close to the deranged state of Hugo van der Goes in the painting by Émile Wauters'. In the light of what happened later that year, Van Gogh's remark has a sense of doom and foreboding. Meanwhile, he tried to get as much sleep as he could, and even that provided him with inspiration for a painting, namely *Vincent's Bedroom*.

554 [F]

[16 October 1888]

My dear Theo,

I'm sending you a little sketch at long last to give you at least some idea of the direction my work is taking. Because I feel quite well again today. My eyes are still tired, but I had a new idea all the same and here is the sketch of it.

As always a size 30 canvas.

This time it's simply my bedroom. Only here everything depends on the colour, and by simplifying it I am lending it more style, creating an overall impression <u>of rest or sleep</u>. In fact, a look at the picture ought to rest the mind, or rather the imagination.

The walls are pale violet. The floor – is red tiles.

The wood of the bed and the chairs is the yellow of fresh butter, the sheet and the pillows very light lime green.

The blanket scarlet.

[554]: enclosed sketch.

The window green.

The washstand orange, the basin blue.

The doors lilac.

And that's all – nothing of any consequence in this shuttered room.

The sturdy lines of the furniture should also express undisturbed rest.

Portraits on the wall, and a mirror, and a hand towel, and some clothes. The frame – because there is no white in the picture – will be white.

This by way of revenge for the enforced rest I have had to take.

I shall work on it again all day tomorrow, but you can see how simple the conception is. The shadows and the cast shadows are left out and it is painted in bright flat tints like the Japanese prints.

It will form a contrast to, for example, the Tarascon diligence and the Night Café.

I am not writing you a long letter because I intend starting very early tomorrow in the cool morning light so as to finish my canvas.

How are your aches and pains? Don't forget to let me know.

I hope you'll write one of these days.

One day I'll do some sketches for you of the other rooms too.

With a good handshake,

Ever yours,
Vincent

On 23 October 1888, just when Van Gogh was beginning to become annoyed at Gauguin's reluctance to turn up, and was thinking of inviting Bernard as an alternative co-tenant for the Yellow House, Gauguin arrived in Arles. Gauguin claimed later that his stay in Arles had seemed to go on for ever, but the notorious association of the two painters in fact lasted for precisely nine weeks.

557 [F]

[24 October 1888]

My dear Theo,

Thanks for your letter and the 50 fr. note. As you learned from my telegram, Gauguin has arrived in good health. He even seems to be in better health than I am.

He is very happy about the sale[1] you made, of course, and I no less so, since some still absolutely essential settling-in expenses will now no longer need to wait, nor will you be saddled with all of them. G. will undoubtedly be writing to you today.

He is very, very interesting as a man, and I have every confidence that we shall achieve a great deal with him. He will undoubtedly be very productive here, and I hope that I may be, too.

And so I dare hope the burden will be <u>a little</u> less heavy for you, I even hope <u>much</u> less heavy.

I realize, to the point of being morally crushed and physically drained by it, that taking all in all, I have absolutely no other means of ever recovering what we have spent.

I cannot help it that my pictures do not sell.

The day will come, however, when people will see they are worth more than the price of the paint and my living expenses, very meagre on the whole, which we put into them.

As far as money or finances are concerned, what I want and what I am interested in is to have no debts in the first place.

But, my dear brother, my debt is so great that by the time I have paid it off, which I'm still sure I'll succeed in doing, the strain of producing pictures will have taken my whole life, and it will seem to me that I haven't lived. The only thing is that producing pictures may become a little more difficult for me, and that, in time, there won't always be so many.

That they are not selling at the moment distresses me because

1 Theo had just sold Gauguin's *Les Bretonnes* for 500 francs.

you suffer for it, but if my bringing nothing in did not inconvenience you, it wouldn't matter much either way to me.

But as far as finances are concerned, all I need is to remember this truth, that a man who lives for 50 years and spends two thousand a year, spends a hundred thousand francs, and that he must therefore also bring in a hundred thousand. To do a thousand pictures at a hundred francs during one's lifetime as an artist is a very, very, very difficult thing to do, and since the pictures do indeed fetch a hundred francs ... then ... our task is very hard at times. But there is nothing we can do to change that.

We shall probably give Tasset[2] a miss altogether, because we are going – to a large extent – to make use of cheaper paints, Gauguin as well as I. As for the canvas, we shall prepare it ourselves for the same reason.

I had the feeling for a time that I was going to be ill, but Gauguin's arrival has so taken my mind off it that I am sure it will pass. I must pay attention to my diet for a while, but that's all – absolutely nothing else. And before very long you will have some work.

Gauguin has brought a magnificent canvas[3] which he'd exchanged with Bernard, Breton women in a green field, white, black, green, and a note of red, and matt flesh tones. So, let's all be of good heart.

I'm sure the day will come when I shall sell as well, but I am so far behind with you, and am still spending without bringing anything in. From time to time that thought saddens me.

I am very, very pleased with what you write about one of the Dutchmen coming to stay with you,[4] so that you too will no longer be alone. It's very, very good news, especially since winter will soon be here.

Anyway, I'm in a hurry now, and must go out and start work again on another size thirty canvas.

2 The paint merchants Tasset & L'Hôte.
3 Émile Bernard, *Breton Women and Children.*
4 The painter Meijer de Haan had moved into Theo's apartment.

Soon, when Gauguin writes to you, I'll add another letter to his.

Of course, I don't know in advance what Gauguin will say about this part of the world, and about our life, but he's very pleased at any rate about the good sale you made for him.

Goodbye for the present, and a good handshake,

Ever yours,
Vincent

In his reply, Theo tried to dispel Vincent's anxieties and would have none of the suggestion that Vincent was in his debt. On the contrary, he, Theo, owed so much to Vincent, who could claim the credit for creating 'a circle of artists & friends' for the two of them. He mentioned that he was now regularly seeing the Dutch artists Joseph Isaäcson and Meijer de Haan.

Initially, Gauguin and Van Gogh worked a great deal together. They painted members of the Ginoux family – Gauguin, too, producing a version of their night café – and explored brothels together. Gauguin encouraged Vincent to work more frequently from memory, and even the arch-realist Van Gogh had to admit that 'things done from memory do indeed assume a more mysterious character'. As a result he produced several works in which he harked back to his Brabant period, amongst them *Woman Reading Novels* and *Memory of the Garden at Etten*. During the second half of November he finished two symbolic portraits of Gauguin and himself in the form of two chairs: the one representing himself was 'wooden, all yellow, rush-bottomed, on red tiles against a wall (<u>by daylight</u>). Then Gauguin's armchair, red and green, night effect, wall and floor red and green as well, on the chair two novels and a candlestick. On thin canvas with thick impasto.'

Thanks to his friendship with the postman Roulin, Vincent at long last obtained the models he so badly needed. At the beginning of December he reported, 'I have done portraits of a <u>whole family</u>, that of the postman whose head I did earlier: husband, wife, baby, the little boy and the 16-year old son, all of them characters and very French, though they look Russian.'

In Paris, Gauguin had admired a still life with sunflowers by Vincent and acquired it, probably by way of exchange. Van Gogh now informed Theo proudly that Gauguin considered the new still lifes with sunflowers he had painted for the Yellow House even finer than a similar work by Claude Monet. It was also as the sunflower painter *par excellence* that Gauguin portrayed his friend in December 1888. Van Gogh, however, seems to have been far from pleased with the painting, apparently saying, 'It's certainly me, but me gone mad.' According to Gauguin, Van Gogh's violent reaction to the portrait one evening was the prelude to the so-called '*grande catastrophe*' of the following week. On the evening in question, Van Gogh is said to have thrown a glass of absinthe at his colleague's head after a loud argument in a café. The incident was smoothed over, apologies offered, and on 17 or 18 December the two painters decided to interrupt their work briefly to pay a joint visit to the Montpellier gallery. Here, amongst other things, they were able to inspect the Bruyas Collection, with work by Delacroix, Courbet and Couture. The heated discussions occasioned by that visit, however, brought to light such vast differences in their respective artistic views that Van Gogh told Theo in a brief note written just before Christmas that their relationship had been impaired.

564 [F]

[second half of December 1888]

My dear Theo,

Yesterday Gauguin and I went to Montpellier to see the gallery there, particularly the Bruyas room, where there are lots of portraits of Bruyas by Delacroix, Ricard, Courbet, Cabanel, Couture, Verdier, Tassaert and others. There are also other paintings by Delacroix, Courbet, Giotto, Paulus Potter, Botticelli, Th. Rousseau, very fine.

Bruyas was a benefactor of artists, and I shall say no more to you than that. In the portrait by Delacroix he is a gentleman with a beard and red hair, who bears an amazing resemblance to you and to me, and made me think of that poem by Musset:

Partout où j'ai touché la terre – un malheureux vêtu de noir auprès de nous venait s'asseoir qui nous regardait comme un frère.[1] It would have the same effect on you, I'm sure.

Do go to that bookshop where they sell lithographs of past and present artists, and try, if it doesn't cost too much, to get the lithograph after Delacroix's Le Tasse dans la prison des fous, since I think that figure must have some connection with this fine portrait of Bruyas.

There are other Delacroixs there, a study of a mulatto woman (which Gauguin copied at one time), Les odalisques, Daniel dans la fosse aux lions, and, by Courbet, 1. Les demoiselles de village, magnificent, a nude woman viewed from behind, another lying on the ground in a landscape, 2. La fileuse (superb), and lots of other Courbets. Anyway, you must know of the existence of this collection, or at least know people who have seen it, and who can talk about it. So I will not dwell on the gallery (except on the Barye drawings and bronzes!).

Gauguin and I discuss Delacroix, Rembrandt, etc., a great deal. The debate is <u>exceedingly electric</u>, and sometimes when we finish our minds are as drained as an electric battery after discharge.

We had been right in the midst of magic, for as Fromentin puts it so well: Rembrandt is above all a magician and Delacroix is a man of God, a fantastic man of God, and that's bloody well all there is to it in the name of God.

I am writing you this in connection with our Dutch friends, De Haan and Isaäcson, who have studied and admired Rembrandt so much, hoping that you will encourage them to continue their research.

There must be no discouragement when it comes to that.

You know the strange and superb portrait of a man by Rembrandt in the Lacaze Gallery? I said to Gauguin that I saw a certain family or racial resemblance to Delacroix or to Gauguin himself in it.

1 'Wherever I touched the earth, a poor wretch dressed in black came and sat down next to us and looked at us like a brother'(inaccurate and incomplete quotation from Alfred de Musset, 'La nuit de Décembre').

I don't know why, but I always call this portrait 'the traveller' or the man come from afar.

It's a similar and parallel idea to the one I've mentioned to you, to see your future self in the portrait of the old Six, that fine portrait with the gloves, and your past and present in Rembrandt's etching entitled Six reading near a window in a ray of sunshine.

So that's where we've got to.

Gauguin said to me this morning, when I asked him how he was, 'that he felt his former self coming back', which gave me great pleasure. When I came here last winter, weary and almost mentally exhausted, I had to suffer a little inwardly too before I could start on my recovery.

How I wish that you could see the gallery in Montpellier some time, there are some very beautiful things there!

Tell Degas that Gauguin and I have been to see the portrait of Bruyas by Delacroix at Montpellier. Because we must dare to believe that what is, is, and the portrait of Bruyas by Delacroix resembles you and me like another brother.

As far as founding an artists' colony for friends is concerned, such strange things have been known, and I'll close with what you're always saying – only time will tell. You can say all that to our friends Isaäcson and De Haan, and even feel free to read this letter to them. I would have written to them already if I had felt the necessary electric charge.

A very hearty handshake to you all on behalf of Gauguin as well as me.

Ever yours,
Vincent

In case you think that Gauguin or I get down to work effortlessly, let me tell you that work does not always come easily to us. And my wish for our Dutch friends, and for you as well, is that they should feel no more discouraged by their difficulties than we do.

565 [F]

[23 December 1888]

My dear Theo,

Thank you very much for your letter, for the 100 fr. note enclosed and also for the money order for 50 fr.

I think that Gauguin was a little disenchanted with the good town of Arles, the little yellow house where we work, and above all with me.

Indeed, there are serious problems to overcome here still, for him as well as for me.

But these problems lie more in ourselves than anywhere else.

In short, I think that he'll either simply leave or he'll simply stay.

I've told him to think it over and weigh up the pros and cons before doing anything.

Gauguin is very strong, very creative, but he needs peace precisely because of that.

Will he find it elsewhere if he doesn't find it here?

I await his decision with absolute equanimity.

With a good handshake,

Vincent

Van Gogh had been describing his discussions with Gauguin in terms of the discharge of an electric battery, and now, on this self-same 23 December, all the fuses blew. While Gauguin worked on a self-portrait and Van Gogh on a version of his portrait of Madame Roulin, the so-called *Berceuse* (Woman Rocking a Cradle), their strained relationship came to a head. In the evening, when Gauguin went for a walk through the small gardens at the place Lamartine, Van Gogh suddenly appeared behind him and threatened his friend with a razor. By looking him straight in the face, Gauguin was able to calm Van Gogh down, but he decided, for safety's sake, not to spend the night in the Yellow House and to go instead to a hotel. At half past eleven that night Van Gogh appeared at a brothel and asked for the prostitute called Rachel. With the words, 'Take good care of this', he handed her a piece he had cut from his earlobe. Next morning, the police found him unconscious in his bed.

What we know about these incidents stems mainly from Gauguin's account, given long after the event. That version can be challenged in several respects, but it certainly conveys the gist of what actually happened. Understandably, Van Gogh's own letters offer no more than a weak echo of the events that were to give his life and artistic career so tragic a turn. However, in the weeks that followed, he let something of what had happened slip out bit by bit, as the implications, especially for his future, gradually dawned on him. He was gripped by deep uncertainty.

Alerted by a telegram from Gauguin, Theo rushed to Arles. Vincent was admitted to the local hospital, where the sympathetic Dr Félix Rey treated him. His condition appeared critical, but on New Year's Eve Theo, back in Paris, received positive news of his brother's recovery. Meanwhile, Vincent's friend Roulin was looking after the Yellow House, which 'because of this episode was in a shambles, all the linen and my clothes being soiled'.

On 2 January, Van Gogh wrote a scribbled note to Theo, who just at this dramatic time had become engaged to Johanna Bonger, the sister of their Dutch friend Andries from Paris. In this note, he asked if he had frightened Gauguin off and why he had heard nothing from him. Alarmed that his dream of an artists' house in the south had now foundered, he enjoined Gauguin two days later not to say 'one bad word about our little yellow house' to colleagues in Paris. He also sent a reassuring note to his mother and Wil in Holland and wrote in a letter to Theo, 'I hope that I have had no more than a perfectly ordinary attack of artistic temperament, followed by high fever as a consequence of the loss of a _very_ great deal of blood because an artery had been severed.'

Having first played down his attack, he gave Theo a more realistic account of what had happened a little later. Gauguin too received another letter in which Van Gogh did his best to put the seriousness of the incident into perspective and was even able to respond soberly and practically to Gauguin's request for his fencing mask and fencing gloves, as well as for Van Gogh's still life with sunflowers.

Hope and resignation alternated in the letters Vincent wrote during the first months following his recovery. He was deeply depressed by the departure of Gauguin, as well as of his good friend Roulin, who had been transferred to Marseilles. After his original delight at the speed of his recovery, Van Gogh now asked himself the existential question, 'What am I getting better for?' On top of that, he could not help fearing a possible relapse. He was aware that his letters still sounded somewhat strained, but, as he remarked wryly, 'in this good land of Tarascon, everyone's a little bit crazy'. He was also relieved that, despite all that had happened, he had not lost his zest for painting. Still holding on to his idea that an artist's oeuvre constitutes an indivisible whole, he wrote to Theo about the fate of his work: 'Well, the paintings may perhaps become scattered beyond recall, but when you see the whole of what I have in mind, then, I hope, you will receive a comforting impression of it.'

570 [F] [part]

[9 January 1889]

My dear Theo,

[...]

Physically I am well. The wound is healing very well, and the great loss of blood is righting itself, as I am eating well and my digestion is good. The thing I <u>dread</u> most is insomnia, but the doctor hasn't mentioned it to me, nor have I mentioned it to him as yet. But I am fighting that myself.

I fight it with a very, very strong dose of camphor in my pillow and my mattress, and if ever you're unable to sleep, I recommend this to you. I very much dreaded the idea of sleeping alone in the house, and I've been worried about not being able to fall asleep, but all that's quite over now and I dare say it won't recur.

In hospital I suffered terribly from it, and yet during it all, when it was worse than losing consciousness, I can tell you as an odd fact that I continued to think about Degas. Gauguin and I had been talking about Degas beforehand, and I had pointed out to Gauguin that Degas had said ... 'I am saving myself for the Arlésiennes.'

Now you know how discerning Degas is, so on your return to Paris, just tell Degas that I confess that up to now I have been powerless to paint the women of Arles without venom, and that he mustn't believe Gauguin if Gauguin is too quick to speak well of my work, since it is nothing more than that of a sick man.

Now if I recover, I must start afresh, but I shall never again be able to reach the heights to which the illness to some extent led me.

[...]

Ever yours,
Vincent

[F] [letter from Vincent to Paul Gauguin]

[*c.* 22 January 1889]

My dear friend Gauguin,

Thank you for your letter. Left behind alone on board my little yellow house – as it was perhaps my duty anyway to be the last to leave – I am not a little put out at my friends' departure.

Roulin got his transfer to Marseilles and has just left. It has been touching to see him these last few days with little Marcelle, making her laugh and dandling her on his knee.

His transfer means his being separated from his family, and you will not be surprised that the one you and I nicknamed 'the passer-by' one evening, was very heavy-hearted. As was I, witnessing that and other upsetting things.

When he sang to his child, his voice took on a strange timbre in which one could hear the voice of a woman rocking a cradle or of a sorrowing wet-nurse, and then another trumpet sound like a clarion call to France.

I reproach myself now that it was I – perhaps insisting too much that you stay on here to await events and giving you so many good reasons for doing so – I reproach myself now that it was I who was perhaps the cause of your departure – unless, of course, that departure was planned beforehand? And that it was therefore perhaps up to me to show I still had the right to be kept fully in the picture.

Be that as it may, I hope we still like each other enough to be able, if need be, to start afresh, assuming that the wolf at the door, alas ever-present for those of us artists without means, should necessitate such a measure.

You mention a canvas of mine in your letter – Sunflowers on a yellow background – and make it plain you'd rather like to have it. I don't think it's altogether a bad choice – for if Jeannin can claim the peony, and Quost the hollyhock, then surely I, above all others, can lay claim to the sunflower.

I think I'll begin by returning what is yours,[1] while observing that it is my intention, after what has happened, categorically to deny your right to the canvas in question. But since I commend your intelligence in choosing this canvas, I'll make the effort to paint two of them exactly alike. In which case it can all be done and settled amicably so that you can have your own in the end all the same.

I made a fresh start today on my canvas of Mme Roulin, the one in which, due to my accident, the hands had been left unfinished.[2] As an arrangement of colours, the reds moving through to pure orange, building up again in the flesh tones to the chromes, passing through the pinks and blending with the olive and Veronese greens – as an impressionist arrangement of colours I have never devised anything better. And I'm sure that if one were to put this canvas just as it is in a fishing boat, even

1 Gauguin's fencing equipment, left behind in Arles.
2 *Augustine Roulin, 'La Berceuse* [Woman Rocking a Cradle]'.

one from Iceland, there would be some among the fishermen who would feel they were there, inside the cradle.

Ah! My dear friend, to achieve in painting what the music of Berlioz and Wagner has already done ... an art that offers consolation for the broken-hearted! There are still just a few who feel it as you and I do!!!

My brother understands you well and when he tells me that you are a poor sort of wretch like me, well, that just proves that he understands us.

I shall send you your things, but I still have bouts of weakness at times during which I'm in no position to lift even a finger to return your things to you. In a few days' time I'll pluck up the courage. And as for the 'fencing masks and gloves' (make as little use as possible of less infantile engines of war), these terrible engines of war will just have to wait until then. I am writing to you very calmly, but packing up what's left is still beyond me.

In my mental or nervous fever, or madness – I am not too sure how to put it or what to call it – my thoughts sailed over many seas. I even dreamed of the phantom Dutch ship and of Le Horla, and it seems that, while thinking what the woman rocking the cradle sang to rock the sailors to sleep, I, who on other occasions cannot even sing a note, came out with an old nursery tune, something I had tried to express in an arrangement of colours before I fell ill, because

I don't know the music of Berlioz.

It would give me great pleasure if you would write to me again soon. Have you finished reading all of Tartarin? The imagination of the south makes for friendship, believe me, and the two of us will always be friends.

Have you read and re-read Uncle Tom's Cabin by Beecher Stowe yet? Perhaps it's not very well written from a literary point of view. Have you read Germinie Lacerteux yet?

With a whole-hearted handshake,

Ever yours,
Vincent

576 [F] [part]

[3 February 1889]

My dear Theo,

I should have preferred to reply at once to your kind letter containing the 100 francs, but since at that precise moment I was very tired and the doctor has given me strict instructions to go out for walks and make no mental exertion, I haven't written to you until today.

As far as work is concerned, this month hasn't been bad on the whole, and as the work takes my mind off things, or rather keeps me in order, I don't deprive myself of it.

I have done La Berceuse three times, and seeing that Mme Roulin was the model and I only the painter, I let her choose between the three, her and her husband, on condition, however, that I could do a duplicate for myself of the one she chose, which I am working on at present.

You ask if I have read Mireille by Mistral – I am like you, I can only read the extracts that have been translated. But what about you, have you <u>heard</u> it yet, for perhaps you know that Gounod has set it to music. At least I think so. I don't know the music, of course, and even if I did go to hear it, I should be watching the musicians rather than listening.

But I can tell you this, that the local dialect spoken here sounds so musical in the mouths of the Arlésiennes that I actually pick up snatches of it every now and then.

Perhaps there is an attempt at a medley of local colour in La Berceuse. It's badly painted, and in a technical sense cheap chromos are infinitely better done, but even so . . .

Here, the so-called worthy town of Arles is such a peculiar sort of a place that it is with good reason our friend Gauguin calls it the filthiest spot in the south. Now, if Rivet[1] saw the population, he'd certainly have some bad moments, and repeat

1 Louis Rivet, Theo's doctor in Paris.

over and over again, 'You're in a sorry state, the lot of you,' just as he says of us. Still, once you've had the local disease, you'll never catch it again.

Which is just to let you know that as far as I am concerned, I have no illusions about myself. Things are going very, very well, and I'll do everything the doctor says, but . . .

When I came out of hospital with good old Roulin, I fancied there'd been nothing wrong with me, it was only <u>afterwards</u> I felt I'd been ill. Well, that's only to be expected, I have moments when I am twisted with enthusiasm or madness or prophecy, like a Greek oracle on his tripod. I display great presence of mind then in my words, and speak like the Arlésiennes, but in spite of all that, my spirits are very low. Especially when my physical strength returns. But I've already told Rey that at the first sign of a serious symptom I would come back and submit myself to the alienists in Aix, or to himself.

What else except pain and suffering can we expect if we are not well, you and I?

Our ambition has been dashed so low. So let us work very calmly, look after ourselves as best we can, and not exhaust ourselves in futile attempts at mutual generosity. You do your duty and I will do mine, and as far as that's concerned, we've both already paid for it – and not just in words – and at the end of the road we may quietly come together again. But when I am in a delirium and everything I love so much is in turmoil, then I don't mistake that for reality, and I don't play the false prophet.

Indeed, illness or death holds no terror for me, but happily for us, ambition is not compatible with the callings we follow. There are so many people in all classes of society, from the highest to the lowest, who believe that, anyway.

But why are you thinking about your marriage contract and the possibility of dying just now? Wouldn't it be better simply to make love to your woman instead? After all, that's normal practice in the north, and it's not for me to say that practices in the north are no good.

It'll all come all right in the end, believe me.

But I, without a penny to my name, I still say that when it

comes down to it, money is one kind of currency and painting is another. And I am even ready to send you a consignment along the lines mentioned in previous letters. And it will get better. If my strength returns.

So, if Gauguin, who is completely infatuated with my sunflowers, takes these two pictures, I should just like him to give your fiancée or you a couple of pictures of his, not second-rate ones but better than that. And should he take a copy of La Berceuse, then all the more reason for him to give a good one in return. Otherwise I wouldn't be able to complete the series I spoke to you about, which should be fit to go on show in that same little display window we have gazed at so often.

In this case, the value of the pictures does not come into it, and I don't claim to be an expert. It remains a fact, however, that I may be entitled to attach as much importance to my social position as you do to yours as a loyal employee. And let me just say this: I think as much of brotherly integrity when it comes to Boussod's money as you do. It has never played us false. And we have sweated far too much doing good work to get annoyed at being called thieves or incompetents.

Anyway, I won't keep on about it.

As for the Indépendants, it seems to me that six pictures are too many by half. To my mind, the Harvest and the White Orchard are enough, with the Provençale Girl or the Sower if you like. But I really don't care. The only thing I really want to do some day is to give you a more comforting impression of this painting business of ours with a collection of about 30 more serious studies. In any case that will prove to our real friends like Gauguin, Guillaumin, Bernard, &c., that we are producing something.

As for the little yellow house, when I paid my rent the landlord's agent was very kind and behaved like an Arlésien, treating me as an equal.

So I told him that I had no need of a lease, nor of a written assurance of preference, and that in the event of my being ill payment would only be made by friendly arrangement.

People here have their hearts in the right place and the

spoken word is more binding than the written word. So I shall keep the house on for the time being, as I need to feel that this is my home if I am to regain my mental health.

[...]

Yesterday I went to see the girl to whom I had gone when I was off my head. They told me that there's nothing surprising about things like that in this part of the world. She'd been upset and had fainted but had regained her composure. And indeed, they spoke well of her.

But it won't do for us to think that I am completely sane. The people from round here who are ill like me have told me the truth. You can be old or young, but there will always be times when you take leave of your senses.

So I don't ask you to tell people that there is nothing wrong with me, or that there never will be. It is just that the explanation of all this is probably not Ricord's but Raspail's.[2] Though I have not yet had the <u>fevers</u> of the region, I might still catch them. But they already know a thing or two about all that here at the hospital, and as long as you have no false shame and say frankly how you feel, you cannot go wrong.

I am bringing this letter to a close for this evening with a good handshake in my thoughts,

Ever yours,
Vincent

On 17 February Van Gogh was discharged from hospital, but continued to eat and sleep there for the time being. The people of Arles saw his return to the town as a threat and, following a petition, the mayor ordered him to be locked up for a month in an isolation cell in the hospital, while the police sealed the Yellow House. Even so, Vincent reassured Theo, 'As far as I can judge I am not really mad. You will see that the canvases I've done in the meantime are untroubled and no

2 Philippe Ricord, French surgeon specializing in syphilis; François Raspail, French chemist and politician who asserted that disease is caused by parasites.

worse than the others.' His spirits were raised by a visit from his faithful friend, the painter Paul Signac, on 23 March. Together they went to the Yellow House and poked fun at the gendarmes.

At the end of March Van Gogh started to paint again, having by then reached the fifth version of his *La Berceuse*. With a show of modesty, he claimed again that all he was trying to achieve was the effect of 'a cheap chromo', the kind of picture 'a sailor who cannot paint might imagine when, out at sea, he thinks of his wife ashore'.

At the beginning of April, Van Gogh resumed his work on orchards in blossom, which he had been forced to abandon the year before because of the change in the weather. However, he felt disoriented, and, seemingly unable to organize his life properly, he shrank from setting up a new studio on his own. For the first time, he mooted the plan to Theo of going to the asylum in nearby Saint-Rémy as a precautionary measure. He assessed his condition very soberly: 'What comforts me is that I am beginning to look upon madness as a disease like any other and to accept it as such.'

His last letters from Arles understandably focus on his health. He found it beneficial to abide by the rules of the hospital because 'I have become timid and hesitant, and live, as it were, mechanically'. He guessed that the possible cause of his attack had been drink and perhaps tobacco as well, though he was quite unable to give up either: 'Each day I take the medicine that the incomparable Dickens prescribes against suicide. It consists of a glass of wine, a piece of bread and cheese and a pipe of tobacco.' The idea of suicide as an escape from his precarious existence crops up in various guises in his letters. However, Theo's support had saved him from that fatal step, or so he reassured his anxious brother. He drew comfort from the poetic view that diseases are to man what ivy is to the oak. In a letter to his sister Wil, who was nursing an elderly cancer patient, he wrote, 'Ivy favours old willows without branches – each spring the ivy seeks out the trunk of an old oak – and that is just how it is with cancer, that mysterious plant which so often fastens on to people whose lives were nothing but love and devotion.'

Although Theo tried to reassure his brother, and implored him not to worry about money, certainly not now when Theo had had a successful year, Van Gogh himself felt crushed 'by a feeling of guilt and inadequacy' when he thought of the money painting cost, adding that 'it would be a good thing if this came to a stop'. To find a way out of the impasse, he even gave serious consideration to the possibility of enlisting in the Foreign Legion, an idea Theo naturally rejected out of hand. However, Theo did see merit in Vincent's plan to move to Saint-Rémy.

While Theo was holding an exhibition of Monet's work in his Parisian gallery, Van Gogh, in his attempts to regain his artistic footing, harked back to the masters he had admired before Impressionism and whom in his heart of hearts he had always held most dear, Millet chief amongst them: 'Sometimes I regret that I didn't simply keep to the Dutch palette with its grey tones, and brush away at landscapes in Montmartre.' True, he would always '[...] preserve a certain passion for impressionism, but I feel I'm increasingly reverting to the ideas I had before I went to Paris [...]. Of course, the progress of colour is an undeniable fact, precisely because of the impressionists, even when they lose their way. But Delacroix was more perfect than they.'

588 [F]

[30 April 1889]

My dear Theo,

On the occasion of the first of May[1] I wish you a tolerably good year, and above all good health.

How I should like to pass on to you some of my physical strength, I have the feeling I've too much of it at the moment. Which does not prevent my head from still not being all that it should be.

How right Delacroix was, who lived on bread and wine alone, and who succeeded in finding a way of life in keeping with his vocation. But the inevitable question of money is ever-present – Delacroix had private means. Corot too. And Millet – Millet was a peasant and the son of a peasant.

You may perhaps be interested in reading this article I cut out

[1] Theo's birthday.

of a Marseilles paper because one catches a glimpse of Monticelli in it, and I find the description of the painting representing a corner of the churchyard very interesting. But alas, it's yet another deplorable story.

How sad it is to think that a painter who succeeds, even if only in part, pulls along half a dozen artists who are worse failures than himself.

However, remember Pangloss, remember Bouvard et Pécuchet – I do – and even that becomes clear then. But perhaps those people don't know Pangloss, or else, fatally marked by real despair and great suffering, they have forgotten all they knew about him.

And anyway, we are falling back again in the name of optimism on a religion that strikes me as the rear end of some sort of Buddhism. No harm in that, on the contrary, if that's what one wants.

I don't like the article on Monet in the Figaro very much – how much better that other article in the 19me Siècle was! One could see the pictures in that, and this one is full of nothing but depressing banalities.

Today I am in the middle of packing a case of pictures and studies. I've stuck some newspapers on to one which is flaking – it's one of the best, and I think that when you've had a look at it you'll understand more clearly what my studio, now come to grief, could have been. This study, just like some of the others, was spoiled by the damp while I was ill.

The flood water came up to within a stone's throw of the house, and more important, since the house wasn't heated during my absence, by the time I got back water and saltpetre were oozing from the walls.

That was a blow for me, since not only the studio had come to grief, but even the studies that would have been reminders of it. It is all so final, and my urge to found something very simple but lasting was so strong. I was fighting a losing battle, or rather it was weakness of character on my part, for I am left with feelings of deep remorse about it, difficult to describe. I think that was the reason I cried out so much during the attacks – I wanted to defend myself and couldn't do it. For it was not to me, it was precisely to painters such as the poor wretch about whom the enclosed article speaks that the studio could have been of use.

In fact, we had several predecessors. Bruyas at Montpellier gave a whole fortune to that, a whole life, and without the slightest apparent result.

Yes – a chilly room in the municipal gallery where you can see a troubled face and many fine pictures, where you certainly feel moved, but, alas, moved as in a graveyard.

Yet it would be difficult to walk through a graveyard that demonstrated more clearly the existence of that Espérance which Puvis de Chavannes has painted.

Pictures fade like flowers – even some of Delacroix's have suffered in this way, the magnificent Daniel, Les odalisques (quite different from those in the Louvre, it was in a single range of purplish-blue), but how they impressed me, those pictures fading there, little understood, that's for sure, by most of the visitors who look at Courbet and Cabanel and Victor Giraud, &c.

What are we, we other painters?

Oh, well, I'm sure Richepin is quite right, for instance when he brutally bursts in and consigns them straight back to the madhouse with his profanities.

However, I assure you that I know of no hospital where they would be willing to take me in for nothing, even supposing that I myself shouldered the painting expenses and left the whole of my work to the hospital.

And that is, I don't say a great, but still a small injustice. Even so, I should feel resigned if one took me in. If I were without your friendship, they would drive me remorselessly to suicide, and coward that I am, I should end by committing it. At this point, I hope, we are permitted to protest against society and to defend ourselves.

You can be fairly sure that the Marseilles artist who committed suicide in no way did it under the influence of absinthe, for the simple reason that no one is likely to have offered him any and he could not have had anything to buy it with. Besides, he would not have drunk it purely for pleasure, but because, being ill already, he kept himself going with it.

M. Salles has been to Saint-Rémy – they are not willing to give me permission to paint outside the institution, nor to take me for less than 100 francs.

So this is pretty bad news.

If I could get out of this mess by joining the Foreign Legion for 5 years, I think I should prefer that.

For on the one hand, being locked up and not working, I should find it hard to get better, and on the other hand, they would make us pay 100 francs a month during the whole long life of a madman.

It's a bad business, and what are we to make of it? But would they be willing to have me as a soldier?

I feel very tired after the conversation with M. Salles, and I don't quite know what to do. I myself advised Bernard to do his service there, so it's hardly surprising that I'm considering going to Arabia as a soldier myself.

I say that so you will not blame me too much if I do go. Everything else is so vague and so strange. And you know how doubtful it is that one will ever get back what it costs to paint. For the rest, it seems I am physically well.

Supposing I am only allowed to work under supervision! And in the institution – my God, is it worth paying money for that? In that case I could certainly work just as well, even better, in the barracks.

Anyway, I'm thinking about it. You do so as well. Let us remember that all is for the best in the best of all worlds – it's not impossible.

A really good handshake,

Ever yours,
Vincent

Here is what I think is worth putting on stretchers from the consignment:

The Night Café	–	The Alyscamps (lane of tombs)
The Green Vineyard	–	ditto
The Red Vineyard	–	Garden with large conifer bush and oleanders
The Bedroom		
The Furrows	–	ditto with cedar & geraniums
ditto		
	–	Sunflowers
Portrait of Boch		Flowers, scabious, &c.
„ „ Laval		ditto, asters, marigolds, &c.
„ „ Gauguin		
„ „ Bernard		

The packing case contains some studies by Gauguin which belong to him, and his two fencing masks and some fencing gloves.

If there is room in the packing case, I'll add some stretchers.

Saint-Rémy

On the same day that he sent his birthday letter to Theo, Van Gogh also wrote to his sister Wil, 'I am going to an asylum in St Rémy, not far from here, for at least three months. In all, I have had 4 major attacks, during which I had no idea what I said, what I wanted or what I did, not to mention the three times before when I had fainting fits for inexplicable reasons, being quite unable to recall what I felt at the time.'

On 8 May, after finishing another four orchard studies and two paintings of the interior of the hospital at Arles, Van Gogh was accompanied by the Protestant pastor, Dr Frédéric Salles, to his new quarters in the asylum of Saint-Paul-de-Mausole. Pastor Salles sent Theo the following report on 10 May: 'Our journey to Saint-Rémy went exceptionally well. M. Vincent was perfectly calm and explained his case himself to the director [Dr Théophile Peyron]. [...] He seemed rather excited at the thought of the completely new life that lay ahead of him in this house.'

Theo sent painting equipment and kept Vincent informed by letter of the latest items of news from the Parisian art world, the Salon, the world exhibition and his meetings with friends. The brothers also corresponded about the paintings Vincent would be entering for the important exhibition of the Indépendants.

At first Van Gogh's doctor confined his freedom of movement to the walled garden of the asylum. There he painted irises, lilac bushes and tree trunks overgrown with ivy. Just as in his Hague days, when he had described the view from his studio in the Schenkweg as a view by Corot, he now compared the prospect from his barred window to a painting by Van Goyen. He observed his fellow patients with interest, and tried to come to terms with his illness, in the knowledge that many fellow artists had preceded him along the same path.

592 [F] [part]

[22 May 1889]

My dear Theo,

[...] Here is a new size 30 canvas, again as run of the mill as a cheap chromo, depicting age-old love nests in the greenery. Large tree trunks covered with ivy, the ground similarly covered with ivy & periwinkle, a stone bench and a bush of roses, pale in the cool shadow. In the foreground, some plants with white calyxes. It is green, violet and pink.

It's all a question – and this is unfortunately missing from the cheap chromos as well as from the barrel organs – of putting some style into it.

Since I've been here, there's been enough work for me to do, what with the neglected garden with its tall pines and long, unkempt grass mixed with all sorts of weeds, and I haven't even been outside.

However, the countryside around St Rémy is very beautiful, and little by little I shall probably make a few short trips.

But while I stay here, the doctor is of course in a better position to see what is wrong, & will have his mind set at rest, I hope, about what he can let me paint.

I assure you that I am all right here, and that for the time being I see no reason at all to take lodgings in or around Paris. I have a small room with greenish-grey paper and two sea-green curtains with a design of very pale roses, brightened with touches of blood red.

These curtains, probably the legacy of some deceased and ruined rich person, are very pretty in design. A very worn armchair, probably from the same source, is covered with a tapestry speckled like a Diaz or a Monticelli in brown, red, pink, white, cream, black, forget-me-not blue and bottle green. Through the iron-barred window I can see an enclosed square of wheat, a prospect like a Van Goyen, above which, in the morning, I watch the sun rise in all its glory.

In addition – as there are more than 30 empty rooms – I have another room for doing my work.

The food is all right as far as it goes. It tastes a bit musty, of course, as in a cockroach-infested restaurant in Paris, or in a boarding house. The poor wretches here, having absolutely nothing to do (not a book, nothing more to distract them than a game of boules or a game of draughts), have no other daily distraction than to stuff themselves with chick peas, haricot beans, lentils and other groceries and colonial produce, in set amounts and at stated hours.

As the digestion of these foodstuffs offers certain difficulties, they fill their days in a manner as inoffensive as it is costly.

But joking apart, my _fear_ of madness is wearing off markedly, since I can see at close quarters those who are affected by it in the same way as I may very easily be in the future.

Previously, I was repelled by these individuals, and I found it distressing to have to reflect that so many in our trade, Troyon, Marchal, Méryon, Jundt, M. Maris, Monticelli, and a whole lot more finished up like that. It was quite impossible for me to picture them in that condition.

Well, now I can think of all that without fear, that's to say, I find it no more dreadful than if those people had died of something else, consumption or syphilis, for example. I see these artists being reinvested with their old serenity, and don't you think it's quite something to meet these old colleagues of ours again? That, joking apart, is what I am profoundly thankful for.

For though there are some who howl or rave a great deal, there is _much_ true friendship here. They say we must tolerate others so that the others may tolerate us, and other very sound arguments, which they put into practice, too. And we understand each other very well. Sometimes, for instance, I can talk with one of them – who can only reply in incoherent sounds – because he is not afraid of me.

[...]

You could take the canvases at Tanguy's or at your place off the stretchers, if they're dry enough, and then put on any new ones you think are worth it.

Gauguin ought to be able to tell you the address of someone who could reline the Bedroom and who won't be too expensive. The restoration ought, I _imagine_, to cost 5 francs. If it is more, then don't have it done. I'm sure Gauguin didn't pay any more on the many occasions when he had his canvases, or Cezanne's, or Pissarro's, relined.

Again – speaking of my condition – I am so grateful for yet another thing. I've noticed that others, too, hear sounds and strange voices during their attacks, as I did, and that things seemed to change before their very eyes. And that lessened the horror with which I remembered my first attack, something that, when it comes upon you unexpectedly, cannot but frighten you terribly. Once you know it is part of the illness, you accept it like anything else. Had I not seen other lunatics close to, I should not have been able to stop myself from thinking about it all the time. For the suffering and the anguish are not funny when you are having an attack.

Most epileptics bite their tongues and injure themselves. Rey told me that he had seen a case who had injured his ear, just as I did, and I think I heard a doctor from here, who came to see me with the director, say that he too had seen it before. I like to think that once you know what it is, once you are conscious of your condition, and of being subject to attacks, then you can do something to prevent your being taken unawares by the anguish or the terror. Now that it has all been abating for 5 months I have high hopes of getting over it, or at least of no longer having such violent attacks.

There is someone here who has been shouting and talking like me <u>all the time</u> for a fortnight. He thinks he hears voices and words in the echo of the corridors, probably because his auditory nerve is diseased and over-sensitive, and in my case it was both sight and hearing at the same time, which is usual at the outset of epilepsy, according to what Rey said one day.

Now, the shock was such that even moving made me feel sick, and nothing would have pleased me more than never to have woken up again. At present this <u>horror of life</u> is already less pronounced, and the melancholy less acute. But I still have no <u>will</u>, and hardly any desires, or none at all that are to do with ordinary life, for example, almost no wish to see friends, although I do think of them. That is why I am still not ready to leave here now or in the near future. I should feel depressed about everything again.

And anyway, it is only recently that my loathing of life has been drastically changed. There is still a long way to go from that to willing and doing.

What a pity that you're condemned to stay full-time in Paris and that you never see any part of the countryside other than that around Paris. I'm sure it's no worse for me to be in the company I now find myself than for you to be with that ill-fated

Goupil & Cie all the time. In that respect, we are pretty equal. For you, too, are only able to act partly in keeping with your ideas. However, once we've got used to these difficulties, it all becomes second nature.

Although the pictures swallow up canvas and paint, &c., nevertheless at the end of the month I'm sure it's more profitable to spend a little more on those, making use of what I've learned, than to abandon it all, when you have to pay for my board and lodging anyway. And that's why I'm carrying on. So this month I have 4 size 30 canvases and two or three drawings.

But the question of money, whatever one does, is always with us, like the enemy facing the troops, and cannot be denied or ignored.

As much as anyone, I know where my duties lie in that respect. And I may yet be able to pay back everything I've spent, for I consider it to have been, if not taken from you, at least taken from the family. So that's why I've been producing pictures and shall be doing some more. This is acting as you yourself are acting. If I were a man of means, perhaps my mind would be freer to produce art for art's sake. Now I content myself with the thought that by working diligently, one may perhaps make some progress even without thinking about it.

Here are the paints I need:

3 emerald green
2 cobalt
1 ultramarine   large tubes
1 orange lead
6 zinc white
5 metres of canvas

Thanking you for your kind letter, I shake your hand warmly, as I do your wife's.

Ever yours,
Vincent

In the middle of June, Vincent ventured beyond the garden to paint a wheat field and his first olive grove – a subject that had been intriguing him for a long time – in the immediate vicinity of the asylum. Despite his speedy recovery, he told his sister Wil that he had little zest for life and that he was anxiously awaiting a letter from Theo. Theo, however, was obviously so taken up by his honeymoon with his bride, Johanna, that the correspondence, which had become Vincent's lifeline, ground to a temporary halt. Many people have speculated on the effect Theo's marriage had on Vincent and to what extent it worsened his condition.

When Theo eventually did write, he was full of praise for Vincent's latest consignment of canvases from Arles (and the first from Saint-Rémy), including such works as *View of Arles with Poplars, Irises* and *Lilacs*: 'They all have an intensity of colour you have not attained before, which is a rare quality in itself, but you have gone even further than that, & while others do violence to the form in order to pursue symbolic ideas, I see that you have achieved that in many of your canvases by conveying the quintessence of your thoughts about nature and living beings, which, you feel, are so closely bound up with them. But how that brain of yours must have laboured, and how you have risked everything in venturing to the very brink, where vertigo is inevitable.' In his answer, Vincent tried to reassure his brother: 'Never fear that I shall venture upon dizzy heights of my own free will. Unfortunately, we are exposed to the conditions and illnesses of our age, whether we like it or not. But with all the precautions I am taking, I am not likely to have a relapse, and I have hopes that the attacks will not recur.'

A month later, Theo wrote just as enthusiastically about a further consignment of paintings. He was also most impressed by some of the drawings he had received: 'The hospital at Arles is outstanding, the butterfly and the branches of eglantine are very beautiful too: simple in colour and very beautifully drawn. The last drawings look as if they were done in a frenzy and are a little further removed from nature [. . .]. I have hung one of the Sunflowers in our dining room against the chimney breast. It looks like a piece of cloth embroidered with satin and gold.'

Despite the weary tone of his letters, Van Gogh was producing one masterpiece after another during this period. In addition to the series of enclosed fields, he also painted *The Reaper, The Starry Night* and the 'bottle-green' *Cypresses*. He had been preoccupied with the thought of depicting cypresses since soon after his arrival in Arles, and was astonished to discover that they 'have not yet been painted as I see them. They are as beautiful as an Egyptian obelisk in their line and proportions. And the green has such a distinctive quality. It is a <u>black</u> patch in a sunny landscape.'

As reading matter he chose Shakespeare's historical plays, with which he was less familiar than with the rest. In them, as in Rembrandt, he found 'that sorrowful tenderness, that momentary revelation of super-human infinitude which then seems so natural'. But reading Shakespeare's plays, full of dramatic incident and the clash of ambitions, was often far from relaxing. When he put the book down, he had always to 'contemplate a blade of grass, a branch of pine, an ear of corn [. . .] to calm myself down again [. . .]. Hours of worry and strife know how to find us, without our going out looking for them.'

His descriptions of the flora and fauna betrayed a growing nostalgia for the Netherlands. He sent Theo a sketch of three cicadas, adding, 'Their chirping in the great heat has the same charm for me as the cricket on the hearth for the peasants at home. Don't let us forget, old fellow, that the minor emotions are the guiding lights of our lives.' In the first letter he had written to his mother for seven months, he summed up what he was missing in the Provence landscape. The fields offered less variety than those in the Netherlands, and he looked in vain for 'those moss-covered farm roofs on the barns or cottages as at home, or any oak copses, any corn spurrey, or any beech hedges with their russet leaves and tangled old whitish trunks. Or any real heather or any birches, which were so lovely in Nuenen.' However, the beauty of the vineyards and the olive groves made up for much.

In her first attempt to write a letter in French, Johanna van Gogh told her brother-in-law on 5 July 1889 that she was expecting a baby. If it turned out to be a boy, and she was certain it would, the child would be called Vincent after him. In Paris, the Belgian impresario Octave Maus had meanwhile called on Theo to invite Vincent to exhibit with the Vingtistes.

In the middle of July Van Gogh had a new attack while out painting in the countryside. Not until 22 August was he well enough to describe the circumstances: 'For days my mind has been wandering wildly, just as in Arles, as bad if not worse, and it must be expected that the attacks will recur in the future. It is <u>frightful</u> [...]. I apparently pick up dirt from the ground and eat it.' A swollen throat made taking food difficult. Because he had also put paint into his mouth and had drunk turpentine, he was ordered not to do any painting until further notice, and Vincent pleaded with Theo to urge Dr Peyron to let him get back to work. He found idleness intolerable and a bar to his recovery. Moreover, the asylum was beginning to get on his nerves. The exaggerated piety of the nuns irritated him and he went in fear of several patients.

Towards the end of August Van Gogh received permission to resume his painting. He thought that Trabuc, the chief attendant at the asylum, a 'real Midi type', looked like an etching of a Spanish nobleman, and while working on a self-portrait he also recalled that portraits by the seventeenth-century masters Rembrandt and Carel Fabritius take on 'something unutterably radiant and comforting'. His rereading of *Le conscrit* by the Flemish writer Hendrik Conscience had a similar effect on him. As in the past, he identified himself with the situations described in books. Dostoevsky's *Memoirs from the House of the Dead* persuaded him to return to his painting of the interior of the hospital at Arles which he had left unfinished, and he drew a parallel between his own depressed mental state and that of the Russian writer 'who also suffered from a nervous illness [...] which brought on terrible attacks from time to time'.

Meanwhile, Dr Peyron, his doctor at the asylum, reported to Theo, 'His suicidal tendencies have gone, the only thing that still troubles him is having unpleasant dreams [...].'

604 [F] [part]

[5 or 6 September 1889]

My dear brother,

I have already written to you, but there are still quite a few things you said to me that I haven't answered yet. Firstly, that you have rented a room in Tanguy's house & that my canvases are there, which is very interesting – provided you aren't paying too much – the expenses go on all the time and the canvases still take so long to bring anything in – it often frightens me.

Be that as it may, I'm sure it's a very good step, and I thank you for taking it, as for so many other things. It is curious that Maus had the idea of inviting young Bernard & me for the next Vingtistes exhibition. I should like to exhibit with them very much, though I'm conscious of my inferiority by the side of so many tremendously talented Belgians.

This Mellery, now, is a great artist. And has been one for a number of years. But I shall try my best to do something good this autumn.

I am working away in my room without interruption which does me good and chases away what I imagine are abnormal ideas.

Thus I've done the canvas of the Bedroom again. That's certainly one of my best studies – and sooner or later it must definitely be <u>relined</u>. It was painted so quickly and has dried in such a way that the turpentine evaporated straight away and the paint hasn't stuck firmly to the canvas at all. That will also have happened with other studies of mine painted very quickly and with a very full brush. Anyway, after some time this thin canvas deteriorates and cannot take a lot of impasto. You've got some excellent stretchers, damn it, if I had some like that to work with, I'd be a lot better off than with these battens you get here which warp in the sun.

They say – and I am very willing to believe it – that it is difficult to know oneself – but it isn't easy to paint oneself either. So I am working on two self-portraits at the moment – for want of another model.

Because it is high time that I did a little figure work. In the one I began the first day I got up, I was thin and deathly pale. It is dark purple-blue, and the head whitish with yellow hair, thus with a colour effect.

But I have since started another, three-quarter length on a light background.

Then I'm retouching this summer's studies – in fact, I am working morning, noon and night.

Are you well? – damn it, I really wish that you were 2 years further on and that these early days of marriage, however lovely they may be at times, were behind you. I'm quite convinced that a marriage grows better with time and that it's <u>then</u> that your constitution improves.

So take things with a pinch of northern phlegm, and look after yourselves, both of you. This confounded life in the art world is exhausting, it seems.

Day by day my own strength is returning, and already I feel I have almost too much of it again. For one doesn't need to be Hercules to remain hard at work at the easel.

What you told me about Maus having been to see my canvases made me think a lot about the Belgian painters these last few days and also during my illness. As a result I was overwhelmed with memories as by an avalanche, and I tried to recall the whole of that school of modern Flemish artists until I felt as homesick as a fish out of water.

Which isn't any good, as our way lies – forwards – and retracing our steps is both impossible and impermissible. In other words one can think about the past without being swamped by an over-melancholic nostalgia.

Anyway, Henri Conscience may not be a perfect writer by any means, but no two ways about it, what a painter! And what loving-kindness in what he said and hoped for. There's a preface in one of his books on my mind all the time (the one to Le conscrit), where he writes that he has been very ill, and says that during his illness, despite all his efforts, he felt his affection for mankind draining away, but that his feelings of love returned on long walks in the countryside.

The inevitability of suffering and despair – well, here I am, bucked up again for a time – and I thank him for it.

I am writing you this letter bit by bit in the intervals when I am worn out with painting. The work is going fairly well. I'm struggling with a canvas I started a few days before my illness – a reaper. The study is all yellow, extremely thickly painted, but the subject was beautiful and simple. For I see in this reaper – a vague figure toiling away for all he's worth in the midst of the heat to finish his task – I see in him the image of death, in the sense that humanity might be the wheat he is reaping. So it is, if you like, the opposite of the sower which I tried to do before. But there is no sadness in this death, this one takes place in broad daylight with a sun flooding everything with a light of pure gold.

Well, here I am, at it again. But I won't give in, and shall try once more on a new canvas. Ah, I could almost believe that I have a new spell of lucidity before me.

So what next – carrying on here for the next few months, or moving elsewhere – I don't know. It's just that the attacks, when they come, are no joke, and running the risk of having a bout like that at your place or at anyone else's is a serious matter.

My dear brother – I always write to you in between bouts of work, & I am working like one truly possessed, more than ever I am in the grip of a pent-up fury of work, and I'm sure it will help to cure me. Perhaps something along the lines of what Eug. Delacroix spoke of will happen to me – 'I discovered painting when I had neither teeth nor breath left,' in the sense that my sad illness makes me work in a pent-up fury – very slowly – but without leaving off from morning till night – and – that is probably the secret – to work long and slowly. But what do I know about it? Still, I think I've one or two canvases on the go which are not too bad, firstly, the reaper in the yellow wheat, and the portrait on a light background which should go to the Vingtistes, if indeed they remember me when the time comes. Actually, I care very little one way or another, it might be preferable if they did forget all about me.

For my part, I do not forget how inspired I am whenever I give my memory of certain Belgians free rein. That is the positive side, and the rest is of no more than secondary importance.

And here we are already in September, soon we'll be in the middle of autumn, and then winter.

I shall continue to work without let-up, and then if I have another attack around Christmas, we'll see, and when that's over, I can't see any objection to my telling the administration here to go to hell, and to my returning north for a fairly long time. To leave now, when I believe I may well have another attack this winter, that's to say in three months' time, would perhaps be too foolhardy.

It's been 6 weeks since I put a foot outdoors, even in the garden. Next week, however, when I've finished the canvases I'm busy with, I'm going to have a go.

But another few months and I'll be so flabby and lethargic that a change will probably do me a lot of good.

That's the way I'm thinking at the moment, though of course nothing is settled.

But I do believe that one shouldn't stand on ceremony with the people of this establishment, any more than with the proprietors of a hotel. We have rented a room from them for a certain length of time, and they are well paid for what they provide, and that's absolutely all there is to it.

Not to mention that they might like nothing better than for my condition to be chronic, and we would be unforgivably stupid to give in to them. They make far too many inquiries, to my mind, not only about what I, but also what you earn, &c.

So let's not quarrel with them and simply give them the slip.

I am continuing this letter again at intervals. Yesterday I began the portrait of the chief attendant, and I may do his wife as well, since he's married and lives in a little farmhouse a stone's throw from the institution.

A most interesting face. There's a beautiful etching by Legros of an old Spanish nobleman – if you remember it, it will give you an idea of the type. He was at the hospital in Marseilles during 2 cholera epidemics, in short, he is a man who has seen an enormous amount of death and suffering, and he has an indefinable expression of quiet contemplation, so that I am irresistibly reminded of Guizot's face – for there is something of that in this head, if different. But he is a man of the people and simpler. Anyway, you will see it if I succeed in doing it and if I make a copy of it.

I am struggling with all my might to keep my work under control by telling myself that success would be the best lightning conductor for my illness. I make sure I don't overdo things, and take care to keep myself to myself. It's selfish, if you like, not getting used to my companions in misfortune here and not going round to see them, but still, I feel none the worse for it, for my work is making headway, and that's what we need, for it is absolutely vital that I do better than before, as that was not enough.

Supposing I get out of here one day, wouldn't it be far better if I came back definitely capable of doing a portrait with some character than if I came back as I started? That's clumsily put, for I'm well aware one cannot say, 'I know how to do a portrait,' without telling a lie, because that is an infinite objective. Still you will understand what I mean, that I must do better than before.

At the moment my mind is working in an orderly way, and I feel completely normal – and when I look at my present condition, in the hope of generally having, between the attacks – if, unfortunately, it has to be expected that they will return from time to time – of having in between times, periods of lucidity and of working – when I look at my present condition, then I do indeed tell myself that it won't do to become obsessed with being sick. And that I must steadfastly continue my humble career as a painter. And so, staying for good in an asylum would probably be going too far.

A few days ago, I was reading in the Figaro about a Russian writer who also suffered from a nervous illness of which, moreover, he sadly died, and which brought on terrible attacks from time to time.[1] But what is one to do? There is no remedy, or if there is one, it is to work with a will.

I am dwelling on this longer than I should.

All in all, I prefer to be definitely ill like this than to be the way I was in Paris when all this was coming on.

You will also see that when you put the portrait with the light background that I've just done next to those portraits I did of myself in Paris, you really will see that I look saner now than I did then, indeed much more so.

[1] Dostoevsky.

I am even inclined to believe that the portrait will tell you better than my letter how I am, and that it will reassure you – it took me a lot of trouble.

And the reaper is also going well, I think – it is very, very simple.

By the end of the month I'd go so far as to say you can count on 12 size 30 canvases, but in most 'cases they will be the same picture twice over, a study and the final painting.

Still, perhaps my journey to the south will yet bear fruit, for the stronger light and the blue sky teaches you to see, especially, or even only, if you see it all for a long time.

The north will undoubtedly seem quite new to me, and I have looked at things so much here that I have become very attached to them, so I shall feel sad for a long time.

Something odd occurs to me – in Manette Salomon there is a discussion of modern art, and some artist or other, talking of 'what will last', says that what will last is 'the landscape painters' – that view has already been proved true to some extent, for Corot, Daubigny, Dupré, Rousseau and Millet do endure as landscape painters, and when Corot said on his deathbed, 'I saw landscapes in a dream with skies all pink, it was charming,' well, yes, we see those skies all pink in Monet, Pissarro and Renoir, so the landscape painters do last very well, it's quite true. We'll leave aside the figure painting of Delacroix and Millet.

In any case, what is it we are now beginning hesitantly to recognize as original and long-lasting? Portraiture. You might say that it's old stuff, but it's also quite new. We'll talk about it again – but we must never stop being on the lookout for portraits, especially by such artists as Guillaumin – that portrait of the young girl by Guillaumin! – and take good care of my portrait by Russell which I'm so fond of. Have you framed Laval's portrait? I don't think you told me what you thought of it. I thought it splendid, that gaze through the glasses, such a frank gaze.

My urge to do portraits is very strong these days, in fact Gauguin and I talked about this and similar matters until our nerves were strained to the point of stifling all human warmth.

But I dare say some good pictures will come out of it, and that's what we're after. And I should imagine they'll be doing some good work in Brittany. I got a letter from G., I think I already told you, and one day I should very much like to see what they are doing.

I must ask you for the following painting requisites.

> 10 metres of canvas
> Large tubes 6 tubes zinc white
> "   "   2 "   emerald green
> "   "   2 "   cobalt
> small tubes
> > 2 carmine
> > 1 vermilion
> 1 large tube ordinary lake
> 6 Sable brushes, black hair

Then I promised the attendant here a copy of Le Monde illustré, No. 1684, 6 July 1889, in which there is a very pretty engraving after Demont-Breton.

Aha! The reaper is finished. I think it'll be one of those you'll keep at home – it's an image of death as the great book of nature speaks of it – but the effect I've been looking for is – 'on the point of smiling'. It's all yellow, except for a line of purple hills. A pale and golden yellow. I find it odd that I saw it like that through the iron bars of a cell.

Well, do you know what I hope for, once I allow myself to begin to hope? It is that the family will be for you what nature, the clods of earth, the grass, the yellow wheat, the peasant, are for me, in other words, that you find in your love for people something not only to work for, but to comfort and restore you when there is a need. So, I beg you not to let yourself get too exhausted by business, but to take good care of yourselves, both of you – perhaps there will still be some good in the not too distant future.

I've a good mind to do the reaper over again for Mother. If not, I'll do another picture for her birthday – it will be coming later, as I'll send it on with the rest.

For I'm convinced Mother would understand it – since it is, in fact, as simple as one of those primitive woodcuts one finds in farmers' almanacs.

Send me the canvas as soon as you can, for if I still want to do other copies for the sisters, and if I am to make a start on the new autumn effects, I'll have enough to fill my time from the beginning of this month to the end.

I'm eating and drinking like a horse at present. I must say the doctor is taking very good care of me.

Yes, I do think that it's a good idea to do some pictures for Holland, for Mother and our two sisters. That will make three, that's to say <u>the Reaper, the Bedroom, the Olive Trees, Wheat Field and Cypress</u>. It will even make four, for there's somebody else I'm going to do one for as well.

I shall work at that, of course, with as much pleasure as for the Vingtistes, and more calmly. Since I feel strong, you may be sure that I shall get through a lot of work.

I am choosing the best from the 12 subjects, so that what they'll get will have been thought about a bit and specially picked. And then, it's a good thing to work for people who don't know what a picture is.

A good handshake for you and Jo,

Vincent

[...]

Theo kept Vincent in touch with the latest work by Pissarro ('the man [who] feels more at ease in clogs than in patent-leather boots') and Gauguin, whose *Belle angèle* had been 'put on the canvas like the large heads on Japanese prints'. Theo also sent a short report of the exhibition by the Indépendants at which Vincent's *Starry Night* and *Irises* compared quite well with the recent work of Seurat, Signac and Toulouse-Lautrec.

In particular, Van Gogh's work was seen and admired there by a number of fellow artists, such as the Belgians Théodore van Rijsselberghe and Octave Maus, and the Dutch artists Isaäc Israëls, Jan Veth and J. J.

Isaäcson, the last of whom intended to write a review. Van Gogh's work was now on show not only in Theo's Paris apartment but also from time to time in the window of Père Tanguy's art and paint shop.

Both brothers continued to hold painters of an earlier generation, such as Delacroix, Daumier and Rousseau among the French, and Weissenbruch among the Hague School, in high regard. Vincent's 'terrible craving' for the countryside in the north was undoubtedly part and parcel of this feeling. To his brother, Vincent characterized his ambivalent attitude to life as that of 'someone who has meant to commit suicide, but then makes for the bank because he finds the water too cold'. He wanted to escape from Saint-Rémy, but his sympathies were torn between the north and the south. He sang the praises of the unsurpassed portrayal of the south by such painters as Delacroix and Fromentin. On the other hand, he was now firmly convinced that he himself would have to return to northern parts. Pont-Aven in Brittany, where most of his friends were staying, put him off, however: 'There are so many people there.' In the circumstances, he felt that it would be more sensible for him to take lodgings with an artist's family, such as that of the landscape painter Victor Vignon, or the Pissarros.

605 [F] [postscript omitted]

[7 or 8 September 1889]

My dear Theo,

I think what you say in your letter is quite right, that Rousseau and artists such as Bodmer are in any case <u>men</u>, and that one would want the world to be peopled with men like them – indeed, yes, that's how I feel as well.

And that J. H. Weissenbruch knows & does the muddy towpaths, the stunted willows, the foreshortenings & the skilful & strange perspectives of the canals, as Daumier does the lawyers, I think that's perfect. Tersteeg has done well to buy some of his work. The reason people like that don't sell is, I think, because there are too many dealers trying to sell other things with which they deceive & mislead the public.

Do you know that even today, when I chance upon the story of some energetic industrialist, or even more of some publisher, I still feel the same indignation, the same rage as I used to when I was with G. & Cie.

Life passes in this way, time does not return, but I am working furiously for the very reason that I know that opportunities for work do not recur.

Especially in my case, where a more violent attack could destroy my ability to paint for good.

During the attacks I feel cowardly in the face of the pain and suffering – more cowardly than is justified – and perhaps it is this moral cowardice itself, which previously I had no desire to cure, that now makes me eat for two, work hard, and limit my relations with the other patients for fear of falling ill again – in short, I am trying to recover, like someone who has meant to commit suicide, but then makes for the bank because he finds the water too cold.

My dear brother, you know that I came to the south and threw myself into work for a thousand reasons – looking for a different light, believing that observing nature under a brighter sky might give one a more accurate idea of the way the Japanese feel and draw. Wanting, finally, to see this stronger sun, because one has the feeling that unless one knows it one would not be able to understand the pictures of Delacroix, as far as execution and technique are concerned, and because one feels that the colours of the prism are veiled in the mists of the north.

All this remains more or less true. Then if one adds that heartfelt leaning towards the south Daudet described in Tartarin, and the fact that from time to time I have also found friends and things to love here, then you will understand that however horrible I find my illness, I have the feeling that I have formed ties here that are a little too strong – ties which could later make me long to come back and work here again. Despite all this it could be that I shall be returning to the north fairly soon.

Yes, for I shall not conceal from you that in the same way that I am at present eating ravenously, so I have a terrible craving to see my friends again and the countryside of the north.

Work is going very well, I am discovering things I have sought in vain for years, and, aware of that, I am constantly reminded of that saying of Delacroix's you know, that he discovered painting when he had neither breath nor teeth left. Oh well, with my mental illness, I think of so many other artists suffering mentally, and tell myself that it doesn't stop one from carrying on one's trade as painter as if nothing had gone wrong.

When I see that here the attacks tend to take an absurdly religious turn, I might almost believe that this actually <u>necessitates</u> a return to the north. Don't say too much about it to the doctor when you see him – but I don't know whether it comes from living so many months both at the hospital in Arles and here in these old cloisters. In fact, I really shouldn't live in such surroundings, the street would be better. I am not indifferent, and even as I suffer, religious thoughts sometimes give me great consolation. I had a piece of bad luck this last time during my illness – that lithograph of Delacroix's, La Pietà, along with some other sheets, fell into some oil and paint and was ruined.

I was very sad about it – so I have been busy painting it and you will see it one day on a size 5 or 6 canvas. I have made a copy of it which I think has some feeling. Besides, having seen Daniel and Les odalisques and the portrait of Bruyas and La mulâtresse in Montpellier not long ago, I am still under the impression they made on me.

That is what uplifts me, and also reading a fine book such as one by Beecher Stowe or by Dickens. But what disturbs me is the constant sight of these good women, who both believe in the Virgin of Lourdes and make up that sort of thing, and realizing that one is a prisoner of an administration that is only too willing to cultivate these unhealthy religious aberrations when it should be concerned with curing them. So I say again, better to go, if not into penal servitude, at least into the army.

I reproach myself with my cowardice, I ought to have defended my studio better, even if it meant coming to blows with the gendarmes & the neighbours. Others would have used a revolver in my place, and had one killed gawking idiots like that, as an artist one would certainly have been acquitted. It would have been better had I done that, but I was cowardly and drunk – ill too, but I wasn't brave.

I'm also very frightened in the face of the suffering brought on by these attacks, and so I don't know if my zeal is anything other than what I said, it is like that of someone who means to commit suicide, but then struggles for the shore because he finds the water too cold.

But listen, to be in board and lodgings as Braat was when I saw him that time – happily long ago – no, and <u>no</u> again.

It would be different if old Pissarro or Vignon, for instance, would care to take me in. Well, I'm a painter myself – it could be arranged, and it would be better if the money went to feed painters than to the excellent nuns.

Yesterday I asked M. Peyron point-blank, since you are going to Paris, what would you say if I suggested that you be kind enough to take me with you? His reply was evasive – that it was too sudden, that he would have to write to you beforehand.

But he is very kind and very indulgent towards me, and while he doesn't have the final say here, far from it, I have him to thank for many liberties.

After all, one shouldn't only make pictures, one should see people too, and every now and then, by associating with others, recuperate a little and stock up on new ideas.

I've abandoned any hope that it won't come back – on the contrary, we must face the fact that I will have an attack from time to time. But at those times I could go into an asylum or even into the town prison where they usually have an isolation cell.

Don't be anxious, in any case – the work is going well, and look, I don't need to tell you that I've still got a lot of things to do, wheat fields, &c.

I've done the portrait of the attendant and have got a copy of it for you. It makes a fairly curious contrast with the portrait I've done of myself, in which the look is vague and veiled, whereas he has a military air and small, lively, black eyes.

I have given it to him, and I'll do his wife as well, if she wants to pose. She is a woman whose looks have faded, a poor soul, resigned to her fate, nothing out of the ordinary and so insignificant that I simply long to paint that dusty blade of grass. I talked to her sometimes when I was doing some olive trees behind their little house, and she told me then that she didn't believe I was ill – in fact, you would now say the same if you saw me working, my mind clear and my fingers so sure that I drew that Pietà by Delacroix without taking a single measurement, though there are those four hands and arms in the foreground – gestures and postures that are not exactly easy or simple.

Please send me the canvas soon, if at all possible, and I think I'm also going to need 10 more tubes of zinc white.

All the same, I'm sure that if one is brave then recovery comes from within, through the complete acceptance of suffering and death, and through the surrender of one's will and love of self. But that's no good to me, I like to paint, to see people and things and everything that makes our life – artificial, if you like. Yes, real life would be something else, but I don't think I belong to that category of souls who are ready to live, and also ready to suffer, at any moment.

What an odd thing the <u>touch</u>, the stroke of the brush, is.

In the open air, exposed to the wind, to the sun, to people's curiosity, one works as best one can, one fills one's canvas regardless. Yet that is how one captures the true and the essential – the most difficult part. But when, after some time, one resumes the study and alters the brushstrokes in keeping with the objects – the result is without doubt more harmonious and pleasant to look at, and one can add whatever serenity and happiness one feels.

Ah, I shall never be able to convey my impressions of some of the figures I have seen here. Certainly, this is the new road, this road to the south, but men from the north find it difficult to follow. And I can already see myself one day in the future enjoying some small success, and missing the solitude and the anguish as I watched the reaper in the field below through the iron bars of my cell. It's an ill wind . . .

To succeed, to enjoy lasting good fortune, one must have a different temperament from mine. I shall never do what I could have done and ought to have wanted and pursued.

But, having these dizzy spells so often, I can never be more than fourth or fifth rate. Although I am well aware of the worth and originality and superiority of Delacroix or Millet, for example, I can still say, yes, I too am something, I too can achieve something. But I must take these artists as my starting point, and then produce the little I am capable of in the same way.

So old Pissarro has been dealt two cruel blows all at once.[1] As soon as I read about it, I thought of asking you if there would be any way of going and staying with him. If you paid him the same as here, he would find it worth his while, for I don't need much – except for work. So ask him straight out, and if he doesn't like the idea, I could easily go and stay with Vignon.

I am a little afraid of Pont-Aven, there are so many people there. But what you say about Gauguin interests me very much. And I still tell myself that Gauguin and I will perhaps work together again. I know that G. can do even better things than he has done, but how to reassure him! I still hope to do his portrait. Have you seen that portrait he did of me painting sunflowers? My face has certainly brightened up since then, but it was really me, extremely tired and charged with electricity as I was then.

Yet to see the country, one must live with the ordinary folk and in the cottages, the inns, &c. And I said that to Boch, who complained he had seen nothing that had tempted him or made an impression on him.

I walked around with him for two days, and I showed him how to do thirty pictures as different from the north as Morocco would be. I'd be curious to know what he's doing at the moment.

And then, do you know why Eug. Delacroix's pictures – the religious and historical pictures, La barque du Christ, La Pietà, Les croisés, have this allure? Because Eug. Delacroix, when he did a Gethsemane, had been beforehand to see what an olive grove was like on the spot, and the same for the sea whipped up by a strong mistral, and because he must have said to himself, these people we know from history, doges of Venice, crusaders,

1 Pissarro's mother had recently died, and he had also had an eye operation.

apostles, holy women, were of the same type as, and lived in a similar way to, their present-day descendants.

And I must tell you, and you can see it in La berceuse, however unsuccessful and feeble that attempt may be, if I had had the strength to continue, then I should have done portraits of saints and holy women from life which would have seemed to belong to another age, and they would have been drawn from the bourgeoisie of today and yet would have had something in common with the very earliest Christians.

The emotions that are aroused are, however, too strong, so I'll leave it at that – but later, later, I don't promise not to return to the charge.

What a great man Fromentin was – he will always be the guide for any who wish to see the east. He, the first to establish a link between Rembrandt and the south, between Potter and what he himself saw.

You are right a thousand times over – I mustn't think about all that – to calm down I must do things – even if they're only studies of cabbages and lettuces, and after calming down, then – whatever I am capable of.

When I see them again, I'll do some copies of those studies of the Diligence of Tarascon, the Vineyard, the Harvest, and above all of the Red Tavern, that Night Café which is the most characteristic of all as far as colour is concerned. But the white figure in the middle must be done all over again for the colour, and better composed. Still, I'd go so far as to say that this is the real south, and a calculated combination of greens and reds.

My strength has been all too quickly exhausted, but in the distance I can see the possibility of others doing an infinite number of fine things. And again and again there is truth in the idea that to make the journey easier for others it would have been a good thing to set up a studio somewhere in this area.

To make the journey in one go from the north to Spain, for example, is not a good thing, you will not see what you should see – you must <u>get your eyes accustomed</u> gradually to the different light.

I really don't need to see the Titians and Velásquezs in the galleries, I've seen so many types in the flesh that have given me a better picture of the south now than before my journey.

My God, my God, those good people among artists who say that Delacroix is not of the true east. Now look, is the true east what Parisians like Gérôme make of it? Because you paint a bit of sunny wall from nature, well and truly according to our northern way of seeing things, does that prove that you have seen the people of the east? That was what Delacroix was searching for, and it in no way prevented him from painting walls in La noce juive and Les odalisques.

Isn't that true? – and then Degas says that it costs too much to drink in the taverns and paint pictures at the same time. I don't deny it, but would he rather I went into the cloisters or the churches? It is there that I myself get frightened. That's why I make a bid to escape with this letter.

With many handshakes for you and Jo,

Ever yours,
Vincent

[. . .]

Theo continued to worry about the repercussions of Vincent's frenetic activity: 'I am always frightened when you work like one possessed, for that is bound to sap your strength.' But Vincent had no choice, for as he told Wil, 'It is only when I stand painting before my easel that I feel in any way alive.' While he was still unable to work in the open, he found satisfaction in painting smaller versions of his own work for his family in the Netherlands, and in copying work by Rembrandt, Delacroix and above all Millet. As the series grew, he came to value it more and more. His pictures were not simply translations into colour of black-and-white prints and photographs, but had a strong interpretative element: 'We painters are always expected to compose our work and to be nothing but composers. So be it, but things aren't like that in music, and when someone plays Beethoven, he adds his personal interpretation – in music and particularly in song, the interpretation of a composer's work matters, and there is no rule that the composer alone should play his own composition.' Looking for solace, he improvised with colour, 'searching for memories' of Delacroix's and Millet's work – 'but the memory, the vague harmony of colours that may not be completely right but approaches the right feeling, that is my own interpretation'. Much as, during his days in The Hague, he had earmarked his prints for distribution among the people, so he now had a social objective for his Millet copies – as soon as the series was large enough, he intended to present it to a school.

In the autumn, lack of vineyards in the area around Saint-Rémy led him to concentrate above all on olive trees, for him the equivalent of willows in the north: 'I am doing all I can to catch them on canvas. They are silvery, sometimes more blue, sometimes whitish and bronze-green, against a yellow, purple-pink or orange to dull red-ochre ground. But very difficult, very difficult. Still, that suits me and working in an abundance of gold and silver appeals to me. And one day I shall no doubt do a personal impression of it, as the sunflowers were for the yellow tones.'

In Paris, Dr Peyron had called on Theo and diagnosed Vincent's attacks as a form of epilepsy. Pissarro, who saw no possibility of taking Vincent into his family home, suggested that he go to Auvers, where he knew someone 'who is a doctor and who paints in his spare time'. This was Dr Paul Gachet, a man on friendly terms not only with Pissarro but also with Cézanne and Guillaumin. Vincent was rather in favour of this idea.

During the third week of October 1889, Van Gogh's thoughts were often with his family in Holland. Now that illness had laid him so low, he hearkened back to 'affections of the past', and had an almost irresistible urge to send something of his work to Holland. He also wanted Margot Begemann to have one of his paintings as a keepsake. He had made four landscape studies and a small version of *The Bedroom*, whose literary inspiration he revealed to Wil: 'I wanted to achieve a simple effect of the kind one finds described in <u>Felix Holt</u> [. . .]. Doing a simple thing with bright colours is not easy, however.' On the wall above the bed could be seen the small self-portrait he had painted for his mother's seventieth birthday, in which he looked like a peasant from Zundert, because 'I plough my canvases as they do their fields'.

A letter from Gauguin during the first half of November revived their old arguments about the painting of religious subjects. Gauguin had enclosed a small sketch meant to give Van Gogh some idea of his recently finished *Le Christ dans le jardin des oliviers*. Theo wrote that Bernard, too, had painted the same subject and that under the influence of the primitives he had added a kneeling figure surrounded by angels, distributing the various figures like pieces on a chessboard. Van Gogh's reply to Theo was unequivocal: '[...] I have never had any truck with their [Gauguin's and Bernard's] biblical interpretations. I said that Rembrandt and Delacroix had done it admirably, that I thought more of that than I did of the primitives [Van Gogh was referring here to the work of Renaissance painters], but let's leave it at that – I don't want to broach that subject again. If I stay here, I shall not try to paint a Christ in the Garden of Olives, but shall paint the olive harvest as one can still see it today, and by giving the human figure its proper place in it, one might perhaps be reminded of it.' He went on to name Puvis de Chavannes, Millais, Pinwell, Rossetti and Holman Hunt as serious painters of religious subjects, a list from which he expressly excluded his French friends. Their work struck him as 'bogus' and 'spurious'. Nor could he refrain from letting Gauguin and Bernard know immediately what he felt about it. Only the letter to Bernard has come down to us. After robust criticism of his 'abstractions', Van Gogh tried to convince his friend, on the basis of his own *View of the Asylum*, 'that one can express anguish without making direct reference to the actual Gethsemane, and that there is no need to portray figures from the Sermon on the Mount in order to express a comforting and gentle motif'.

B21 [F] [letter from Vincent to Émile Bernard]
[postscript omitted]
[translated from the Dutch]

[*c.* 20 November 1889]

My dear friend Bernard,

Thanks for your letter and thanks above all for the photographs, which give me some idea of your work. In fact, my brother wrote to me on the subject not long ago, and told me he was greatly taken with the harmony of the colours and the dignity of many of the figures.

But now look, though I found the landscape in L'adoration des Mages so beautiful that I wouldn't dare say a word against it, you surely can't seriously imagine a confinement like that, in the middle of the road, with the mother starting to pray instead of suckling her child? Those bloated frogs of priests on their knees as though they're having an epileptic fit are also part of it, God alone knows how and why!

No, I can't call that sound, for if I am at all capable of spiritual ecstasy, then I feel exalted in the face of truth, of what is possible, which means I bow down before the study – one that had enough power in it to make a Millet tremble – of peasants carrying a calf born in the fields back home to the farm. That, my friend, is what people everywhere, from France to America, have felt. And having performed a feat like that, can you really contemplate reverting to medieval tapestries? Can that really be what you mean to do? No! You can do better than that, and know that you must look for what is possible, logical and true, even if that means turning your back on those Parisian things à la Baudelaire. How I prefer Daumier to that fellow!

An <u>Annunciation</u>? Of what? I see figures of angels – quite elegant, no doubt – a terrace with two cypresses which I like very much. There is an enormous amount of sky, of brightness ... but, once over this first impression, I wonder if the whole thing is not a misrepresentation, and then the figures lose their meaning for me.

Let me make it perfectly clear that I was looking forward to seeing the sort of things that are in that painting of yours which Gauguin has, those Breton women walking in a meadow, so beautifully composed, the colour with such naïve distinction. And you are trading that in for something – I won't prevaricate – bogus, spurious!

Last year you did a painting[1] which – according to what

---

1 *Madeleine au Bois d'Amour.*

Gauguin told me – looked, I believe, something like this: on a grassy foreground, the figure of a young girl in a blue or whitish dress, lying stretched out full-length; on  the second plane the edge of a beech wood, the ground covered with fallen red leaves, vertical grey-green tree trunks across it. Her hair, I think, is in a tint that serves as a complementary colour to the white dress: black if that garment is white, orange if it is blue. Well, I said to myself, what a simple subject and how well he knows how to create grace from nothing!

Gauguin also mentioned another subject, just three trees, the effect of orange foliage against a blue sky, but with very clear outlines, very strictly divided into planes of contrasting, clear colours – splendid!

And when I compare that with the nightmare of a Christ au jardin des oliviers, then, good God, I mourn, and with this letter I ask you once more, shouting at the top of my voice: please try to be yourself again! Le Christ portant sa croix is appalling. Are those touches of colour in it meant to be harmonious? I cannot forgive your using a <u>cliché</u>, yes, a cliché, for your composition.

When Gauguin was in Arles, I once or twice allowed myself to be led astray into abstraction, as you know, for instance in the Berceuse, in the Woman Reading a Novel, black against a yellow bookcase. At the time, I considered abstraction an attractive method. But that was delusion, dear friend, and one soon comes up against a brick wall.

I don't say one might not try one's hand at it after a whole life long of experimentation, of hand-to-hand struggle with nature, but personally, I don't want to trouble my head with such things. All year I was doing little things after nature, without giving a thought to impressionism or whatever else. And yet, once again I allowed myself to be led astray into reaching for stars that are too big – another failure – and I have had my fill of that.

So right now I'm working in the olive grove, in search of all sorts of effects of grey sky against yellow soil, with a grey-green hue in the foliage, and then again with the soil and the leaves all purple against a yellow sky, or a red-ochre soil and green-pink sky. Yes, I do find that more interesting than the above-named abstractions.

The reason I haven't written for so long is that I've been trying to keep on top of my illness and was reluctant to enter into discussions, sensing danger in those abstractions. If one carries on working quietly, beautiful subjects come of their own accord. Believe me, it is of the utmost importance to immerse oneself in reality, without any preconceived ideas, without any Parisian prejudice.

As it happens, I'm not at all satisfied with this year, but it may yet provide a solid basis for the next. I have feasted upon the air in the hills and the orchards. For the rest I shall have to wait and see. My ambition reaches no further than a few clods of earth, sprouting wheat, an olive grove, a cypress – the last, for instance, far from easy to do.

How is it possible that you, who like the primitives and study them, don't know Giotto? Gauguin and I saw a tiny little panel of his in Montpellier, the death of some holy woman or other. In it, the expression of pain and ecstasy is so human that, even though we are in the middle of the 19th century, one could think and feel one was there, so much does one share the emotion.

If I were to see the canvases themselves, I might well be enchanted by the colour, but you also mention portraits you've done that are striking likenesses. That's good, and you will have put more of yourself into them.

Now a description of a canvas that is in front of me at the moment. A view of the garden of the asylum where I am staying: to the right a grey terrace and a part of the house. A few faded rose bushes, the garden to the left – red ochre – scorched by the sun, covered with pine needles. The edge of the garden is planted with large pines with red-ochre trunks and branches, the green foliage darkened with a mixture of black. These tall trees stand out against a yellow evening sky crossed with purple stripes, the yellow yielding to pink and green higher up. A wall – also red ochre – bars the view and only a purple and yellow-ochre hill appears above it. The nearest tree has an enormous trunk but has been struck by lightning and sawn off. However, a branch still juts high up into the air and sends down a rain of dark green needles. This sombre giant – with its hurt pride – contrasts, if you were to lend it human characteristics, with the pale smile of a last rose on the fading bush in front of it. Under the big trees, empty stone benches, mournful little box trees; the sky is reflected – yellow – in a puddle after the rain. A ray of sun turns the dark ochre into orange with its last reflection. Small black figures wander about here and there among the tree trunks.

Of course, you realize that the combination of red ochre, green darkened with grey and the black stripes indicating the contours, arouses that anguished feeling, the so-called 'black-and-reds', with which some of my fellow patients are afflicted. Moreover, the motif of the great tree, struck by lightning, the wan pink-green smile of the last autumn flower, serve to reinforce this impression.

Another canvas shows a rising sun above a field of young wheat – receding lines, furrows that run to the top of the canvas, towards a wall and a row of lilac hills. The field is purple and yellow-green. The white sun is surrounded by a large yellow halo. Here, in contrast to the first canvas, I have tried to express calmness, great peace.

I am telling you about these canvases, and about the first one in particular, to remind you that one can express anguish without making direct reference to the actual Gethsemane, and that there is no need to portray figures from the Sermon on the Mount in order to express a comforting and gentle motif.

Oh, it is only right and proper to be moved by the Bible, but present-day reality has so strong a hold over us that even when we try to imagine the past the minor events in our lives immediately wrench us out of our musings, and our own adventures throw us back irrevocably upon our personal feelings: joy, boredom, suffering, anger or a smile.

The Bible, the Bible! Millet, who grew up with it from childhood, did nothing but read that book! And yet he never, or hardly ever, painted biblical pictures. Corot did do a Mount of Olives, with Christ and the evening star, sublime. In his work you can feel Homer, Aeschylus, Sophocles and sometimes the Gospels as well, but so discreetly and always taking account of all the modern feelings that all of us share.

But what of Delacroix, you may ask. Yes, Delacroix – but then you would have to study quite a lot more, indeed, you would have to make a study of history before you could depict things as he did.

So, my dear fellow, those biblical paintings of yours are hopeless. There are only a few who make such a mistake, and a mistake it is, but once you have turned your back on it, I dare say the results will be marvellous! Sometimes our mistakes show us the right way.

Come now, make up for it by painting your garden just as it is, or any way you like. Anyhow, it's a good idea to put something worthy, something noble, into your figures, studies take real effort and hence are never a waste of time. Being able to divide a canvas into large intermingling planes, to devise contrasting lines and forms – that is technique, tricks of the trade, if you like, but ultimately a sign that your craftsmanship is being strengthened, and that is all to the good.

No matter how odious and burdensome painting may be at present, those who have chosen this profession – if only they pursue it with zeal – are dutiful, sound and faithful men. Society often renders our existence hard, and that is the source of our impotence and of the imperfection of our work. I believe that even Gauguin suffers greatly from this and cannot develop, although he has it in him to do so. I myself am frustrated by a total lack of models. On the other hand, there are some very beautiful spots around here. I have just finished 5 size 30 canvases of olive groves. And the reason I am still here is that my health is making good progress. What I am doing is hard, harsh, but that is because I am trying to get back on my feet with work that is a bit rough, having been afraid that I would go soft with abstractions.

Have you seen my study of a small reaper, a yellow wheat field and a yellow sun? It isn't the real thing yet, but at least I have tackled the devilish problem of yellow in it. I am referring to the one with the thick impasto and done on the spot, and not to the copy with the hatchings, which has a much weaker effect. I'd like to do it in deep sulphur-yellow.

I still have a great deal more to say to you, and though I can tell you today that my head has grown somewhat calmer, I used to be afraid of getting excited before I got cured. With a very cordial handshake in my thoughts, for Anquetin too, and any other friends should you see them, believe me,

Ever yours,
Vincent

[...]

During the last two months of 1889, Van Gogh continued to paint copies after Millet and also finished his *Wheat Field with Rising Sun, A Corner of the Asylum Garden, Pines Against the Evening Sky* and *Women Picking Olives.* Then, one year after the first crisis in Arles, he had another violent attack that continued for the whole of the last week in December. Because he had again tried to poison himself by swallowing paint, Dr Peyron decided once more that until further notice he must confine himself to drawing.

Early in January 1890, Vincent wrote to Theo and Johanna, setting out the circumstances surrounding his latest attack: 'Oddly enough I had been working quite calmly on canvases you will shortly be seeing, when suddenly, without any reason, I once again became confused. [...] Oh, while I was ill there was a fall of wet, melting snow. I got out of my bed at night to look at the landscape – never, never has nature had such an affecting, such a moving impression on me. The rather superstitious ideas people here have about painting make me feel sadder than I can tell you, because in essence it is really quite true that a painter, as a human being, is too absorbed in what his eyes see to have enough grasp on other things in his life.'

After the latest attack Van Gogh felt 'a broken vessel'. In his continued search for alternatives to Saint-Rémy, he discovered an asylum at Montevergues, where people worked on the land and where there would therefore be more models for him. He even repeated his proposal for sharing an apartment with Gauguin in Paris, something Gauguin rejected immediately. Instead Gauguin suggested that he and Meijer de Haan look for a studio in Antwerp, where it was cheaper.

On 21 January, Van Gogh had yet another attack. In the meantime, a highly favourable article on his work had appeared in *Le Mercure de France* under the title of 'Les Isolés: Vincent van Gogh'. Its author was the authoritative though still young critic Albert Aurier.

On 31 January 1890 Johanna van Gogh gave birth to a boy, who was named after Vincent, as promised. Theo expressed the wish that the boy might be 'as steadfast & courageous as you'. The letter in which the slowly recovering Vincent congratulated Theo on the birth of his son was, however, largely devoted to his own reactions to Aurier's article. Despite his joy at the recognition for which he had had to wait for so long, Van Gogh felt that the eulogy placed a heavy responsibility upon him. He then sent Aurier a singular letter in which he maintained that Aurier should have reserved his praises for Monticelli.

625 [F]

[2 February 1890]

My dear Theo,

I have just received your good news that you are a father at last, that Jo is over the most critical period, and finally that the little boy is doing well. That has done me more good and given me more pleasure than I can put into words. Bravo – and how pleased Mother will be! The day before yesterday I received a fairly long, very calm letter from her as well. So what I have been longing for so much and for such a long time has happened at last. No need to tell you that my thoughts have often turned to you of late, and it touched me very much that Jo had the kindness to write to me only the night before. How brave and calm she was at her moment of peril, it touched me very much.

Well, it all helps a great deal in making me forget these last days when I was ill – at such times I no longer know where I am and my mind wanders.

I was extremely surprised by the article on my paintings you sent me. No need to tell you that I hope to keep thinking that I don't paint like that, but I do gather from it how I ought to be painting. For the article is absolutely right in the way it shows the gap to be filled, and I think that the writer really wrote it to guide, not only me, but all the other impressionists, and even to help them make the breach in the right place. So he proposes an ideal collective ego to the others quite as much as to me. He simply tells me that here and there he can see something good, if you like, even in my work which is so imperfect, and that is the comforting part, which I appreciate and for which I hope I am grateful. Only it ought to be understood that my back is not broad enough to be saddled with that task, and I need not tell you that, in concentrating the article on me, he has made me feel steeped in flattery. In my opinion it is all as exaggerated as a certain article by Isaäcson about you which claimed that present-day artists had given up quarrelling, and that an important movement was silently taking shape in the little shop on the Boulevard Montmartre. I admit that it is difficult to say what one means, to express oneself properly – just as one cannot paint things as one sees them – and so this isn't really a criticism of Isaäcson's rashness, or that of the other critic, but as far as we are concerned, well, we are merely serving as model, and that is surely a duty and a task like any other. So, should you or I acquire some sort of reputation, then we must simply try to take it as calmly as possible, and to keep our heads.

Why not say what he said of my sunflowers, and with far greater justification, of those magnificent and quite perfect holly-hocks of Quost's and his yellow irises, and those splendid peonies of Jeannin's? You know as well as I do that there is always another side of the coin to such praise. But I am glad, and very grateful for the article, or rather 'la coeur à l'aise',[1] as the

1 Glad at heart.

revue song has it, since one may need it, as one may indeed have need of a coin. Moreover, an article like that has its own merit as a critical work of art. As such I think it is to be respected and the writer must raise the tone, harness his conclusions, &c.

But from the outset, you should guard against allowing your young family too much contact with the artistic world. Old Goupil guided his household well through the Parisian undergrowth, and I imagine you still think of him often. Things have changed so much, today. His cold aloofness would meet resistance today, yet his capacity to weather so many storms was something special.

Gauguin proposed, very vaguely it is true, that we found a studio in his name, he, De Haan and I, but he insisted on seeing his Tonkin project through first. He seems to have cooled off a great deal, I'm not sure exactly why, about continuing to paint. And he is just the kind of man to clear off to Tonkin, in fact he needs some room to expand, and finds the life of an artist – and there is some truth in this – a mean one.

With all his experience of travel, what is one to say to him?

So I hope that he will feel that you and I are indeed his friends, without counting on us too much, which, it must be added, he in no way does. He writes with a great deal of reserve, and more seriously than last year. I have just sent another note to Russell to jog his memory about Gauguin, for I know that Russell is very reliable and a sound character. And should I get back together with Gauguin, then we would have need of Russell. Gauguin and Russell are countrymen at heart – not uncivilized, but with the innate mellowness of distant fields, probably much more than you or I – that is how they look to me.

True enough, one must sometimes have a little faith to see that. If I, for my part, wanted to go on with, let us call it the translation of certain pages of Millet, then to prevent people – not from criticizing me, that would be all right – but from hampering or stopping me by making out that all I do is produce copies – then – I need the support of people like Russell or Gauguin from among the artists to carry my project through and to make a serious job of it. I have scruples of conscience about doing the things by Millet you sent me, for example, and which seemed to me perfectly chosen, and so I took the pile of photographs and sent them straight to Russell, lest I see them again before I have thought it over. I don't want to do it before having heard something of what you and certain others think of the things you will soon be receiving.

Else I should be having scruples of conscience, fearing that it might be plagiarism. And not now, but in a few months' time, I shall try to obtain the frank opinion of Russell himself on the real usefulness of the thing. In any case, Russell is on a short fuse, he gets angry, and says what's what, and that is what I sometimes need. You know that I find the Virgin so dazzling that I haven't dared look at it. I felt an immediate 'not yet'. My illness makes me very sensitive right now, and I don't feel capable for the moment of continuing these 'translations' when such masterpieces are involved. I am stopping with the Sower on which I am working, and which is not coming on as I would wish. Being ill, however, I have thought a great deal about going on with the work. When I do it, I do it calmly, as you will soon see when I send you the five or 6 finished canvases.

I hope that M. Lauzet will come, I very much wish to make his acquaintance.[2] I trust his opinion and when he says it [my painting] is Provence, he begs the question, and like the other critic he talks more about something yet to be done than about something already accomplished. Landscapes with cypresses! Ah, that wouldn't be easy – Aurier is aware of that, too, when he says that even black is a colour, and refers to their flaming appearance. I am thinking about it, but dare do nothing more, and like the cautious Isaäcson, I say that I don't think we are there yet. One needs a dose of inspiration, a ray from on high that is not in ourselves, to do beautiful things. When I had done those Sunflowers, I looked for the opposite and yet the equivalent, and said – it's the cypress.

I'm going to stop here – I am a little anxious about a friend

2 Auguste M. Lauzet, lithographer who had reproduced work by Monticelli.

who, it seems, is still ill, and whom I should like to see. She is the one whose portrait I did in yellow and black,[3] and she has changed very much. She has nervous attacks, complicated by a premature change of life, in short, very painful. She looked like an old grandfather the last time. I had promised to come back in a fortnight, but was taken ill again myself.

Anyhow, as far as I'm concerned, the good news you've given me, and that article, and a whole lot of things have made me feel quite well today. I'm sorry that M. Salles did not find you. I want to thank Wil once again for her kind letter. I should have liked to have replied to it today, but am putting it off for a few days. Tell her that Mother has written me another long letter from Amsterdam. How happy she will be, Wil too!

I am with you all in my thoughts, though ending my letter. May Jo long remain for us what she is now. As for the little boy, why don't you name him Theo, in memory of our Father, that would certainly give me much pleasure.

A handshake,

Ever yours,
Vincent

In the meantime, if you see him, thank M. Aurier very much for his article. I shall of course be sending you a note for him, and a study.

626a [F] [letter from Vincent to Albert Aurier]

[10 or 11 February 1890]

Dear M. Aurier,

Thank you very much for your article in the <u>Mercure de France</u>, which surprised me a good deal. I admire it very much as a work of art in itself, it seems to me that you paint with words; in fact, I encounter my canvases anew in your article, but better than they

3 Mme Ginoux.

are in reality, richer, more meaningful. Reflecting, however, that what you say would be more relevant to others than to myself, I feel uneasy. Monticelli in particular is a case in point. Since you say that 'he is, so far as I know, the only painter who perceives the range of colour of things with this intensity, with this metallic, gem-like quality', please go to see, at my brother's, a certain bouquet[1] by Monticelli – a bouquet in white, forget-me-not blue & orange – and then you will understand what I mean. But for some time now the best, the most wonderful Monticellis have been in Scotland and England. There should still be a marvellous one of his in a gallery in the North – the one in Lille, I think – as rich and certainly no less French than Le départ pour Cythère by Watteau. At this moment M. Lauzet is in the process of reproducing about thirty Monticellis. As far as I know, there is no colourist who stems so directly from Delacroix, and yet it is probable, in my opinion, that Monticelli knew of Delacroix's colour theories at second-hand only; he had them in particular from Diaz and Ziem. Monticelli's artistic temperament seems to me exactly the same as that of the author of the Decameron – Boccaccio – a melancholy, rather resigned, unhappy man, watching the fashionable wedding party and the lovers of his time pass him by, painting them and analysing them – he, the outsider. Oh! He no more imitated Boccaccio than Henri Leys imitated the primitives.

Anyway – what I am trying to say is that things seem to have mistakenly become attached to my name that you would do better to link to Monticelli, to whom I owe so much. I also owe a great deal to Paul Gauguin, with whom I worked for several months in Arles, and whom, moreover, I already knew in Paris.

Gauguin, that curious artist, that strange individual, whose demeanour and look vaguely recall Rembrandt's Portrait of a Man at the Galerie Lacaze – that friend who likes to make one feel that a good picture should be equivalent to a good deed, not that he says so, but it is in fact difficult to be much in his company without being mindful of a certain moral responsibility.

1 Adolphe Monticelli, *Vase with Flowers.*

A few days before we parted company, when my illness forced me to go into an asylum, I tried to paint 'his empty place'.

It is a study of his wooden armchair, brown and dark red, the seat of greenish straw, and in place of the absent person, a lighted candle in a candlestick and some modern novels. Should the opportunity arise, do please take another look at this study by way of a reminder of him. It is done throughout in broken tones of green and red.

You may realize now that your article would have been fairer and – it seems to me – consequently more powerful, if, when dealing with the question of the future of 'tropical painting' and the question of colour, you had – before speaking of me – done justice to Gauguin and Monticelli. <u>For the role attaching to me, or that will be attached to me, will remain, I assure you, of very secondary importance</u>.

Besides, I should like to ask you another question. Let us suppose that the two canvases of sunflowers which are at present at the Vingtistes have certain qualities of colour, and that they also symbolize 'gratitude'. Are they any different from so many other pictures of flowers, more skilfully painted, which are not yet appreciated enough – the Roses trémières and the Iris jaunes by old Quost, the magnificent bunches of peonies which Jeannin produces in such abundance? You see, I find it very difficult to make a distinction between impressionism and other things. I do not see any use for much of the sectarian thinking we have seen these last few years, <u>but the absurdity of it frightens me</u>.

And in conclusion, I confess I do not understand why you should vilify Meissonier. It may have been from the excellent Mauve that I have inherited a boundless admiration for Meissonier; Mauve was tireless in his praise of Troyon and Meissonier – a strange combination.

I say this in order to draw your attention to how much people from other countries admire the artists of France without attaching the slightest importance to what, unfortunately, so often divides them. An often-repeated saying of Mauve's was something like, 'If one wants to use colour, one should also be able to draw an inglenook or an interior like Meissonier.'

If you will do me the pleasure of accepting it, I shall include a study of cypresses for you in the next batch I send to my brother, in remembrance of your article. I am still working on it at the moment, as I want to put a small figure into it. The cypress is so characteristic of the Provence landscape. You will feel it, and say, 'Even the colour black.' Until now, I have not been able to do them as I feel them; the emotions that come over me in the face of nature can be so intense that I lose conscious-ness, and the result is a fortnight during which I cannot do any work. However, before leaving here, I mean to have one more try at tackling the cypresses. The study I intend for you repre-sents a group of them in the corner of a wheat field during the mistral on a summer's day. It is thus a kind of black note in the shifting blue of the flowing wide sky, with the vermilion of the poppies contrasting with the note of black. You will see that it forms something like the combination of tones found in those agreeable Scottish tartans of green, blue, red, yellow and black, which seemed so charming to you and to me at the time, and which, alas, we hardly see any more these days.

In the meantime, dear Sir, please accept my grateful thanks for your article. If I come to Paris in the spring, I certainly shall not fail to thank you in person.

Vincent v. Gogh

It will be a year before the study I am going to send you will be thoroughly dry, particularly the impasto – I think it might be a good idea to give it a good coat of varnish.

And in the meantime, it should be washed several times with plenty of water to get the oil out completely. This study is painted in pure Prussian blue, that much-maligned colour which Delacroix nevertheless used so much. I think that once the tones of Prussian blue are quite dry, you will, by varnishing, get the black, the very black tones that are needed to bring out the various dark greens.

I am not quite sure how this study should be framed, but since it makes one think of those much-esteemed Scottish fabrics, I have noticed that a <u>very simple flat frame in BRIGHT ORANGE</u>

LEAD gives the desired effect along with the blues of the background and the black-green of the trees. Without that there might not be enough red in the canvas, and the upper part would seem rather cold.

On 19 February Vincent received news from Theo that at the exhibition of the Vingtistes in Brussels one of his paintings had been sold for 400 francs to Anna Boch, the sister of his friend Eugène Boch.

While he was continually being admonished to take things easy after his attacks, Van Gogh himself stressed the necessity of a large output: 'What some consider working too fast is really nothing out of the ordinary, the normal condition of regular production, seeing that a painter really ought to work just as hard as, say, a shoemaker.' The 'overwrought' way in which all Impressionists worked, moreover, 'renders us very sensitive to colours and their special language, and to the effects of complementary colours, of contrasts and harmony'. Sometimes he felt like turning his back on reality and creating 'a melody of tones with colour', but he knew he had to stick to the real world if only for the sake of his health. For his new nephew he painted a study of branches of almond blossom against a blue sky. Most of his paintings, however, were less serene, and he apologized to Wil for the fact that his current pictures were 'almost a cry of anguish, though they may symbolize gratitude in the motif of the rustic sunflower'.

Epileptic seizures were now following one another more quickly. On 22 February 1890, during an outing to Arles, where he intended to present Mme Ginoux with a version of her portrait, he had another attack. Dr Peyron saw a causal link between these seizures and such trips with their emotional reunions. This time it took Van Gogh much longer to recover than it had in the past. In letters dated 19 and 29 March, Theo tried to cheer his brother up with a report of his successes at the Vingtistes' exhibition in Brussels and at the Salon des Indépendants in Paris, where Vincent was now represented by no fewer than ten works. Pissarro had said that Van Gogh had scored a real success with his fellow artists. A note from Gauguin confirmed this impression: '[. . .] many artists think your work has been the most striking at the exhibition'.

He added that he would be delighted to exchange Van Gogh's picture *Ravine* for one of his own canvases.

A month later, in a letter to Vincent of 23 April 1890, Theo had reluctantly to conclude that 'to us, your silence is proof that you are not yet well'. This time Vincent replied without delay, apologizing for still being depressed and confused: 'Work was going well, you will see that the last canvas with the branches in blossom was perhaps the best, the one on which I worked most patiently, painted calmly and with a greater assurance of touch. And the next day I was completely done in. Difficult to understand things like that.' A week later he wrote that during his illness he had done a few small canvases from memory, chiefly recollections of the north. He was planning new versions of *The Potato Eaters*, *The Cottage* and *The Old Tower*, which he had done in Nuenen, and asked Theo to send him his figure drawings from his time in Brabant.

After all Vincent's doubts about whether he was taking the right course with his Millet copies, and his fear that they might even be considered downright plagiarism, Theo's enthusiasm over his latest consignment of paintings to Paris must have done him a world of good: 'The copies after Millet are possibly the finest things you've done.' And Theo called Vincent's present to Aurier, the picture of a large cypress, 'as rich as a peacock's tail'.

Van Gogh's letters of 2 and 3 May 1890 reflected considerably more energy. He was now firmly resolved to implement his new plans in the north. He expected a great deal from his stay with Dr Gachet, 'this doctor in the country. [...] since he likes painting there is a real chance that a lasting friendship will come of it'.

Before leaving for Auvers, Van Gogh wanted first to spend a few days in Paris to see Theo, Johanna and little Vincent, and to look up a number of old friends. Also on his programme were visits to an exhibition of Japanese prints and to the Salon des Indépendants. He even knew what he would still want to paint in Paris: '[...] a bookshop with a yellow and pink front window, in the evening, with dark passers-by. It is such a thoroughly modern motif. For the source of light is metaphorical as well. The subject – a scattering of books and prints – is bound to go well, don't you think, between an olive grove and a wheat field? I have set my heart on doing it, as a light in the darkness.'

During his last week in Saint-Rémy he managed to finish four large still lifes with flowers. On the eve of his departure from the south, which he saw as the conclusion of an important chapter, he thought back to his departure from Paris at the beginning of 1888: 'It's another remarkable thing that, just as we were so struck by Seurat's canvases that day [the day Van Gogh left for Arles], these last few days here have again been like a revelation of colours to me.' Despite his dislike of the asylum, which he even compared with a penal colony, his departure was attended by sadness as a result of which '[...] packing my cases seems to me much more difficult than painting'. Theo voiced his concern about whether Vincent would be able to stand up to the journey.

631 [F]

[4 May 1890]

My dear brother,

Thank you for your kind letter and the portrait of Jo, which is very pretty & a very successful pose. Now look, I'm going to be very straightforward in my reply & as practical as possible. First, I categorically reject what you say, that I must be accompanied the whole way. Once on the train, I will be quite safe, I am not one of those who are dangerous – and even supposing I do have an attack, there are other passengers in the carriage, aren't there, and anyway, don't they know at every station what to do in such cases? You have so many qualms about this that they weigh me down heavily enough to discourage me completely.

I have just said the same thing to M. Peyron, and I pointed out to him that attacks like the one I have just had have invariably been followed by three or four months of complete calm. I want to take advantage of this period to move – I must move in any case, my intention to leave is now unshakeable.

I do not feel competent to judge the way disorders are treated here. I don't feel like going into details – but please remember that I warned you about 6 months ago that if I had another attack of the same kind I should wish to change asylums. And I have already delayed too long, having allowed an attack to go by in the meantime. I was in the middle of my work then and I wanted to finish the canvas I had started. But for that I should no longer be here. Right, so now I'm saying that it seems to me that a fortnight at most (although I'd be happier with a week) should be enough to prepare the move. I shall have myself accompanied as far as Tarascon – even one or two stations further on, if you insist. When I arrive in Paris (I'll send a telegram on leaving here) you could come and pick me up at the Gare de Lyon.

Now I should think it would be as well to go and see this doctor in the country as soon as possible, and we could leave the luggage at the station. So I should not be staying with you for more than, let's say, 2 or 3 days. I would then leave for this village, where I could stay at the inn to begin with.

What I think you might do one of these days – without delay – is to write to our future friend, the doctor in question, 'My brother greatly desires to make your acquaintance, and preferring to consult you before prolonging his stay in Paris, hopes that you will approve of his coming and spending a few weeks in your village in order to do some studies; he has every confidence in reaching an understanding with you, believing that his illness will abate with a return to the north, whereas his condition would threaten to become more acute if he stayed any longer in the south.'

There, you write him something like that, we can send him a telegram the day after I arrive in Paris, or the day after that, and he would probably meet me at the station.

The surroundings here are beginning to weigh me down more than I can say – heavens above, I've been patient for more than a year – I need some air, I feel overwhelmed by boredom and grief.

Also the work is pressing, and I should be wasting my time here. Why then, I ask you, are you so afraid of accidents? That's not what should be frightening you. Heavens above, every day since I've been here I've watched people falling down, or going out of their minds – what is more important is to try and take misfortune into account.

I assure you that it's quite something to resign oneself to living under surveillance, even if it is sympathetic, and to sacrifice one's liberty, to remain outside society with nothing but one's work as distraction.

This has given me wrinkles which will not be smoothed out in a hurry. Now that things are beginning to weigh me down <u>too heavily</u> here, I think it only fair that they should be brought to an end.

So please ask M. Peyron to allow me to leave, let's say by the 15th at the latest. If I wait, I shall be letting the favourable period of calm between two attacks go by, and by leaving now, I should have the time I need to make the acquaintance of the other doctor. Then if the illness does come back in a little while, it would not be unexpected, and depending upon how serious it is, we could see if I can continue to be at liberty, or if I must settle down in a lunatic asylum for good. In the latter case – as I told you in my last letter, I would go into a home where the patients work in the fields & the workshop. I'm sure I'd find even more subjects to paint there than here.

So remember that the journey costs a lot, that it is pointless [to provide an escort], and that I have every right to change homes if I wish. I am not demanding my complete liberty.

I have tried to be patient up till now, I haven't done anybody any harm, is it fair to have me accompanied like some dangerous animal? No, thank you, I protest. If I should have an attack, they know what to do at every station, and I should let them get on with it.

But I'm sure that my nerve will not desert me. I am so distressed at leaving like this that the distress will be stronger than the madness. So I'm sure I shall have what nerve it takes.

M. Peyron won't commit himself, because he doesn't want to take the responsibility, he says, but that way we'll never, ever, get to the end of it, the thing will drag on and on, and we'll end up by getting angry with each other. As for me, my dear brother, my patience is at an end, quite at an end, I cannot go on, I must make a change, even if it's only a stopgap.

However, there really is a chance that the change will do me good – the work is going well, I've done 2 canvases of the newly cut grass in the grounds, one of which is extremely simple. Here is a hasty sketch of it – a pine trunk, pink and purple, and then

the grass with some white flowers and dandelions, a little rose bush and some other tree trunks in the background right at the top of the canvas. I shall be out of doors over there. I'm sure that my zest for work will get the better of me and make me indifferent to everything else, as well as put me in a good humour. And I shall let myself go there, not without thought, but without brooding over what might have been.

They say that in painting one should look for nothing more and hope for nothing more than a good picture and a good talk and a good dinner as the height of happiness, and ignore the less brilliant digressions. That may well be true, so why shouldn't one seize the hour, particularly if in so doing one steals a march on one's illness?

A good handshake for you and Jo. I think I shall do a painting for myself after the portrait, it may not be a resemblance, but anyway I'll try.

See you soon, I hope – and come on now, spare me this imposed travel companion.

Ever yours,
Vincent

Auvers-sur-Oise

In Paris, Van Gogh met his sister-in-law for the first time. Johanna van Gogh herself later described their meeting. 'I had expected a sick man, but here was a sturdy, broad-shouldered man, with a healthy colour, a smile on his face, and a very resolute appearance.' Van Gogh's own impressions of Johanna were also very positive ('charming and very simple and nice'). Both brothers were moved as they stood side by side over little Vincent's cradle. Despite far from ideal storage conditions for his old canvases, it did Vincent good to see the work again, both at Theo's and also at Père Tanguy's 'flea pit'. However, he was no longer used to the commotion of city life. After three days, on 20 May 1890, 'taking fright at the noise and bustle of Paris', he left for what was to be the last stop on his pilgrimage. In Auvers he took lodgings at the Auberge Ravoux, opposite the town hall in the place de la Mairie. Dr Gachet, to whose care he was now entrusted, was a homoeopathic doctor and psychiatrist who had written a thesis on neurosis in artists. Gachet, however, was not only an eccentric but seemed to be at least as neurotic as the afflicted artist, which caused Van Gogh to observe, 'Now when one blind man leads another blind man, don't they both end up in the ditch?'

Van Gogh's output during the two months he was granted in Auvers was impressive. His first paintings were of old houses with moss-covered thatched roofs, of the kind he had loved in Brabant and had also painted in Saint-Rémy in his *Souvenir du nord*. His famous painting of the little church in Auvers must be considered another example of a new approach to an old subject, recalling as it did the church tower he had done in Nuenen. He now found a willing model in Adeline Ravoux, his landlord's daughter, of whom three small portraits in deep blue and yellow are known. In view of his yearning to renew his ties with the traditions of northern painting, he was intrigued to find that the widows of Daubigny and Daumier, two artists he so greatly admired, were living in Auvers: 'At least, I'm sure that the former still does.' In order to maintain the quality of his draughtsmanship, he asked Theo to send him Bargue's book *Les exercises au fusain.*

A letter Van Gogh wrote on 25 May 1890 to the Dutch painter Joseph Isaäcson was in many respects a sequel to his letter to Albert Aurier. Isaäcson, too, was about to write an enthusiastic article devoted to Van Gogh's work and Vincent was worried about its possible tenor. His tone was once again unassuming, but he had a very concrete objective, namely that Isaäcson should stress the importance of the series of olive orchards done in Saint-Rémy. Much as he had stood up for Monticelli in his letter to Aurier, so he now held up Puvis de Chavannes as the most important painter of his day. In particular, that artist's *Inter Artes et Naturam,* a canvas shown at the world exhibition on the Champ de Mars, had made a great impression on Van Gogh during his visit to Paris.

'His canvas now at the Champ de Mars seems, among other things, to allude to an equivalence, to a strange and providential meeting between <u>far</u> distant antiquities and the <u>crude</u> modern age. Because his recent canvases are, if anything, even vaguer and more prophetic than the work of Delacroix, they fill you with the sense of being present at the continuation of all that went before, an inevitable but benevolent renaissance. But it seems better not to dwell on this point as one stands musing in gratitude before as perfect a painting as Le sermon sur la montagne. Oh, he ought to be doing them, the olive trees of the south – he, <u>the Seer</u>. I must tell you as a friend, that faced with such natural force I feel impotent, my northern spirit having fallen prey to nightmares in those peaceful surroundings, because I felt that I ought to be doing better with them. And yet I did not want to leave without making any effort <u>at all</u> – but that was confined to the depiction of those two things: cypresses and olive trees. Let others who may be better and more capable than I, convey their symbolic language. Millet is the voice of the wheat, and so is Jules Breton. Well, let me assure you that I can no longer think of Puvis de Chavannes without the presentiment that he, or perhaps someone else, will one day interpret the olive trees for us. I can see from this distance that a new art of painting may perhaps be on the horizon [. . .].'

To Wil, too, Vincent wrote about Puvis de Chavannes's painting, enclosing a small sketch he had made of it for her. He went on to confide his anxiety about Theo's deteriorating health and his hope that he might be able to persuade Theo and his family to go and live outside Paris in the healthy air of the countryside. To Theo and Johanna he wrote, 'I see in it, or think I see, a Puvis de Chavannes-like peace, no factories, but a profusion of lovely, well-tended greenery.'

Dr Gachet had meanwhile become a second brother to Van Gogh. As Theo had written, they even resembled each other in character and appearance. Johanna van Gogh was later to compare Gachet's house to 'the workshop of an alchemist of the Middle Ages'. And Van Gogh's account bore her out: '[. . .] his house is as full as an antique shop, full to bursting with things that are not always worth bothering about, awful, even. But the good thing about it is that there is always something for arranging flowers or for still lifes.' Moreover, Gachet himself and his daughter Marguérite sat for new portraits. It seemed Van Gogh had still not given up his ambitions as a painter of the modern portrait.

W22 [F] [letter from Vincent to Wil]

[3 June 1890]

My dear sister,

I should have replied long ago to your two letters, which I received while still at St Rémy, but the journey, the work, and a great many new emotions made me put off writing from one day to the next until now. I was very interested to learn that you had been nursing patients at the Walloon hospital. That is certainly the way to learn a great deal, the best & the most useful things one can learn, and I for one regret that I know nothing, or at any rate not enough, about it all.

It gave me great joy to see Theo again, and to make the acquaintance of Jo and the little one. Theo's cough was worse than when I last saw him more than 2 years ago, but in talking to him and seeing him close at hand, I certainly found him, all things considered, changed somewhat for the better, and Jo is full of good sense and good will. The little one isn't sickly, but he isn't strong either. If one lives in a big city, it is a good system for the wife to go to the country for her confinement and to stay there with the baby for the first few months. But seeing that the first confinement is especially difficult they certainly could not have done better or otherwise than they did. I am hoping that they will come here to Auvers soon for a few days.

As for me, the journey & everything else have gone well so far, and coming back north has taken my mind off things a great deal. And then I have found a perfect friend in Dr Gachet, something like another brother – so alike are we physically, and mentally, too. He is very nervous and most odd himself and has been a great friend & help, so far as he was able, to the artists of the new school. I did his portrait the other day and am also going to do one of his daughter, who is 19 years old. He lost his wife some years ago, which was the main reason for his being laid low. We became instant friends, so to speak, and I shall go and stay with him one or two days every week to work in his garden, of which I have already painted two studies, one with plants of the south, aloes, cypresses, marigolds, and the other with some white roses, a vine and a figure, and then a clump of ranunculus. As well as that, I've done a larger picture of the village church – with an effect in which the building appears purplish-blue against a sky of deep & simple blue, pure cobalt. The stained-glass windows appear as patches of ultramarine, the roof is purple and partly orange. In the foreground a little greenery in bloom and some pink sunlit sand. Again, it's very similar to the studies I did in Nuenen of the old tower and the churchyard. Only now the colour is probably more expressive, more sumptuous. But towards the end at St Rémy I was still working like one possessed, especially on bunches of flowers, roses and purple irises.

I brought back quite a large picture for Theo and Jo's little one – which they have hung above the piano – white almond blossom – large branches against a sky-blue background, and they've also got a new portrait of the Arlésienne in their apartment. My friend Dr Gachet is <u>decidedly enthusiastic</u> about this last portrait of the Arlésienne, of which I have also kept a copy for myself, and about a self-portrait, and I was pleased about that, as he's persuading me to do some figure painting and will be finding me some interesting models to do, I hope. What fascinates me much, much more than it does all the others in my trade – is the portrait, the modern portrait. I am attempting it with colour, and am certainly not alone in attempting it this way. I should like – you see, I'm far from saying that I can, but I'm going to try anyway – I should like to do portraits which will appear as revelations to people in a hundred years' time. In other words, I am not trying to achieve this by photographic likeness but by rendering our impassioned expressions, by using our modern knowledge and appreciation of colour as a means of rendering and exalting character. So the portrait of Dr Gachet shows you a face the colour of an overheated brick, burnt by the sun, with red hair and a white cap, against a landscape with a background of blue hills. His clothes are ultramarine, which brings out his face and makes it look pale even though it is brick-coloured. His hands, the hands of an obstetrician, are paler than his face. In front of him on a red garden table are yellow novels and a dark red foxglove flower. My self-portrait is done in almost the same way, but the blue is a delicate southern blue, and the clothes are pale lilac. The portrait of the Arlésienne has a colourless and matt flesh tone, the eyes are calm and very simple, the clothing is black, the background pink, and she is leaning on a green table with green books. But in the copy that Theo has, the clothing is pink, the background yellowy-white, and

the front of the open bodice is muslin in a white that merges into green. Among all these light colours, only the hair, the eyelashes and the eyes form black patches.

I'm not managing to do a very good sketch of it.

There is a superb picture by Puvis de Chavannes at the exhibition.[1] The figures are dressed in bright colours, and one cannot tell if they are present-day costumes or clothes from olden times. On one side two women in simple long gowns are talking, on the other side men who look like artists, and in the centre a woman with a child in her arms is picking a flower from an apple tree in blossom. One figure is forget-me-not blue, another bright lemon yellow, another soft pink, another white, another violet. They are shown on a meadow dotted with little white and yellow flowers. The far distance is blue, with a white town and a river. All humanity, all nature simplified, as they might be, if they are not already so.

This description tells you nothing, but on seeing the picture, and looking at it for a long time, you might think you are present at a renaissance, inevitable but benevolent, of all things in which one has believed, which one has longed for, a strange and happy meeting of far distant antiquities with crude modernity.

I was also pleased to see André Bonger again, who appeared strong and calm, and argued, upon my word, with much soundness about art.

I was delighted that he came while I was in Paris.

Thank you again for your letters, goodbye for now, I embrace you in thought,

Ever yours,
Vincent

The brothers' correspondence reflected a guarded optimism that Vincent's change of surroundings might prove salutary. After a visit to

1 *Inter Artes et Naturam.*

Auvers by Theo, Johanna and little Vincent, Van Gogh wrote, 'It is as if the nightmare had lifted completely.' Theo missed no opportunity of telling his brother about the growing esteem in which his work was being held by fellow artists. The Neo-Impressionist painter Leo Gausson wanted to exchange a work with him, and through Theo, Eugène Boch exchanged a canvas of the Borinage for Van Gogh's *Mountain Landscape*, done in Saint-Rémy. Albert Aurier was very taken with *The Cypress*, which Van Gogh had sent him by way of thanks, and Gauguin wrote to say how much he admired the portrait of Mme Ginoux: 'Despite your illness you have never before done such well-balanced work, without sacrificing any feeling or any of the inner warmth demanded by a work of art, and this at a time when art has turned into a business ruled by cold calculation.' Gauguin himself was thinking of going to Madagascar, staying in a mud hut amidst 'gentle people who have no money and who live on what the soil yields'. Such conditions, he hoped, might beget the John the Baptist of the new art.

From Arles, Van Gogh received the warm regards of the Ginoux family. He also drew comfort from his closer ties with his mother and the spontaneous letters of his sister Wil. In his penultimate letter to his mother, tenderness and longing for Brabant went hand in hand with reflections on the transitory nature of life. Referring to 1 Corinthians, chapter 13, he wrote to the pastor's widow about death and loneliness.

To his sister he once again revealed his ambition of becoming a landscape painter and a modern portraitist.

641a [D] [letter from Vincent to his mother]

[*c.* 12 June 1890]

Dear Mother,

I was struck by what you say in your letter about having been to Nuenen. You saw everything again, 'with gratitude that once it was yours' – and are now able to leave it to others with an easy mind. As through a glass, darkly – so it has remained; life, the why or wherefore of parting, passing away, the permanence of turmoil – one grasps no more of it than that.

For me, life may well continue in solitude. I have never perceived those to whom I have been most attached other than as through a glass, darkly.

And yet there is good reason why my work is sometimes more harmonious nowadays. Painting is unlike anything else. Last year I read somewhere that writing a book or painting a picture was like having a child. I don't go so far as to make that claim for myself, however – I have always considered the last-named the most natural and the best of these three – if indeed they were comparable. That is why I at times try my very hardest, although it is this very work that turns out to be the least understood, and though for me it is the only link between the past and the present.

There are a lot of painters in this village – next door a whole family of Americans who paint away day in, day out. I haven't seen any of their work yet – it's unlikely to be up to much.

Theo, his wife and his child were here last Sunday and we lunched at Dr Gachet's. There my little namesake made his acquaintance of the animal world for the first time, as there are 8 cats, 3 dogs, as well as chickens, rabbits, ducks, pigeons, etc., in large numbers. As yet he doesn't understand much of it all, I think. But he looked well, and so did Theo and Jo. It is a very reassuring feeling for me to live so much closer to them. You too will probably be seeing them soon.

Once again thanks for your letter, and hoping that you and Wil remain in good health, I embrace you in my thoughts,

Your loving
<u>Vincent</u>

W23 [F] [letter from Vincent to Wil]

[11 or 12 June 1890]

My dear sister,

I am adding à few words for you to Mother's letter. Last Sunday I had a visit from Theo and his family. It's very pleasant to be living less far away from them. Recently I've been working very hard and quickly; in this way I try to express the desperately fast passage of things in modern life.

Yesterday, in the rain, I painted a large landscape with fields as far as the eye can see, viewed from a height, different kinds of greenery, a dark green field of potatoes, the rich purple earth between the regular rows of plants, to one side a field of peas white with bloom, a field of clover with pink flowers and the little figure of a mower, a field of tall, ripe, fawn-coloured grass, then some wheat, some poplars, on the horizon a last line of blue hills at the foot of which a train is passing, leaving an immense trail of white smoke over the greenery. A white road crosses the canvas, on the road a little carriage, and some white houses with bright red roofs alongside the road. Fine drizzle streaks the whole with blue or grey lines.

There is another landscape with a vineyard and meadows in the foreground, the roofs of the village appearing beyond them.

And yet another with nothing but a green field of wheat, stretching away to a white villa, surrounded by a white wall with a solitary tree.

I've done the portrait of M. Gachet with a melancholy expression, which might well seem like a grimace to those who see it. And yet I had to paint it like that to convey how much expression and passion there is in our present-day heads in comparison with the old calm portraits, and how much longing and crying out. Sad but gentle, yet clear and intelligent, that is how many portraits ought to be done. At times it might well make some impression on people.

There are modern heads that may be looked at for a long

time, and that may perhaps be looked back on with longing a hundred years later. If I were ten years younger and knew what I know now, with how much ambition should I not be working on this! Under the circumstances I can't do much, I neither keep company with, nor know how to keep company with, the sort of people I should like to influence.

I very much hope to do your portrait one day.

I'm greatly looking forward to another letter from you. I do hope to see you soon, I embrace you warmly in my thoughts,

Ever yours,
Vincent

Van Gogh continued his efforts to forge links between his painted works, the better to create a solidly structured overall 'oeuvre'. In a letter to Theo written a few days later, he called the landscape he had described in such detail to his sister in the preceding letter 'a study in the style of the Harvest'.

Because Gachet was a keen amateur printmaker, Van Gogh felt inspired to try his hand at etching again. In particular, he planned to make prints of his Arlésienne and of the landscape with cypress. Under the influence of the series of lithographs the artist Auguste Lauzet had made after Monticelli's work, he wrote, 'I shall probably be making etchings of this and other landscapes and subjects, so many memories of Provence [...]'. His trial attempt, a print of his portrait of Dr Gachet, earned him Theo's admiration: 'It is a real painter's etching. No refinement in the execution, but a drawing on metal.' It was to be the only print he managed to do before his death.

At the end of June, Van Gogh did several paintings of flowers, and planned to paint Daubigny's garden, of which he had already made a small study. On narrow, elongated canvases, possibly based on dimensions favoured by Puvis de Chavannes, he painted panoramic landscapes and a 'sousbois [undergrowth]', as well as a portrait of Gachet's daughter, Marguérite, playing the piano, with a landscape in complementary colours as a pendant. His reason for doing so was that 'people are still a long way from appreciating the remarkable links between one piece of nature and another, even when the two clarify and enhance each other'. He was also hoping to paint Marguérite at a small organ, as a modern St Cecilia.

In Paris, Theo and his family were suddenly beset with problems. In late June, in what for him was an unusually emotional letter, Theo made his brother privy to his worries about his job, his finances and his little boy's health. Should he leave 'those skinflints Boussod & Valadon' and set up in business as an independent art dealer? Ought they to move to Auvers, or to Holland? Whatever was decided they would all have to tighten their belts. However, he took comfort from the knowledge that Vincent was in good health: 'You have found your way, dear brother, your carriage is already nearing its destination and can stand up to a good many knocks.'

The fact that Vincent was suddenly expected to take over the role of fraternal adviser came as a shock. He was far from convinced that his own situation had become so much rosier: 'I must tell you honestly that I dare not count on my health never letting me down again. And don't hold it against me if my illness should return.' Theo, by contrast, enjoyed Johanna's constant support, while marriage was something Vincent could no longer depend on: 'I still love art and life very much, but as for ever having a wife of my own, I have no great faith in that. I am rather afraid that towards, let's say, the age of forty – or rather, let's not say anything at all, for I must tell you that I absolutely, and I mean absolutely, do not know what course things are going to take with me.' Although Vincent had felt certain that his presence in Paris would only make things worse, out of concern he did visit his brother all the same. We know from Johanna that Vincent's first instinct had been the right one, and that the visit turned out to be an especially unhappy one. The child's illness had made everyone overtired. The brothers did have serious discussions about Theo's leaving Boussod & Valadon, but even these were constantly interrupted by the many callers who came during his visit. Moreover, Vincent was dissatisfied with the way in which his paintings had been stored. The short note he sent Theo upon his return to Auvers makes it clear that there had been much irritation on both sides. A sweet letter from Johanna helped clear the air, however, as we can tell from what Vincent wrote to his brother and his sister-in-law on about 10 July, shortly before they left for a short holiday in the Netherlands.

647 [F]

[7 July 1890]

Dear brother and sister,

My impression is that since we are not quite ourselves, and rather preoccupied anyway, there is relatively little point in insisting on a clear definition of the position we are in. It rather surprises me that, there being no agreement, you seem to want to force the situation. Can I do anything about it? Perhaps not – but have I done anything wrong, or is there anything you would like me to do?

Anyhow, once again a good handshake in my thoughts, and despite everything it gave me a great deal of pleasure to see you all again. Be very sure of that.

Ever yours,
V.

649 [F]

[*c.* 10 July 1890]

Dear brother and sister,

The letter from Jo has really been like a gospel for me, a deliverance from the distress caused by the hours I shared with you, which were rather difficult & trying for us all. It is no small matter when we are all made aware that our daily bread is at risk, no small matter when for different reasons we are also made aware of the precariousness of our existence.

Back here, I, too, still felt very sad, and the storm which threatens you continued to weigh heavily on me as well. What is there to be done? Look, I try to be reasonably good-humoured in general, but my life is also under attack at its very root, my step is also unsteady.

I was afraid – not entirely – but a little nevertheless – that my being a burden to you was something you found intolerable – but Jo's letter proves to me clearly that you do realize that I am working and making an effort just as much as you are.

So – having arrived back here, I have set to work again – although the brush is nearly falling from my hands – and because I knew exactly what I wanted to do, I have painted three more large canvases. They are vast stretches of wheat under troubled skies, and I didn't have to put myself out very much in order to try and express sadness and extreme loneliness. I hope you'll be seeing them shortly since I'd like to bring them to you in Paris as soon as possible. I'm fairly sure these canvases will tell you what I cannot say in words, that is, how healthy and invigorating I find the countryside.

The third canvas is Daubigny's garden, a picture I've had in mind ever since I came here.

I hope with all my heart that the proposed journey will help a little to take your minds off things.

I often think of the little one, I don't doubt it's better to bring up children than to spend all one's nervous energy on making pictures, but it can't be helped, I am, or at least I feel I am, too old now to retrace my steps or to long for anything else. That longing has left me, but the mental suffering remains.

I was very sorry not to have seen Guillaumin again, but am pleased he's looked at my canvases. If I had waited for him, I should probably have stayed talking to him so long I would have missed my train.

Wishing you both luck, a stout heart and comparative prosperity, may I ask you to tell Mother and our sister once again that I think of them very often. Indeed, I had a letter from them this morning and will be replying soon.

Handshakes in thought,

Ever yours,
Vincent

My money won't last me very long this time, for on my return I had to pay the bill for the luggage from Arles. I have some very good memories of that journey to Paris. A few months ago I hardly dared hoped to see my friends again. I think that Dutch lady is most talented.[1] Lautrec's picture, Portrait de musicienne, is quite wonderful, it moved me when I saw it.

Vincent wrote to his mother and Wil that he was 'absorbed in that immense plain with wheat fields up as far as the hills, big as the ocean, delicate yellow, delicate soft green, the delicate purple of a tilled and weeded piece of ground, with the regular speckle of the green of flowering potato plants, everything under a sky of delicate tones of blue, white, pink and violet. I am in a mood of almost too much calm, just the mood needed for painting this.'

Following Johanna's letter, Theo, too, tried to boost Vincent's spirits. In a letter dated 14 July, he repeated the simile of the horse and cart he had used in an earlier letter, writing, 'Disappointments – certainly, but we are no beginners & are like wagoners who by their horses' supreme efforts almost reach the top of the hill, do an about-turn, and then, often with one more push, manage to gain the top.' Another letter from Theo, written a week later, tells us of new tensions during the third week of July. Theo had gathered from one of Vincent's letters that Vincent thought there was trouble between Theo and his brother-in-law Andries Bonger, who lived in the same house, and Theo did his best to refute the story. In turn, Theo was worried by Vincent's remark that he was having difficulties with writing, and advised him to consult Dr Gachet.

A short, unfinished note to Theo dated 24 July 1890 was long thought to have been the last letter Van Gogh wrote. Theo had marked the note with, 'Letter he had with him on 29 July'. In reality, it was a draft for a somewhat longer letter with illustrations that Vincent did post. He may have decided not to send the earlier version because its tone was somewhat gloomy. The central theme once again was the conflict between artist and art dealer, and for many years its dramatic conclusion was – quite understandably in the light of subsequent developments – taken for a farewell message. That passage reads: 'Well, I have risked my life for my work, and it has cost me half my reason – all right

1 The Dutch sculptor Saar de Swart.

[...] as far as I can tell, you are not one of those traders in human beings, I am sure you act with real humanity. But what do you expect? ...'

In the letter he actually posted, these musings had been toned down. The main topic was again Van Gogh's ideal of an association of artists. Although the letter was disillusioned in tone, it contained the usual order for paints, and he ended with the description of one of his last paintings, *Daubigny's Garden*.

651 [F]

[24 July 1890]

My dear brother,

Thank you for your letter of today and the enclosed 50 fr. note.

I should try, perhaps, to write to you about a great many things, but in the first place I have completely lost the inclination, and then, it seems useless to me.

I hope you found those gentlemen favourably disposed towards you.

As far as the peace of your household is concerned, I am as much convinced that it can be preserved as I am that it is threatened by storms.

I would rather not forget the little French I know, and am certainly unable to see the sense in delving deeper into the rights or wrongs of one side or the other in any discussions. It wouldn't be my concern anyway.

Things move quickly here. Aren't Dries, you and I rather more convinced of that, don't we understand that rather better than those ladies? So much the better for them – but in the long run we can't even count on talking coolly about it.

As far as I am concerned, I am giving my canvases my undivided attention. I am trying to do as well as some painters I have greatly loved and admired.

Now I have returned, my feeling is that the painters themselves are increasingly at bay these days.

All right ... but hasn't the moment for trying to make them understand the usefulness of an association already passed? On the other hand an association, should it come about, would go under if the rest were to go under. In that case, you might say, the dealers could throw their lot in with the impressionists – but that would be very short-lived. All in all, it seems to me that personal initiative is of no avail, and given the experience we've had, should we really be starting all over again?

I've noted with pleasure that the Gauguin from Brittany I saw is very beautiful, and it seems to me that the others he's done there will probably be so as well.

Perhaps you'll take a look at this sketch of Daubigny's garden – it is one of my most carefully thought-out canvases. I am adding a sketch of old thatched roofs and sketches of two size 30 canvases representing vast stretches of wheat after the rain. Hirschig has asked if you would be kind enough to order him the enclosed list of paints from the same dealer where you buy my paints.

Tasset could send them to him direct, cash on delivery, but then he'd have to give him the 20% discount, which would be the simplest. Or else you could put them in the batch of paints for me, adding the bill, or telling me how much the total amount comes to, and then he would send the money to you. You can't get good paints here. I have cut my own order to the absolute minimum.

Hirschig is beginning to get a better idea of things, it seems to me. He has done a portrait of the old schoolmaster, who has given him a 'well done'. And then he has some landscape studies which are almost the same colour as the Konings at your place. They may turn out to be just like these, or like the things by Voerman we saw together.

Goodbye for now, keep well and good luck in business, etc., remember me to Jo and handshakes in thought,

Ever yours,
Vincent

Daubigny's garden.

   Foreground of green & pink grass, to the left a green & lilac bush and a low clump of plants with whitish foliage. In the middle a rose bed, to the right a wicket gate, a wall, and above the wall a hazel tree with purple foliage. Then a lilac hedge, a row of rounded yellow lime trees. The house itself in the background, pink, with a roof of bluish tiles. A bench and 3 chairs, a black figure with a yellow hat, and in the foreground a black cat. Sky pale green.

According to Johanna, Theo had difficulty in making sense of this letter. At any event, the shot that rang out on 27 July in the wheat fields behind the château in Auvers took him completely by surprise. Johanna van Gogh wrote later, 'Fear of the illness that was threatening him once again, or an actual attack, drove him to his death.' Severely wounded, Van Gogh stumbled to the Auberge Ravoux, where Dr Gachet was summoned when the suicide attempt was discovered. At first, Van Gogh seemed to be holding his own and, despite the severe pain, lay on his bed smoking a pipe. Theo, sent for from Paris by a note from Dr Gachet, also thought at first that things were not as bad as he had feared. The doctor probably underestimated the severity of the wound, and no attempt was made to remove the bullet. Vincent finally fell into a coma, and died in the early hours of 29 July in his brother's arms.

In the presence of a number of his painter friends – Bernard, Laval, Lucien Pissarro and Père Tanguy – Van Gogh was buried in a sunny spot among the wheat fields. Bernard described to Aurier how the coffin had been covered with yellow flowers, 'his favourite colour [...] a symbol of the light of which he dreamed both in his heart and in his work. Close by, too, his easel, his camp stool and his brushes had been placed on the ground beside the coffin.'

Theo's already failing health was not up to this loss. Bernard ended his account of the funeral with the words, 'Theodorus van Gogh is broken by grief.' To what extent Theo blamed himself for having been unable to prevent his brother's death, we do not know. In a sense, his last actions seemed to be carrying out Vincent's last will and testament. In September, and with Bernard's help, Theo held a memorial exhibition of Vincent's work in his Paris apartment.

At the end of that month, Theo began to suffer from violent headaches and giddy spells and his nights were plagued by hallucinations and nightmares. According to Camille Pissarro, Theo, embittered by the way he was being treated by his employers, resigned his post and soon afterwards, at the Café Le Tambourin, by then thoroughly confused, tried to set up the association of painters Vincent had so enthusiastically championed. In the middle of October, Theo broke down completely and was admitted to a Paris clinic with signs of paralysis. On about 19 November, beyond hope of recovery, he was taken to Holland, where he died on 25 January 1891.

Select Bibliography

Blotkamp, Carel, et al., *The Age of Van Gogh: Dutch Painting 1880–1895*, Amsterdam and Zwolle 1990

Cooper, Douglas, *Paul Gauguin. 45 Lettres à Vincent, Théo et Jo van Gogh*, Collection Rijksmuseum Vincent van Gogh, Amsterdam, The Hague and Lausanne 1983

Crimpen, Han van, et al., *De brieven van Vincent van Gogh*, The Hague 1990

Faille, J.-B. de la, *The Works of Vincent van Gogh. His Paintings and Drawings*, Amsterdam 1970

Hulsker, Jan, *The Complete Van Gogh: Paintings, Drawings, Sketches*, New York 1980

— *Vincent and Theo van Gogh: A Dual Biography*, Ann Arbor 1985

— (ed.), *The Mythology of Vincent van Gogh*, Tokyo, Amsterdam and Philadelphia 1993

Kodera, Tsukasa, *Vincent van Gogh, Christianity Versus Nature*, Amsterdam and Philadelphia 1993

Leeuw, Ronald de, et al., *The Hague School: Dutch Masters of the Nineteenth Century* [with a chapter on Van Gogh], London 1983

— *The Van Gogh Museum. Paintings and Pastels*, Zwolle 1994

Pabst, Fieke, *Vincent van Gogh's Poetry Albums*, series 'Cahiers Vincent' no. 1, Amsterdam and Zwolle 1988

Pickvance, Ronald, *Van Gogh in Arles*, New York 1984

— *Van Gogh in St Rémy and Auvers*, New York 1986

— 'A great artist is dead', *Letters of Condolence on Vincent van Gogh's Death*, series 'Cahiers Vincent' no. 4, Amsterdam and Zwolle 1992

Pollock, Griselda, 'Artists, mythologies and media. Genius, madness and art history', *Screen 21* (1980), no. 3, pp. 57–96

Rewald, John, *Post-Impressionism from Van Gogh to Gauguin*, New York 1956

— 'Theo van Gogh as art dealer', *Studies in Post-Impressionism*, 1986, pp. 7–15

Stein, Susan A., *Van Gogh. A Retrospective*, New York 1986

Tilborgh, Louis van, et al., *Van Gogh and Millet*, Amsterdam and Zwolle 1988

— *Vincent van Gogh: Paintings* (catalogue of the 1990 Van Gogh retrospective), Milan 1990

— *The Potato Eaters by Vincent van Gogh*, series 'Cahiers Vincent' no. 5, Amsterdam and Zwolle 1993

Uitert, Evert van, et al. (eds.), *The Rijksmuseum Vincent van Gogh*, Amsterdam 1987

Welsh-Ovcharov, Bogomila, *Vincent van Gogh and the Birth of Cloisonism*, Toronto 1981

— *Van Gogh à Paris*, Paris 1988

Zemel, Carol, *The Formation of a Legend. Van Gogh Criticism 1890–1920*, Ann Arbor 1980

Index